Latin America at 200

Joe R. and Teresa Lozano Long Series
in Latin American and Latino Art and Culture

Latin America at 200

A New Introduction

PHILLIP BERRYMAN

UNIVERSITY OF TEXAS PRESS ⟡ AUSTIN

Requests for permission to reproduce material from this work
should be sent to:
    Permissions
    University of Texas Press
    P.O. Box 7819
    Austin, TX 78713-7819
    http://utpress.utexas.edu/index.php/rp-form

♾ The paper used in this book meets the minimum requirements
of ANSI/NISO Z39.48-1992 (R1997) (Permanence of Paper).

LIBRARY OF CONGRESS CATALOGING-IN-PUBLICATION DATA

Berryman, Phillip, author.
    Latin America at 200 : a new introduction / Phillip Berryman.
— First edition.
        pages   cm — (Joe R. and Teresa Lozano Long series in
Latin American and Latino art and culture)
    Includes bibliographical references and index.
    ISBN 978-1-4773-0827-1 (cloth : alk. paper) — ISBN 978-1-4773-
0867-7 (pbk. : alk. paper) — ISBN 978-1-4773-0868-4 (library
e-book) — ISBN 978-1-4773-0869-1 (nonlibrary e-book)
1. Latin America—21st century. 2. Latin America—Forecasting.
I. Title. II. Series: Joe R. and Teresa Lozano Long series in Latin
American and Latino art and culture.
    F1409.3.B475   2016
    980.04—dc23
                                                    2015029021
doi:10.7560/308271

Contents

Acknowledgments

The impetus for this book goes back to discussions with friends starting around 2000, as I began to sense new developments in Latin American countries and as I taught an introductory course on the region at Temple University. In 2008, I began writing drafts and interviewing people in various countries. Among those who were helpful with ideas, encouragement, hosting me, or other forms of assistance were Eduard Barrebes, Edgar Bermúdez, Joe Broderick, Aurora Camacho de Schmidt, Mark Castro, Jesús Abad Colorado, Guillermo Corado and Isabel de Corado, Héctor Endara, Dick Erstad, Phil Evanson, Karen Faulkner, Dave Farrel, Jean Friedman-Rudovsky, Noah Friedman-Rudovsky, Martín Gárate, Ana María Gómez, Mary Day Kent, Dan Levine, Milton Machuca, Elsie Monge, David Murray, Gene Palumbo, Valeria Rezende, Amanda Romero, Art Schmidt, Oscar Tabares, Leandro Vetcher, Joe Walsh, Ron Webb, and María Zúñiga. Reading the manuscript or portions of it and offering helpful comments were John Chasteen, Tony Equale, June Erlick, Phil Evanson, Ann Farnsworth-Alvear, Ann Helwege, Manuel Lombera, Josh Markel, Art Schmidt, and Tom Quigley. I wish to thank Noah Friedman-Rudovsky, Tommie Sue Montgomery, Edgar Romero, and Julián García for their fine photographs, and Sigfus Breidfjord for preparing the graphs and maps. None of those named are responsible for errors and shortcomings.

I would like to thank Theresa May of the University of Texas Press for her enthusiastic acceptance of the proposal and manuscript; the anonymous readers for their criticisms; Kerry Webb, Angelica Lopez, Lynne Chapman, and other staff at the Press for bringing it to completion; and Nancy Warrington for her thorough copyediting. As always, I am in debt to my wife, Angela Berryman, who has been my partner in involvement with Latin America for several decades.

Latin America at 200

Entering a Third Century

In 1810, what we now know as Latin America still belonged to the Spanish and Portuguese colonial empires; by 1825, most of the present nations in the region had been born. The actual year of celebration varies from one nation to another; some emphasize the proclamation of independence and others the moment when the colonial armies were defeated in their land. Broadly speaking, however, most of the region is now celebrating two centuries of independent life as nations.

As I write, Latin Americans have some positive developments to celebrate. By 2010, most countries had entered periods of sustained growth. More surprisingly, inequality in the most unequal region in the world was showing modest declines, and both researchers and ordinary observers saw signs of an expanding middle class. People had entered the digital world: heads of state were tweeting, young people were on social media, and people in poor neighborhoods were creating their own news media.

Most Latin American countries were only moderately affected by the post-2007 recession and had returned to growth by 2010. Brazil was acknowledged to be an "emerging power," Chile foresaw a time when it would no longer be regarded as an "underdeveloped" country, and some other countries such as Colombia seemed to be poised for sustained growth. Dictatorships had been left behind, and all major political actors seemed to have accepted the democratic rules of the game, as disappointing as the results in practice might sometimes be. Even in small countries, US ambassadors could no longer act as proconsuls. The title of a 2010 special report in *The Economist* expressed the new situation: "Nobody's Backyard: The Rise of Latin America."

Chronic problems still plagued the region: high crime rates, including organized international drug organizations defying governments; high levels of inequality, with a significant proportion of the population in poverty; poorly performing governments and uncompetitive businesses; and racial, ethnic, and gender discrimination. In the indexes ranking the countries of the world on crime, corruption, ease of starting or running a business, educational performance, and so forth that have been developed by the World Bank, the World Economic Forum, and other international agencies, the performance of Latin American countries was generally mediocre.

This book is the outgrowth of over a decade of attempts to come to grips with new developments in Latin America. While teaching survey courses on the region, I sensed a growing gap between the standard books and what I observed in visits to the region, in news reports, and in the newer specialist literature. Each semester I looked for an overview to use in my class and was disappointed that even new editions of standard works had only minor updates. After waiting in vain for such a work, I began the drafts that have led to this book.

During this bicentennial period, Latin Americans themselves are taking a fresh look at their own history and their prospects in the twenty-first century. A shift in leadership is under way: most of today's heads of state came of age in the 1960–1990 period of revolution and counterrevolution, but by 2025 they will be replaced by "bicentennials," who were children when the Cold War ended but are accustomed to viewing China as rival, customer, and possible partner. In that light, this survey seeks to examine major trends in the countries of the region from various angles.

The book's unconventional outline may require explanation. In organizing an interdisciplinary introduction, one has to decide what to do with history: treat it separately or incorporate aspects of it into thematic chapters? A common approach is to begin with geography, history, economics, and politics, followed by chapters on society (class, gender, race/ethnicity, religion, culture). In this introduction, the first nine chapters pursue current developments thematically (geography and demography, urbanization, agriculture, environment, class, race, gender, religion). A survey of history follows (chapters 10–12), leading to more systematic treatment of economics, politics, and international relations (chapters 13–17), and a conclusion, which draws together the various strands. Placing the thematic chapters first helps keep the focus on the present. In particular, the fact that 75 or 80 percent of Latin Americans are now urban suggests that it makes sense to emphasize cities at the outset. The chapters on history may offer insight into the various thematic chapters. In addition to the historical survey from precolonial times to the middle of the last century, a whole chapter is devoted to the experience of the past half century, which is still a living memory for older adults in the region today and serves as a background to the chapters on economics and politics.[1]

Chapter 1 begins by considering the commonalities and differences between the nineteen countries of the region, as well as the human impacts of geography and demography. Chapters 2 (urbanization and cities) and 3 (food and agriculture) are opposite sides of the same coin: the massive movement of millions of people from the countryside to the city. The future of Latin Americans largely depends on the cities they live in: Will they be segregated or inclusionary? Will everyone have a "right to the city," including workable transportation? Agriculture is being transformed by the "supermarket revolution," which is changing the food production chain from the field to the table. Brazil is now an agricultural powerhouse whose agroexports rival those of United States.

Chapter 4 (business and labor) enters into economics not from grand theories but from an examination of types of businesses ranging from family-operated corner stores to *multilatinas*, large enterprises that are now going global.[2] Chapter 5 surveys environmental issues (rain forests, mining, water and sanitation, urban transportation), with the accent on examples of practical steps being taken.

Chapter 6 (inequality, poverty, class) takes up two seemingly contradictory propositions: Latin America is highly unequal, and yet it is witnessing the emergence of a strong middle class. Chapter 7 traces efforts to overcome racial and ethnic discrimination. Gender and family matters are taken up in chapter 8 around two poles: long-standing machismo and women's efforts to claim their rights in both the public and the domestic spheres. The story of religion (chapter 9) includes the role of church activists in struggles for justice, and the shift from a Catholic monopoly to an emergent religious pluralism, particularly through the spread of Pentecostal Christianity.

In chapter 10, Latin American history is situated in global history, first emphasizing the emergence of increasingly complex societies before the arrival of the Europeans in the late fifteenth century, and then discussing the legacy of the three centuries of colonial society. Chapter 11 considers the formation of new nations after 1810, their role as suppliers of agricultural products and minerals, and the post-1930 crisis and incipient modernization. Chapter 12 recounts the past half century of contemporary history as a struggle for economic and social development.

The next five chapters examine the economic and political challenges of the present. Chapter 13 considers the ingredients of economic success, based on examples from the past two decades. Chapter 14 considers political evolution and what kinds of changes are needed to make democracy more effective. The emphasis is not only on elections but includes more humdrum aspects of governance such as civil service and taxes. Chapter 15 considers how crime and corruption might be reduced and the rule of law enhanced based on efforts already under way in some places, particularly those tackling drug trafficking and organized crime. Chapter 16 takes up health and education, two areas in which Latin Americans have made great strides (e.g., dramatically increasing longevity) but where much remains to be done.

Latin America's external relations (chapter 17) were long seen as primarily revolving around its relationship to the United States or its efforts to break free of US domination. In a globalized world, relations with other countries are becoming more important: China is now the number-one trading partner of some countries, and Brazil is becoming a player in Africa. With Latinos now the largest "minority" in the United States, boundaries are being blurred. The book concludes by pulling together the major themes and considering prospects for the coming years.

A central thread through the book is the pursuit of development, understood not simply as economic growth, but as the means whereby all members of society can enjoy a decent standard of living in a society that works equitably for all. The work is not driven by any overarching theory of how to bring that about. In the 1960s, many Latin American intellectuals and scholars of the region rejected a paradigm of modernization, which proposed that underdeveloped societies needed to follow the footsteps of already developed nations, and do so under their tutelage. They largely adopted variants of "dependency theory," according to which the key issue was to break free of the domination of the United States and to develop in terms of their own needs, through revolution if necessary. Although that view has persisted in some left-wing circles, most countries have settled on more pragmatic, less ideological approaches to development. For example, governments of both right and left have adapted "conditional cash transfers" (direct payments to the poorest families) because the benefits seem clear: poverty is alleviated, and local economies are stimulated with money that goes directly to the family, often the woman.

For decades, overviews of Latin America have served to explain its failures. A classic example is Eduardo Galeano's *Open Veins of Latin America*, whose subtitle—*Five Centuries of the Pillage of a Continent*—summarizes its thesis.[3] That angle of vision made sense as recently as the 1980s, when the policies of the US government enormously aggravated the wars in Nicaragua, El Salvador, and Guatemala. The debt crisis and "lost decade" of the 1980s, which lasted into the 1990s, and the imposition of neoliberal policies by the World Bank and others seemed to be the latest chapter in the story. Books on Latin America continued to present pessimistic analyses, with the implication that nothing short of a new model of society was required.

A leitmotif in this book is that a workable and decent society may be within reach, at least in some countries. Without underestimating problems such as crime and corruption already mentioned, the emphasis here is on what Latin Americans are doing to meet the challenges of the twenty-first century.

PART I

Society

Lands and Peoples

The Constraints and Opportunities of Geography and Demography

This survey begins with some elementary information on Latin American countries, their main geographical features, population size, racial/ethnic combinations, and how Latin America compares to other world regions. In addition to basic data, the human implications are considered: for example, the consequences of living in the tropics or in a continent-sized country like Brazil as opposed to a small one like El Salvador.

DOES "LATIN AMERICA" REALLY EXIST?

But does it even make sense to speak of Latin America and Latin Americans? After all, Colombian or Mexican schoolchildren learn their own Colombian or Mexican history, not a generic "Latin American" history. Downtown plazas have statues of different independence heroes: Miguel Hidalgo and José Morelos in Mexico, Simón Bolívar in Venezuela and Colombia, José de San Martín in Argentina, Francisco Morazán in Honduras. Each country has its own national anthem, its own historical heroes and villains. Individuals live within the confines of their own country; its borders form their horizon. People living across those borders speak Spanish differently and have different customs. Brazil seems to be a world unto itself, speaking Portuguese and being geographically closer to Africa than to Mexico. "Latin America" would seem to be an abstraction, perhaps most useful to people outside the region. Nevertheless, underlying commonalities among the peoples of the nineteen countries[1] make it meaningful to speak of Latin America. Argentina and Mexico are thousands of miles apart, and yet an Argentine visiting a provincial Mexican town will feel at home in the central plaza, with the church on one side and colonial or nineteenth-century buildings on the other.

Although Latin American countries have been independent nations for two centuries, those nations themselves grew out of the colonial societies set up by Spain and Portugal and thus share common cultural roots, including Roman Catholicism. Pop stars give concerts and sell their music throughout the region,[2] and brand names, such as for digital phone companies, cross borders and are increasingly multinational.

Poets like Pablo Neruda (Chile) and Ernesto Cardenal (Nicaragua) have composed book-length poems invoking the wonders of the continent beyond the borders of their own countries. In the 1960s, intellectuals and writers spoke of Latin America as the Patria Grande (Great Homeland), with the implication that someday it might be a single nation. In his trilogy *Memory of Fire*, the Uruguayan writer Eduardo Galeano presents the region's history from precolonial times to the present in short vignettes, drawing on material from every country in the hemisphere. The popularity of this work attests to the fact that many identify with Latin America as well as their own country. In short, it is meaningful to speak of "Latin America" and "Latin Americans," provided we realize that the terms are abstractions, albeit useful ones.[3]

"Latin America" is here understood, then, as the countries that arose out of Spanish and Portuguese colonization. Puerto Rico and Haiti are borderline cases. In language and culture, Puerto Rico is quite similar to the Dominican Republic or Panama. However, Puerto Ricans have been United States citizens since 1917, even while their status as a "commonwealth"—neither a US state nor an independent nation—places them in a unique situation. Haiti shares the island of Hispaniola with the Dominican Republic and a similar colonial history, and its independence struggle occurred a few years before that of the rest of Latin America. However, its languages, French and Creole, and stronger elements of African culture set it apart. It could be claimed that Latin Americans in the United States constitute a twentieth Latin American country; Los Angeles is the second-largest Mexican and Salvadoran city, and the same is true of Miami for Cuba.

MAJOR GEOGRAPHICAL FEATURES

In the film *The Motorcycle Diaries* (2004), two young Argentines, Ernesto and Alberto, set out on a motorcycle from Buenos Aires in the early 1950s. They first head south through the pampas, and then turn west to cross the Andes, where they encounter blizzards. Moving north through the temperate central valley of Chile, they reach the arid deserts of the far north and cross into the Peruvian Andes (hitching rides after the motorcycle breaks down). Along the way they encounter estate owners, fish marketers, exploited miners, and indigenous peasants. The film climaxes at a leper colony in the Peruvian Amazon, where Ernesto—the future revolutionary "Che" Guevara—proposes a toast to Latin American unity and swims across the Amazon at night. He and Alberto continue on a makeshift raft toward Colombia, touch a corner of Amazonian Brazil, and end their journey in Venezuela. Through their encounters with the grandeur of the continent's geography and the variety of its peoples, they have transcended their Argentine identity and become Latin Americans.

From Tijuana, across the Mexico-US border from San Diego, to Tierra del Fuego, facing Antarctica, Latin America stretches over 6,500 miles. Although the terrain varies, most of it is in the tropics, as opposed to the United States, almost all of which

MAP 1.1. *Latin America*

is in the temperate zone.[4] Two-thirds of Mexico is composed of mountains or the plateaus between mountain ranges. The northern part of the country is arid desert, but other regions are tropical. The mountains from Mexico continue through the Central American isthmus, dividing it into Pacific and Atlantic sides, the latter generally receiving considerably more rainfall and being more sparsely populated. The Caribbean Latin American nations (Cuba, Dominican Republic, Haiti, Puerto Rico) are part of a larger set of islands, which are in effect mountains arising out of the sea.

An obvious feature in South America is the Andes mountain range, which begins in Venezuela and Colombia, where snow-capped peaks can be found not far from the Caribbean, and continues down along the western edge of South America without interruption to southern Chile. The Andes, which average at least half again as high as the Rockies and the Sierra Nevada,[5] affect all the countries of western South America. They account for the peculiar shape of Chile, which is almost 2,700 miles long but averages only a little over 100 miles in width.

A second major feature is the Amazon River, whose tributaries reach from Brazil into Venezuela, Colombia, Ecuador, Peru, and Bolivia. The Amazon River is virtually as long as the Nile, and its volume as it enters the Atlantic Ocean is by far the largest of any river in the world (and in fact is as large as that of the next six or seven largest rivers combined).

Although most Latin American countries have nothing like the flat productive plains of the American Midwest, a partial exception are the pampas or grasslands in central Argentina, Uruguay, Paraguay, and a portion of southern Brazil. They have long served for cattle ranching and also today for large-scale commercial agriculture. Colombia and Venezuela also have extensive low-level tropical grasslands called *llanos*. Terrain in Chile and Argentina ranges from desert in the north (the Atacama Desert in northern Chile is the driest in the world) to forests, with glaciers in the south where both countries approach Antarctica.

Dominican Republic farmlands. © Inter-American Development Bank.

Settlement along the Amazon River, Brazil. © Tommie Sue Montgomery.

Arica, Chile—driest desert in the world. © Tommie Sue Montgomery.

Vineyards with Andes in the background, Mendoza, Argentina. © Tommie Sue Montgomery.

Fishermen selling catch on the beach, Manta, Ecuador. © Tommie Sue Montgomery.

HUMAN IMPACTS OF GEOGRAPHY

Relatively few Brazilians have been to the Amazon, and likewise, few Chileans have been to the deserts of the north or the portion of their country across from Antarctica. The geography that matters most is the one that affects everyday life, so we now consider the more immediate impacts of geography on the people of the region.

An obvious starting point is climate. Most Latin Americans live in the tropics, which stretch from central Mexico to northern Argentina and Paraguay. The tropics typically have only two seasons, rainy and dry, in contrast to the four seasons of the temperate zones. Likewise, in the tropics the length of the days and nights varies little year-round, with the sun rising around 6:00 a.m. and setting twelve hours later, as opposed to the greater contrast between the summer and winter solstices the farther one is from the equator.

However, there is no sharp break between the temperate and tropical zones but rather a broad subtropical zone, which has something of a four-season pattern in which winters are relatively mild. In the northern hemisphere, that zone reaches from Southern California and northern Mexico across the South and into the lower Mid-Atlantic states. The corresponding area in South America includes the middle sections of Chile and Argentina and parts of southern Brazil, including the city of São Paulo.

Most land in Latin America thus lies in the tropics. People who live near sea level have hot and humid weather, like that of July and August in the US Midwest, year-round. In Central America, the rainy season lasts seven or eight months of the year (approximately April to November), during which it may rain two out of every three days, typically with a strong but short downpour (*aguacero*); during other months it never rains, so that by the end of the dry season, everything may be covered by dust kicked up by passing vehicles. Farmers plant corn, beans, rice, and other crops at the start of the rainy season, and harvest them toward its close.

Even in the tropics, as soon as one rises in altitude, the weather becomes cooler. Caracas, located roughly 2,000 feet above sea level, has pleasant weather. Guatemala City, at 4,900 feet, has weather like spring in the temperate zone. In Bogotá (8,000 feet) and Quito (9,000 feet), people are typically in long sleeves and even jackets during the day, and nights are cool. In fact, most Latin American capital cities are somewhat elevated. The climate in Lima, Peru, is kept moderate by the cool Humboldt Current in the Pacific. Truly tropical capital cities include Managua, Panama City, Santo Domingo, and Asunción (Paraguay). Buenos Aires, Santiago, and Montevideo are in the subtropical zone and have climates comparable to that of Southern California. The same country can have widely varying climates. Weather in La Paz, Bolivia, located at close to 12,000 feet, is generally cool; Santa Cruz on the savanna east of the Andes is tropical; Cochabamba, about halfway between them, is moderate.

The variation in climate depending on altitude has advantages other than being able to escape the heat of the coastal or rain-forest regions. In Colombia and other Andean countries, markets have an enormous variety of fruits and vegetables; people in the temperate highlands can buy pineapples, and people in the tropical lowlands, plums or apples. Even in pre-Columbian times, indigenous peoples took advantage of their geography by planting crops at different altitudes and trading with one another.

Those who live in sea-level tropical cities like Rio de Janeiro, Panama City, or Asunción must find ways to live with the heat. To some extent, it is a matter of becoming accustomed to it, seeking the shade where possible, rising at sunrise to take advantage of the cool of the morning, slowing down in the early afternoon but keeping businesses open longer in the evening. Architects can design buildings and houses with shade features and make them open so as to favor a breeze. The effects of a tropical climate are increasingly being mitigated by air-conditioning in offices and retail stores.

GEOGRAPHY: FATE OR OPPORTUNITY?

A glance at a world map shows that the most developed countries in the world (Japan and those of Western Europe and North America) are generally in the temperate zone, and the poorest are in the tropics (sub-Saharan Africa). A century ago that disparity was sometimes given the pseudo-sociological explanation that living in the tropics inclined people to indolence, whereas living with harsh winters and a limited growing season impelled them to be hardworking and inventive—conveniently ignoring colonial domination by Europe and North America. Partly out of embarrassment over the racism in such views, for decades scholars shied away from considering the impact of geography on development.[6] Since the 1990s, researchers have been exploring its impact, both positive and negative, on the assumption that each nation must confront the geographical hand that it has been dealt. We turn here to some examples.

One area where geography and climate impact ordinary people is the ease (or difficulty) of transportation. Most Latin American countries have nothing like the US interstate highway system, which is facilitated by hundreds of miles of flat or gently undulating land. Much of Colombia, Ecuador, Peru, and Bolivia is mountainous, and land travel from one place to another is over two-lane curving roads where passing is difficult and dangerous. In Central America, traffic can move readily on the flatlands along the Pacific coast, but not in the hills and mountains running through the center of the isthmus. Few roads exist on the sparsely populated Atlantic side (especially in Nicaragua and Honduras). Most roads in the Amazon and other rain forests are unpaved and hence muddy in the rainy season and dusty in the dry season. There are no roads whatsoever in a 60-mile section of Panama leading to Colombia (the Darién Gap). Likewise, until 2011 there was no all-weather road through the Amazon Basin in Brazil over the Andes and to the Pacific Ocean, although such roads are now being completed—over the objections of environmentalists and indigenous groups.

The tropics have their own diseases. Efforts to combat malaria, yellow fever, and other diseases go back a century and help account for rising longevity. However, a number of tropical diseases of various kinds (Chagas disease, dengue, hookworm) are still causing chronic ill health and even death. The victims are disproportionately indigenous and Afro-descendant. Large pharmaceutical companies have little incentive to invest in research because medications for these diseases offer little likelihood of large profits.

Given the region's lush vegetation, it is perhaps surprising that tropical agriculture has not been as productive as agriculture in temperate lands. That is partly because the soil itself is thin and easily eroded, but it is also because northern-hemisphere agricultural yields have benefited from over a century of applied research. Only recently have similar efforts been applied to the specific features of tropical agriculture. Brazil has led the way, with government-sponsored research institutes and partnerships between universities and the private sector, in developing crops, such as new feed grasses for livestock and soybean varieties suitable for the tropics. It has transformed the large area of brushland known as the *cerrado*, once considered to have little economic value, into a highly productive area.

Mexico and Central American countries are increasingly attempting to take advantage of their geographical proximity to the United States and Canada. They did so in the last decades of the twentieth century, particularly with the assembly plants along the US border. In the early 2000s, many of these operations were closed as manufacturers moved to China. However, as labor there and transportation have become more expensive, companies are again recognizing the advantages of "near-sourcing," including being in the same time zone, and are again locating operations in Mexico and Central America.

A final potential geographical advantage is that of tourism, particularly nature tourism. For decades, tourists have gone to Mexico and the Caribbean for beaches; to Guatemala and Peru for archaeological sites; and to Brazil for Rio de Janeiro and Iguazú Falls. Since the 1970s, Costa Rica has pioneered ecotourism, opportunities to see the rain forest, and "adventure tourism" (white-water rafting or flying on zip lines through the trees). However, many potential natural sites remain little developed. Tourism is likely to expand dramatically in Colombia, where 10 percent of the country is set aside as national parks and protected areas. Tourism in Latin America is projected to keep growing, because of rising incomes and customers from newly developing countries, particularly China. Domestic and regional tourism is expected to grow as the expanding middle classes become increasingly interested in experiencing the natural world.

DOES SIZE MATTER?

As of 2015, the total number of Latin Americans was around 600 million, considerably larger than the total US population of 317 million. Two countries have large populations (Brazil and Mexico), some have only a few million people, and several countries have medium-sized populations.

An obvious advantage of being in a large country is the size of the domestic market and hence the possibilities of the economy. Brazil is the sixth-largest economy in the

TABLE 1.1. Populations of Latin American Countries (in Millions)

Over 100 million	Brazil (196)	
	Mexico (118)	
30–50 million	Colombia (47)	Peru (30)
	Argentina (41)	Venezuela (30)
10–30 million	Chile (17)	Cuba (11)
	Ecuador (16)	Bolivia (10)
	Guatemala (15)	
Under 10 million	Dominican Republic (9.7)	Costa Rica (4.6)
	Honduras (8)	Puerto Rico (4)
	Paraguay (6.7)	Panama (3.6)
	El Salvador (6.6)	Uruguay (3)
	Nicaragua (6)	

Figures from official sources; figures for countries with over 10 million inhabitants have been rounded; decimals have been left for those under 10 million.

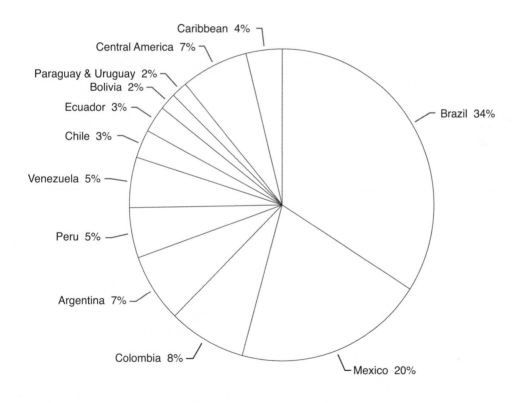

GRAPH 1.1. *Relative Populations. Based on official sources, 2014.*

world, and Mexico the tenth. Both have had auto industries for over a half century, thereby spurring related industries (auto parts, tires, steel, rubber). A larger market allows not only for greater size but greater complexity; for example, the Brazilian company Embraer is the world's third-largest aircraft manufacturer (after Airbus and Boeing) and sells planes to US commercial airlines and to the Pentagon. In a large country, the size of the domestic market is itself a source of growth. By contrast, small countries are inevitably more dependent on foreign trade. Despite these constraints, Costa Rica and Uruguay have successfully attained a decent standard of living.

There are also less tangible aspects to the size of a country and how it affects its citizens. Living in a continent-sized country may make Brazilians more expansive in their personalities; one's horizon is different in El Salvador, where in one or two hours one reaches the border of another country. On the other hand, countries of a few million people have the advantage of a more human scale.[7]

ETHNIC/RACIAL DIVERSITY AND MIXTURE

Although the United States prides itself on being a "melting pot," ethnic and racial diversity is at least as great in most Latin American countries. Because the Spanish and Portuguese colonizers usually came as single men or did not bring their families, they took indigenous or African women as partners, giving rise to mixed-blood children, either mestizo or mulatto. New waves of European immigration in the nineteenth and twentieth centuries added new streams, especially in the Southern Cone (Chile, Argentina, Uruguay, and southern Brazil). Most Latin Americans have some combination of two or more of these groups, but the mix in each country is different, reflecting its different history. Countries may be classified according to the prevailing strain(s) as shown in table 1.2.

TABLE 1.2. Predominant Ethnic/Racial Characteristics of Latin American Countries

Indigenous & European	Afro-descendant & European	Mestizo	European
Clear divide between indigenous and nonindigenous (including mestizos)	Continuum from European to African appearance	Prevalence of mixed indigenous and European features	Predominantly European with some mestizo features
Guatemala	Brazil	Mexico	Chile
Bolivia	Dominican Republic	Colombia	Costa Rica
Ecuador	Cuba	Venezuela	Argentina
Peru	Panama	El Salvador	Uruguay
		Honduras	
		Nicaragua	
		Paraguay	

TABLE 1.3. Human Development Index Rankings

VERY HIGH HUMAN DEVELOPMENT

[1–5 Norway, Australia, Switzerland, Netherlands, United States] [14—United Kingdom]	41—Chile 49—Argentina

HIGH HUMAN DEVELOPMENT

50—Uruguay	67—Venezuela
59—Cuba	77—Peru
59—Panama	85—Brazil
61—Mexico	89—Ecuador
62—Costa Rica	91—Colombia

MEDIUM HUMAN DEVELOPMENT

96—Dominican Republic	111—Paraguay
[101—China]	120—Honduras
107—El Salvador	129—Nicaragua
108—Bolivia	133—Guatemala

LOW HUMAN DEVELOPMENT

161—Haiti
[183–187—Burkina Faso, Chad, Mozambique, Dem. Rep. of the Congo, Niger]

Note: Bracketed countries are for purposes of comparison.
Source: United Nations Human Development Index, 2013.

This broad characterization needs further refinement. In fact, Afro-descendant and indigenous populations are found in almost all countries. In Mexico, for example, indigenous people make up 12 percent of the population; indeed, Mexico has more indigenous people than Ecuador. On the whole, the upper classes have more European features than average citizens, and the poor are disproportionately indigenous or Afro-descendant.

LATIN AMERICA COMPARED TO OTHER WORLD REGIONS

Some readers might be surprised to learn that Latin America is categorized as "middle income" by the World Bank and United Nations agencies (roughly comparable to the Middle East and North Africa and ranking above South Asia and sub-Saharan Africa). How various Latin American countries compare among themselves and to other countries may be seen in the Human Development Index (HDI), which was devised by the United Nations as a tool for measuring the performance of governments in improving the welfare of their people. The HDI measures education (including literacy), life expectancy at birth, and purchasing power.[8] These can stand as rough indicators of people's welfare, especially when taken together. The 2013 HDI rankings include 187 countries. Table 1.3 shows the ranking of all Latin American countries together with some other countries for comparative purposes, including the highest and lowest five.

Not surprisingly, the countries with the highest rankings are in Europe and North America, along with Australia and Japan. The first Latin American country on the list is Chile, which, together with Argentina, is in the top quarter of countries. Uruguay, Cuba, Mexico, and Costa Rica are toward the top of the second quarter. Several Latin American countries fall into the second half, but none (except Haiti) appear in the "Low Human Development" column.[9] Brazil's HDI is close to that of the Ukraine, Argentina's is close to that of Portugal, while Bolivia's and Paraguay's are just above Egypt.

After these introductory observations on geography and demography, the next four chapters deal with urbanization (2), changes in agriculture (3), business and labor (4), and environmental challenges (5).

FURTHER READING

Standard surveys of Latin America by single (or dual) authors include Green (2013); Holden and Villars (2013); Munck (2003); Reid (2007); Skidmore and Smith (1992); Vanden and Prevost (2009); and Winn (2006). Multiauthor surveys include Black (2011); Gwynne and Kay (1999); and Hillman and D'Agostino (2011). From the discipline of geography, see Clawson (2006). On the relationship between geography and development, see Gallup, Gaviria, and Lora (2003).

Two quarterly reviews are recommended: *Americas Quarterly*, published by the Council of the Americas, and *ReVista*, published by the David Rockefeller Center for Latin American Studies at Harvard. Each presents articles on a major theme by scholars or experts for nonspecialists and has a website.

CHAPTER 2

Confronting Urban Challenges

In 1952, Eurídice Ferreira de Melo took her children from their home in northeast Brazil to São Paulo to join her husband, who had gone there earlier. They traveled in the back of a truck for thirteen days. Finding that her husband now had a family with another woman, she had to raise her children on her own. One of her sons, Luiz, began working even while attending school, and left school permanently after fourth grade. He found factory work, was trained as a lathe operator, became involved in union organizing, rose to leadership positions, and eventually got involved in politics.

That child was Luiz Inácio Lula da Silva (Lula), who in 2002 was elected president of Brazil. Many Brazilians could identify with his story. Tens of millions of people had moved from rural areas to towns and cities and had struggled to adapt to this new environment. Two or three generations ago, when Lula was born, the typical Latin American was a small farmer working the land; today he or she lives in a town or city. Latin America is now 75 to 80 percent urban, roughly equal to the rate in Europe or the United States.

RAPID URBAN SHIFT

Although the first cities were built about six thousand years ago in the Middle East, until recently only a minority of people were urban. As late as 1900 only one country in the world, Great Britain, had an urban majority, and a majority of Americans were rural until the 1920 census. The world population was 10 percent urban in 1900, crossed the 50 percent mark in 2007, and is expected to be 75 percent urban in 2050. In 1950, only seven cities in Latin America had a population of one million or more, and 10.6 percent of the population lived in them. By 1995 there were forty-two such cities, and 30.2 percent of the population lived in them. Besides these large cities, there are many medium-sized cities and smaller towns, existing on a continuum down to villages and isolated settlements.[1]

The movement from countryside to city follows a curve: starting from a low figure, the number of people in urban areas grows over time at an accelerating pace but then

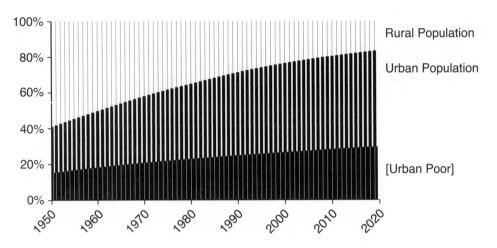

GRAPH 2.1. *Urban Population in Latin America, 1950–2020. Source: United Nations.*

begins to level off at around the 80 percent mark. The movement to the largest cities like São Paulo and Mexico City was already slowing in the 1980s but continued in medium-sized cities. For several decades, countries struggled to deal with rapid urbanization. Now that most Latin Americans are urban, the primary challenge is to make existing cities function well for their inhabitants.

Urbanization is an incremental and generally undramatic process, unlike revolutionary movements or attempts to suppress them, or even changes in government through electoral politics. However, the shift from a rural to an urban majority is arguably the most important change in Latin America since the mid-twentieth century. We consider urbanization at the outset because it is crucially related to changes in the economy, including the rural economy, and the recent expansion of the middle class.

SHAPE OF THE CITY

Latin American cities tend to resemble one another to the point where it is possible to construct a model of them, based on their characteristic features. For comparison purposes, consider the shape of US cities: a downtown business district, perhaps one or more manufacturing districts, and large areas of suburbs, all served by networks of roads and freeways, since almost all travel is by car. In Latin American cities, corresponding to "downtown" is likely to be a "historic center," which may date to its foundation in the sixteenth century. A prominent feature is a plaza with the Catholic cathedral on one side, one or more government buildings, and a statue of a hero of independence. Besides this main plaza, there are likely to be other plazas, also faced by churches. Somewhere in the downtown there will be a large market with hundreds of stalls. The business and banking center may no longer be located downtown but in clusters of high-rise buildings some distance away. Spreading out from the center are traditional residential areas.

In the outlying areas are poor neighborhoods that have grown up in the past half century. In Caracas, they are visible on hills, especially at either end of the city. In Guayaquil, Ecuador, they are on flatland, much of it originally swampy. In Bogotá, they are largely in the south. Much of the middle class lives in apartment buildings, usually either four-story walkups or towers with elevators. Ownership is often defined on a condominium model. US suburban-style neighborhoods of houses with large front and back yards are not common.

Local geography often shapes the city: Caracas runs along the base of a mountain ridge that rises several thousand feet above the city, so it runs east and west, with extensions to the south. Guatemala City was constrained by sharp canyons on all sides, although now it has extended beyond them. Quito runs in a valley between two mountain ridges. The metropolitan area is typically larger than the city proper; for example, Mexico City itself is around nine million, but Greater Mexico City is over twenty-two million. Many capital cities are disproportionately large: Greater Mexico City is four or five times larger than Guadalajara, the second-largest city in Mexico; Guatemala City is ten times as large as Quetzaltenango; and one-third of all Chileans live in or near Santiago. This "urban primacy" is characteristic of most Latin American countries; partial exceptions are Brazil, with two megacities, São Paulo and Rio de Janeiro, and several other cities of over one million inhabitants; Colombia, with several large cities besides Bogotá; and Ecuador and Honduras, where Guayaquil and San Pedro Sula counterbalance the capitals, Quito and Tegucigalpa.

Residences and high-rises, Caracas, Venezuela. © Noah Friedman-Rudovsky.

URBANIZATION PROCESS

The mass migration to the cities during the second half of the twentieth century was driven by both push and pull factors. Driving people from the countryside was rural poverty and a general lack of prospects in the countryside. With the best land in the hands of large landholders, small farmers had been left with marginal plots, whose size dwindled as they were divided among male children, and no new land was available. In El Salvador, Guatemala, Peru, and Colombia, violence against civilians by armies and paramilitaries (and, in the case of Peru, by the Shining Path guerrillas) drove many people out of the countryside and into the cities, especially in the 1980s and even later in Colombia.

Pull factors included opportunities not available in the countryside, such as employment, schools, and electricity. Governments tended to have an "urban bias," spending more money per capita in cities because urban constituencies can exert stronger political pressure. Finally, there were simply the "bright lights" of the city and the promise of a more interesting life, spurred by reports from family members who had migrated. The net result was that over several decades tens of millions of Latin Americans moved to towns and cities.

These immigrants might arrive as single men or women or, like Lula's mother, as the head of the household. They initially stayed with relatives or other contacts but at some time would need a home of their own. At that point they would seize an opportunity to get a small piece of land on the outskirts of the city as part of an organized invasion or upon hearing of an available piece of land that they could buy or rent (even if the seller might not actually have title to it). People set up temporary shelter using whatever materials could be found: scrap lumber, plywood, and corrugated metal. Such shantytown communities often first had to stand up to police attempts to evict them.

TABLE 2.1. Population Growth of Latin American Cities (in Millions)

CITY	YEARS			
	1950	1970	1990	2010
Bogotá	.6	2.92	4.85	8.5
Buenos Aires	4.6	8.3	10.9	14.5
Lima	.6	3.3	6.4	8.5
Mexico City	3.1	8.9	15	22.7
Rio de Janeiro	2.9	6.7	9.6	12.2
São Paulo	2.3	7.9	15.2	20.5

Note: Figures refer to metropolitan areas.

Housing of Haitian sugarcane cutters, Dominican Republic. © Noah Friedman-Rudovsky.

With no electricity, residents of these shantytowns used candles or lanterns at night; they hauled water from the closest spigot or bought it from trucks that sold it by the barrel; and their bathroom was a latrine in the back of the house. Shantytown dwellers became organized based on their needs. Electricians among them would connect up to a live power line and bring current to the community and to individual houses. They organized to pressure politicians or the municipal water company to run pipes to the community and install public outlets; sewer service would only come much later. Depending on circumstances, bus routes might come to the outskirts of the community or wind their way through it. Schools and public clinics might follow. Local businesses (stores with basic items, butcher shops, barber and beauty shops) would be started by some of the residents themselves. Some worked from home (e.g., as seamstresses or tailors).

Meanwhile, families gradually built permanent houses on their site. Materials were bought, and construction took place as time permitted. Building materials and style could vary widely. In tropical areas, walls could be lighter because a breeze is advantageous; in cooler areas, materials had to be more solid and walls thicker. By the 1960s, the favelas of Rio de Janeiro were emblematic of this situation, but all countries had their shantytowns and their own names for them; in Chile, they were called *callampas* (mushrooms) because they sprang up on their own. They were on

Hillside self-built housing, Caracas, Venezuela. © Noah Friedman-Rudovsky.

the outskirts of the city, generally on hilly or swampy land not suited for commercial development.

Governments and the public were initially negatively disposed toward these settlements and their inhabitants, viewing them as a problem to be solved by bulldozing. In reply to the growing "housing deficit," governments and international agencies sponsored housing developments for low-income families, often in the form of several hundred identical homes with low-interest loans. Such schemes, however, could never meet the demand, and in fact were out of reach of the very poorest, who did not have incomes steady enough to allow for regular house payments. Home mortgages did not exist, even for the middle class.

Shantytowns seemed to be an indictment of the existing socioeconomic system, in both the countryside and the city. Critics implicitly assumed that the true soul of their society, embodied in the peasant, was being lost in the degrading poverty of the shantytowns. Latin American factories employed relatively few people, and so it was assumed that the new immigrants were becoming surplus labor with high unemployment rates. To stem the flow to the cities, land reform was urged, but it was resisted by politically powerful rural landholders.[2] Eventually such assumptions were challenged. In *The Myth of Marginality* (1976), based on field research in Rio de Janeiro, Janice Perlman found that favela residents were not as "marginal" as had often been assumed by journalists and even social scientists. The people she studied were quite integrated into the economy of the city, many working in the formal economy, while others were self-employed by providing services.

Ideas changed among policy makers and government officials as well. Shanty-towns erected spontaneously with houses packed together left room only for narrow footpaths, not for vehicles. Their location on hillsides or low-lying swamps made it hard to retrofit infrastructure. An alternative began to take shape: rather than resist shantytowns, why not recognize that they were inevitable and organize the entire process? An early example took place in Panama City in 1966. A group of squatters in an area called Veranillo, in discussion with the government housing agency, agreed to move to another location where they would be provided with lots with urban services and financing to pay for them. Plots were assigned by lottery on a Saturday morning; by Sunday night, all the families had erected their provisional structure and Nuevo Veranillo (New Veranillo) was beginning to function.[3]

This model became increasingly common: the "urbanization" was designed, with provision for roads, water, electric power, green spaces, and areas for future schools and other services. Each household could then be provided with a lot, access to water and electricity, building materials, and perhaps even a concrete foundation. The entire package would be paid for with a low-interest loan. The advantages of this approach were that infrastructure was in place from the beginning, the tech-nically best use was made of the land, and the community organized itself around specific tasks and did not have to spend years in an antagonistic relationship with local government.

A well-known example of such a pre-planned "invasion" is Villa El Salvador in Greater Lima. A group of people invaded lands intended for upper-class residential development and were met with police resistance. In the clash, a young man was killed, and in the ensuing dialogue process, a plan was reached that would make available a large tract of sandy land in the southern outskirts of Lima. From the beginning, it was a planned community with blocks, zones, and sectors, all with public spaces. Settlement began in May 1971 as people built initial shelters from woven mats, which were sufficient for the moment because it seldom rains in Lima and the climate is moderate. Within a year, a hundred thousand people were living in Villa El Salvador.

Twenty-five years after its founding, Villa El Salvador had 350,000 residents, and as families grew, new squatter settlements developed beyond it. It had an industrial park where 1,200 small businesses were providing employment for 15,000 people and turning out many products, such as artisan-made furniture, and attracting buyers from elsewhere in the city. Universities had set up campuses in the area. The veterans from the early years were proud of what they and their generation had achieved.

An example of more recent growth is El Alto, Bolivia, located on a high plain above La Paz, which grew from a few thousand people in the 1960s to 650,000 in 2001, and to over a million people today (more than La Paz itself). Its population is almost entirely indigenous, and it is a thriving commercial center.

El Alto, Bolivia. The city has grown from a small population in the 1960s to over a million people today, almost all indigenous.
© *Phillip Berryman.*

FROM SHANTYTOWNS TO NEIGHBORHOODS

Based on journalistic reports, documentary films, or books like Mike Davis's *Planet of Slums* (2006), it might be assumed that shantytown residents are trapped in poverty from generation to generation. Recent research, however, suggests a more nuanced interpretation. In 2005, researchers surveyed a random sample of 1,092 households in four large favelas of Greater São Paulo. They found that over time people had built substantial houses. A municipal program had helped people gain title to their land, thus making their investment more secure. Adult children were often living in the same house or compound. What began as informal settlements became part of the formal side of the economy; for example, people were now paying water and electricity bills. The researchers commented that the outside appearance of the modest brick houses did not "prepare a visitor for the quantity and quality of durable goods to be found inside. All homes have refrigerators, with 64 percent of them financed" (Guedes and Oliveira 2006, 11). The families averaged 1.5 television sets—thus indirectly indicating a degree of privacy in the sense that two sets could be playing at once. The researchers found DVD players and cell phones, and 29 percent of the households had automobiles, while others hoped to get one. The homes averaged five rooms each.[4] The researchers titled their paper "The Democratization of Consumption," meaning that something of a consumer society was spreading even in the favelas that outsiders assumed were concentrations of desperate poverty. The authors remark on the lively commerce in these communities. A number of their interviewees were successfully running small businesses.

In the late 1990s and early 2000s, Janice Perlman returned to the favelas of Rio seeking to find out how the people she had studied in the 1970s had fared, and she encountered several surprises. One was that many had moved out of the favela: 34 percent of the original subjects, 44 percent of their children, and 51 percent of the grandchildren were in a formal neighborhood. Only 37 percent of the subjects were still in a favela, and some had remained by choice. Children had generally fared better than their parents in terms of schooling and job classification, and many had attended the university. Families had refrigerators and domestic appliances, and almost all had mobile phones. On the other hand, many expressed regret that people were less community-minded than in the early days of the favela. Crime and drug gangs made them feel more insecure. Simply living in a favela was a stigma in dealing with people elsewhere in Rio (Perlman 2010).[5]

The urban anthropologist Caroline Moser has likewise published a longitudinal study of the community of Indio Guayas in Guayaquil, Ecuador, where she lived in 1978 when the houses were still perched on stilts over swampy mangroves, and where she continued to do research at various times over three decades. The mangroves were eventually filled in, and by 2004, Indio Guayas was regarded as a neighborhood in Greater Guayaquil. Broadly speaking, Moser found that the poor in the community declined from four-fifths to one-third.[6] The fate of people in Indio Guayas has been conditioned by changes in Ecuador and Guayaquil (economic growth in the 1980s; crisis in the 1990s, culminating at the end of the decade; some recovery by 2004). Moser (2009) analyzes how households accumulate assets: first, a permanent house; then perhaps some productive capital for a small business; then human capital in the form of training for themselves and especially for their children, even paying for private school; and, finally, consumption goods.

Households change over time, often in response to changes in the economic context. For example, when jobs are plentiful, women may stay at home; in hard times, they and other family members seek to earn cash incomes. A daughter with children may move back into her parents' house or build a house on the original property. Thus, what began typically as nuclear families end up over time as multigenerational households, whose combined incomes may help them advance or simply survive.

The patterns found by both Perlman and Moser concur with what long-term observers of the evolution of Latin American barrios find: over time and between generations, families do better economically; children and grandchildren are on the whole better educated and are more likely to work in the formal economy, even as some people remain trapped in poverty. Generational differences can be discerned between those who built the original community and their children, and the grandchildren, who have largely lost contact with the countryside, who play video games or use social media but would get blisters on their hands if they used a machete for any length of time. People who were part of the early days of the community, and especially community leaders, lament the fact that most people no longer participate in community organizations, and they often decry the rise of crime, drug consumption and trafficking, and gangs.

EXCLUSIONARY OR INCLUSIONARY CITIES?

In the 1960s and 1970s, residents of Latin American cities might have been concerned about pickpockets or break-ins, but they did not fear for their safety from crime or random violence (despite the political violence in some places). Since the 1980s, however, people voice fears of carjacking at red lights, of being robbed by a rogue taxi driver, and of "express kidnappings" in which victims are taken to bank machines and forced to remove cash. Those responsible could be petty criminals, members of youth gangs, or hard-core criminals involved in drug trafficking and other forms of organized crime. "Citizen security" is perhaps the most acute aspect of a larger question, namely, what kinds of cities are being formed and whether they will be livable and workable.[7]

One approach households take is to insulate themselves from the rest of the city. A notable example was Alphaville, 23 kilometers from São Paulo, which came to have thirty-three gated communities with 20,000 residents, along with businesses, shopping, and recreational facilities. Even the infrastructure (water, electricity, roads) was built and is managed not by a municipal entity but by the real-estate developers. The area of Santa Fe in Greater Mexico City is similar, an enclave of business property and high-priced residences with little connection to the rest of the city. Even if they do not live in such enclaves, many wealthier Latin Americans move between homes in exclusive neighborhoods to office buildings with security, pick up their children from private schools, and socialize in private clubs. They can spend their lives largely contacting people of their own class and have little interaction with people in other situations. São Paulo has the world's largest helicopter fleet (500), more than New York or Tokyo, carrying busy executives to appointments. At the extreme, some people can in effect secede from the rest of the city.

Many middle-class Latin American families live in apartment buildings or condominiums, with a private security guard controlling access and entry (unlike the model of a single house situated on a large lot in US suburbia). Gated communities have become common in Guatemala City; even modest middle-class areas have been retrofitted with some version of security control.

Most city dwellers cannot insulate themselves, however, and in fact the danger is that such attempts end up sacrificing a central reason for living in cities: the kaleidoscope of human variety. The remainder of this chapter takes up examples of urban initiatives (social movements, municipal actions, and planning) that move in the opposite direction, seeking to make the city work for everyone.

As an initial example, consider the experience of the Viva Rio movement. In the early 1990s, Rio de Janeiro seemed to be in a downward spiral. Two incidents in 1993—a group of men opening fire on street children sleeping outside the Candelária church, killing eight, and police killing twenty-one innocent residents in a favela, supposedly in retaliation for the killings of four police officers by drug traffickers— prompted activists, academics, and others to come together united by a common sense of indignation: "Enough!" The first action of their new organization, Viva Rio, took place on a day in mid-December. As a sign of adherence, people were invited to wear white clothing, to put white cloths in their windows, and to pause in silence, wherever they were at noon, to reflect for two minutes on their city. In subsequent years, the organization frequently arranged mass marches and demonstrations, particularly around issues of gun violence. In one early action, the movement took a boat through Guanabara Bay to illustrate its fundamental conviction: We're all in the same boat, in other words, the kind of city we have will affect us all. In 2000, Viva Rio sponsored a campaign against violence. A television celebrity encouraged people to turn off the lights in their house and place a candle in the windows. They were also urged to wear white clothes to work as a sign of the campaign. Volunteers gathered 1,300,000 signatures in Rio, petitioning for gun-control legislation.[8]

Concerted efforts to confront urban problems at the city level are relatively recent. Throughout most of the twentieth century, the functions of government, such as education or infrastructure, were managed by national government ministries. Mayors were appointed, not elected, and had relatively little power. This began to change in the 1980s and 1990s as part of a trend toward the decentralization of politics and government. An example of the shift is the "participatory budget" pioneered in 1989 by the Workers Party in Porto Alegre in southern Brazil. The process starts in January and February as specialists present budget possibilities and constraints to people in the city's sixteen districts, who discuss and vote on budget items in a series of meetings, sometimes with as many as a thousand people attending. Eventually the entire budget is approved and signed by the mayor. In the intervening two decades, sewerage coverage in Porto Alegre has risen from 75 percent to 98 percent of households, and schooling and health-care coverage have improved. Some of this no doubt would have occurred in any case, but the participatory budget has assured that the people's own priorities are more respected. It also makes even ordinary citizens more sophisticated and realistic about how their city works. Hundreds of municipalities in Brazil and elsewhere in Latin America, and even Europe and Canada, have borrowed the idea and attempted their own forms of participatory budgeting.

MAKING THE CITY WORK

In 1960, Brazil shifted its capital from coastal Rio de Janeiro inland to Brasília, which had been constructed from bare ground to brand-new city in less than three years. Lúcio Costa, the planner who proposed the layout of the city, and Oscar Niemeyer, the architect who designed many of its signature buildings, made it an outstanding example of modernist architecture, a symbol of Brazil's desire to be advanced. President Juscelino Kubitschek claimed that the country was leaping ahead fifty years in five. The buildings of the presidency, the legislature, the supreme court, and the cathedral were built along sleek modern lines. Viewed from overhead, the city was symmetrical in design, suggesting an airplane or a dragonfly. Government ministries were housed in opposing rows of identical rectangular blocks; residential areas were composed of clusters of apartment buildings, spreading out from the main axis of the city.

Very soon, however, the shortcomings of building an entire city from a seemingly rationalistic angle became apparent. Satellite cities of poor people sprang up almost instantly, starting with the thousands of construction workers laid off when the building projects were completed. The city had been planned for salaried government employees, not for poor people. The vast open distances, impressive from a vehicle, are barren when one is walking, and in fact the design made no provision for pedestrians. The planners' rationalistic design of segregating residences from businesses proved troublesome to residents. For example, if they had a car problem, they had to take the vehicle to the part of town where auto repair was located rather than to a mechanic shop in the neighborhood. Viewed abstractly, the city was a masterpiece of modern art and aesthetics; however, the bold planners and architects seem to have forgotten the people who would inhabit it.

Architects and planners are rarely given the opportunity to design a city from scratch; they must work with the city as it exists. Moreover, during the decades of rapid urbanization, municipal governments had little ability to plan effectively, and thus cities expanded rather chaotically. Now that the growth rate has leveled off, the task is to address cities as they are and to make them more livable and workable. An obvious issue is that of traffic and transportation.

Traffic jams with cars, taxis, minibuses, and buses crawling along are a feature of large and even medium-sized Latin American cities. In São Paulo, radio and television traffic reports speak of traffic crawling for dozens of kilometers. Class differences are embodied in vehicle types: private cars for those who can afford them, taxis for some, and buses and vans of various kinds for most people. A number of cities (Mexico City, São Paulo, Rio de Janeiro, Brasília, Buenos Aires, Medellín, Santiago, Caracas) have metro systems, but these reach only a portion of the city. Buses can be dangerous because a driver's earnings depend on fares collected, so drivers compete to pick up passengers, even cutting one another off. Air pollution from vehicles is high. There is constant pressure to build more streets and widen them, but the number of vehicles continues to grow.[9] Starting with Mexico City in the 1980s, many cities have set up systems whereby cars are prevented from entering the downtown on certain days (or during peak hours on those days), based on one's license plate number.[10] Such measures may provide temporary alleviation, but they are stopgaps.

The most interesting transportation initiative is a system called bus rapid transit (BRT), pioneered in the southern Brazilian city of Curitiba in the 1970s and adapted decades later by a number of cities, such as Mexico City, Quito, Cali, and Santiago.

BRT (bus rapid transit) station, Lima, Peru. © Inter-American Development Bank.

The largest such system is the TransMilenio in Bogotá, which transports 1.4 million passengers a day. It is as fast as a metro system because buses have exclusive traffic lanes. Passengers prepay in special stations, and hence drivers are not distracted by collecting fares. The vehicles themselves are often double buses with a swivel section in the middle, allowing them to turn. They run on schedules and on average move faster than cars stuck in traffic. The routes operate along main arteries, supplemented by a system of feeder buses at the nodes that allows passengers from large portions of the city to use the system. These systems are clean and safe and a source of pride to city residents, even though they are packed at peak hours.

Former Bogotá mayor Enrique Peñalosa, who proposed and oversaw construction of the TransMilenio, believes that these systems are more than pragmatic solutions. Private automobiles are inherently undemocratic in societies where only a minority of people have them. Construction of roads disproportionately benefits car owners and absorbs revenues that could otherwise be spent on education or health care. Parking spaces take up more room and diminish public spaces. Peñalosa is an advocate not only of mass transit but of bicycles, and Bogotá has constructed many kilometers of bike paths. "A bikeway is a symbol that shows that a citizen on a $30 bicycle is as important as a citizen in a $30,000 car," he says.[11] Cities have been slow to foster bicycling for ordinary transportation (job, school, or errands), in part perhaps because of weather (frequent tropical rains) or hilly terrain and the attitudes of automobile drivers. However, Buenos Aires and Santiago have begun exclusive bike lanes (sometimes with barriers to protect cyclists from cars), and in 2012 Mexico City expanded its bike-share program to 4,000 bikes available at 275 stations (Romig 2012).

In addition to its bus system, Curitiba is known for several other initiatives and for the overall approach to the city of its three-term mayor, the architect Jaime Lerner. In the early 1970s, for example, flooding was becoming a problem. Rather than taking the conventional route of channeling rainwater into underground conduits, the city used money from the federal government to literally "go with the flow," that is, to buy land downhill from the usual flooding routes and let the water accumulate there, building parks around the resulting new lakes. The creation of these parks made the amount of green space per inhabitant rise from 2 to 150 square feet per inhabitant, making Curitiba one of the "greenest" cities in the world.

The people of Curitiba recycle 70 percent of their waste, partly stimulated by a program that exchanges groceries and school supplies for the waste collected by low-income residents. Although Curitiba has the highest per capita auto ownership of any city in Brazil, its pollution is the lowest of major Brazilian cities because so many people use the public transportation system (2.3 million per day). In the past forty years, Curitiba has shown that innovative design can make cities work better for their inhabitants.

PUBLIC SPACES

Latin American cities were built around public spaces, the plazas lined by churches and cathedrals, often reworked in the nineteenth and early twentieth centuries, when they took the names of the heroes of the independence movement. Those plazas have been meeting grounds, iconic landmarks, and sites of large political rallies and marches. However, as the cities grew in recent decades, the functions that once took place in the old downtown have been dispersed, sometimes to the point where a sense of a common meeting ground is being lost. The center of Guatemala City, the Parque Central, has been left to the poor; the rich and the middle class work, shop, and recreate elsewhere.

How important public space is—and even what it is—is admittedly elusive. London, Rome, and Paris all have spaces where one walks and enjoys being with one's fellow citizens, most of them strangers. It may be a piazza, a park, or a riverfront walk. San Francisco has them; Los Angeles does not, and indeed, many Americans in the suburbs or their equivalent drive from home to job to school to mall with little concern for public space.

The Ecuadorean urbanist Francisco Carrión says Latin American cities no longer have a "center," but rather a series of "centralities." Carrión also suggests that the aim should be not simply to make a historic center a place to attract tourists, but to assure that the historic center remains a functioning part of the city.[12]

Some cities have created pedestrian walkways. One of the first was in Curitiba in the 1970s. Two notable ones are in Santiago, Chile, and Caracas, Venezuela, both of which are above the metro systems, which run for several stops below. In the 1980s, the municipality of Guayaquil proposed to redo the area along the Guayas River, which had fallen into disrepair and was regarded as dangerous. The result is Malecón 2000, a restored promenade stretching a mile and a half along which are a variety of gardens, exhibits, children's play areas, and restaurants, with a mall at one end and an Imax theater at the other. The Malecón, which is managed by a nonprofit association, has helped revitalize the traditional downtown of the city.

In the largest cities, most people may rarely come to the historic area and may see the iconic spaces only on television. In medium-sized provincial cities, the same public spaces may be shared by a larger proportion of the population, such as the ridge at one end of town in Manizales, Colombia, where hundreds of people stroll and watch spectacular sunsets, or the plaza in the center of Santa Cruz, Bolivia, where park benches in the shade are usually occupied. In poor neighborhoods, soccer fields may function as public spaces, along with green areas or parks if the area was planned. Public space is less likely in suburbs, where most transport takes place by private car.

For over a decade, Mexico City has undertaken a vast effort to revitalize the historic downtown. The public-private effort involving left-wing administrations in city hall and business leaders has focused on improving lighting, making areas more pedestrian-friendly, and restoring the façades of buildings. Besides the vast Zócalo (large plaza), the downtown has arguably the largest stock of nineteenth-century and colonial buildings in the Americas. One focus is Alameda Park, in the heart of downtown, which had come to be regarded as dangerous and dirty. Marcelo Ebrard,

Pedestrian mall, San José, Costa Rica. © Tommie Sue Montgomery.

elected mayor of the Federal District in 2006, has spoken of public space as a human right of all, especially the poor.

It could be argued that the malls now proliferating offer some public space. A notable example is in Brasília, where the planners made no provision for gathering places because they envisioned a city in which people would move about by vehicle. The popularity of the Conjunto Nacional mall, built in the 1970s, may have derived from the lack of public spaces. Malls are clean and safe and give even poor people a vicarious experience of the consumer society. Some malls are clearly exclusionary; they are accessed by cars, not by public transportation, and many of the businesses sell luxury goods. Others, however, are filled with people of different classes, and some large malls are built in or near poor sections of cities. One may at least wonder whether the popularity of malls with large food courts owes something to a desire for what the public plaza used to be, a space to mix with other people.

Considering public space might seem trivial when compared to needs like sewer service, clinics, and adequate schools. However, for the poor, it embodies their "right to the city," the sense that the city is theirs. For the better off, it manifests a refusal to succumb to the temptation to secede into purely private domains.

URBAN TURNAROUND

How Latin Americans live will increasingly depend on the cities they live in—for the obvious reason that three-quarters of them now live in cities. There is a subtler reason, however, that requires a little reflection. People identify as citizens of nation-states; they participate in elections, pay taxes, observe the politics of presidents and legislatures; and their worldview is often shaped by the national political party to which they adhere. However, they spend their days in a city or metropolitan region, traveling to work or school, stopping to buy groceries or going downtown to a restaurant, moving about within a radius (on foot, bicycle, bus, or automobile). Their well-being depends on what goes on within that radius, whether they regularly see flowers and trees and hear birds in a park; whether they feel reasonably safe while going about their business; whether children and youth have adequate schools; and whether they breathe clean air. Institutionally, these depend on local police, school systems, transportation systems. In short, people's welfare depends at least as much on the kind of neighborhood and city they live in as on their nation as a whole.[13] We have already noted the innovations made in Curitiba, and we now turn to some other examples of innovations at the municipal level.

In the 1990s and early 2000s, the mayor's office in Bogotá was occupied by two idiosyncratic mayors, both independent of traditional parties. In 1995, Antanus Mockus, a mathematician from the world of academia, campaigned as a quirky outsider and was elected mayor. Under his administration, the police were professionalized and corrupt police were fired. He dismissed the traffic police, who were not respected, and hired four hundred mimes to work in traffic and change behavior through humor and shaming. (The same technique was later used in Caracas.) Mockus donned a superhero outfit—calling himself Supercitizen—and went about picking up trash in the streets. To draw attention to a water shortage, he had himself filmed taking a shower, turning off the water to lather up, and water usage in fact dropped significantly. One of his emphases was personal honesty, awarding public contracts on merit rather than patronage and corruption. Under Mockus, traffic fatalities dropped 50 percent (a good part of it due to the declaration and enforcement of a 1 a.m. curfew) as did homicide rates.

Mockus's approach was ethical and artistic. His successor, Enrique Peñalosa, mentioned earlier, proposed to make the city more livable and democratic through smart design. To do so, he brought business people ("doers rather than thinkers") into the municipal government. His most ambitious initiative was the TransMilenio described earlier, along with bike lanes. Fifteen libraries were built, designed by excellent architects and with contemporary technology, and were soon receiving 400,000 visitors a week. Mockus returned as mayor after Peñalosa, continuing his approach and even retaining many of his staff.

During the same period, remarkable changes were also taking place in Medellín. By the 1990s, the city had a murder rate of 381 per 100,000, perhaps the highest in the world. The murder rate was brought down, partly as a result of blows dealt against organized drug traffic (and its displacement elsewhere). Under Mayor Sergio Fajardo (2004–2007), major attention was given to building libraries in the poor areas on the hills overlooking the city. Cable cars connected poor hillside barrios like Santo Domingo Savio to the metro system in minutes. The city has extensive sports programs with coaches sent to the neighborhoods and acres of sports facilities near the city center. Three thousand youths participate in classical music programs. "A child who picks up a violin won't pick up a gun," it is said. The Botanical Garden, which had become a run-down, dangerous site where youths from a neighborhood barrio did drugs, was restored with the cooperation of neighbors, and it now receives two and a half million visitors a year. One ingredient in the turnaround in Medellín was the organized participation of business people as volunteers in projects in poor areas (Kimmelman 2012).

Under the leadership of Mayor Marcelo Ebrard, Mexico City initiated a number of steps under the general rubric of environmental sustainability, after first securing an approval vote (Green Consultation) in which over a million people cast ballots. Perhaps the most notable reforms were in transportation: construction of new metro lines, replacement of older buses with larger hybrid and natural-gas buses; retrofitting of 80,000 taxis with greener technology; installation of charging stations for electric vehicles. Because 30 percent of traffic at peak hours was found to be private automobiles transporting children to and from school, the decision was made to incentivize families to use public transportation, and the use of private vehicles declined 30 percent. Because traffic volume was lessened, average speeds increased and auto pollution was reduced. A bike-share program was established with 258 stations, and it was soon recording 10,000 trips daily. With bike lanes and other infrastructure changes, bicycling was becoming a common mode of transportation. In the downtown area, over a thousand colonial-era façades were restored, along with traditional monuments, parks, and pedestrian areas. The iconic Paseo de la Reforma was closed to vehicles on Sundays from 8:00 a.m. to 2:00 p.m. to open it up to pedestrians, cyclists, people in wheelchairs, and pet owners. Other steps were taken in river restoration, wastewater treatment, and recycling. As Ebrard (2014) readily admitted, these small steps were only a beginning, but they proved that progress could be made even in a megacity.

Rio de Janeiro has used two major events as reasons for attempting its own turnaround, the 2014 FIFA World Cup and the 2016 Summer Olympics. Much attention was focused on whether the many stadiums, hotels, airports, and other facilities would be completed on time and adequately, and whether crowds of visitors would be able to enjoy the events with security. The temptation was to simply assure that the zones closest to where the events take place are safe for visitors. Police and army units reoccupied some favelas that were in the hands of drug lords. The test will be whether after the spotlight of world attention is gone, the poor residents will find that their city works better for them.

LOOKING AHEAD

In one sense, Latin American urbanization is now nearly complete—at least quantitatively. The half-century move to the city is nearing completion, and most city residents are now children or grandchildren of those who made the move. The fate of Latin Americans depends largely on what kinds of cities they will live in. The effectiveness of the municipal government may matter at least as much as the ideological stripe of the party occupying the presidency. Some issues, such as crime prevention, are primarily local.

Some of the issues mentioned here (inequality and poverty, discrimination, crime) will be dealt with in subsequent chapters. The next chapter turns to the quarter of the population remaining in the countryside, as we consider changes in agriculture.

FURTHER READING

Although inevitably dated, Gilbert (1994) is a useful introduction. McGuirk (2014) is a report on urban design innovations in over a half dozen cities. The longitudinal studies by Perlman (2010) and Moser (2009) are especially valuable because they trace the lives of poor people over several decades and three generations. Cadena et al. (2011) and The Economist Intelligence Unit (2010) provide examples of urban innovation. Schwartz (2004) tells the story of Curitiba, including the politics. The Winter 2014 issue of *Americas Quarterly* (vol. 8, no. 1) is devoted to "Our Cities, Our Future." The Winter 2003 issue of *ReVista* offers a number of pointed short essays on aspects of Latin American cities. For an inside look at Rio favelas, see the half-hour video produced by Catalytic Communities at http://www.youtube.com/watch?v=2sT8rhhbCUA#t=1020.

CHAPTER 3

Agriculture in Transition

Food and Farmers

Although the typical Latin American is now a city dweller, roughly a quarter of the population live in the countryside. Not all are farmers, however: the percentage of the population engaged in agriculture ranges from the higher end in Honduras (39.2%) and Guatemala (38%) to a low in Mexico and Chile (13%) and Argentina (12%). Worldwide, as countries develop, the proportion of people engaged in agriculture tends to decline, even as agricultural productivity rises, and hence it is no surprise that a similar pattern can be discerned in Latin America, albeit with its own features.

A quick comparison with the historical experience of the United States offers a useful perspective. In 1900, 40 percent of the US population worked in agriculture; by 1930, the figure was 21 percent, and it continued to decline. Today around 16 percent of the US population is classified as rural, but only about 2 percent of the labor force is engaged in agriculture—there are ten times as many teachers as farmers in the United States[1]—and yet the United States is the world's largest agricultural exporter (now being challenged by Brazil). Europe has seen a similar evolution, although the percentage of farmers in the labor force is higher because Europe has favored a family as opposed to a corporate model of farming. Corporate farming dominates in commodities like corn, soybeans, hogs, and poultry. Increasingly in the 1980s, many family farms closed; those that survived did so by modernizing and expanding acreage. Some farm families find a niche, particularly with organic farming, but they need nonfarm income to survive.

This chapter outlines major features and trends in Latin American agriculture today, tracing patterns, land reforms, modernization, the supermarket revolution, and prospects for viable family farming.

PATTERNS OF AGRICULTURE

Latin American countries have long had a dual system of agriculture: large plantations producing export crops and small subsistence farms. In Guatemala, for example, the flat Pacific coast area has been devoted to plantations producing coffee, sugar, cotton,

Guatemalan corn farmer spreading fertilizer. © Noah Friedman-Rudovsky.

and cattle, generally run by managers for absentee owners. In the highlands, indigenous families worked tens of thousands of small plots, often just a few acres. Only about 10 percent of all agricultural land was in what might be called "family farms," that is, owner-operated farms with enough land for a family to make a decent living.

These two primary forms (plantations and subsistence farms) were interrelated. The permanent labor force on the plantations was not large, but during harvest season (roughly October to January), labor was needed to cut sugarcane and to pick cotton and coffee beans. That was also the fallow period between the harvest of corn and beans in the highlands late in the year and planting in the following April or May. Labor contractors brought truckloads of indigenous subsistence farmers and their families down from the highlands to the Pacific coast to work for a month at a time for the minimum agricultural wage (in the 1970s, about a dollar a day). They lived in crowded open-air sheds that were simply a roof and a space to hang hammocks. A farm family could go to the coast for a month or two and bring back a small amount of cash to supplement their earnings. They were often in debt to the labor contractor, however, and their meager earnings could be squandered in a bar.

Versions of this pattern of subsistence farming alongside large agroexport plantations have existed throughout Latin America, with some partial exceptions, such as Costa Rica, where coffee was largely family farmed. Coffee is labor-intensive, and if a family had enough land, it could make a decent living, provided coffee prices did not plunge too low. Such family coffee farms were also common in the coffee region of Colombia and some parts of Brazil.

This pattern of large plantations and ranches is rooted in history. After subjugating the indigenous inhabitants, the sixteenth-century conquistadors took tracts of land for themselves and put local labor to work on them. Sugar plantations were being set up in northeastern Brazil and later in the Caribbean, using African slave labor. The plantation was a self-sufficient entity, growing food and producing sugarcane, which was processed at sugar mills that at the time were advanced industrial operations. The processed sugar was shaped in molds and exported by ship. Another model of farming was the hacienda (*fazenda* in Portuguese), which might best be translated as "ranch," since it emphasized the production of cattle. The hacienda did not produce primarily for export; landholding was itself an expression of power and prestige. Alongside these large enterprises were many small farmers who continued to live in their communities, producing their own food at a subsistence level. This dual structure remained through the colonial period and the decades after independence. It began to change in the later nineteenth century when European and American demand for beef, coffee, sugar, tobacco, bananas, and other products led to a great agroexport boom (1870–1930). The export boom produced a class of prosperous landholders who constituted the ruling elites. The land-tenure pattern that made a few wealthy while condemning the vast majority to poverty eventually led to calls for change.

A 2011 study provides a typology of Latin American farm types, showing the prevalence of this dual pattern, but also indicating the gradations between large operations and subsistence farming (table 3.1).

TABLE 3.1. Typology of Latin American Farms (by Size)

TYPE OF FARM	CHARACTER-ISTICS	NUMBER	LAND AREA (IN HECTARES)	PERCENTAGE OF TOTAL LAND AREA
Corporate	Absentee owned—large mechanized operations, often for export	0.5 million	500 million	55%
Family a. Commercial	Family operated; commercial, competitive, hires labor	1 million	100 million	45%
b. Subsistence	Family does almost all work	4 million	200 million	
c. Sub-subsistence	Family needs nonfarm income	10 million	100 million	

Source: Berdegué and Fuentealba (2011).

Bolivian Aymara women planting potatoes. © Noah Friedman-Rudovsky.

A half million corporate farms and ranches have over half the agricultural land and often produce for export. The other three categories are all classified as "family" farms.[2] However, fourteen million are described as either subsistence or sub-subsistence. Being a subsistence farmer means growing one's own food and selling a little of one's surplus in order to buy a few needs such as fabric for clothes or cooking oil. Until a few decades ago, that was how the rural poor lived, only marginally in the cash economy as producers and consumers, but in the twenty-first century subsistence farming is increasingly nonviable, because even the rural poor have increasing needs that can only be supplied by the cash economy. Moreover, as table 3.1 indicates, the largest number of farmers are classified as "sub-subsistence," that is, they have too little land even for subsistence.

Only one million agricultural operations (one-ninth of land farmed) are described as both "family" and "commercial," meaning they are owner-operated farms on which a family can make a decent living. Such farmers are connected to the market and can afford perhaps a pickup truck or other equipment needed for a modern operation.

Thus, of the roughly 25 percent of Latin Americans classified as rural, some work as employees on large enterprises (whether corporate or family operated), some live primarily from what they produce on their land, some work in nonfarm employment, and some live from a combination of farm and nonfarm employment. These models of farming, as well as the fact that farms produce both for domestic consumption and for export, should be kept in mind as we consider current trends in agriculture. First, however, we consider historical efforts to address inequality of land tenure.

LAND REFORMS AND THEIR LEGACY

The cry for land attributed to Emiliano Zapata in the Mexican Revolution ("La tierra es de quien la trabaja"; "The land belongs to those who till it") echoed throughout the twentieth century in all Latin American countries. The fact that profits from agriculture went largely to absentee owners seemed to call for a more just division of agricultural lands. To those objecting on the grounds of the owners' property rights, it could be replied that the plantations and haciendas were the result of an unjust expropriation, either in colonial times or in the later nineteenth century when the wealthy took lands from the indigenous people and from Catholic religious orders in order to grow export crops. For centuries, large landholders had held on to their land through violence, perpetrated either by their own henchmen or by government troops.

Land reforms were unleashed by revolutions in Mexico (1910), Bolivia (1952), and Cuba (1959). In Mexico, the large landholding system was broken, and land was distributed to peasants to be worked as *ejidos*, a communal form of working the land. The Bolivian land reform broke the power of large landholders in the highlands, but it did not enable small farmers to rise out of poverty. In Cuba, land was initially taken from the allies of the Fulgencio Batista regime who had fled the country. Eventually, all large estates were nationalized and converted into state farms.

Spurred by the Cuban Revolution, in the 1960s the US government urged land reform in Latin America, partly to undercut the appeal of revolution but also as a step toward modernizing economies. The argument was that much land on plantations was idle or underutilized and could be farmed more intensively by small farmers.

Large landowners were unpersuaded. For example, in the mid-1970s, the Salvadoran military-led government, with support from the US embassy, proposed a moderate land reform and invoked the example of Taiwan, where land reform had helped pave the way for rapid industrial growth. Landholders and the right wing fought back with propaganda campaigns in the press; bombs were set off in the Jesuit university, which had supported the reform. As a result, the government backed away from land reform proposals. The events were symptomatic of the resistance of landholders and their ability to wield power when their perceived interests were threatened. A major ingredient in the wars in Nicaragua, El Salvador, and Guatemala in the 1970s and 1980s was pressure for land reform and resistance from landholders.

The implementation of land reform varied considerably from country to country. If given their preference, small farmers typically wished to receive a sufficient portion of land and then be left in peace. Few land reforms did so, however. In Cuba, the prevailing model was a state farm; farmers ended up being state employees, with job security and with benefits (electricity, schools, clinics, housing). Other land reforms encouraged a more communal form of ownership or operation, such as cooperatives. Obtaining land, though, is not sufficient: farmers need seeds, fertilizers, pesticides, market access, credit, agricultural extension service, crop insurance, and so forth. Cooperatives are a way of addressing these needs.

Another question was whether and how the owners whose land was expropriated might be compensated, and whether the beneficiaries of the land reform would pay for their land (generally at below-market rates). Table 3.2 illustrates some of these variations, along with the eventual outcomes.

When poor small farmers were half or more of the population, land reform seemed to be required by the demands of justice and economic modernization. Its advocates often assumed that peasants with enough land would no longer feel the need to migrate, and thus rapid urbanization would be curbed. As an examination of the table indicates, however, the historical examples of land reform have not solved the problems of the countryside or of nations as a whole. Some land reforms were simply reversed, often with violence (Guatemala, Chile). Some affected only a portion of the country (Peru, Bolivia). In Mexico, the *ejido* system functioned from the 1930s to the 1990s. Meanwhile, a prosperous commercial agriculture grew up, especially in the north, aimed at the US market. In 1992, President Salinas formally nullified the land reform law: farmers would now own their land individually and could sell it. The most devastating blow came in 1994 when the market was opened to the import of cheap corn from the United States under the North American Free Trade Agreement (NAFTA). An estimated two million found that farming was no longer viable for them, and they opted to move to the cities or to go to the United States looking for work. In Cuba, for three decades the revolutionary government supplied sugar to the Soviet Union, was paid above-market prices, and had access to oil and other goods. The collapse of communism and low world sugar prices led to sugar mill closures in Cuba, but private farming was permitted only slowly.

The MST (Landless Workers' Movement) in Brazil, which arose in the mid-1980s, has been the most well-known and successful land reform effort in recent decades. Its primary organizing tactic has been occupation of underutilized lands on large farms. It then negotiates with the government to be allowed to settle and farm the land. Between the Cardoso (1995–2002) and Lula (2003–2010) governments, almost a million households were settled this way. However, those settled have not always had other things necessary for success: credit, market access, irrigation. The MST was very disappointed with the Lula government, both for its response to their demands and for its acceptance of the model of commercial agriculture now ascendant in Brazil.

Few today would advocate land reform based on breaking up existing large farms. Rather, efforts should be aimed at fostering viable family farms and assuring that jobs in the rural economy can provide a living wage and adequate working conditions.

TRANSFORMATIONS IN AGRICULTURE

The United States was the world's largest exporter of soybeans until 2006, when it was surpassed by Brazil, which is now one of the world's leading agricultural economies. Brazil also has the world's largest beef herd, double the size of that of the United

TABLE 3.2. Latin American Land Reforms

COUNTRY AND TIME	POLITICAL CIRCUM-STANCES	MODEL	OUTCOME
Mexico, declared in 1917; accelerated in 1930s	Revolution	Expropriation, creation of communal *ejidos*	Existing large estates divided among small farmers in some parts of country but not all (e.g., Chiapas) Large-scale commercial farming grows up in northern Mexico Land reform reversed in 1992; small farmers devastated by import of cheap corn from United States under globalization
Bolivia, 1950s	Revolution	Underutilized land distributed	Power of large landholders broken Land reform does not really bring fundamental change for indigenous people Large-scale commercial farming later develops and expands in eastern Bolivian lowlands
Guatemala, 1950s	Democratic government	Land to small farmers; with compensation to previous owners	Reversed with 1954 CIA overthrow of Arbenz government; large landholders and military regain power, and country remains under military and oligarchical control for decades
Cuba, 1960s	Revolution	Expropriation, creation of state farms	After attempts at diversification fail, Cuba enters pact with USSR to supply sugar in return for oil; sugar dependency increased Agriculture declines; Cuba importing 80% of its food in 2000s
Chile, 1960s	Democratic government	Land to small farmers; encouragement of cooperatives	Reversed by Pinochet dictatorship Emphasis placed on export of fruits and wine Small farming declines
Peru, late 1960s	Leftist military government	Imposed by force; organization into cooperatives	Power of traditional landholders broken on coast; little effect in indigenous highland Cooperatives broken into individual plots in 1980s
Nicaragua, 1980s	Revolution	Expropriation of absentee owners' lands; state farms, cooperatives, and individual plots	Sandinista Revolution at first favors state-farm model *Contra* (counterrevolutionary) forces take advantage of peasant discontent; Sandinistas later favor individual plots Effect of land reform undone by post-1990 governments and poor economic conditions

TABLE 3.2. Latin American Land Reforms (continued)

COUNTRY AND TIME	POLITICAL CIRCUM-STANCES	MODEL	OUTCOME
El Salvador, early 1980s	Program imposed by the United States to undercut appeal of revolution	Land to farmers; compensation to owners; organization of cooperatives	Cooperatives function in the 1980s under war conditions By mid-1990s, right-wing ARENA government economic strategy de-emphasizes agriculture
Brazil, 1990s–2000s	Democratic governments; MST (Landless Workers' Movement) applies pressure	Compensation to owners; cooperatives	Hundreds of thousands of families settled on land under Cardoso and Lula governments Insufficient credit and agricultural assistance for some farmers

States. Brazil leads the world in the production of coffee, cane sugar, oranges and orange juice, and dry beans, and is one of the top three producers of soybeans, corn, beef, poultry, and various other products. From colonial times until the Great Depression, the Brazilian economy was based on agroexport, which continued even during the industrialization of the mid-twentieth century. What is new is how Brazilian commercial agriculture has modernized and expanded. The value of Brazilian crops rose 365 percent in ten years (1996–2006), aided partly by rising commodity prices.

What happened in the *cerrado*, a large savanna area in the middle of the country south of the Amazon basin, is emblematic. Until three or four decades ago, the *cerrado* was considered agriculturally unproductive, among other reasons because of poor soil. In the 1970s, the government agency EMBRAPA (Brazilian Agricultural Research Corporation), working with commercial farmers, made a number of innovations. The soils have been made productive with the addition of lime and phosphorus. An African grass was crossbred to produce a variety more productive than the native grass, to be used as pasture and so expand the beef herd. Another innovation was no-till agriculture: crops are harvested on the stalk and the remains of the plant are left to rot in place, where seeds for the next crop can be planted with no need for plowing.

EMBRAPA scientists have developed thirty varieties of soybean, which is normally a temperate-climate crop, now adapted for growing in the tropics. The upshot is that a highly productive area has been developed in the heart of South America. It is now common to plant corn after harvesting soybeans and thus get two (or sometimes three) crops in a year. Brazilian scientists and farmers have not simply imported technology but have developed techniques and bred new varieties, the patents for which are held in Brazil. This area, which some call "Soylandia," rivals the

Soy farm in Brazil. © Noah Friedman-Rudovsky.

US Midwest in productivity, and includes portions of northern Argentina, Paraguay, and eastern Bolivia.[3]

Mexican commercial agriculture has developed quite differently. In the decades after the revolution, the aftermath of which divided up traditional haciendas in much of the country, a new type of commercial agriculture arose in the country's northern and western states: irrigated agriculture aimed at the US market. NAFTA in 1994 further linked Mexican agriculture to the United States, which receives three-quarters of Mexican agricultural exports. By comparison, only 6 percent of Brazil's agricultural exports go to the United States; most go to a variety of markets, the largest being the European Union (24%) followed by China (18%). The types of products also differ notably. Mexico's exports are primarily fruits and vegetables: tomatoes (15%), avocados (8%), peppers (7%), and a large variety of other products. Brazil's exports are heavily in commodities, especially soybeans, which are largely used in animal feeds. The rising demand and high prices owe much to growing appetites for meat in China.

Argentina is yet another interesting point of comparison. Its agricultural and grazing land is temperate rather than tropical. Agriculture constitutes only 7 percent of GDP, but it is 52 percent of exports, primarily in commodity crops. In Colombia, some argue that the country's *llanos* (grasslands) in the east are similar to the Brazilian *cerrado* and could be developed similarly.

Genetically modified organisms (GMOs) have entered Latin American agriculture significantly, but countries are divided over them. Agricultural GMOs are varieties developed through genetic engineering that are easier and cheaper to grow. In using them, farmers must buy seeds and particular fertilizers and pesticides from a company like Monsanto. Although GMOs have been approved for use in the United States after extensive testing has shown no harm to human beings and the environment, critics object to their use on several grounds. Use of GMO single-variety corns could mean the loss of the hundreds of varieties existing now. GMO corn could pollinate other varieties and change their genetic makeup. GMO-growing farmers become dependent on the chemical company that provides their inputs. Finally, it can be argued that even though no harmful effects have been found in testing, we should err on the side of caution. The European Union and individual countries in Europe have taken a go-slow approach, with extensive restrictions and labeling requirements. Argentina, Brazil, and Paraguay quickly accepted GMOs for soybeans, corn, and some other commodity crops. As of 2014, Peru had banned cultivation of GMOs, on the grounds that its rich biodiversity of native crops could be threatened. At that time, the use of GMOs in Mexico was being battled in court.

FAIR-TRADE COFFEE

Most patrons of coffee chains and food shoppers are now familiar with the term "fair trade," especially when applied to coffee. How it came about illustrates important aspects of farming and the food production chain.

In the late 1970s, activists noted that most of the several dollars paid for a can of coffee went to the brand-name company; very little was passed on to the coffee grower, and only pennies went to the laborers who picked it. Critics began to draw attention to this injustice and call for fair trade.

Some NGOs and church-related organizations did this by buying the coffee in beans from the farmers, typically through a cooperative, and transporting it to sympathetic buyers in church organizations or shops offering fair-trade coffee. The price might be higher than the mass-production coffee sold in the supermarket, but these consumers were willing to pay. By implication, conventional coffee was unjust. The obvious disadvantage of this system was that only an infinitesimal amount could be sold this way, and only if connections were made between a local farmers coop and an organization in the developed world.

Other developments made it possible for fair trade to become more mainstream. One possibility was to put pressure on well-known name brands. Most important was the introduction of standards for labor and environmental practices and mechanisms for monitoring and issuing certification. The entity certified was not the individual farmer but the growers cooperative or perhaps second-level cooperative, which was serving as a marketing agent. Under fair-trade arrangements, farmers are guaranteed a minimum price, even when world prices drop; when prices rise, they may receive a premium. The amount of coffee being produced and sold in this way grew from the 1990s onward.

Changing tastes have helped make fair-trade certification possible. Forty years ago, coffee was a commodity that consumers bought by brand names like Folgers or Maxwell House, just as they bought gasoline for their cars. Over a twenty-five-year period, so-called "specialty coffees" grew from 1 percent to 20 percent of the US coffee market by 2007. Consumers now have a variety of flavors from which to choose, and many are aware of the country of origin and type of bean. Even so, only about 4 percent of coffee exported to developed countries is fair-trade certified.

Fair trade in itself does not resolve all problems for coffee growers. Farmers sometimes find that meeting all the requirements for certification, particularly organic practices, does not make economic sense for them. Or they may find that it is better to sell a portion of their production as ordinary commodity coffee to mass buyers.

By 2012, Fair Trade USA, which is part of a global network of such organizations headquartered in Bonn, Germany, was working with 360 farmers cooperatives, mainly in Latin America, and was working with 740 companies, including Starbucks, Dunkin' Donuts, Costco, and Whole Foods. However, when it proposed extending certification beyond cooperatives to large plantations and individual small farmers, it was roundly condemned by others in the movement for betraying the "democratic" principles of the fair-trade movement.[4]

Before returning to prospects for Latin America's rural people, the subsistence farmers and farm laborers, we must consider an important development on the domestic consumption side.

THE SUPERMARKET REVOLUTION

Supermarkets have existed in Latin America for a half century, but for most of that time they served primarily the upper 10 percent or so of the population. In the last two or three decades, however, ordinary households have done more and more of their shopping in supermarkets. The chains themselves have been expanding from large cities to secondary cities and even towns, and from upper- and middle-class neighborhoods to poorer areas. From 1992 to 2002, the percentage of food bought through supermarkets leaped from 10–20 percent to 50–60 percent in the larger Latin American countries (Reardon and Gulati 2008).

How is this rapid growth to be explained? One obvious answer is investment by supermarket chains, sometimes with foreign capital, but that does not explain people's readiness to change their food-buying habits. The first generations of immigrants to cities continue to eat as they did in the countryside, often a diet based on a

Supermarket, Santiago, Chile. © Tommie Sue Montgomery.

few staples (corn tortillas, rice and beans, or potatoes), which are grown primarily by small farmers. As they become more urban and earn more, they consume more bread, meat, dairy, processed foods, and fresh produce. Having a refrigerator makes it possible to keep foods and plan more than one meal ahead. As women increasingly work outside the home, they favor meals that can be prepared quickly. Consumers shop at supermarkets for a combination of price, variety, convenience, and food safety.

One of the reasons that supermarkets can offer foods at attractive prices is that they bypass the traditional supply chain, in which farmers sell their crops to intermediaries, who in turn sell to wholesalers in the cities, who then sell to retailers. Supermarkets need to operate systems with timely supply at agreed-upon standards: so many cartons of eggs, so many pounds of beef or pork, so many pounds of tomatoes of a given quality, on a given date, and hence they have contractual arrangements with producers.

To see this development from another angle, traditionally, large commercial agriculture was primarily for export, while basic staples like corn and beans were produced by small farmers who sold to intermediaries. As the diets of urban consumers have changed, more domestic food production follows a commercial model, although the farms in question may be family operated. These changes represent both a challenge and an opportunity to small farmers.

Large commercial farms obviously have an advantage over small farmers: a supermarket chain will prefer to deal with a manageable number of suppliers and cannot make individual contracts with hundreds or thousands of small farmers, even if they could meet the other requirements. If small farmers wish to sell to supermarkets, they have to form larger units such as cooperatives and organize themselves as efficiently as commercial farms to provide products with the same degree of reliability and quality.

From the farmers' standpoint, selling to supermarkets means that from the moment of planting they know that they have a customer and an assured price. They may earn 20–50 percent more than in traditional markets.[5]

PROSPECTS FOR FARMERS

As noted previously, Latin American agriculture is being transformed. At one pole are highly modernized operations, typified by farms in "Soylandia." Such large operations are appropriate for agricultural commodities like soybeans, corn, sorghum, and other grains for animal feed. These commodities do not compete on quality, and their price is set by market factors. They require large mechanized operations and so lend themselves to corporate farming.

At the other pole is subsistence—and sub-subsistence—farming, which is declining, as households need a cash income and as young people seek other opportunities.[6] In Mexico, NAFTA accelerated this process by allowing cheap US corn into the Mexican market, driving down prices and convincing many small farmers that there was no future in traditional corn farming. The crucial question is not how to preserve subsistence farming but how to develop models of farming in which a family can make a reasonably prosperous and reliable living.

An ongoing factor is world food prices. Starting in the 1960s, prices of foods (cereals, oilseeds, meats, dairy, and sugar products) generally trended downward, but in the early 2000s, they started to rise, and spiked in 2006–2008. After that they flattened at a generally higher rate, where they are expected to remain. Higher prices for food seem to have become a permanent reality after decades in which progress in agriculture had kept prices low. World demand is projected to grow faster than supply. The reasons include land going into biofuel production and thus away from grains; demand from emerging countries, especially China; a growing worldwide middle class changing its diet from traditional grains toward meats and processed foods, which require more grain; and crop failures due to weather disasters. Those most immediately affected are poor people worldwide who already spend most of their income on food, typically grains.

The effects of higher food prices on Latin America have been mixed. Countries like Brazil and Argentina, which are net exporters of grains, have fared well (indeed, such prices were largely responsible for Argentina's economic turnaround from the collapse of its economic system and default on its loans in 2000–2001). However, those benefiting are producers of commodity foods. Countries and regions that are net food importers, such as Central America, have suffered the consequences. Those worst affected have been poor households; in Mexico, hikes in the price of tortillas led to street demonstrations.

A 2008 World Bank study exploring the relationship between agriculture and development in the twenty-first century observed that agriculture can "help reduce the remaining rural poverty if smallholders become direct suppliers in modern food markets, good jobs are created in agriculture and agro industry, and markets for environmental services are introduced" (World Bank 2008). To unpack the development jargon, "modern food markets" are supermarkets, which in some Latin American countries already handle close to half of food purchasing. The implication is that of a partnership between supermarkets and family farmers, particularly in supplying fresh produce, especially if it is produced organically. Small producers need to be able to match the quality and reliability of commercial farms. One way of doing that is to band together in producer associations, ideally in a partnership with the supermarket and relevant government agencies.[7]

As noted earlier, "family farms" can include commercial farms, subsistence farms, and sub-subsistence farms, or plots on which the family must seek off-farm employment. The longer-range goal is for agriculture to serve as a route out of poverty for the rural population. Besides technical assistance, farmers need credit and some form of insurance against crop failure. These are areas where governments need to do more. Stated most broadly, the aim should be the fostering of family farms—areas primarily worked by the family on-site—which have enough land, technology, and market access to allow the family to make a decent living. Thus, even if they grow much of what they themselves consume, they produce for the market, whether it be a supermarket or even for export. As noted, they are at a disadvantage vis-à-vis commercial farms, particularly in making contracts with supermarkets, but those disadvantages can be overcome. Some steps that can be taken are:

- grouping of small farmers in cooperatives or other arrangements so that they can become part of modern production chains;
- government purchases of production from family farms for reselling;
- providing government insurance to help family farms deal with price volatility;
- creating farmers markets, perhaps in association with supermarkets, where farmers can sell directly to the final consumer.

After this survey of agriculture, from small farmers to large-scale commercial farming, we turn to surveying businesses, likewise small and large.

FURTHER READING

World Bank (2008) provides an overview of agriculture and development worldwide. On Latin America, see FAO (2011); on agriculture and development, see Byerlee, de Janvry, and Sadoulet (2009). On small farmers, see Berdegué and Fuentealba (2011); on the *cerrado*, Hecht and Mann (2008); on the implications for Latin America of the supermarket revolution, Reardon and Berdegué (2002).

Corner Stores and *Multilatinas*

Business, Industry, and Labor in a Globalized World

Anyone walking through an ordinary Latin American neighborhood is soon likely to see a small shop selling soda, candy, medicines, or elementary groceries. Within a few minutes, one may see other businesses catering to immediate needs, such as a bakery, grocery store, or drugstore. Taking a bus, one will see businesses interspersed with residences: auto or tire repair, beauty and barber shops, doctors' and lawyers' offices, restaurants, gas stations, small shopping centers with parking lots, and perhaps even a mall; another route would pass factories or warehouse operations. In fact, like people everywhere, Latin Americans are surrounded by many businesses, ranging from street stalls to large corporations.

Although omnipresent, business is not prominent in academic writing about Latin America, which tends to speak of abstractions like "capitalism" or "neoliberalism." Scholars and activists in Latin America and elsewhere have often assumed that business was inherently exploitative. Such assumptions were still common in 2002 when Lula became president of Brazil, since he had been a labor leader and his party was considered socialist. To the surprise of many, however, Lula appointed business figures to key cabinet positions, and Brazilian businesses large and small thrived during his eight years as president, benefiting even the poor.

The private sector matters to Latin America for the obvious reason that most people work in it, even if they are self-employed. It also matters because the quality of goods and services people receive depends on the quality of the businesses providing them.

In 2010, Chilean president Sebastián Piñera pointed to a major challenge when he wrote:

> Latin America arrived late to the 19th-century industrial revolution and that helps explain why we are still an underdeveloped continent. But we cannot be late for the 21st-century revolution: the knowledge, technology and information society will be very generous to those countries that wish to embrace it, but indifferent—and even cruel—to those that let it pass by. (Piñera 2010)

Small business selling mobile phones, Asunción, Paraguay. © Noah Friedman-Rudovsky.

Piñera was referring to the fact that after independence in the early nineteenth century, Latin American elites accepted the region's assigned role in the international division of labor as a supplier of raw materials. With the proceeds, those elites could import the results of that revolution (street lighting in capital cities, automobiles), at least for themselves. When demand for raw materials plummeted during the Great Depression of the 1930s, the larger countries, especially Brazil, Mexico, and Argentina, began belated state-led industrialization programs, and over the next several decades industries grew with the help of high import tariffs and other protectionist measures. American and European multinational companies set up operations to supply local markets. Likewise, Latin American family-owned enterprises arose in some lines of industry (clothing, food, beverages), but the goods produced could not compete on the world market in terms of price and quality without tariff protection. Starting in the 1980s, Latin American countries shifted from a protectionist to a free-trade model, as was happening elsewhere in the world. The process was painful (many businesses closed), but starting in the early 2000s, the region in general returned to growth, partly as a result of improved financial stability.

A general historical pattern can be discerned worldwide in which national economies move from agriculture, to manufacturing, to services. The move to a service economy has been taking place in the United States for decades.[1] As implied by

Piñera, Latin America was late in industrializing and did so to varying degrees, but over half of Latin Americans now work in the service sector.

This chapter surveys some current developments in the private sector, generally moving from smaller to larger businesses. Topics include the formal and informal economy, the emergence of large Latin American corporations called *multilatinas*, and the role of technology. The focus is generally on the situation of firms, leaving economic policy for chapter 13.

SMALL BUSINESS AND THE INFORMAL SECTOR

The vast majority of Latin American businesses are microenterprises employing ten or fewer people. Relatively few are large enterprises (i.e., those with 250 or more employees). In between these are small and medium enterprises. It should be kept in mind that what is considered a "large" business in a country like Nicaragua (with five million people) might seem quite ordinary in Brazil (with two hundred million).

With the debt crisis of the 1980s and the subsequent "lost decade," hiring slowed at large firms and in the government, and it was "microenterprise"—essentially the informal economy or self-employment—that served as a "sponge" to soak up workers

Market in El Alto, Bolivia, offering a wide variety of goods. © *Phillip Berryman.*

unable to obtain formal-sector jobs. In Latin America, a large portion of workers and businesses are off the books: their businesses are not registered, they do not pay taxes, and they are not enrolled in pension programs. They are often simply self-employed people, such as street vendors or repairmen, but also businesses such as the corner store invoked at the beginning of this chapter. Together they constitute the "informal sector."

A common form of informal labor is domestic service. A few decades ago, well-off families had live-in maids, and often more than one. Today, many households pay women to come in to clean, prepare foods, or take care of children. If they work a given number of hours per week, labor legislation may require that they be formally registered and subject to deductions for benefits, so commonly they work below that threshold on different days for different families and are paid in cash.

The informal sector existed long before it was labeled: people were hired as needed and paid in cash. The formal sector rose slowly as governments kept records and began to tax businesses, and as social-insurance schemes were put in place in the middle decades of the twentieth century. Even at the height of the 1930–1980 period, only a minority of workers were in the formal sector, primarily public employees and those employed by large companies. These formal workers often had their own health-care network.

During and after the "lost decade" of the 1980s, as the formal sector stagnated or shrank, the informal sector expanded, absorbing labor. People from shantytowns such as Indio Guayas (chapter 2) typically work in the informal sector, making clothes to order at home, hiring out as day laborers in construction, or repairing shoes or electrical appliances.

The degree of informality varies considerably from Chile, Argentina, and Costa Rica to Peru and Bolivia.[2] The figures in table 4.1 also indicate a correlation between informality and poverty: Bolivia, where two-thirds of the economy is informal, is far poorer than Chile, where the figure is only one-fifth.

The informal sector is less productive than the formal sector; for example, in one hour a supermarket checkout clerk handles many times the value of what a corner store employee sells in a day. It should not be assumed, however, that all informal workers are poor. For instance, skilled builders can operate a business constructing entire houses for clients, operating on a cash basis, and employing assistants as needed.

Some would add a third sector: the illicit or criminal economy, most obviously drug production and trafficking, including a series of illegal forms of commerce. Speaking of Peru, Francisco Durand lists various types of contraband (agricultural products and food, beverages, tobacco, petroleum derivates, software, and piracy) estimated to total $1.8 billion. Contraband is thus not simply carried out by individuals crossing borders and reselling small amounts but has a far greater reach (Durand 2007, 88–104). The weight and composition of the third, or criminal, sector is difficult to measure and varies by country and region, but it should be taken into account when considering the nature of Latin American economies.

TABLE 4.1. Degree of Informality of Latin American Economies, 1999–2007

WORLD RANKING	COUNTRY	PERCENTAGE OF GDP
[1]	[Switzerland]	[8.5]
[2]	[United States]	[8.6]
35	Chile	19.3
45	Argentina	25.3
46	Costa Rica	25.8
62	Mexico	30.0
70	Dominican Republic	31.9
74	Ecuador	32.4
MIDWAY POINT		
86	Venezuela	33.8
98	Colombia	37.3
103	Paraguay	38.8
105	Brazil	39.0
127	Nicaragua	44.6
129	El Salvador	45.1
138	Honduras	48.3
142	Guatemala	50.5
144	Uruguay	50.6
147	Peru	58.0
151	Bolivia	66.1

Source: Schneider, Buehn, and Montenegro (2010). Countries in brackets are for purposes of comparison.

In the 1980s, the Peruvian economist Hernando de Soto argued that the informal economy was a potential force for development. He staked his position against both the left, which saw the informal sector as an indictment of capitalism, and the right, which generally ignored the poor. He saw those engaged in self-built housing, unregistered transport of goods and passengers, and off-the-books businesses as incipient entrepreneurs whose potential should be unleashed. In his view, government regulation was the single largest impediment to that economic takeoff.[3] A key point of de Soto's argument is that without title to their home or land, poor people cannot use what they have as collateral for starting small businesses. He thus urged that regulations for opening businesses and acquiring title to land and houses should be streamlined (de Soto 1989).[4]

There is much to be said for making it easy to start and operate small businesses, but de Soto overstates his case. Although the many bureaucratic hurdles to registering a business (now documented elsewhere in Latin America and around the world), foster the informal economy, it is also true that entering the formal economy often does not make economic sense for small business owners. People are understandably reluctant to place their home in jeopardy to have collateral to open or expand a small business, when that home is the only form of security they have. Likewise, a man who builds houses by paying his workers out of his household wallet may not be willing to register his business if that means paying taxes and paying his workers a salary with benefits even for days when they do not work. Similarly, a woman who does domestic service might understandably prefer to be paid in cash now rather than receive a check at the end of the month with deductions. An off-the-books business may provide a better income than a low-paying formal-sector job. Although policy changes can be helpful, the informal sector will diminish primarily when formal-sector jobs are more plentiful and when it makes economic sense for small businesses to become formal.

SHIFT TO RETAIL

The Fundadores Mall, which opened in 2009 in Manizales, a traditional city in the heart of the coffee country of Colombia, offers insight into shifts taking place in retailing and indeed the economy. On the top floor is a food court with over twenty offerings (mainly Colombian food chains) and a large seating area. It has over one hundred retail stores and a multiplex theater, and the bottom level is occupied by a hypermarket of the Colombian chain Éxito. The underground parking has space for hundreds of cars and motorcycles, but many shoppers arrive by public transport.

Entering from the front of the Éxito store in Manizales, one finds a well-stocked supermarket with the accent on commonly consumed food items. The store is a hypermarket, so the other portion is a department store, with clothing, electronic consumer items, exercise equipment, and a half dozen motorcycles. This hypermarket model originated in Europe and was tried in the 1980s in the United States, especially by the French company Carrefour, but did not catch on. It has had more success in Brazil, Mexico, and some other Latin American countries. The premise of the hypermarket is that customers find everything they are looking for under one roof; the appeal may be partly psychological, a pleasure in being surrounded by goods, even if one is not shopping for, or cannot afford, them. One attraction of buying from a company like Éxito is that it offers its own credit: the motorcycles for sale display both the total price and the monthly payment. Indeed, many stores offer their own credit card.

Like supermarkets, malls have existed in Latin America for decades, but the pace

Mall, Buenos Aires, Argentina. © Tommie Sue Montgomery.

of construction picked up in the 2000s as malls were built in provincial cities and adjacent to poor urban barrios. In Brazil, the number went from 338 in 2006 to over 500 in 2013. Malls differ in style and in the type of customer they target; some obviously target upper-income customers and offer largely luxury goods affordable only to elites. Others are clearly spaces where a broader cross section of society can be seen, including whole families from grandma to infants on an outing. Some people no doubt come primarily for window-shopping and perhaps to have fast food or ice cream. Physical security is one factor in the popularity of malls, along with air-conditioning and an overall order and cleanliness.

Malls are a sign of a larger shift that has taken place in the world economy. In the mid-twentieth century, the heart of the economy was symbolized by the industrial giants with familiar names: US Steel, General Motors, Ford, General Mills, General Electric, Westinghouse, Motorola, Unilever, and so forth. After the 1970s, however, portions of manufacturing were shifted to low-wage countries, especially China, and production became a chain whose links could be located on different continents. The brand loyalty of consumers has largely passed from the manufacturers to the large retail companies (Walmart, Target, IKEA, Best Buy, Home Depot), which sign contracts with suppliers from around the world. A similar shift is under way in Latin America. The continued expansion of malls reflects changes in society, such as more women in the workforce and an expanding middle class.

TABLE 4.2. Top Food Franchises in Latin America, 2012

COMPANY	NO. OF LOCATIONS
McDonald's	3,350
Subway	1,804
7-Eleven	1,351
Cacau Show (Brazil)	1,126
Burger King	1,079
Grido Helado (Argentina)	925
KFC	900
Bob's (Brazil)	739
Pizza Hut	700
Domino's Pizza	598
Starbucks	503
Casa do Pão de Queijo (Brazil)	400
Havanna (Argentina)	213
Dunkin' Donuts	140
Taco Bell	100

Source: Barnes (2012, 45).

A related phenomenon is franchising. US fast-food franchises in Latin America date back at least to the 1970s, often lamented as a loss of local culture.[5] Nevertheless, franchising represents a significant development in Latin American business.

It should be noted that five of the chains listed in table 4.2 are Latin American. One of them is Casa do Pão de Queijo, which began in 1967 when Mario Carneiro opened a shop in São Paulo using his mother's recipe for *pão de queijo* (cheese bread); it caught on and expanded as a franchise chain. In 2003, Woods Staton, a Colombian national, formed a consortium with private equity firms from Brazil and the United States and paid $700 million for the Latin American McDonald's outlets, now called Arcos Dorados (Golden Arches), which has 86,000 employees. In 2010, a Brazilian investment group bought a majority stake in Burger King worldwide.

In short, Latin America has embraced the franchising business model. Brazil has more than 1,890 franchise brands, with more than 90,000 outlets. Mexican franchises employ almost a half million people and generate 6 percent of the country's GDP. Most of these are retail chains for higher-end consumer products, though, not restaurants.

RISE OF THE *MULTILATINAS*

In 2010, the Mexican Carlos Slim became the richest person in the world, surpassing Bill Gates. His many holdings include América Móvil, the largest telecom company in

Food court in a mall, Caracas, Venezuela. © *Noah Friedman-Rudovsky.*

Latin America. Slim's innovation was prepaid calling cards (as opposed to requiring people to pay a monthly bill), thereby making mobile phones much more accessible to lower-income people. By 2007, the company had fifty million customers in Mexico, far more than the competition. Slim was accused of using political connections to buy companies and of exploiting a quasi monopoly with América Móvil, whose rates were said to be artificially high as a result of its stranglehold on the market. In 2013, the Mexican government moved to open competition in the telecom industry, and Slim returned to second place behind Gates.

This example suggests how business is changing in the age of globalization. Two or three decades ago, the largest companies in Latin America were usually subsidiaries of US and European companies, producing for the local market. Some large family-owned conglomerates operated in São Paulo, Mexico City, and other large cities, but most companies were modest in scale. Manufacturing companies enjoyed the protection of high tariffs and often a comfortable quasi monopoly. When tariffs and other barriers were removed, the companies suddenly had to face stiff competition, and some went out of business.

Now, however, some Latin American companies have learned to compete and even go global themselves. Such companies, which first expand to neighboring countries and then to Europe, North America, or Asia, are called *multilatinas*, and include:[6]

- The Brazilian company Embraer is the third-largest aircraft manufacturer in the world (after Airbus and Boeing), specializing in regional jets and smaller planes but also producing some military aircraft. Fifty-five percent of its orders come from the United States.
- The Brazilian oil company Petrobras is a semipublic oil company with operations in twenty-eight countries, valued at $218 billion.
- The Bimbo Group, the world's largest bread-making company, began in Mexico in 1945 and for decades was known primarily for producing sliced white bread there. It began expanding in the 1980s, and in recent years acquired brands such as Entenmann's, Sara Lee, and Thomas's English Muffins. It has revenues of $5 billion and operates in nineteen countries.
- CEMEX, originally a Mexican cement company, is now the third-largest building materials company in the world, with annual revenues of over $18 billion.
- The Brazilian company Vale is the second-largest mining company in the world and operates on five continents. In 2006, it purchased the Canadian nickel company Inco for $18.9 billion in cash, the biggest foreign takeover ever by a Latin American company.
- The Brazilian cosmetics and personal-care-product company Natura Cosméticos has revenues of $3.1 billion and 6,700 employees, in addition to over a half million independent person-to-person sales representatives (like Avon, from which the model was borrowed). The company makes only natural products, is continually innovating based on laboratory work, and seeks to practice environmental sustainability and make that part of its image. It is the seventh-largest personal-care-product company in the world (and Brazil is the third-largest market for such products) and operates in eight countries in Latin America and Europe.
- Pollo Campero is a fast-food franchise company concentrating on fried chicken, which began in Guatemala, expanded to Central America, and now has around three hundred restaurants, including fifty in the United States.

A *multilatina* operates in several Latin American countries; a "global *latina*" is a *multilatina* that has operations in at least one other continent and generates "a minimum of US$500 million in annual revenues" (Casanova and Fraser 2009, 3).[7] The impact of these firms has been seen in company ownership: in 2000, foreign companies accounted for 41 percent of the revenues of the largest five hundred companies in Latin America; by 2005, that figure had dropped to 25 percent.

A study of the top five hundred Latin American companies in 2010 found that the largest were Petrobras, Pemex, Vale, and América Móvil.[8] Most of the first fifty have $10–$50 billion in revenues, followed by many in the $5–$10 billion category. The largest companies are concentrated in Brazil and Mexico, reflecting their larger populations (200 and 120 million respectively). Although many Chilean companies are well run and innovative, they are less likely to become very large when their domestic market is only 15 million people. To keep matters in perspective, even large Latin

American firms are modest-sized on the world stage: only ten of the top five hundred are on the Fortune 500 of global firms (vs. 153 from the United States and 29 from China), and all of those are from Brazil and Mexico. Carlos Slim's América Móvil is fourth in Latin America but 330th in the world on the Fortune list.[9]

Indeed, pinning down the nationality of many large enterprises can be elusive. Consider AmBev, listed as #27 in Latin America. It was formed in 1999 by a merger of the two largest brewery companies in Brazil, making it the largest in South America. In 2004, it merged with Interbrew, a Belgian company, to form InBev, which in 2008 merged with Anheuser-Busch (for $52 billion), and the new firm was named Anheuser-Busch InBev, thus becoming the world's largest beverage company. Through mergers and acquisitions, a Brazilian company thus became part of the world's largest beer company (the CEO is Brazilian), which markets two hundred brands (including Budweiser, Stella Artois, and Becks), and employs 116,000 people. Few beer drinkers are aware of these developments, because the brand names themselves are unaffected.

The automobile industry provides other examples of the changes under way. Until around 1990, American and European auto companies assembled autos in the larger Latin American countries for their domestic markets. Since then, the entire auto industry has been transformed, and national borders have largely dissolved. In 2013, Mexico produced 3.1 million vehicles (more than Canada), four-fifths of which were for the United States. One of GM's global design centers is located in São Paulo, and new model cars are now designed and developed in Brazil. Both Brazil and Mexico are regarded as having a great potential for increasing auto ownership. In Brazil, for every thousand inhabitants there are only 165 cars (as opposed to 812 in the United States). As incomes rise and the middle class expands, the mass auto market is expected to grow as it is elsewhere in emerging economies.[10] Individual countries vary in the manner in which they fit into the international auto industry; in most countries, there is no auto industry: any car in the country rolls off a ship in a port. Argentina has assembly plants that put together the major elements of the car, which are manufactured elsewhere. Only Brazil and Mexico can be said to not only assemble the components but to manufacture them as well.

CORPORATE SOCIAL RESPONSIBILITY

In recent decades, the notion of corporate social responsibility has gained ground in Latin America as elsewhere. Behind it is a sense that businesses should act as good citizens, serving a circle of stakeholders wider than their employees, customers, and shareholders. This stance runs contrary to the commonly uttered dictum that the only obligation of a business is to its owners or shareholders. Critics dismiss corporate social responsibility as public relations or an attempt to divert attention away from the harmful effects of businesses.

Corporate social responsibility had antecedents insofar as traditional family-owned businesses often made donations to projects or occasionally set up foundations, but they were operating primarily on a philanthropic model. Today a new generation of businesspeople believes that it can make a positive contribution to development and can partner positively with organizations in the nonprofit sector. The trend is away from a model in which a company sponsors a project that bears its name to one in which it forms partnerships with civil society organizations, recognizing their experience and expertise. A further step entails moving beyond a simple "giving back" model to one in which a company makes corporate responsibility a part of its entire operation, particularly taking into account the environmental effects of its business activity.[11]

A perhaps surprising example comes from Walmart's operations in Brazil. It began with four stores in the 1990s, but then a decade later expanded by acquiring 258 more. Its US business model of ordering large quantities from producers and transporting them inexpensively to mass-consumer outlets was not directly transferable to Brazil. A nonprofit institute founded by the company worked to develop the capacity of suppliers in the regions where it had stores. A key element was the promotion of Producers Clubs in each region "to locate, recruit, train, and help equip indigenous suppliers for the full range of the chain's products and to work with these suppliers to improve their quality and reliability." Included was a commitment to buy only fairtrade products. In addition, it set up an office to promote the export of the products of its Brazilian suppliers. By 2007, the producers had fostered 324 small companies supplying Walmart outlets (Salamon 2010, 94–96; quote on p. 95).

Walmart is one of the eight partners of the Ethos Institute, the leading Brazilian proponent of corporate social responsibility, which has 1,368 member companies, representing a sizable portion of the Brazilian economy. The Ethos Institute was founded by businesspeople in 1998 and seeks to encourage companies to integrate practices of corporate sustainability into their entire operation, including sound environmental and labor practices and cooperative relations with local communities.

LABOR STRUGGLES AND TRADE UNIONS

Most workers in Latin America are not unionized (obviously not in the informal sector but also not in most small and medium formal enterprises). The unionized labor force is primarily public-sector workers and those in large companies. Unionization rates average around 12–13 percent of the workforce (similar to the US rate of 12 percent) and range as high as 28.9 percent (Argentina) and 25 percent (Bolivia) and as low as 5 percent (Peru) (Hall-Jones 2007).

Organized labor was a major protagonist in society for a half century or more after 1930. In the wake of the Great Depression, governments promoted the development of industry, especially in Brazil, Mexico, and Argentina, sometimes through an explicit three-way partnership between government, industry, and labor unions, which were state sponsored. Consequently, unionized workers enjoyed relatively good pay, benefits, and even extras like sports facilities or vacation areas. Labor unions concentrated on defending their gains and maintaining political alliances. The collective bargaining they engaged in was typically across a whole industry. Many of the enterprises themselves were state enterprises, such as oil in Venezuela and Mexico and steel in Brazil.

Unions typically saw themselves as struggling for more than "bread-and-butter issues" (as in the United States); they were generally on the left politically and sometimes had alliances with leftist parties. In Bolivia, starting in the 1950s, the Bolivian Labor Confederation (COB, or Central Obrera Boliviana), the core of which was mine workers, struggled for its members but also for the rights of the poor as a whole, and was usually at odds with the national government. The military and military-run governments of the 1960s to the 1980s in Brazil, Chile, Uruguay, Argentina, Guatemala, and El Salvador actively persecuted union leaders, seeing them as enemies in a "dirty war"; some were imprisoned, tortured, murdered, or "disappeared." Labor unions in Colombia waged a heroic struggle in the face of violence: between 1986 and 2010, over 2,800 labor union members were murdered, by both right-wing paramilitary groups and government forces. Labor unions in the United States and Europe have made alliances with those in Central America and Colombia, particularly in connection with their opposition to free-trade agreements that did not make sufficient provision for workers' rights.

As a result of labor union struggles, formal-sector workers in some countries enjoy established rights, particularly job stability. For example, a worker who is dismissed is entitled to severance pay, typically a month's wages for every year worked. Although that is beneficial to a worker, it can be a hindrance to hiring: employers are more reluctant to hire permanent workers if the cost of subsequently dismissing them seems prohibitive. Worker benefits (pensions, unemployment) in all modern countries add to the cost of hiring in the formal sector. As is the case elsewhere, labor unions struggle to defend the interests of their members while seeking to expand and find their place in the changed circumstances of the twenty-first-century economy (i.e., globalization and the shift toward a service economy).

INNOVATION AND THE KNOWLEDGE ECONOMY

In considering Latin America's participation in the "knowledge, technology, and information society" mentioned by President Piñera, it is well to be reminded of how recent it is. It was only in the mid-1980s that computers replaced typewriters; the Internet came into common use in the mid-1990s; the public began to turn to Google in the late 1990s, followed by iPhones and apps in the 2000s.[12]

Latin America came into the IT revolution somewhat belatedly, although the elites adopted consumer items as soon as they became common in the developed world.[13] The primary "digital gap" was that most households could not afford a computer, either a desktop or a portable. Nevertheless, adoption was surprisingly rapid; the middle classes did buy devices; many people had Internet access through their workplace; and wherever there was electricity, cybercafés allowed young people to go online for the equivalent of 25 cents an hour. In 2009, taking advantage of the "one laptop per child" program developed at M.I.T., Uruguay became the first country in the world to equip all primary school children with laptop computers. By 2010, there were more mobile phones than people in Colombia. The 2011 Venezuelan mystery-thriller telenovela *La Viuda Joven* (called *The Black Widow* in English) had a million online followers discussing who the killer was.

What Piñera and others have in mind, however, is not simply adaptation of new technologies as consumers, but using them in ways that make businesses more productive. The supermarkets and the businesses in the malls already mentioned depend on modern systems of inventory management. The percentage of people who use computers in their work in countries like Brazil and Chile is similar to that of Europe or North America. The metro system in Santiago adopted a smart-card system years before transport systems in the United States did so.

Examples of applications of the new technologies include the following:

- MercadoLibre, which was begun by an Argentine business student in 1999, operates like eBay: visitors to a site agree to buy an item and pay for it as agreed upon. The company spread to other Latin American countries and is listed on the NASDAQ. Rather than compete with it, eBay bought a 20 percent interest in the company.
- Softtek, a Mexican company headed by Blanca Treviño since 2000, is the largest IT provider in Latin America. In 1997 it pioneered the concept of "nearsourcing," that is, taking advantage of Mexico's geographical proximity to the United States to offer business outsourcing services. Even if Mexican wages are somewhat higher than those in Asia, it makes sense for US businesses to outsource in their own time zone, with shorter shipping distances, and with intangibles like understanding one another's cultures.
- A Brazilian company called Netshoes began in 2000 and became the largest online supplier of sports goods in Brazil, with 565 employees.
- In 2011, an Argentine company named Kuepa launched a platform for education management. Student enrollment, attendance, grades, and grade reports are all managed online and are accessible to teachers, administrators, students, and parents in a differentiated way. The company founder, Gonzalo Pulit, says that the system frees teachers from administrative tasks and enables them to give students individualized attention. From the outset, the company marketed its products throughout Latin America.

Orlando Rincón is an entrepreneur who grew up poor in Cali, Colombia, but received a good university education. After achieving success in a software business, he sold his shares to start what became Parquesoft. As the name implies, it is a kind of "park" for startups in technology projects. The main part of the headquarters is a large open space with dividers between the work spaces, each housing a startup company. Parquesoft exists to provide software entrepreneurs (primarily in business-to-business services) with office space, the Parquesoft brand, and the opportunity to learn from others.

Rincón bristles with ideas and believes that entrepreneurs are born, not made, but that it helps to learn from others and from failure; he says it took Parquesoft five years to understand just what they were trying to do. By 2012, Parquesoft had operations in ten Colombian cities. From the start, Parquesoft has been open to young people from the kinds of barrios where Rincón grew up. Rincón believes that in today's world, technology levels the playing field. When an American told him that Parquesoft is a great idea but should be located in Silicon Valley, he replied that he is in the right place and that young people from Cali who have had to contend with problems like war and poverty are at least as talented as Swiss or Americans.[14] Parquesoft is one approach to developing entrepreneurship along the lines of what President Piñera was urging.

This chapter has offered a series of snapshots of various aspects of business and labor. Some related issues are taken up later in the book, but next we turn to issues of the environment.

FURTHER READING

For an up-to-date textbook on business trends, see Robles, Wiese, and Torres-Baumgarten (2014). *Latin Trade*, published every two months in Miami, covers business developments in glossy magazine format.

On the informal economy, see de Soto (1989); on *multilatinas*, Casanova and Fraser (2009) and Santiso (2013); on corporate social responsibility, Salamon (2010).

Growth with Sustainability

Meeting the New Environmental Challenge

When confronted by objections to the deforestation of the Amazon in the 1970s, a Brazilian general harrumphed, "Now it's our turn to pollute."[1] He had a point: the vast plains of the American Midwest stretching from the Alleghenies to the Rockies were a sea of grass until the nineteenth century, when they were turned into farms. Only a few remnants of that habitat remain, primarily in miniscule nature reserves of a few hundred acres. Likewise, the forests of the eastern United States were thoroughly cut down for lumber and farming; the trees have largely grown back but now as second-growth forests. The landscapes of Europe also reflect centuries of human interference. So Latin Americans were understandably resistant to being dictated to from North America or Europe and initially resisted the modern environmental movement.

Nevertheless, Latin American governments and publics have taken environmentalism seriously at least since 1992, when Brazil hosted the United Nations Earth Summit in Rio de Janeiro. In Latin America, even right-wing parties and business organizations accept the consensus of environmental scientists on human-wrought climate change (unlike many US politicians, pundits, and citizens). One reason is that they see and experience the evidence of climate change. Glaciers in the Andes have shrunk by 20–30 percent since 1970, and the rate may be accelerating, threatening water supplies for farmers and for cities like La Paz and Lima.

At the same time, Latin Americans insist that environmental concerns must not trump development. That concern is often expressed with the term "sustainable development," defined as "development that meets the needs of the present without compromising the ability of future generations to meet their own needs."[2] The expression has become a bureaucratic buzzword, but it enshrines a crucial challenge: Latin American nations must pursue growth and development while maintaining harmony with the environment.

The 2008 Ecuadorean constitution speaks of earth as Pacha Mama (Earth Mother) and invokes the Quechua term *sumak kawsay* ("living well" or "good living") to endow

The glacier on Huayna Potosí in Bolivia is visibly receding. © Noah Friedman-Rudovsky.

nature with rights: the right to function as it does in balance and to be restored where necessary; people also have rights to enjoy the goods of nature. In 2010, the Bolivian legislature likewise passed a Law of Mother Earth with similar expressions. Both Ecuadoreans and Bolivians boast that their legislations are the first to recognize the "rights" of nature, a position that reflects the influence of indigenous grassroots movements and was intended as a rejection of conventional Western notions of development. Just how these laws were to be applied remained fuzzy, however, particularly when the governments of Bolivia and Peru pursued highways and mining projects in environmentally sensitive terrain.

An example from Venezuela provided by Forrest Colburn illustrates the limits of framing environmental issues in simplistic terms. Two communities near Lake Maracaibo accused the national oil company, Petróleos de Venezuela S.A. (PDVSA), of pollution that was harming them, as shown, for example, in an abnormal number of birth defects. The obvious villain was the oil company, which had been polluting for decades and had abandoned networks of pipes in the bottom of the lake. Although it did not admit wrongdoing, the company agreed to pay to resettle the communities in another area with new housing. The case seemed to have a clear villain, and in this instance people had successfully fought back.

PDVSA was far from the only culprit, however. Approximately 120 industries around the lakeshore were dumping their waste, and dozens of communities also emptied their untreated sewer water there. Finally, the Catatombo River, which begins in Colombia and empties into Lake Maracaibo, is also a source of pollution. Even if the PDVSA agreement helped the two communities, truly restoring Lake Maracaibo (actually an estuary) would be elusive (Colburn 2002, 56–60).

Discussion of environmental issues tends to move in two directions. Sometimes the issue is clearly defined and is amenable to solution, such as air pollution levels that are maintained under control by imposing and enforcing fuel emission standards, or encouraging people to shop with reusable bags in order to reduce plastic bags in landfills. However, issues such as climate change accelerated by human activity have no ready fix and would require fundamental changes agreed to by countries around the world. Some environmental scientists warn that the present course of the planet is unsustainable, and that radical alternatives, such as drastically reducing the use of fossil fuels, must be undertaken.

In what follows we will be concerned primarily with several environmental issues that can and are being addressed. The examples have to do with rain forests and other natural environments, mining and other extractive industries, and urban environmental problems, with an accent on what Latin Americans are doing to meet the environmental challenge. However, the more fundamental question of the overall path of development worldwide must not be ignored.

RAIN FORESTS AND OTHER HABITATS: THREATS AND RESPONSES

The largest tropical rain forest in the world lies in the Amazon basin, primarily in Brazil, but also in eight surrounding countries. Smaller rain forests exist in Central America and Mexico. During colonial times and into the nineteenth century, Brazilians remained largely on the Atlantic coast. The rubber boom of the late nineteenth century brought settlement to some areas in the Amazon region, but it was only under the military government (1964–1985) that systematic efforts were made to settle the Amazon rain forest, because the military regarded populating the center of the country as a matter of national security. A north–south road was built between the capital, Brasília, and Belem at the mouth of the river; the Trans-Amazon Highway was completed in 1974; and other roads followed. Until the 1980s, the federal government offered incentives for ranchers and settlers. The upshot was deforestation in the name of "development."

The settling of the Amazon tends to take place along a "frontier" closely associated with roads, whether they are highways built by the government or roads privately cut for logging. Sometimes those who enter first are loggers seeking the most valuable trees, particularly mahogany. Later, other trees are cut down for lumber, and then the land is used for farming or ranching. Or small farmers may clear-cut and burn the trees for farming. Although the native forest is abundant with life, the soil itself is thin and poor after clear-cutting, and after a few years it is exhausted and serves, at best, for cattle grazing.

It is now universally agreed that allowing the world's rain forests to be destroyed

MAP 5.1. *The Amazon Basin*

for the short-term gains of loggers and ranchers would be disastrous in terms of climate change, carbon absorption, and species extinction.

Climate change. The rain forest absorbs moisture and then returns it to the atmosphere. Farmers far from the Amazon (e.g., to the west and the south and perhaps even as far as the American Midwest) depend on that moisture. The present cycle of rain, absorption by soil and plants, and re-evaporation may be permanently disrupted. By the mid-2000s, the normal dry season in the Amazon was growing longer and droughts were occurring. Environmental biologists fear that a tipping point could be reached in which droughts would increase, leading to large out-of-control

Deforestation by cutting trees and burning in the Amazon basin in northeastern Bolivia. © Noah Friedman-Rudovsky.

fires that could destroy more forests, to the point that what was once rain forest could turn dry, with incalculable results elsewhere.

Carbon emissions. Vegetation absorbs carbon dioxide from the atmosphere. When trees are cut and burned, they emit that carbon into the atmosphere. It is estimated that 10 percent of carbon emissions worldwide comes from deforestation.

Species extinction. Rain-forest ecologies have far more species of plant and animal life than other ecosystems. In the Yasuni National Park in Ecuador, a single hectare (100 meters by 100 meters) contained 655 species of trees (more species than in the United States and Canada combined). It also contained 271 species of reptiles and amphibians, and by one researcher's estimate, 100,000 unique insect species.

Biologists have catalogued only a fraction of these species and are far from having explored their properties, which may well include useful chemicals, particularly for medications. For years pharmaceutical companies have been seeking potential drugs from rain-forest plants, sometimes drawing on the knowledge of indigenous healers.[3] Estimates of species extinction are quite imprecise; indeed, the total number of species on earth is not known. However, it seems clear that human activity, particularly habitat destruction, is causing many species to go extinct. Whether or not the species being lost potentially contain "miracle" drugs (e.g., cures for cancer), it is quite reckless to allow such extinction to continue.

Sister Dorothy Stang in Amazon near Santarém, Brazil. © Sisters of Notre Dame de Namur.

DEFENDERS OF THE AMAZON

A Brazilian union leader and an American Catholic nun, both murdered for defending the Amazon, are venerated in Brazil. Chico Mendes (Fernando Alves Mendes Filho) was born in 1944 in the Amazonian state of Acre bordering on Bolivia. With little schooling, he followed his father to work as a rubber gatherer. Over time he became a leader, and in the 1980s helped form a rubber gatherers association and also ran for office for the then incipient Workers Party. He led rubber gatherers in opposing loggers and ranchers who were taking land, sometimes with nonviolent standoffs to halt crews with chainsaws.

By the mid-1980s, Mendes was becoming known as a spokesperson for rubber tappers and for the rain forest. He and others developed the concept of "extractive reserves," areas of land set aside not simply as wilderness but for sustainable economic exploitation for products like rubber, fish, nuts, and so forth. In 1987, he made the case for these reserves in Washington, DC, before the Inter-American Development Bank and the US Congress.

Mendes was threatened and brought to court by local loggers and ranchers. In December 1988, he was gunned down at the entrance of his house. The killers assumed that they would not be brought to justice, since by that time hundreds of small farmers had been killed with impunity in Brazil. In this case, because of the international outcry, a local landholder, his son, and another man were eventually found guilty and imprisoned.

Mendes became known throughout Brazil. Books were written about him; documentaries and a biopic were filmed. His death catalyzed the movement for extractive reserves, and there are now 43 of them, totaling 8.6 million hectares and serving 40,000 families. When the status of the land has been legally set as an extractive reserve, the families can obtain loans, and governments provide schools and clinics.

Roughly a thousand miles to the northeast, Sister Dorothy Stang worked with poor people for thirty years in the state of Pará. Over time, she developed an ecological vision and was also helping small groups of poor people in the forest develop extractive reserves. Local loggers and ranchers also threatened her. In February 2005, while on her way to a meeting, she was accosted by two gunmen, who shot her as she opened her Bible. Again, her killers must have assumed that they could act with impunity: fifty-three rural workers had been murdered the previous year, nineteen in the state of Pará. Under pressure from the federal government, three men, including the rancher who paid for the killing, were eventually jailed. In the years after her death, the federal government accelerated the pace of designating areas of the rain forest for protection.

In 2011 it was reported that eight hundred activists had been killed in the state of Pará in the previous forty years. Even though the federal government in principle wishes to protect the forests and assure the rule of law, it has often been unable to prevail over rural landholders, who control local governments.

By 2010, encouraging signs of progress in halting Amazon deforestation could be seen. Starting in 2002, Virgilio Viana, secretary for environment for the state of Amazonas, the largest state in Brazil, worked with the governor on a new approach, based on the slogan "Forests are worth more standing than cut."[4] Although over half of the state is protected area, enforcement of the law was difficult. The aim was to increase both incentives (making forest products more valuable) and disincentives (strengthening enforcement and sanctions) and to enlist the cooperation of local people. A variety of measures were taken:

- To combat contraband logging, licensing was made more effective. The value of legal logging rose fourfold from 2002 to 2008.[5]
- Similarly, by cracking down on illegal fishing, the value of legal fishing increased.
- Taxes were reduced or eliminated on forest products.
- State agencies provided loans and technical assistance.
- Scientific research related to the forest was enhanced.
- Market access was improved so that forest products could be purchased by supermarket chains and sold in cities labeled as forest products.
- The government itself made arrangements to buy sustainable forest products.
- Paperwork was streamlined, and legislation was explained to people in clear terms at community meetings.
- The Bolsa Floresta (Forest Allowance) Program (BFP), through which people living in a protected area are paid for their services of protecting the area, was established.

These examples come from a single state, albeit a huge one, but the principles are to some extent being applied elsewhere. In particular, it is increasingly acknowledged that the best guardians of the forest are indigenous people living there.

The approach in the state of Amazonas placed the emphasis on changing how incentives operate, but better enforcement is also needed. One difficulty has been the impossibility of patrolling vast areas of the Amazon with small numbers of inspectors. Brazilian agencies are now using satellites and drones. Over the 2003–2009 period, annual deforestation in the state dropped from 1,558 to 405 square kilometers, a 74 percent drop. Protected areas increased by 160 percent over that same time.

In 2009, a Greenpeace report, "Slaughtering the Amazon," focused on the connection between illegal cattle raising in the Amazon; large Brazilian beef slaughtering and processing operations; and their customers for both beef and leather, including companies such as automakers (BMW, Ford, Honda, Toyota), retailers (Carrefour, Kraft, Walmart, IKEA), and clothing manufacturers (Adidas, Gucci, Nike). The reaction was swift, and soon the companies were insisting on receiving legal products. Twenty thousand ranchers registered legally, and the beef companies were promising to comply. The public prosecutor fined ranchers and slaughterhouses $1.2 billion (Greenpeace International 2009).

Brazil has the world's largest cattle herd, but the animals typically graze inefficiently on large areas. The environmentalist Roberto Smeraldi, of Amigos da Terra, has called for a "technological revolution" to intensify the cattle-raising process by increasing the number of cattle per hectare from one to three. That would make it possible to reduce the grazing area by two-thirds and allow the forest to return on the vacated land. Such a change would also provide more jobs for the local population. Smeraldi pointed out that cattle raising produces only 1 percent of GDP but was producing a third of the carbon emissions of Brazil, itself the third- or fourth-largest producer of emissions in the world (Butler 2009).

An experience in Central America suggests that restoring forests is not so far-fetched. When the political ecologist Susanna Hecht first went to El Salvador in 1999, she heard the conventional view that the country's forests had all been cleared, and that any trees standing are not old-growth but secondary forests. However, Hecht found that the forests had grown significantly since the war of the 1980s. The reason was that less land was being used for corn in subsistence agriculture because imported corn was cheaper and many families now had access to remittances. They were letting forest return to their marginal land or, in some instances, growing forest products for sale (Mertens 2008).

At first glance, this seems like poor consolation for the loss of original forest, but Hecht and others insist that it shows that the issue need not be framed in all-or-nothing terms. They also suggest that the notion of a primeval forest untouched by humans may be something of a Western myth. Research is now indicating that several million people inhabited the Amazon before the arrival of Europeans, and although they left no stone monuments, they developed complex societies with sophisticated ways of life that included fish farming, improving soil for farming, and fostering the growth of favorable products.[6] Their example is relevant to developing sustainable uses of the rain forest today.

Besides the well-known struggle to "save the Amazon," Latin Americans are involved in other kinds of conservation efforts. The Atlantic Forest, for example, was once a wooded area in eastern Brazil twice the size of Texas. Due to settlement and agriculture, it has been reduced to about 15 percent of its original size. Nevertheless, it has a biological diversity similar to that of the Amazon: 2,200 species of birds, mammals, reptiles, and amphibians, some of which are found nowhere else. In just two and a half acres, researchers counted 458 tree species—more than double the number in the entire Eastern Seaboard of the United States. Many species are endangered, particularly because what is left of the forest is spread out in many small areas. An effort is under way to protect and restore 30 million acres of the forest by creating a corridor of these lands, enabling the species of birds and animals to move about in it. Because the proposed corridor runs through populated areas, part of the effort means making people aware of its importance. Only 3 percent of the forest is legally protected, hence a good part of the effort is to achieve cooperation from owners of private lands. In 2008, the Nature Conservancy launched a campaign to plant a billion trees in the Atlantic Forest (at a cost of one dollar per tree).

A similar concept is behind the Mesoamerican Biological Corridor, which was initiated in 1997 and runs from Mexico through Central America to Panama. Because the isthmus is the meeting point of North and South America, biodiversity is especially high there: Central America has 1 percent of the earth's landmass but 7 percent of its species. Lands along the corridor are classified into four types: natural areas (strictly protected for species); buffer areas (where use is restricted); corridors (intended to allow wildlife to pass); and multiple use (areas used for agriculture, fisheries, or silviculture). As in the Atlantic Forest Corridor, the aim is to assure cooperation across different types of lands.

Latin American countries have designated significant proportions of their land as national parks and other protected areas. Colombia has fifty-six national parks coordinated in a system; Brazil has over eighteen hundred designated protected areas. In general, these are not exactly like designated wilderness areas in the United States, since people live in them, especially indigenous peoples. On the whole, protected lands constitute 20 percent of Latin America, as compared to a world average of 10–15 percent.[7]

HIGHWAY CONFLICTS

In 2011, a group of mainly indigenous Bolivians began a 375-mile protest march from their lowlands up to the chilly heights of La Paz. They were from an area known by its acronym TIPNIS[8] and represented three indigenous peoples (Tsimané, Yuracaré, and Mojeño-Trinitario). Until that point, these peoples had been largely isolated, but they were concerned that a 152-mile highway proposed by the Bolivian government, and the inevitable development and population influx that it would bring, would threaten their hunter-gatherer way of life. They were joined by allies, particularly urban-based environmentalists.

From afar it might seem surprising that they were marching against Evo Morales, Bolivia's first indigenous president and a symbol of their struggle, who had risen to prominence by leading large public demonstrations and marches, some of them similar to this one. It might also seem obvious that a major highway should not be routed through their land, which had been set aside in 1965 for both indigenous peoples and forest protection. However, these three peoples numbered only 12,000 people and had virtually no contact with the rest of Bolivia. Farther to the south in the same region were more recent immigrants, some also indigenous, including some coca growers. These poor people were also part of Morales's constituency and generally supported the highway project.

This proposed road would connect the Bolivian departments of El Beni and Cochabamba, but more importantly it was a crucial final link in a Brazilian project to complete a highway from the Brazilian states of Acre and Rondônia, over the Andes, and through Peru to the Pacific. The dream of integrating the South American continent goes back to the eighteenth century (including proposals along this route in Bolivia). However, the interior of Brazil was largely unsettled as late as the mid-twentieth century. As noted, Brazil's military government sponsored highway projects, which are generally regarded as ecological and economic failures. To this day, the Trans-Amazon Highway comes to a halt in western Brazil.

In 2000, under Brazilian leadership, twelve South American governments formed IIRSA (Iniciativa para la Integración de la Infraestructura Regional Suramericana; Initiative for the Integration of Regional Infrastructure in South America). Over the next decade proposals were made for hundreds of projects, primarily highways, but also railways, bridges, seaports, waterways, and energy development. The projects extend from Uruguay to Suriname and have funding from major international

Sixty-five-day march from lowlands to La Paz, to protest road in TIPNIS area (2011). © Noah Friedman-Rudovsky.

lending agencies. Because Brazil has more expertise and its national development bank is able to supply funding, it has led the initiative not only in Brazil but elsewhere. Thus, seen from Bolivia's perspective, the entire TIPNIS project looked like Brazil flexing its muscles and getting its way (Friedman-Rudovsky 2012).

In mid-2012, further protests brought the project in Bolivia to a temporary halt while the government carried out a series of consultations with local people, as it was in fact obligated to do. At the end of the year, the government announced that it had consulted the peoples of the region and that the majority had indicated that they favored the road. Critics saw the consultation as a formality with a foregone conclusion. Among other things, it seemed to give equal or more weight to recent settlers in the region as to those whose ancestral land it is. Government spokespersons further said that the government would begin by setting up economic development, healthcare, and education projects in the region. Indications were that the road would not be built quickly, because it was not even designed yet. Opponents vowed to continue their struggle, even internationally.

If the road goes through the TIPNIS—another route bypassing it could conceivably be chosen—it will almost certainly bring destruction of forest and species extinction. Since oil exploration permits have already been issued, oil operations could bring far greater destruction. How should the desires and rights of native peoples, who in this case number only 12,000, be weighed against the benefits of greater movement of people and goods, such as the understandable desire of Brazilians to have access to the Pacific?

In 2012, the last stages of a road farther north connecting Pacific ports in Peru with the Peruvian Amazon and Brazil were completed, and passengers and goods could travel by bus from São Paulo to Lima (a five-day journey) by road. Other transcontinental routes were at various stages of development, and their ultimate impact was unclear.

MINES, OIL, AND GAS: CAN NATURAL RESOURCE EXTRACTION BE DONE RIGHT?

A major component of the commodities boom that started in the 1990s and has driven Latin American growth is in extractive industries: mining and hydrocarbons (oil and gas). Mining has existed in Latin America for five centuries—Columbus himself was looking for gold, as were the first generations of conquerors. Silver from Bolivia and Mexico made Spain rich starting in the sixteenth century. Brazil underwent a mining boom in the eighteenth century, and other booms came later. Small-scale mining exists throughout the continent. Venezuela and Mexico have been major petroleum exporters for almost a century. The fact that Latin Americans remained poor demonstrates that extractive riches usually do not translate into prosperity for ordinary people.

More recent examples reinforce that impression. Starting in the 1970s, Texaco developed oil fields in the Ecuadorean Amazon, which is thinly populated by indigenous people. Oil spills destroyed habitats, and the communities were divided when some people accepted jobs from the oil companies. Their traditional way of life was destroyed, and those who remained were reduced to poverty, while some opted to move deeper into the Amazon.

Another example comes from western Honduras, where the Canadian company Greenstone Resources Limited arrived in the 1990s. The area had been settled since colonial times when Spanish settlers did some mining. One community was forced by the government to resettle with only a few days' notice, and promises of new land were not honored. Greenstone went bankrupt, and the mine has changed hands twice since then. The mine operation is typical of modern gold mining, made possible by new technologies. Water laced with cyanide is run through the ore and gathered in ponds, where gold and silver can be extracted. In 2003 and 2009, water overflowed from the cyanide pools into streams and rivers, leaving thousands of fish dead. Honduran government agencies sided with the mining companies, not local communities. They have arrested protesters, and two leaders had to flee after assassination attempts.

By 2010, Latin America was attracting 27 percent of global investment in mining, making it the leading region in the world for mining exploration. Investment in mining was projected to reach $200 billion for the 2010–2019 period. New mining operations were opening in virtually every country, and governments were issuing licenses to explore for minerals and for petroleum and natural gas. The boom was being driven by various trends: sustained high and rising prices for natural resources, especially due to demand from China and other emerging economies; new technologies that made it possible to exploit ores and hydrocarbons previously too difficult to extract; and encouragement from governments in the form of tax breaks and favorable regulations.

Both Bolivia and Ecuador, whose constitutions supposedly recognize the "rights of nature" and embrace the ideal of Buen Vivir (living well, understood as meaning in harmony with nature), were making extractive industries central to their development strategy. In 2012, President Rafael Correa of Ecuador signed a concession contract for an open-pit mine in the Amazon region. The royalties for the government were estimated at $5.4 billion, but it would affect around 450,000 acres of cloud forest inhabited by the Shuar people. "We cannot be beggars sitting on a sack of gold," Correa said repeatedly (Castelli 2012). Correa insists that these resources should be utilized for the benefit of all Ecuadoreans, primarily those who are poor. In this instance, left-wing leaders like Correa and Morales seem not very different from right-wing leaders elsewhere, who might stress the notion of "development" more abstractly. However, the logic was the same in both cases: neither the "rights of nature" nor those of people close to mines and other extractive projects would be allowed to stand in the way of revenues from resource exploitation.

These projects were arousing opposition from local communities and from their environmentalist allies. Based on historical experience, they criticize these industries on the following grounds:

- *Environmental destruction*: Open-pit mining bulldozes large areas: 70 tons of waste are generated to produce one ounce of gold.
- *Water supply*: Mining requires large amounts of water from local supplies, depriving local farmers and communities of this precious resource.
- *Toxic chemicals*: Arsenic and cyanide can make their way into the atmosphere or the watershed.
- *Displacement and destruction of communities*: As in the example from Honduras above, people may be expelled from where they live.
- *Boom and bust*: Prices rise and fall abruptly, causing activity to increase and decrease or even end.
- *Uneven benefits*: Historically, it is typically foreign companies that benefit the most; governments gain revenues, but local communities end up paying the costs. Most employment goes to experienced workers from outside the community or the country; the jobs offered to local people are low-paying unskilled positions.
- *"Natural resource curse"*: Evidence shows that economies based on natural resource extraction grow more slowly than others and are a magnet for corruption.

These criticisms are largely borne out by experience, particularly since the early

2000s. Why, then, are hundreds of extractive projects under way throughout Latin America, even under governments that claim to be defending the interests of the poor or indigenous? The words of President Correa quoted above offer a clue: governments see these industries as a tempting source of revenue that can be used for government expenses and development projects, including social programs for the poor.

The impact of mining is asymmetrical: extractive industries take place at a specific point, and the costs are borne by the environment and the local community, while the benefits are widespread: for the company (if it is private), the government, and people elsewhere. But benefits for the local community may be very limited, particularly if their way of life has been destroyed.

By the historical record, most major mining projects have one or more of the problems listed above. On the whole, however, Chile seems to provide an instance where mining has generally worked to the good. For example, Chilean legislation lays down requirements for how much revenue from copper can go into current expenses and how much must be set aside in investments for use in the future when prices decline.[9] Chilean copper mines, however, are located in the sparsely inhabited deserts of the north, not in environmentally sensitive rain forests.

Based on past experience, some guidelines may be suggested for what should be done if the current mining boom is not to repeat the historical pattern:

- *Full participation*: Indigenous and other local communities should be involved in a genuine (not pro-forma) consultation at every stage and be provided with accurate information. They should be able to make decisions through their customary procedures (not simply by majority vote).
- *Saying "no"*: Proof that such consultations are working will come when some projects are rejected or halted. When the Colombian coal mining company Cerrejón wished to divert a river in order to get at the coal underneath it, it spent a decade in discussion with members of the Wayuu people about the project and about the benefits the community would receive.[10] In 2008, the Salvadoran government declared a moratorium on approvals for mining on the grounds that the government and the country needed to be better prepared.
- *Nonmonetary value recognition*: Nations and companies need to consider that no price tag can be put on some things, such as unique species of animals and plants or the language and way of life of a people.
- *Impact studies*: Extractive industries should be allowed to go forward only after full studies of the likely impacts in the near and long run have been completed.
- *Up-to-date equipment:* To minimize environmental damage, modern equipment and procedures should be used.
- *Commitment to the restoration of nature*: Forest and plant cover should be replaced after open-pit mining ceases.
- *Comprehensive local development*: Communities should receive not only jobs but also schools, clinics, and infrastructure development.

- *Fair balance between local, regional, and national interests*: This should be the goal with regard to the sharing of revenues from extractive projects.
- *Transparency and good corporate citizenship*: Mining companies should be held to high standards of openness and cooperation with local communities.
- *Administrative competence and institutional adequacy*: In the past, elected and appointed government officials have often lacked the expertise and administrative ability needed to handle complex environmental matters. Moreover, they have tended to operate from a clientelistic mind-set in which those in power reward their allies and patrons. Chile furnishes a counterexample, in which institutions generally work well and officials are assumed to be competent and honest.

Meeting these requirements would not be easy, especially given past performance. But setting them as goals would suggest that governments should not be hasty about proceeding with or approving specific projects.

URBAN INITIATIVES

As crucial as the issues surveyed above are, they can seem somewhat abstract to most Latin Americans who live in cities or towns. The Amazon is as far from the actual experience of most Brazilians as Alaska is to Americans, and most have seen it only on television. The environmental issues that they experience most directly have to do with urban life. This chapter closes with a sample of how urban environmental issues are being addressed.[11]

Air quality. In 1992, Mexico City had the most polluted air in the world, according to the United Nations, due to the population of twenty million people, large numbers of vehicles with no emissions requirements, and the "inversion layer" of air trapped between mountains (similar to the situation in Los Angeles and Santiago, Chile). Other large cities, such as São Paulo, have also had poor air quality. Initially, it seemed difficult to reverse these patterns, for example, by eliminating lead from gasoline or initiating and enforcing emissions standards, since these changes would entail costs to vehicle owners.

In fact, however, cities have been tackling their air-quality problems in a variety of ways. Through a combination of policies instituted over a period of two decades, Mexico City reduced lead by 90 percent, particles by 70 percent, and ozone by 75 percent. Part of the success came from requiring catalytic converters on vehicles. Although air-quality indicators in Mexico City sometimes exceed international standards, the city's air quality is now on a par with that in Los Angeles, which has also improved over the decades. The city is continuing to address the issue with more initiatives. Major Latin American cities monitor air quality and advise the public on air-quality levels. Some have instituted strict emissions standards, sometimes employing random stops and fines.

Transportation. Latin American cities have dual or triple transportation systems:

Bicycle lane in Miraflores, a Lima suburb. © Tommie Sue Montgomery.

mass transit, taxis, and private automobiles. Most have moderate to maddening traffic jams, especially at peak times. Perhaps the biggest problem now and in the future facing all Latin American cities is that new vehicles are increasing at a rate of over 5 percent per year. As noted in chapter 2, Latin American cities have led the way in BRT (bus rapid transit) systems, first pioneered in Curitiba, Brazil, in the 1970s. Curitiba has proven that a well-functioning public transportation system can attract even vehicle owners. Santiago, Chile, has the best integrated public transport system, in which the metro, BRT, and bus system work together. Some cities have taken steps to encourage bicycling as a mode of transportation. Bogotá has 300 kilometers of dedicated bike paths, and 300,000 to 400,000 trips are taken daily. Buenos Aires established bike lanes, which included physical barriers for protection from cars. Mexico City and Medellín have started card-operated bike-share systems.

Water and sanitation. Three interrelated matters come into play here: supply of safe drinking water, a sewerage system to remove water, and treatment of the resulting wastewater. A survey of seventeen major Latin American cities found that 98 percent of residents had access to potable water, and 94 percent had access to sanitation. (Those figures were open to question, however, because they did not necessarily include informal settlements.) Only 52 percent of the wastewater was treated; in other words, half of the sewage went directly into rivers or the ocean. Estimates of water loss averaged around 35 percent, due in many cases to aging pipes, but also perhaps to informal settlements using unmetered water.

In Mexico City, although the water supply is in principle potable or drinkable, many residents do not regard it as trustworthy. On average, the city's inhabitants consume 61.8 gallons of bottled water a year, more than any other city in the world. They buy it largely in 5-gallon jugs, costing a family an average of $140 a year. The suppliers are large soft drink and food companies, which advertise it heavily.

Waste disposal. The study of seventeen cities showed average waste creation to be at a rate of 465 kilograms per person per year (only about 10%–15% less than the European average). Waste generally goes into landfills, but Curitiba pioneered a program whereby poor people could turn in recyclable materials in return for groceries or transportation passes. Through a variety of programs, the city reached a recycling rate of 70 percent. In some cities, poor people who once scavenged dump sites for possible items to use or sell have organized and become recognized as recycling cooperatives. In Puebla, Mexico, the private sector organized a program called "Green Wallet": participants brought recyclable waste to depots and received electronic credit redeemable at stores. Within a half year, 22 tons of solid and electronic waste had been collected. In general, however, Latin American cities are just beginning the process of separating and recycling trash.

Land use and environmental governance. All major cities make efforts to conserve existing green spaces, such as parks, but few are able to create new ones, especially in areas of spontaneous growth. In response to a 2001 study urging more tree cover, and using a variety of programs, the city of Quito has had hundreds of thousands of trees planted in the city and its environs. The aim is to absorb air pollution, provide

Workers separating recyclable materials from trash, Brazil. © Inter-American Development Bank.

shade, and improve rainwater runoff absorption. São Paulo has set energy-efficiency standards for all new municipal buildings and has mandated that existing buildings be retrofitted with energy-saving technology. In 2008, Buenos Aires initiated a program to improve the efficiency of one hundred existing buildings, starting with energy audits, and to eliminate 5,000 tons of carbon emissions by 2012.

ULTIMATE ENVIRONMENTAL QUESTIONS

This chapter has surveyed several major areas of ecological concern (rain forests and natural habitats, mining and hydrocarbons, and urban environment) and noted how they are being addressed. To focus on such matters implicitly assumes that "sustainable development" is a genuine possibility under present conditions. Some environmental specialists paint a far bleaker picture, namely, that the planet is approaching or has even crossed some kind of threshold beyond which feedback mechanisms will make climate change irreversible. One sign that the tipping point has been reached is rapidly melting polar ice. Their conclusion is that present models of development are unsustainable: if China were to reach US levels of energy usage, particularly greenhouse gas emissions, the results would be catastrophic. All attempts to reach binding agreements on carbon emissions between governments have thus far failed, not least because the US public and government cannot come to agreement on the seriousness of the problem.

Latin Americans leave only a fraction of the ecological "footprint" of the wealthier nations because their level of consumption of fossil fuels, water, wood, and so forth is only a fraction of what it is in North America and Europe, and the region has abundant water and other natural resources. Those facts should not lead to complacency, however, and especially not to a thoughtless yearning to reach the levels of consumption of richer nations. The aim should be to find innovative approaches to meeting needs for energy, transportation, housing, agriculture, and manufacturing that do not confuse higher consumption with greater human welfare.

FURTHER READING

A number of concrete examples of environmental activism are provided in Collinson (1996).

On water, see *ReVista* (Winter 2013b); on mining, *Americas Quarterly: Natural Resource Extraction in Latin America* 7, no. 1 (Winter 2013), and *ReVista* 13, no. 2 (Winter 2014); on environmental issues in cities, *Americas Quarterly* 8, no. 1 (Winter 2014), and The Economist Intelligence Unit (2010).

Highly Unequal— and Middle Class?

Visitors to Latin America used to comment that most people were poor, a few were very rich, and there was "no middle class." Indeed, Latin America is statistically the most unequal region in the world. Academics have also taken it for granted that the middle classes are relatively small in the region. Decades ago, Latin American activists and their academic allies would scoff at the very notion of a development strategy aimed at expanding the middle class. More recently, the stagnation resulting from the "lost decade" of the 1980s made the notion of an expanding middle class implausible.

Yet in the first two decades of the twenty-first century, signs of a growing middle class were evident.[1] In 2007, the respected Getúlio Vargas Foundation published a study concluding that 52 percent of Brazilian households could be considered middle class. According to former Mexican foreign minister Jorge Castañeda, 60 percent of Mexicans are middle class (Castañeda 2011, chap. 2, 34–67). By 2010, the notion of an emerging middle class in Latin America (and in other developing regions) was becoming a journalistic commonplace.

This chapter takes up the three intertwined issues of poverty, inequality, and class. In each case it is important to examine how they are measured and defined. At the same time, it should be kept in mind that poverty cannot be captured solely in numbers: being poor means being excluded and powerless; ending poverty would ultimately mean creating a society in which no one is excluded.

DECLINING POVERTY

Statistically, the proportion of Latin Americans living in poverty has been declining in recent years from almost half of the population in 1990 to about a third of the population by 2010: two-thirds of Latin Americans can now be regarded as non-poor. Nevertheless, 177 million people were in poverty in 2010, including 70 million in extreme poverty or "indigence," defined as not having sufficient income to meet nutritional requirements. However, the rate varies considerably from country to country, from a

Woman carrying water from river, eastern Bolivia. © Noah Friedman-Rudovsky.

high in Honduras and Nicaragua, where 60 percent of the population is classified as poor, to Chile, Uruguay, and Argentina, where the figure hovers around 10 percent.

A reader may wonder how it is possible to come to such precise figures for poverty. Governments and international development agencies draw "poverty lines" by determining a "basket of goods" that a typical family would need. In poor countries, that means primarily food (rice, beans, cooking oil, etc.), but it might include rent, bus fare, or other items, depending on the country. These items are totaled and a figure is determined, say, for a household of four or five people. Census departments regularly conduct household surveys and inquire about a family's monthly income. Suppose the "basket of goods" needed costs $300 a month; if household surveys then show that 25 percent of the households in the country are receiving less than that amount, they are below the "poverty line."[2]

Poverty lines vary from country to country: the amount of income needed in Costa Rica will be different from what is needed in neighboring Nicaragua. A particular country's poverty line is useful primarily for measuring progress or deterioration in that country, not for making comparisons between countries. In the 1980s and into the 1990s, poverty rates increased as income did not keep pace with inflation. As incomes rose in the 2000s, the rates declined.

As a very rough measure for poverty worldwide, around the year 2000 the World Bank began to define "extreme poverty" as living on a dollar a day per person[3] and "moderate poverty" as living on two dollars a day. It should be noted that these are per capita figures: thus a family of five with an income of five dollars a day (or $150 a month) or less would be living in extreme poverty and one with ten dollars a day ($300 a month) or less would be living in moderate poverty.

A moment's reflection will serve to show how imprecise such figures are. Consider two families, each with $150 cash income a month, one in the countryside with a plot of land on which it grows corn and beans for its own food, and the other in the city where it has to buy all its food, may be paying rent, and has expenses of bus fare, school supplies, and so forth. Statistically, they are both in a situation of extreme poverty, but it is considerably harder for the urban family to meet its needs. Since three-quarters of Latin Americans are city dwellers, the two-dollar-a-day mark is more realistic as the poverty line, and by 2010 some researchers were saying it should be four dollars.[4]

Focusing on income leaves out important aspects. It makes a difference whether a family has piped-in safe drinking water or has to carry it from a community water spout or a creek, even though that difference is not recorded as income. The same is true of access to a public clinic, and the quality of health care received there. Such public services as water and sewerage, health care, schooling, and police protection make a difference, but they do not show up on income statistics.

At a special session of the United Nations in 2000, representatives of 190 nations pledged to achieve the Millennium Development Goals, summarized as cutting worldwide poverty in half by 2015. That general aim was further divided into eight goals, each of which was further specified.

1. Eradicating extreme poverty and hunger
2. Achieving universal primary education
3. Promoting gender equality and empowering women
4. Reducing child mortality rates
5. Improving maternal health
6. Combating HIV/AIDS, malaria, and other diseases
7. Ensuring environmental sustainability
8. Developing a global partnership for development

The Millennium Development Goals were designed to be a set of measurable targets for which governments could be held accountable. Latin American countries generally succeeded in cutting poverty rates in half, and made significant progress on various fronts. In September 2015 representatives of governments around the world met at the United Nations and pledged to advance on what were now being called the Sustainable Development Goals, with the stated aim of leaving no one behind in eliminating poverty by 2030.

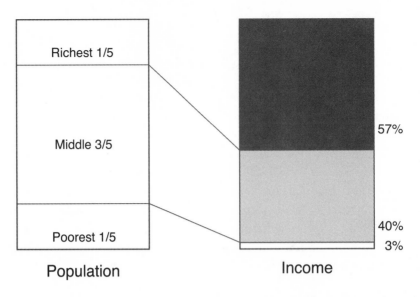

Richest 1/5

Middle 3/5

Poorest 1/5

Population

Income

57%

40%

3%

GRAPH 6.1. *Income Distribution, Latin America and Caribbean. Based on official sources, 2008.*

INEQUALITY

Inequality is not synonymous with poverty: consider a rich but unequal country where even the poor are well off by world standards (e.g., Canada), and a relatively equal country where almost everyone is poor (e.g., North Korea). Nevertheless, Latin American poverty is very much aggravated by its high level of inequality.

The graph above indicates the extreme disparity between the top 20 percent and bottom 20 percent of the population in terms of income. The high degree of inequality in Latin America may be illustrated by comparing it to other developing regions of the world, where the bottom fifth receives a considerably larger share of total income.

According to a United Nations study, Brazil and Hungary have a similar GDP per capita, but poverty is far higher in Brazil. In Hungary, the richest fifth receive 4.5 times as much as the poorest fifth, whereas the ratio in Brazil is 30 times (Soubbotina 2004).

The degree of inequality in nations is measured by the Gini coefficient, a number between 0 (hypothetical complete equality) and 1 (complete inequality). Thus all countries can be compared by the degree of inequality. Among the most developed countries, the Scandinavian countries are the most equal and the United States the most unequal. Latin America is the most unequal region in the world, but some countries such as Argentina, Ecuador, and Venezuela are in a range similar to that of the United States, while Brazil, Chile, and Colombia are far more unequal. As inequality rises in the United States and declines in Mexico, the Gini coefficients of the two countries have been converging.

Since the early 2000s, poverty rates have declined in Latin America, inequality has been reduced in most countries, and a middle class marked by changes in consumption has been emerging. The implications are considered below, but first it should be noted that inequality has been rooted in Latin American societies for

TABLE 6.1. Poorest Fifth's Share of Total Income by Region, 2008

REGIONS	PERCENTAGE OF INCOME RECEIVED BY POOREST *FIFTH*
South Asia	8.7
Eastern Europe, Central Asia	6.6
East Asia & Pacific	5.2
Middle East & North Africa	5.1
Sub-Saharan Africa	3.6
Latin America & Caribbean	2.9

Source: Soubbotina (2004, chap. 5).

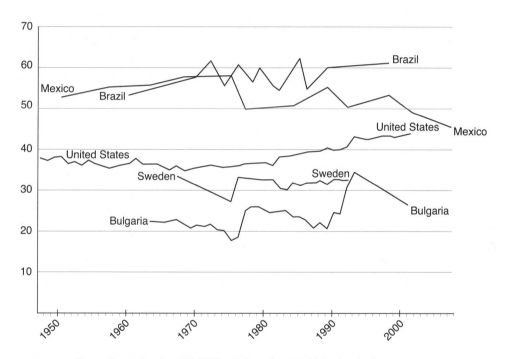

GRAPH 6.2. *Income Inequality since World War II. Data from World Bank and other sources.*

centuries, beginning with the subjection of the native peoples at the conquest and the imposition of slavery. During the agroexport boom from the late nineteenth century until 1930, there was little incentive to develop an internal market. Governments represented the agricultural and mining oligarchies. A small middle class developed in some countries around management of export and commercial activities, and it expanded under state-led industrialization (roughly 1930–1980), as there was some effort to develop the domestic market. Starting in the "lost decade" of the 1980s, government employment declined, some businesses closed, labor unions lost power, and the informal sector swelled.

Those trends have reversed in recent years. In Brazil, a notable turning point came in 1994, when inflation, which had raged for decades, was brought under control. That benefited the entire economy, but especially the poor, who have no way to shield themselves from inflation. Consumption patterns changed at the household level as families bought refrigerators, washing machines, and electronic devices. Conditional cash transfers put money into poor people's hands. Merchandisers discovered the purchasing power of the poor. Credit and credit cards have allowed more people to buy larger-ticket items, whose prices have come down. Mortgage lending has expanded, admittedly from a very low base.

In the past, the appeal of socialism in Latin America was driven by the extremes of wealth and poverty, symbolized by shantytowns and high-rise apartments in close proximity. Given the failure of state socialism, few today would advocate absolute equality, and in fact, economic conservatives are unperturbed by inequality as the result of the market. However, it can be argued that extremes of inequality should be avoided, first on simply ethical grounds. Every member of society should have the opportunity to enjoy a decent standard of living within the possibilities of that society. Moreover, a society in which purchasing power is widely distributed should be of interest to businesses serving the domestic economy. In other words, there are pragmatic as well as ethical grounds for eliminating poverty and reducing inequality.

UNDERSTANDINGS OF CLASS

If our understanding of poverty and inequality depends on how they are measured, that is all the more true of the elusive terms "class" and "middle class." We start the discussion with more commonsense notions and then consider other measures.

One way to measure class is simply to survey people to ask them to identify the class to which they belong. When so asked, the vast majority of people in the United States will identify themselves as "middle class."[5] A 2007 survey in seven Latin American countries asked a sample of urban dwellers to locate themselves in terms of social class. The responses were surprisingly similar. On average, only around 16 percent identified themselves as "lower class"; the vast majority (73%) saw themselves as middle class or lower middle class. Astonishingly, 50 percent of Guatemalans identified themselves as middle class. The striking exception was Brazil, where people were twice as willing to classify themselves as "lower class" and correspondingly less inclined to identify themselves as middle class. People's self-identification and changes in such perception are certainly interesting, not least to politicians and political parties, but they are obviously quite subjective.

Sociologists have tended to define social class in terms of status and occupation: the middle classes might be said to include professional people, small business owners, and white-collar workers in general.[6] Decades ago business consulting firms in Latin America developed systems for analyzing markets based on income and

TABLE 6.2. Self-Designation of Class by Respondents in Seven Latin American Countries (Percentages)

	UPPER AND UPPER MIDDLE CLASS	MIDDLE CLASS	LOWER MIDDLE CLASS	LOWER CLASS
Argentina	5	49	32	13
Brazil	12	23	33	32
Chile	4	47	34	13
Colombia	11	43	28	14
Guatemala	8	50	26	15
Mexico	7	47	29	15
Peru	6	40	34	17
Total	8	42	31	16

Answers to the question "In our society people tend to locate themselves in different social classes. Do you feel you belong to any of these classes?" ECosociAL 2007 survey.

consumption levels, commonly divided into strata identified with letters: A, B, C, D, and E. Classes A and B were both wealthy, and C was a generic middle. Most of the population was in the bottom categories, D being roughly equivalent to the urban poor and E the rural poor. Most attention went to the top categories, for example, an auto dealer was interested in classes A and B, even though they were numerically very small, and could ignore D and E.

The Colombian government classifies all households into six strata, ranging from the very poor in stratum 1 and extending to the prosperous at strata 5 and 6. The formula for calculating each stratum is centered on housing and neighborhood, not the income of individual households. Those in strata 1 and 2 in particular are entitled to lower rates for utilities payments and day care.

In recent years, merchandisers in Latin America have put aside their previous attitudes and have discovered the purchasing power of the poor. One sign of this change is the construction of malls near large poor neighborhoods. In chapter 2, we noted that researchers in São Paulo were surprised at the degree of penetration of consumer goods such as electronics into what they had regarded as poor favelas. Because businesspeople are more interested in measuring purchasing power and how it can be tapped than in constructing a theoretically coherent model, their findings offer clues for evolving class structures.

Journalistically, the new middle classes have been defined around consumption, as summarized in the "six Cs": *casa propia, carro, celular, cable, computadora, cinema*: owning a house, car, cell phone, cable TV, and computer, and going to the movies. The "house" envisioned here is not necessarily along the lines of a US suburban stand-alone house surrounded by large yards; it may be a condominium. Automobile

Middle-class patrons at Larco Museum restaurant, Lima, Peru. © Tommie Sue Montgomery.

ownership is expanding faster than the population, and the growing middle classes at least aspire to owning a car. The "computer" may or may not be a desktop at home, but Latin Americans are part of the Internet age in various ways (including wide use of social networking by young people). Malls, supermarkets, fast foods, and franchise operations are already signs of the consumer dimension of the middle class. Another C (at least in Portuguese) that should be on the list is *cartão de crédito* (credit card), which facilitates larger purchases. In Latin American countries, a common form of card is a store card, one issued by a merchandiser, such as the Éxito chain in Colombia.

Another such sign is domestic tourism: the new middle classes are traveling to the beaches, national parks, and historic sites of their own countries. Yet another sign is schooling: already 30 percent of Colombian young people are in some form of post-secondary education, and President Juan Manuel Santos pledged to raise that figure to 50 percent, surely another marker of an expanding middle class.

A further indication of middle-class behavior is the use of the Internet, which in 2011 was rising faster than in any other global region. In absolute numbers, the largest numbers of users were in Brazil, Mexico, Argentina, and Colombia. In 2011, social networking accounted for nearly 30 percent of time spent on the Internet. One report summarized that "an average internet user in Latin America spent 24 hours online

TABLE 6.3. Internet Penetration in Latin America, 2014

Argentina	75.0
Colombia	61.6
Chile	67.3
Brazil	54.2
Dominican Rep.	58.5
Ecuador	77.4
Venezuela	50.4
Mexico	49.2
Peru	41.7
Guatemala	19.7

Note: Figures represent the percentage of the population over age fifteen using the Internet; the corresponding figure for North America is 87.7%.

Source: Miniwatts Marketing Group (2014).

during January 2011, consuming 1,795 pages of content and visiting the internet nearly 50 times during the month" (Israel 2013).

Economists define social class through measurements, particularly household income. One approach is to start with household income, find the median (the absolute midpoint, with half of households earning more and half less), and define a band on either side, say from 75 percent to 150 percent of the median family income. If the median household income per year in a country was $10,000, the "middle class" would be those households earning between $7,500 and $15,000. Thus any country will by definition have a middle class. An advantage to that approach is that the definition focuses on what is economically "middle" in that particular society.

Another approach is to assume that being middle class means having discretionary income. Thus, households could be said to be middle class if after meeting basic expenses for food, housing, clothing, and transportation, they have a third of their income left for spending on household appliances, eating out, or private schooling for the children.

As should be evident at this point, understandings of social class vary considerably, ranging from commonsense understandings, such as how people classify themselves when surveyed, to functional definitions as in traditional sociology, to behavior and consumer patterns, to measurements of income. Each approach reflects aspects of class, and together they demonstrate the complexity of understanding what class means.

Earlier in this chapter it was noted that around 2000, World Bank economists were proposing a worldwide poverty line of $1.25 per capita a day, or $2.00 per capita

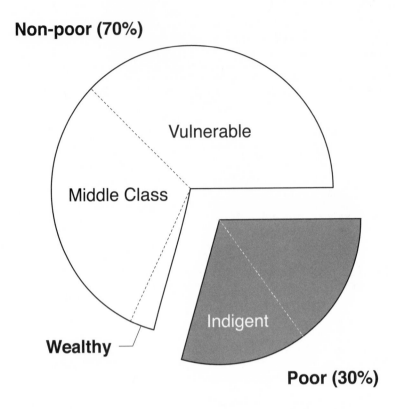

Non-poor (70%)

Vulnerable

Middle Class

Indigent

Wealthy

Poor (30%)

GRAPH 6.3. *Class Structure: Poor and Non-poor. Data from Ferreira et al. 2013.*

for urban areas. A decade later, economists were saying that the real poverty line for Latin America should be $4.00 per capita per day, and a World Bank study proposed that the middle class be defined as those receiving between $10 and $50 per day (again, these figures are per capita and should be multiplied by the number of people in the household). The poor are those living on $4 a day or less, and the wealthy are the upper 2 percent.

In this approach the largest class (37.5%) is neither poor nor middle class. Although these people are not poor and enjoy some aspects of middle-class life, they are "vulnerable" (defined as having at least a 10% chance of falling into poverty in the next five years). If asked to define themselves, the people in the "vulnerable" category would probably prefer a label like "lower middle class."

TOWARD MIDDLE-CLASS SOCIETIES?

This chapter thus far has noted three interrelated (but not identical) phenomena: declining poverty, modest declines in inequality, and expanding middle classes (however they might be defined). Is it possible that Latin American countries may be on the way to eliminating poverty, or perhaps to becoming "middle-class societies"?

We should bear in mind the broad trends that have favored these developments (discussed elsewhere in this book):

- steady growth since the early 2000s, driven by demand for Latin American exports
- sound macroeconomic management, and particularly low inflation
- growth in formal sector employment
- conditional cash transfers to the poorest people (110 million people benefiting)
- credit available (mortgage loans, other consumer loans, credit cards)
- small business formation
- expansion of schooling, especially universities
- expansion of other public services, such as safe drinking water and sewerage.

These developments are mutually reinforcing, that is, conditional cash transfers put money in the hands of the poor, who spend it at local businesses or may even open small businesses themselves. Growth has thus been driven by consumer demand, even by those labeled "vulnerable" in the World Bank study.

Political party appeals and electoral outcomes offer some corroboration of the expanding middle classes. Lula, a former labor leader in a party with strong Marxist factions, tailored his 2002 campaign to suit the sensitivities of the Brazilian middle classes, and he governed with policies that favored the internal market. For example, in 2009, in response to the worldwide recession, he announced a federal government–directed program to promote the building of one million homes by the private sector (thus stimulating the construction sector as well as home ownership). His successor, Dilma Rousseff, pledged to double the number to two million. The 2006 election in Mexico showed a split: Felipe Calderón won very narrowly by appealing to younger voters on "middle-class" issues, while Manuel López Obrador pledged to use the power of government to help the poor.

Eliminating poverty is an explicit goal of the Chilean government and is accepted by the country at large as part of making Chile a "developed" country.[7] Uruguay, a small nation, could perhaps do the same, and Brazil seems to have similar ambitions, although it would no doubt take some years, and a commitment across class and party lines. The effort is partly driven by national pride, a sense that as a powerful and rich country, Brazil cannot do less than eliminate poverty.

Looking toward the future role of the middle class, the World Bank study raises the question of what the impact of the new middle classes will be on the "social contract," which it defines as "the combination of implicit and explicit arrangements that determine what each group contributes to and receives from the state" (Ferreira et al. 2012, 11). In Latin America, that social contract has generally been characterized by a small state, for which taxes were limited, averaging 20.4 percent of GDP, as opposed to 33.7 percent in OECD (Organisation for Economic Co-operation and Development) countries. Pensions, disability, labor benefits, and health insurance went to a relatively small group. The upper and middle classes tended to opt out of public

Isla Trinitaria shantytown, Guayaquil, Ecuador. © Phillip Berryman.

education and health services—and sometimes even electricity (i.e., having private generators for power outages).

If Latin America wishes to continue to develop, it will need investments in education, health care, and infrastructure, which would call for higher taxes. The authors say Latin America stands at a crossroads:

> Will it break (further) with the fragmented social contract it inherited from its colonial past and continue to pursue greater parity of opportunities, or will it embrace even more forcefully a perverse model where the middle class opts out and fends for itself? (Ferreira et al. 2012, 12)

The report calls for continuing reforms, such as improving public education, developing cognitive skills in early education, undertaking a new set of reforms in social protection, particularly taking into account the "vulnerable" (non-poor, non–middle class) sector, and breaking the vicious cycle of "low taxation and low quality of public services that leads the middle and upper classes to opt out" (Ferreira et al. 2012, 12–13).

The authors of the study are thus expressing a wish that Latin American societies will collectively opt to be inclusive societies. In this optimistic scenario, the expansion of the middle classes would reach so far as to encompass the poor, so that even if the resulting societies were not egalitarian, all citizens would reasonably believe that they had opportunities. However, there are reasons to suspect that large numbers of people will be left in self-reinforcing poverty. A prominent factor is unequal education: middle- and upper-class children would attend the university for which they have been prepared in private schools, while poor children would find it difficult to pass entrance examinations or to finance their education. These trends could be reinforced by segregation of the poor into neighborhoods of higher crime and patterns of less stable households, leading to generational poverty.

Thus, it is by no means assured that Latin American societies will evolve toward relative equality—where all citizens feel that they are in principle equal. One of the obstacles will be racial and ethnic disparities, to which we now turn.

FURTHER READING

On declining poverty, see Helwege and Birch (2007); on inequality, Birdsall, Lustig, and McLeod (2011). On the middle classes, see especially *Americas Quarterly* 6, no. 4 (Fall 2012), which is devoted to the topic and which presents the findings of recent research in a nontechnical fashion. Castañeda (2011) devotes a chapter to the emerging Mexican middle class. A thorough World Bank study is Ferreira et al. (2012).

Overcoming Legacies of Conquest and Slavery

Indigenous Peoples and Afro-descendants

As noted in chapter 1, Latin American countries can be divided into four broad categories of racial-ethnic mix:

- indigenous/European (Guatemala, Bolivia, Ecuador, Peru)
- Afro-descendant/European (Brazil, Dominican Republic, Cuba, Panama)
- mestizo (Mexico, El Salvador, Honduras, Nicaragua, Colombia, Venezuela, Paraguay)
- European (Chile, Costa Rica, Argentina, Uruguay)

In the countries classified as "indigenous/European," a large proportion of the population speaks an indigenous language and identifies as indigenous. Yet in those same countries, such as Guatemala, many people show no sign of indigenous ancestry or culture. Indigenous peoples also live in "mestizo" and "European" countries. For instance, about 8 percent of Mexicans and 2.4 percent of Costa Ricans are indigenous. Likewise, most countries have some Afro-descendants, but there is generally no sharp line separating "black" from "white." Paraguay is a unique case: less than 2 percent of the nation is fully indigenous, and yet 90 percent of the nation speaks Guaraní (as well as Spanish).

In most countries, a representative group of business or government elites or university students and professors will show largely "European" features, and a representative group of the rural or urban poor will show disproportionately indigenous or Afro-descendant features. That division was not institutionalized in legal forms like Jim Crow laws in the American South and apartheid in South Africa. Its origins lie rather in the nature of colonial society after the conquest of the native peoples and the import of African slaves. The upshot is that indigenous people and Afro-descendants suffer exclusion to the present day.

Indications of the second-class status of indigenous peoples in the recent past and even in the present have been visible to anyone with eyes to see. Indigenous women

Indigenous Guatemalan man carrying burden. © *Tommie Sue Montgomery.*

served as live-in maids on duty from early morning to late at night, with Sunday after-noon their only time off. In Guatemala and elsewhere, indigenous men were rounded up by force to serve in the military, but were not trained as officers and could not rise through the ranks. Medical services were not available in the countryside, and schools were scarce and poorly served, so many indigenous people remained illiterate. Afro-descendants likewise lived in poor neighborhoods and were disproportionately employed in domestic service and manual labor.

VARIETIES OF INDIGENOUS PEOPLE

Approximately five hundred indigenous languages are still spoken in Latin America (out of an estimated two thousand at the time of the conquest). In many instances, there are only a few hundred or even a few dozen speakers of a language. The indig-enous peoples can be broadly divided into "highland" and "lowland."

Highland Indians, such as the Quechua and Aymara in the Andes, are the descen-dants of those who were conquered in the sixteenth century by the Spanish armies led by Francisco Pizarro in Peru. They and similar groups have lived under the control of the dominant society since that time. Throughout what is now southern Mexico to Guatemala, and in what is now Peru, Ecuador, and Bolivia, the Spanish forced the Indians to live in designated towns and villages, and even to wear particular dress to identify themselves; the colorful clothing that distinguishes people from one Gua-temalan highland town from another was imposed by their colonial masters. The indigenous people were converted to Catholicism by force, although they retained much of their worldview and some practices and rituals. These highland Indians already practiced intensive agriculture, and they continued to do so, cultivating their traditional crops (corn in Mesoamerica and potatoes in the Andes). Under various regimes, they were forced to work in the mines, on plantations, and on public works like roads. Otherwise they retained elements of their village life.

Hundreds of other lowland Indian groups were not immediately so subjected. In Brazil, for example, peoples with a hunter-gatherer way of life moved inland beyond the reach of the Portuguese, who settled along the coast and did not venture far into the interior. The peoples in the Amazon (Brazil, Peru, Ecuador, Bolivia, Colombia, Venezuela) have maintained their traditional ways of life with little or no contact with the rest of the population, and a few peoples even remain "uncontacted" in the twenty-first century. Throughout the Americas, some peoples survived on the far frontiers of the colonies and even after independence.[1]

In four countries indigenous people compose from 30 percent to almost 60 per-cent of the population: Guatemala, 44%; Bolivia, 57%; Peru, 41%; and Ecuador, 30% (Schwerin 2011, 43). Together with indigenous communities in southern Mexico, they constitute what may be called "Indo-America," regions where the indigenous people are not a minority in large portions of the country, or in the case of Bolivia, in the country itself.[2]

By way of example, let us consider the indigenous people of Guatemala. They are

Highland indigenous women in market, La Paz, Bolivia. © Noah Friedman-Rudovsky.

Chiquitano family in the Santa Cruz region of Bolivia. © Noah Friedman-Rudovsky.

descendants of the ancient Maya and speak over twenty related languages, although four predominate. After the conquest, most of the indigenous people lived in towns, villages, and hamlets in the highlands. In the later nineteenth century, indigenous communal lands were appropriated by the local elites who wanted to expand coffee cultivation to meet demand from Europe.

The Guatemalan population was divided into elites with European ancestry, indigenous people, and mixed-race mestizos in some parts of the country. Indigenous people in the highlands had largely self-sufficient economies, producing corn, beans, some vegetables, chickens, a little livestock, and some cash crops. They also sold their surpluses of corn and beans to intermediaries to earn some cash. Because their plots were small, in the mid-twentieth century many indigenous people would sign up with labor contractors to go down to the plantations on the Pacific coastal plain from October to February (when their own lands were lying fallow) and would harvest coffee, cut sugarcane, or pick cotton for about a dollar a day.

The local power structure (public officials, larger merchants) in indigenous towns was usually composed of ladinos (non-Indians). Government health services did not reach far into the countryside; illiteracy was high among indigenous people, especially women; and many did not speak Spanish. The indigenous people were important to the economy of the country for their labor on the agroexport plantations and as suppliers of corn and beans, which were the basis of the diet of ordinary people in the cities, but they had too little cash income to be very significant for the domestic economy. They were almost invisible in public life: they rarely appeared in the newspapers or on television, although colorful images of them were used to attract tourists.

In the early 1970s, however, leftist guerrillas began organizing in the indigenous highlands, and the Guatemalan army reacted by attacking areas where people were suspected of guerrilla sympathies. In 1978, the army opened fire on indigenous people protesting peacefully in the town of Panzós, killing several dozen. That was the prelude to several years in which the army carried out approximately 440 massacres, the vast majority in indigenous towns and villages, as part of what it regarded as a counterinsurgency, even though almost all the victims were unarmed civilians. The army forced people to be gathered in "model villages," and organized all males into "civil patrols," which were obliged to go out into the countryside against the guerrillas.

Whole villages were left deserted and people fled to Guatemala City, across the border into Mexico, and even to the United States. Anthropologists familiar with the area as researchers spoke of genocide, meaning that people were being killed simply because they were indigenous. Virtually no one has been brought to justice for any of these massacres.[3] Exact figures for the numbers killed in Guatemala cannot be obtained, but it is 100,000 or more, and the vast majority of victims were indigenous. In the 1990s, tens of thousands returned from exile. The upshot is that the trauma still affects families and communities.

By the twenty-first century, other developments were taking place. Paved roads had reached towns, and most indigenous children, even girls, were attending elementary school. Teachers were now more likely to be indigenous, and some instruction was being given in the indigenous languages. Traditional village-level subsistence farming seemed less and less viable in the twenty-first century. It did not provide much cash income, and young people were increasingly unwilling to spend their lives doing it, especially after having had a few years of schooling. Many who had fled the violence to Guatemala City did not return to their towns and villages. Guatemalan indigenous people had continued to make their way north to the United States, despite the obstacles and dangers, and were sending back remittances to their families. The signs of these remittances could be seen in the building boom in indigenous towns as migrants sent money to build large houses in a nontraditional style more for conspicuous display than for use. Drugs were being run through Guatemala by many routes, including through the indigenous highlands.

These developments raised questions of identity: What happens when indigenous people are no longer in the indigenous town, working in agriculture, and participating in the annual cycle of religious holidays? Is an indigenous lawyer who lives in Guatemala City still indigenous, even if he speaks his language only at home (if even there)?

The life of highland indigenous people elsewhere was also being disrupted. In 1980, a radical fanatic guerrilla movement called Shining Path was organized in the Peruvian highlands. Unlike guerrilla movements elsewhere that sought to win over the peasantry, Shining Path was willing to use terrorism, including assassination, against indigenous people to cow them into submission and allegiance. Tens of thousands of indigenous people lost their lives at the hands of either the guerrillas or the Peruvian army, and many fled to Lima and other cities. Indigenous peoples in Ecuador and Bolivia have likewise emigrated from their highland towns and villages.

As one example of the twenty-first-century situation of indigenous people, consider El Alto, Bolivia,[4] which two generations ago was a poor satellite of La Paz and is now larger, with over a million inhabitants. In the 2001 census, 74 percent of people in El Alto identified themselves as Aymara, even though only 48 percent spoke the language. The anthropologist Xavier Albó, who has lived in El Alto for decades, describes it as a "hinge city" between La Paz, to which 200,000 of its residents descend to work each day, and the rural communities of the altiplano (highlands), from which they came and to which most retain ties. Some of the neighborhoods are made up of people from a particular community in the highlands. The city has hundreds of local neighborhood boards, which are influential in resolving local conflicts and in obtaining and apportioning funding for community projects. At the same time, Albó admits that despite the signs of community, many households are disconnected from their neighborhoods, like city dwellers elsewhere (Albó 2011).

A key feature of the city is the open-air market held Sundays and Thursdays with thousands of booths and businesses selling all kinds of goods, from food and clothing to electronics, construction goods, and auto parts. A visitor is surprised to find lavish six-story buildings put up by successful merchants and professionals, with a great deal of postmodern color and swirling designs, in what is clearly a demonstration of worldly success. Even though it is a unique case, El Alto exemplifies the tensions of being indigenous in the twenty-first century.

Likewise, consider Nebaj in highland Guatemala, which the army occupied in the 1980s, killing many civilians and driving many from the surrounding countryside into exile. Because of that history, the town attracted many international aid projects in the subsequent two decades, some aimed at enabling the people to improve their agriculture and become self-sufficient. However, due to a high birth rate causing the population to double every twenty-five years, available farmland per family has dwindled to the point that subsistence farming is no longer sufficient. The people of the area are entrepreneurial and thus many started small businesses, but the local market was soon saturated. Some have gone to Guatemala City to work, but with only partial success. Thus, starting in the early 2000s, many men from Nebaj went to the United States, especially to sites in Florida, northern Virginia, and Ohio, where pioneers from Nebaj had established beachheads.

Unable to obtain visas, these emigrants had to hire traffickers, at a rate of around $5,000 per head. While some might be able to borrow the money from relatives already in the United States, the sum was usually obtained by borrowing from moneylenders in the town, who customarily charged 10 percent per month (not compounded), possibly putting up a house or farmland as collateral. An anthropologist delving into this situation found that the moneylenders themselves were borrowing from the many microcredit projects set up in the town (he counted twenty-three agencies lending at low interest rates).[5] Enterprising people were borrowing at 2 percent and relending at 10 percent. If the migrant could earn money and send remittances, the loans could be paid. That scheme was not always working, however, even before the US recession of 2008, and at that point it became a crisis. The borrowing, relending, and financing migration to the United States had become an inadvertent Ponzi scheme, a bubble ready to burst. Those left holding the bag, and also thoroughly involved in the wheeling and dealing, were typically women, spouses trying to repay their husbands' debt by becoming moneylenders themselves (Stoll 2010).

What matters here is not the details of the cases of El Alto and Nebaj in themselves, but the recognition that the life of indigenous people in the twenty-first century is not that of their grandparents, even if they still speak an indigenous language and wear indigenous dress.

The main distinguishing feature of lowland indigenous people is that they were not integrated into the colonial order as were the survivors of the Inca and Aztec Empires and the Mayans, but either fled or lived on the frontiers and were only gradually subjugated. They were thus able to retain more of their traditional way of life. Their total numbers are small, but they constitute hundreds of individual societies with their own languages, customs, and worldviews. In Colombia, for example, there are a hundred distinct indigenous peoples, totaling 800,000 people.

A large number live in the Amazon basin, others in remote areas of Central America and Mexico. They typically practice extensive agriculture (as opposed to the intensive agriculture of highland peoples), combined with fishing and hunting. In more remote regions of the Amazon, most of these peoples had little contact with outsiders until recent decades. Some of these peoples remain uncontacted; by one estimate, thirty such tribes exist in Brazil, and possibly a total of forty to sixty in the Amazon (Wallace 2007).

Events in the northern Ecuadorean Amazon offer insight into what is happening to lowland Indians. Until the 1960s, the area was inhabited by several peoples who maintained their customary way of life, with occasional contacts with Catholic and Protestant missionaries. In 1967, oil was discovered, and production began in earnest in the 1970s. Texaco built a pipeline over the Andes and drilled wells. Encouraged by government policy and incentives, nonindigenous settlers came into the area, and the population rose from 25,000 in 1962 to 370,000 in 1992. Nearly a fifth of the Ecuadorean Amazon had been cleared by 1995.

According to Judith Kimerling, a lawyer and academic who has advocated for the Huaorani people, the government regarded the Amazon "as a frontier to be conquered, a source of wealth for the State, and an escape valve for land distribution pressures in the highland and coastal regions" (Kimerling 2013, 47). At first, the government treated the lands as uninhabited, in other words, available for being occupied and claimed by nonindigenous settlers. Eventually a tract of land was titled to the Huaorani, but with the provision that title could be revoked if they impeded oil or mining activities. The areas titled to the Huaorani are about a third of their traditional lands.

The Huaorani people, who had a reputation as warriors, sought to resist these encroachments. They were pacified, however, by both the Ecuadorean government and missionaries; many gave up their nomadic way of life and established permanent settlements. New diseases decimated them. "As a group, the Huaorani have been thrust into a process of rapid change, external pressures, and loss of territory and access to natural resources that endangers their survival as a people," writes Kimerling (2013, 52).

Texaco extracted nearly 1.5 billion barrels of crude oil from 1964 to 1992. By the time Texaco handed over control to the Ecuadorean state company Petroecuador in 1990, it was producing over 213,000 barrels a day from two hundred wells. It was also generating more than 3.2 million gallons of toxic wastewater a day, which it placed in open-air waste pits with no treatment or monitoring. It flared natural gas as a waste product and spilled vast amounts of oil, both from the main line and elsewhere. Kimerling says, "No cleanup activities were undertaken and no assistance or compensation was provided to affected communities" (2013, 61). The crisscrossing oil lines can foul waters and leave chronic pollution.

The outside world has learned of this situation primarily as a result of lawsuits in the United States and then in Ecuadorean courts. In 2011, an Ecuadorean court ordered Chevron, which had taken over Texaco in a merger, to pay $18 billion in damages, the largest judgment ever in an environmental lawsuit, but the oil company continued to fight the verdict and had deep pockets to do so.[6]

The Huaorani and other peoples have responded to the loss of their lands by becoming organized to defend their interests and by seeking allies. However, their own communities have been divided: some people, including leaders, accepted jobs with the oil companies or the government, but that in itself entails giving up more of their way of life. The organizations themselves have different approaches, some simply resisting "development" and others seeking to make sure that their people get their fair share of the proceeds. It should be noted that the plaintiffs in the legal cases have been primarily nonindigenous settlers, but the lawyers and others have displayed indigenous people in their international public relations campaigns as well as in the courtroom.

The Huaorani have been faced with a cruel choice: agree to accept some of the benefits of contact with the outside world and sacrifice their independence and way of life, or withdraw farther away into a forest reserve (which does not provide ultimate protection, since the subsoil rights remain with the government).

INDIGENOUS ACTIVISM

In June 1990, indigenous groups in Ecuador from the lowlands and the highlands carried out a weeklong uprising (*levantamiento*) that paralyzed the country, because they cut down trees and placed boulders to block highways. It was a signal that something new was happening, and that the rest of the country would have to pay more attention to the indigenous people and their demands. The shutdown was organized by CONAIE (Confederation of Indigenous Nationalities of Ecuador), which had been founded in 1986, building on earlier federations. CONAIE is a coalition of a dozen indigenous peoples from the Amazon, together with the Quechua of the highlands— by far the largest group—and some people on the coast, including Afro-Ecuadoreans. Similar mass mobilizations intended to halt normal activity and force the nation to deal with their issues took place in 1992, 1994, 1997, 2000, and 2005.

CONAIE was the outgrowth of literacy and leadership training by both Catholic and Protestant churches in the previous decades. As a result of missionary work and population pressures from settlers, some indigenous peoples, like the Shuar, gradually turned from their previous nomadic way of life and became grouped in settled communities. Contact with the wider world was a mixed blessing, but it gave people the tools with which to become organized and press their case. The issues pursued by CONAIE included recognition of the various indigenous groups as "nations," land and water rights, fair prices for basic necessities, education and health care, and resistance to "neoliberal" policies imposed by international agencies and the United States.

After initially eschewing party politics, CONAIE played a key role in the 2000 coup that overthrew a president and installed a three-man junta, including a CONAIE representative. It later supported the presidential campaign of Col. Lucio Gutiérrez, who had been involved in the coup, but then broke with him after he was elected, and then participated in the demonstrations by which he was ousted in 2005. Organized indigenous groups were prominent in the activism that deposed three presidents and led to the emergence of the populist economist Rafael Correa, who was elected president in 2007.

*Bolivian indigenous people marching 150 miles toward La Paz to demand nationalization of the country's natural gas, 2005.
© Noah Friedman-Rudovsky.*

Bolivia shows significant parallels to Ecuador, including a thirty-five-day "March for Territory and Dignity" in 1990, which started in the lowland department of El Beni and continued for 400 miles up to the capital, La Paz. Subsequent marches of indigenous peoples were organized in 1996, 2000, 2002, and beyond. In Bolivia, street demonstrations also intersected with national politics, especially around the 2000 "water wars" in Cochabamba,[7] and in the resistance of coca growers to government violence against them. Out of these struggles emerged Evo Morales, an Aymara-speaking Bolivian who grew up in a poor family and had only a few years of schooling, as a founder and leader of the Movimiento al Socialismo (MAS; Movement toward Socialism). Morales, elected president in 2006, represents the emergence of the indigenous majority, along with other poor Bolivians who have been excluded from national life.

By 1990, when these major national marches took place in Ecuador and Bolivia, indigenous groups in almost all Latin American countries had established networks among themselves and with sympathetic allies abroad (other indigenous organizations, anthropologists and other academics, environmentalists, and NGOs). The impending five-hundred-year anniversary of the landing of Christopher Columbus became a focal point for organizing, starting with the very name of what happened in 1492. The traditional term, the "discovery" of the Americas, put the emphasis on the Europeans. Indigenous people tended to use the word "conquest" and emphasized the terrible price paid by their ancestors and their people: decimating diseases, loss of lands, servitude, and humiliation.

Those debates came to a head in Guatemala, when Rigoberta Menchú was awarded the 1992 Nobel Peace Prize. Menchú had arisen to prominence after 1982, traveling the world as a young woman telling the story of her family, her people, and her country. In 1980, her father, Vicente Menchú, had been part of a delegation that occupied the Spanish embassy in Guatemala City to protest army violence in the department of Quiché. Police surrounded the building, a fire broke out, firefighters were not allowed to enter, and thirty-nine people, occupiers and embassy staff, were burned to death. Starting with her personal story, Menchú had become a spokesperson for Guatemalan indigenous people and so was honored with the prize, to the extreme chagrin of the Guatemalan army and its supporters.[8]

In the wake of the slaughter in Guatemala, some indigenous groups came to the conclusion that their people had had to pay the price for leftist insurgency and popular organizing. They created what came to be called the Pan-Mayanist movement, rejecting the notion that the indigenous people were part of a larger coalition of popular forces and insisting that they should work on their own agenda, with a particular stress on cultural affirmation, language, education, and access to professions.

On January 1, 1994, Mexico and the world were startled by the emergence of what appeared to be a new indigenous insurgency led by the Zapatista National Liberation Army, which occupied San Cristóbal de las Casas and a number of other towns in the southern Mexican state of Chiapas. After about two weeks of hostilities, a truce was arranged. The Zapatista movement was the result of a decade of clandestine organizing by a small Marxist group in Chiapas, taking advantage of previous leadership development, particularly under the aegis of the Catholic Church. By the time the movement went public, it had abandoned the dream of taking state power and saw itself as a force for pressing indigenous demands before the Mexican state and society. Much attention was focused on "Subcomandante Marcos,"[9] the ski-masked, pipe-smoking spokesman for the group, who issued rambling poetic communiqués composed on a laptop. However, the Zapatistas themselves were indigenous, and they were forcing the nation to pay attention to their plight.

Since the 1990s, as a result of organizing and pressure, indigenous peoples have forced national states and public opinion to take them into account, but progress in resolving fundamental inequities remains elusive. New constitutions in recent decades (in Colombia, Brazil, and Ecuador) have explicitly recognized the special relationship of indigenous people to their lands. In this regard they take their cue from the International Labour Organisation (ILO) Indigenous and Tribal Peoples Convention (1989; ILO-Convention 169), which was signed by only about twenty countries, almost all in Latin America. In 2007, the United Nations approved a Declaration of the Rights of Indigenous Peoples. Both of these documents recognize a collective right of native peoples to their traditional lands. In that spirit, various countries have allocated territories for them. For example, in Brazil, 672 parcels, constituting 13 percent of the country, are set aside as reserves for indigenous groups, who constitute only about 0.4 percent of the population. Other nations have similar provisions. As noted in chapter 5, recent constitutions and legislation of Ecuador and Bolivia enshrine the indigenous notion of "living well," meaning living in harmony with nature.

In practice, however, these legislative provisions prove imprecise and difficult to enforce. Landholding elites object to granting collective rights to indigenous peoples. Colonists and loggers are likely to ignore such reserves. National governments, which legally retain the rights to minerals and hydrocarbons in the soil, make contracts with oil and mining companies, and at most offer to resettle the local inhabitants.

Advances have been made in formal politics. Until about thirty years ago, literacy requirements kept many indigenous people from even voting. More indigenous people, including women, hold seats in national parliaments and even more in mayorships. No longer are nonindigenous politicians likely to represent an area whose population is overwhelmingly indigenous. Indigenous parties as such, however, do not fare well. Leftist parties tend to take the support of indigenous groups for granted and to regard class exploitation as the more fundamental issue. A notable example is the MAS headed by Evo Morales in Bolivia. Although he drew on the indigenous vote and emphasized that he was the first (self-identified) indigenous president of Bolivia, in office he tended to act as the head of a left-wing coalition, to the dismay of many of

Nobel Prize winner Rigoberta Menchú and President Evo Morales. © Noah Friedman-Rudovsky.

his indigenous supporters, as in the TIPNIS conflict regarding the proposal to build highways through an indigenous reserve.[10]

An interesting case is that of the "uncontacted" peoples mentioned earlier. "Uncontacted" means that they do not have known contacts with the dominant national society, but they may be known through neighboring indigenous groups who occasionally get a glimpse of them. The governments of Brazil, Ecuador, Peru, Bolivia, and Colombia have adopted, to one degree or another, policies of respecting the rights of these peoples to remain in "voluntary isolation."

As a result of pressures from grassroots organizations, governments have been extending schooling and health care into indigenous areas. Illiteracy is being eliminated, and people are living longer. As a result of increased schooling, indigenous people now have access to professions. By and large more indigenous people have roles in public life, both locally and in national parliaments. However, the relationship to party politics remains problematic: Should indigenous people pursue their own agenda, even forming indigenous parties, or be part of a larger leftist coalition?

The sharpest contradiction appears in struggles over natural resources, particularly mining and petroleum and gas extraction. The pattern is for companies to enter an area, offer jobs, and divide the existing community. Governments argue that this development is necessary for the good of the entire population and should not be blocked by relatively small local groups and their environmentalist allies.

AFRO-LATIN AMERICA

Approximately a quarter of Latin Americans are black or mulatto—160 million out of 600 million—although it must be admitted immediately that such statistics are necessarily imprecise. The countries where the African presence is most notable are Brazil, the Dominican Republic, Cuba, and Panama. Notable black populations can also be found in Colombia, Venezuela, Ecuador, Peru, and even Uruguay. By one estimate, Brazil is 45 percent black or mulatto; it has been called the "second-largest black nation" following Nigeria. The Dominican Republic is said to be 73 percent mixed race, 16 percent white, and 11 percent black, and Colombia, to be 19 to 26 percent Afro-Colombian, although only 11 percent self-identified as black in the 2005 census.

As early as the 1530s, the Portuguese and Spanish began to import African slaves, and by the nineteenth century, 10 or 12 million had been brought to Latin America. The largest numbers went to work on sugar plantations in Brazil and the Caribbean, but slavery existed throughout the Americas, even in countries like Argentina where no discernible Afro-descendants remain today. Slaves from different areas of Africa were mixed together, and in the process, they lost their languages, ways of life, and cultures. Traces of African culture can be found in capoeira, the Brazilian martial art and dance, and in Afro-Brazilian and Afro-Cuban religions. In Brazil, Colombia, Panama, and elsewhere, some slaves managed to escape and set up free colonies. Slavery was not abolished until the nineteenth century; the last country in the hemisphere to abolish it was Brazil (1888).

Afro-Colombian youth painting mural in Medellín, Colombia. © Julián García.

Because Iberian men bore children by African women from the onset of slavery, there is no "color line" in Latin American countries. Although some individuals appear to be all European or all African in ancestry, many people fall somewhere along a continuum. People who would clearly be regarded as "black" in the United States with its color line, generally do not call themselves "black." These attitudes are rooted in history, but they have unfolded differently from one country to another.

Most people in the Dominican Republic show some African ancestry, but very few people would consider themselves black, and they describe themselves with a variety of terms other than "black." These attitudes are partly explained by their relationship with Haiti, which occupies the western side of the island of Hispaniola. Almost immediately after the Dominican Republic achieved independence from Spain (1821), it was invaded by Haiti, which feared that Spain or France might use the Dominican Republic to attack Haiti (which had won its own independence as a black republic in 1804). It was not until 1844 that Dominicans won back their independence, this time from Haiti. In Dominican eyes, Haitians are truly black, and this historical memory of occupation helps explain the reluctance of Dominicans to consider themselves black. Because living standards are considerably higher in the Dominican Republic, an estimated 800,000 Haitians live there doing agricultural and other low-paying work.

In the late nineteenth and early twentieth centuries, the elites of Brazil and other

The Redemption of Ham *(1895). Modesto Brocos portrays "whitening": a black grandmother thanks God for the appearance of the child of her mulatta daughter and her European immigrant son-in-law. Museu Nacional de Belas Artes, Rio de Janeiro.*

countries encouraged immigration from Europe, partly because Europe embodied the progress they wished to emulate, and they even spoke of "whitening" (*branqueamento*) their population. The 1895 painting *The Redemption of Ham*, by Modesto Brocos, depicts that process, showing a black grandmother, a mulatta mother, and an even lighter child as the result of marrying a European man.

In the 1930s, the Brazilian sociologist and writer Gilberto Freyre provided a new interpretation of race in Brazil that proved influential. He claimed that because of the free miscegenation of masters and slaves on plantations, Brazilians were racially tolerant, and he contrasted that tolerance with legally enforced segregation in the US South. This claim came to be called "racial democracy."[11] For decades, the notion served to convince many Brazilians that their society was not racist.

It is extremely difficult to obtain accurate and consistent statistics on Afro-descendants in Latin America. Consider the problem of census agencies: Should census takers make their own judgment? Should they ask people to name their race or skin color? Or should the question even appear on the census? The upshot is that figures vary from time to time; in some censuses, the question is not asked, and varying criteria yield different answers.

Despite the imprecision of who is "black," it is clear that Afro-descendants are disproportionately poor, making up almost 50 percent of the region's poor. For example, in the Ecuadorean province of Esmeraldas, which is 80 percent Afro-Ecuadorean, infant mortality is double the national rate. In Brazil, although 45 percent of the population claimed some African ancestry, only about 3 percent (17 out of 594) of congressional representatives in 2007 self-identified as Afro-Brazilian. In 2000, only 2 percent of the three million university students were black (Seelke 2008). Another way to examine racial prejudice is to look at films, television, and advertising. For example, in Brazilian films and television, there is no equivalent to Oprah Winfrey or Denzel Washington.

The sociologist Edward Telles uses the concepts of vertical and horizontal relationships to show how race (or skin color) works in Brazil and how it is different from the United States. *Horizontally*, Brazilians are not separated by skin color: they are not residentially segregated, and intermarriage is not a taboo. He is referring primarily to the poor: in a favela, mulattos, whites, and blacks live side by side. *Vertically*, however, it is harder for blacks to enter the middle class (and almost impossible to enter the wealthy elite). To enter the middle class, people need a middle-class income. That in turn increasingly requires greater educational attainment, particularly a university degree, but entering the university has required passing difficult entrance examinations. Because of the poor quality of Brazil's public schools, middle-class families send their children to private schools, where they receive a better education and consequently score higher on entrance exams.

> Poor whites tend to be preferred to poor browns and especially blacks in schooling and in the market for middle-class jobs, especially when middle-class whites are not available. Aside from being granted greater social prestige on the basis of their appearance, poor whites also have greater access than non-whites of similar social standing to the networks and patronage that are important in the Brazilian labor market. (Telles 2004, 223)

Such attitudes are internalized and taken for granted.

In contrasting how race operates in Brazil and the United States, Telles says that, horizontally, Brazilians of different colors intermarry more and are more likely to live in proximity to one another than in the United States—at least among the poor. In the United States, while blacks are disproportionately poor, significant numbers have entered the middle class. In Telles's terms, "On the horizontal plane, racial boundaries in Brazil are much more easily traversed than in the United States. However, on the vertical dimension, racial barriers are more insurmountable than in the United States" (2004, 225). Telles notes the importance of location, contrasting largely white southern Brazil to the state of Bahia, which is heavily mulatto and black, although the middle and upper classes and business and political elites are largely white.

Angela Figueiredo (2010) casts an interesting light on the experience of blacks who do manage to rise to middle-class status. She surveyed thirty mulatto-to-black owners of businesses employing from six to one hundred employees. Economically, all were middle class, most of them first-generation. She found numerous instances in which middle-class blacks had encountered surprise at their very presence in certain places: for example, a black woman registers at a five-star hotel in São Paulo where she is scheduled to give a course, and the hotel staff act as though she does not belong; an accountant shows up at a company and the client registers surprise—that he is not white. Figueiredo notes that her interviewees are reluctant to interpret such treatment as discrimination, and they train their children, all in private schools, not to react when they find themselves in such situations.

ORGANIZING AROUND RACE?

On the basis of US experience, one might think that Afro-descendants would welcome becoming mobilized in campaigns akin to the civil rights movement in the 1950s and 1960s. Indeed, "black power" movements were formed in Brazil and elsewhere in the 1970s, but they gained little traction and did not become large mass organizations, unlike the indigenous movements in Ecuador and Bolivia, which could bring the nation to a halt.

At least three reasons can be suggested for the inability to create mass movements around skin color. First, contrary to the Jim Crow South, racial discrimination in Latin America is not enshrined in legislation and does not offer targets for legal action (occupying buses, sitting at lunch counters, registering to vote). Even though blacks are disproportionately poor and public services in predominantly black areas are of lesser quality, it is difficult to isolate race as the sole cause or factor.

Second, it is difficult to distinguish the effects of race from class, and those striving for justice have tended to emphasize class. This is particularly true in Brazil, where focusing on race is easily branded "divisive."

Third, in the absence of a clear color line, people are reluctant to consider themselves black, as we have already noted for Dominicans. In the 1990 census, when asked to choose, only 4.9 percent of Brazilians classified themselves as black; 39.3 percent chose mulatto; 55.3 percent, white; and 0.5 percent, Asian.[12] It is not surprising, then, that specifically black organizations have focused on consciousness-raising, cultural activities (music, dance, and capoeira), and encouraging people to proudly affirm that they are black.

Somewhat by way of exception, Colombia offers an example of people who have organized around their African identity. Afro-Colombians have lived largely on the Pacific coastal areas of the country in relatively isolated rural areas, often since colonial times. Afro-Colombian activists have insisted that their communities are "peoples," with ties to particular areas of land, similar to those of indigenous peoples, and that that relationship should be officially recognized. Despite initial resistance, the 1991 constitution recognized those claims, which were spelled out in a 1993 law, "Law 70 . . . In Recognition of the Right of Black Colombians to Collectively Own and Occupy Their Ancestral Lands."

One specific attempt to remedy discrimination is occurring with affirmative action in higher education in Brazil. As already noted, until the early 2000s, very few Afro-descendant faces were visible on Brazilian university campuses among the students, and even fewer in the faculty. This was not due to any specific exclusion on the basis of skin color but rather primarily to the fact that admission to the state universities is through a highly competitive entrance exam, which has the effect of eliminating students from inferior public schools who generally do not perform as well. Students who pass the examination enjoy free tuition to the most prestigious universities in Brazil. In the early 2000s, universities began to experiment with various approaches to "affirmative action," using quotas. As a result of a 2012 Supreme Court ruling, affirmative action is now mandated at all fifty-nine federal universities and thirty-nine government technical schools: half of the students accepted must come from public schools, and half of the latter must come from families earning less than $503 per month. In addition, schools must allocate spaces in accordance with the racial makeup of the state, that is, higher black and mulatto enrollment is expected in Bahia and other northern states, but the numbers would be lower in southern states like São Paulo. What has changed is that poor students now have access to the free higher education that was previously the monopoly of the middle and upper classes. It should mean that the complexion of the professional classes, including the teaching profession, will change over time.[13]

Each of the nineteen or so Latin American countries has its own ethnic/racial mix, its own history, and its own built-in assumptions, and in all of them a racial/ethnic divide is significant. In this chapter we have sought to characterize the features of these relationships and of efforts to overcome racial and ethnic discrimination. We have noted a key difference between the situation of indigenous peoples and Afro-descendants: it has been possible to organize politically around indigenous identity to some extent because the line between indigenous groups and others is relatively sharp, whereas the lack of a clear "color line" has meant that mass movements around race have not emerged. The focus here has largely been on patterns of discrimination and exclusion and efforts to challenge them.

In making a presentation to the International Olympic Committee for what became Brazil's successful bid to host the 2016 Summer Olympics, President Lula showed a three-minute film in which Brazilians welcome delegations from around the world to Rio under the slogan "Our Enthusiasm Unites Us." The film was an apotheosis of national pride and international solidarity, showing Brazilians of all hues and hairstyles united in harmonious celebration. Strictly speaking, it was of a Brazil that did not exist—at least not yet—but it expressed an aspiration for one that might come to be. Similar aspirations are gestating elsewhere in Latin American societies.

FURTHER READING

Canby (1992) offers portraits of contemporary indigenous life in Guatemala and southern Mexico, making excellent connections to their Maya ancestors. Insight into the way of life of lowland indigenous people may be found in Kopenawa (2013), a Yanomami leader's story and philosophy, and in Harry Walker (2012), a study of the Urarina people in the Peruvian Amazon, with a strong emphasis on infant and child rearing. Cleary and Steigenga (2004) provide an overview and case studies of indigenous organizing. Andrews (2004) presents an overview of Afro–Latin American history. See Klein and Vinson (2007) for an account of slavery. The four-part documentary *Black in Latin America* and companion book of the same name (Gates 2011) present an accessible introduction to the topic with a focus on Brazil, Cuba, Dominican Republic/Haiti, and (surprisingly) Mexico.

Machismo Contested

Changing Gender Roles and Expectations

The word "machismo," based on Spanish *macho* (male), has been used in various languages to designate patriarchy or male domination. Although machismo has flourished for centuries in Latin America, it is now being challenged, both inside and outside the household. For example, six Latin American countries (Nicaragua, Chile, Panama, Brazil, Costa Rica, and Argentina) have elected female presidents. Women are now equaling and even surpassing men in educational attainment.

This chapter considers models of family and their roots in history, women's activism in challenging repressive regimes, women in the workplace, organized feminism challenging domestic violence and seeking reproductive rights, the changing status of gays and lesbians, and emerging new patterns of masculinity.

PATTERNS FROM THE PAST

Major aspects of sexuality, gender, and family in Latin America can be traced to the early colonial period. The Iberian colonizers arrived as single men, or left their existing families in Spain and Portugal. They had sexual liaisons and fathered children with indigenous and African women. Hernán Cortés, the conqueror of Mexico, had approximately ten children, evenly divided between "natural" children, primarily by women from indigenous elite families, and "legitimate" children by his second wife.

Until the nineteenth century, all marriages were ecclesiastical. The respectable elites had church marriages, but many unions were not formal, particularly among slaves. Where the Catholic Church was able to establish hegemony, ecclesiastical marriage became the norm; where it was weaker, consensual unions were common. In highland villages, something like a nuclear family might well be the norm: a man and his wife and their children doing subsistence agriculture. Neither slave owners nor the Catholic clergy encouraged formal marriage among slaves.

Status, race/ethnicity, and marriage were intertwined: the highest standard of respectability was that of European-descended families closely observing the norms

President Dilma Rousseff at her 2011 inauguration (accompanied by her daughter). © Edgar Romero.

of ecclesiastical marriage (even if males had amorous liaisons or forced sex with female servants). Others might or might not observe the formalities of marriage. Civil marriage was introduced in the nineteenth century as liberal anticlerical governments sought to curtail the Church's power.

The results may be seen to this day in varying patterns of marriage. In upper- and middle-class circles, a full church wedding remains the ideal. In some areas, such as the Caribbean, Central America, and coastal South America, many couples live in common-law arrangements, which are recognized as legal. When men father children out of wedlock, it is considered "honorable" to "recognize" the child, that is, be identified as the father on the birth certificate, even if they are not living with the mother. Birth certificate forms often have spaces for indicating whether the child is legitimate or illegitimate.

These observable patterns are confirmed by demographers and social scientists who discern two broad types of "nuptiality" in Latin America: formal marriages and consensual unions. Formal marriage is correlated with educational level and wealth; consensual union is more common among the poor and the less educated. However, other factors enter in, such as custom and tradition. Formal marriage is far less common among coastal and tropical communities than in the highlands. Susan DeVos notes that in Ecuador, "less than 10 percent of the women 20–24 or men 23–27 who were in a union in 1982 were in a consensual union if they lived in the mountains, but over half were in a consensual union if they lived on the coast" (2000, 24). Comparing nations, Teresa Castro Martín finds that almost two-thirds of women aged fifteen to forty-nine in the Dominican Republic are in consensual unions, whereas the figure for Chile is less than 20 percent. Other countries ranged from 30 percent to 60 percent (Castro Martín 2010).

Likewise, three types of households may be discerned in Latin America: those headed by formally married couples, consensual unions, and female-headed households. The proportions vary considerably from country to country and sometimes regionally within countries. In her decades of observation of Guayaquil, the urban anthropologist Caroline Moser found changes in the model of family. The pioneering young couples she got to know in the 1970s went through various changes of fortune into the early 2000s. As fathers abandoned their families and daughters moved back into the family home, with or without a spouse, the axis of stability over the decades was often the mother—and then grandmother (Moser 2009).

Assumptions about family and gender relations are expressed in common expressions. "El hombre es para la calle; la mujer es para la casa" (Man is for the street; woman is for the house) is one such expression. Men can be out drinking with their buddies, but women are expected to stay at home, taking care of children, cooking, and maintaining the house. Another such expression is: "Mujeres hay muchas, pero madre hay una sola" (There are lots of women, but only one mother). In other words, one's bond to one's mother is deeper than to one's spouse or partner at any particular time.

The journalist David Lida explores some of these assumptions, based on his observations of two decades in Mexico City and interviews with psychologists specializing in sexual issues. Male and female children are raised differently. Male children are pampered and are not responsible for any domestic chores, which fall to their sisters. In seeking potential wives, they look for women like their mothers, a yearning that undermines viewing women as sexual partners.

> Mexican families are matriarchies because fathers are frequently absent, and men who live with their wives and children tend to offer economic support but little in the way of emotional or practical guidance. Male adultery is nearly universal, accepted openly or tacitly. This is one reason that mothers cling so tightly to their children; they get no physical or emotional satisfaction from their husbands. (Lida 2008, 144)

Adult children continue to live with their parents until they marry. Lida asserts that these "overage children" are ill prepared for marriage and repeat the patterns in which they have been raised. One result is sexual dissatisfaction. "In 2006, 78 percent of Mexican men and 71 percent of women, responding to a Pfizer-sponsored survey, said they were sexually unsatisfied" (Lida 2008, 148). Both men and women are unable to communicate about sex. Women distrust men, and men distrust women, albeit for different reasons. Some Mexicans and others would question the universality of Lida's assertions, but the picture of machismo that he paints is recognizable to ordinary observers in Latin America and is in line with the findings of social scientists.

A study by the sociologist Cecilia Menjívar (2011) in a community in Guatemala sheds light on the situation of women more broadly. She went to a rural town in eastern Guatemala that she calls San Alejo, initially as part of a study of mother and child health matters, but then began studying women's lives more broadly. She conducted in-depth interviews with thirty women, primarily poor, but some in better-off circumstances. Over a period of five years, she continued to conduct the interviews and had follow-up visits. The people in San Alejo are what Guatemalans call ladinos (nonindigenous) culturally and linguistically, and are similar to people of nearby Honduras and El Salvador. For comparative purposes, Menjívar did a similar study of a community in the indigenous highlands.

Her title *Enduring Violence: Ladina Women's Lives in Guatemala* reflects her findings. "Enduring" has a double meaning; it refers to the violence that women *bear*, but also to the fact that that violence is *persisting*. However, what she has in mind is primarily everyday violence, typically that of a husband or companion who beats his spouse or threatens to do so. One chapter is entitled "Marital Unions and the Normalization of Suffering" and is organized primarily around a triad of violence, alcohol, and infidelity by the male partner. These are considered to be part of being a man. Menjívar devotes particular attention to the fact that women go to their mothers or other relatives and express their suffering and are consoled, but at the same time they are encouraged to bear with it. Their social networks—relatives, friends, acquaintances—all contribute to "normalizing" the situation, both the man's behavior and her duty to endure. Menjívar believes she is examining "the everyday, routinized forms of visible and invisible forms of violence. The women (and their relatives and friends) recognized behavior such as direct physical maltreatment as violence, and often they would interpret abuse and mistreatment—whether in its direct or indirect form—as the way things were" (Menjívar 2011, 128).

What is significant about Menjívar's study is that it could be duplicated in other San Alejos in Guatemala and elsewhere. In that sense, "violence" means more than the instances of striking or beating the woman, or threatening to do so; it refers to the violence that is internalized by women and reinforced by the immediate community and the larger society. The central assertion of this chapter is that machismo in practice and ideology is being challenged on several fronts.

WOMEN STANDING UP

The first-generation leaders of the modern feminist movement that took shape around 1970 in the United States have often said that they had earlier participated in other movements (civil rights, antiwar) where they were expected to work but were not recognized as leaders. That experience led them to conclude that the depth of oppression against women required consciousness-raising and organizing around

Madres de la Plaza de Mayo defying the military government by demanding to know the whereabouts of their disappeared children and grandchildren, Buenos Aires, Argentina, November 1977. © AP Images.

issues specifically pertinent to women. Something similar happened in Latin America, that is, women first were involved in struggles for justice and subsequently came to address women's issues as such.

A remarkable example is that of the Mothers of the Plaza de Mayo in Argentina. In 1976, a military junta took power in Argentina and stepped up its "dirty war" against its opponents, abducting, torturing, and "disappearing" political activists. The technique of disappearance itself was intended to sow terror in the population. In April 1977, fourteen women wearing white scarves gathered in the Plaza de Mayo in front of the presidential palace. That very act was illegal, since gatherings of all kinds were prohibited. They then began to walk in silent procession around the plaza. That act became a weekly event, and over time they were joined by dozens and then hundreds of others. Their demand was simple: we want our loved ones back, or we want to know what happened to them.

The Mothers of the Plaza de Mayo were largely women aged forty to sixty, most of modest means. Over the years they often met with violence: some were beaten or jailed, and some who worked with them were "disappeared." However, they were acting out of the most basic roles of women: as mothers, spouses, or grandmothers.[1] Because other forces in society (the press, political parties, lawyers' organizations, and the Catholic Church) had been silenced or were even in complicity, the Mothers became the lone public voice of conscience throughout the "dirty war." Foreign journalists began to cover the Mothers, and in 1979 the Inter-American Commission on Human Rights visited Argentina and held hearings.

Women in Chile likewise played key roles in resisting the regime that took power in a 1973 military coup and systematically tortured and murdered unarmed opponents. With Church support, women organized neighborhood soup kitchens, which were especially important during the mass unemployment of the 1970s. Women were encouraged to do the traditional craft of sewing *arpilleras*, appliqué representations of real-life situations, to earn a little through the overseas sale of their work. On *arpilleras* they expressed their demands for the appearance of lost family members. In the 1980s, similar organizations of women were pursuing the fate of disappeared family members in El Salvador and Guatemala.

These organizations were political in the sense that they were challenging repressive political regimes. However, in all of them women were acting as wives and mothers and were motivated by what had happened to their spouses or children, not themselves. In Chile during the mid- and late 1980s, women played prominent roles in the increasingly public opposition to the dictatorship of General Pinochet, which, for its part, expected women to conform to traditional roles and be submissive to authority.

Jo Fisher (1993) describes how a grassroots movement in the shantytowns of Santiago evolved from opposition to the Pinochet dictatorship to embracing women's issues. In 1982, they formed MOMUPO (Movimiento de Mujeres Pobladoras; Movement of Shantytown Women) in the north of the city. In response to economic crisis, they marched in protests and held workshops where women could learn skills to earn money. In the mid-1980s, MOMUPO worked in alliance with antidictatorial forces, including (male-led) political parties and middle-class feminist organizations. By 1988, they were able to acquire a modest wooden house to serve as their office. They continued with courses in hairdressing, bread making, and alternative medicine.

One of their first "feminist" issues was domestic violence, which they had all experienced. They also held workshops on sex education in terms of their own situation—for example, the limitations of life in wooden houses without a private bedroom—and discussed topics like contraception and abortion. In some instances, they brought about improvements in their households (husbands no longer beating them and even beginning to take on more household responsibilities).

Fisher uses a slogan from Chile as a chapter heading: "Democracy for the Country, Democracy for the Home." It was the experience of struggling for a return to democracy in public life, based on respect for human rights, that led many women in Chile and elsewhere to insist that the same principles should apply domestically.

CHANGING WORKPLACE

The notion that women are "for the home" expresses the traditional notion that men provide the family with needed income while women do the (unpaid) domestic labor. Among the well-off, that might mean directing the household help, while for the rural poor it used to include carrying water containers on their heads from a stream. In reality, some women have earned income outside the home for a long time, whether by selling vegetables in the market or as teachers and nurses. However, the proportion of women in the paid workforce has risen steadily in recent decades. That helps account for the rapid rise of supermarkets: meals must now be prepared quickly because there is no longer a stay-at-home mother or grandmother. In the expanding middle classes, both spouses typically now have jobs.

From 1990 to 1998, the number of Brazilian women in the workforce jumped from 23 to 31 million. The proportion of women in the workforce rose in all Latin American countries, as indicated in table 8.1. Two generations ago, approximately 20 percent of women were in the paid labor force; by 2005, figures ranged from 40 to 60 percent. The second set of figures indicates that in 1960, women were only 30 percent as likely to be in the paid labor force as men, but by 2005 that figure had risen to 60 to 80 percent.

TABLE 8.1. Labor Force Participation Rates for Working-Age Women

COUNTRY	PERCENTAGE OF WOMEN EMPLOYED		PERCENTAGE OF FEMALE-TO-MALE EMPLOYMENT	
	1960	2005	1960	2005
Argentina	24.4	49.0	26.3	80.1
Brazil	18.2	57.5	35.7	82.4
Chile	28.6	40.6	33.1	71.4
Colombia	19.0	56.6	19.5	81.9
Costa Rica	18.6	41.4	19.2	67.8
Ecuador	17.7	47.8	18.1	73.1
Guatemala	13.1	40.9	13.6	67.0
Honduras	7.7	37.4	18.2	61.8
Mexico	19.1	41.0	19.8	68.1
Panama	24.9	45.5	40.9	72.2
Peru	22.7	59.2	31.8	84.8
Uruguay	32.0	51.9	34.4	82.3
Venezuela	22.1	40.7	39.3	71.4

Source: Tiano (2011, 296–297), which draws from World Bank and other statistical sources.

Apprentice jewelry makers, H. Stern, Rio de Janeiro, Brazil. © Tommie Sue Montgomery.

Several factors help account for the large-scale movement of women into paid labor. In many instances, it was a requirement of survival. For roughly two decades starting in the 1980s, growth in most countries was slow, pay was stagnant, businesses closed, and governments reduced payroll. In Chile in the 1970s and 1980s, factory closings triggered by the Pinochet government's economic policies made many men chronically unemployed at the same time as the expansion of fruit exports provided jobs for women in the fields and in packing houses. The maquiladora plants along the US-Mexico border and in Central American free-trade zones hired thousands of young women for assembly jobs. The shift toward a service economy also helps account for greater female employment. However, in many cases women joined the rapidly expanding informal sector.

Domestic service was a traditional form of women's employment. Decades ago, live-in maids were common, often young peasant or indigenous women from the countryside, but that pattern has declined in recent decades. In some countries, labor legislation made domestic service a part of the formal economy: employers were required to register the job and pay benefits if the person worked above a given number of hours per week. It then might be more convenient to arrange to have a woman come in once or twice a week and pay her in cash. By working for several households, she could receive her pay directly and retain flexibility. Similarly, poor women could make a living by taking in laundry from several families, washing, drying, ironing, and returning it. But the spread of washers and driers in middle-class families is reducing that avenue of domestic employment.

A 2005 study showed that women are making significant advances in the corporate world. Sylvia Maxfield led a project researching the situation of women in Argentina, Brazil, Mexico, Colombia, El Salvador, and Venezuela, and found that 25 to 35 percent of management positions were held by women (as compared to 45 percent in the United States). The figure is higher in the public sector (e.g., education and government offices), higher in companies selling to consumers (e.g., cosmetic or pharmaceutical companies), and lower in construction, transportation, or oil. Moreover, women tend to be more represented in customer services, marketing, law, and human resources, and less so in production and finance. Likewise, they run into a corporate glass ceiling: there are few women CEOs, and corporate boards are still overwhelmingly male (as they are elsewhere). The women executives Maxfield interviewed generally did not see themselves as having suffered discrimination, but they felt that as women they had to work harder than men. Older women tended to have remained at their present company for many years and were loyal to the company but were not rewarded with promotion; younger women were more focused on rising professionally and more willing to shift companies if necessary (Maxfield 2005).

Women are likely to continue to rise in business. Insofar as women are underrepresented, they constitute a talent pool remaining to be tapped; businesses more willing to hire women in managerial positions should have a competitive advantage. Fortune 500 companies are said to be more open to hiring women as a result of the implementation of diversity policies already in effect in their parent companies.

Two further relevant factors in the rising role of women in the workforce are education levels and fertility behavior. In 1960, a schooling "gender gap" still existed, notably in the countryside where many families did not send their daughters to school. By 1990, schools had expanded to the point where almost all school-age children were in class, and by 2010 the gender gap had been eliminated. Indeed, in most countries women slightly outnumbered men in university enrollment, although they were still underrepresented in areas typically considered male, such as engineering. Today the male and female labor pool is equally well educated.

In the 1960s and for decades thereafter, demographers warned of a "population explosion," driven by the tendency for families in developing countries to have many children. The Latin American average was then around six children per woman. Development experts urged the spread of birth control information and medicines. That push was resisted by the Catholic Church, and also by nationalistic forces of both left and right, which regarded birth-control programs as imperialistic attempts to weaken Latin America. To the surprise of the experts, birth rates have fallen dramatically, primarily, it would seem, due to the decisions of women themselves. Several factors help account for the change. The spread of modern medicine has dramatically lowered infant and child mortality. In the countryside, children represented farm labor, but in the city, they are an expense. As more women entered the labor force, having fewer children made obvious sense. Today fertility rates in most countries hover around 2.1 children per woman, the rate at which a society simply reproduces itself and does not grow.

Feminists around the world have pointed to a "double day" for working women: when they return from work, they are expected to handle cooking, cleaning, washing clothes, shopping, child care, and so forth. Based on her research in Guayaquil, Caroline Moser (1993) noted a "triple day," with the "third day" coming from the fact that women did more than their share of participating in community organizations, although the president of an association was typically a man. What Moser observed is broadly true throughout Latin America: women are disproportionately present at meetings and street demonstrations. Moser made the further observation that women had to juggle commitments to family, paid employment, and community participation and, consciously or not, had to triage their priorities. One consequence was that they would turn out in force when the aims were most concrete and most necessary, but would tend to withdraw after the basic gains had been made (electricity, water, roads, bus service, clinics, schools). Organizers and activists, seeing sparsely attended meetings, might complain of the lack of community spirit, but from the standpoint of women negotiating their "triple day," it was understandable. This applied mainly to poor, not middle-class, women.

Moser also noted that women tended to step into paid employment when the family could not rely on the earnings of the male head of the house, because of periodic economic crisis, his own behavior or abilities, or both. Over time, the female partner often became more reliably employed. Now that women have broadly equaled and may surpass male educational achievement, and as services become the predominant sector of the economy, they may be at least as employable as men.[2]

ORGANIZED FEMINISM AND WOMEN'S ISSUES

The women who played important roles in the struggles against dictatorships in South America and during the 1980s in Central America were generally reluctant to call themselves "feminists," a term they associated with the United States and Europe. By the 1990s, however, many were turning their energy to women's issues and were more willing to accept the term, albeit from their own standpoint. Developments in Latin America took place against worldwide efforts to raise women's issues and to establish legal frameworks for protection of rights. Latin American governments are signatories to some of those agreements and standards that have served as a basis for legislation.[3]

Organized women's movements have had to fight an uphill battle in the decades since the return to democracy. To take Chile as an example, with the return to democracy after 1989, governance returned to the (male-dominated) political parties: women had no more cabinet positions than under Pinochet. The government formed an agency to deal with women's issues, SERNAM (Servicio Nacional de la Mujer— National Women's Service), and the activists that it hired were thereby absorbed into the government and possibly co-opted.

A further complication came from the evolving nature of women's organizations, which had arisen during a long emergency period of state repression, with help from development agencies, largely in Europe. After 1990, their mainly European funders turned to areas deemed more critical than Latin America (Eastern Europe and Africa), and so they found themselves competing for declining available funds. They now began to take on a more permanent nature as NGOs (nongovernmental organizations), and staff members became professionalized. A growing body of research by Latin American academics and policy institutions provided data and analysis for the decentralized women's movements. Three major issues were women's participation in politics, domestic violence, and reproductive matters.

Women in politics. In 2006, Chileans, generally regarded as culturally conservative, elected as president Michelle Bachelet, a leftist and agnostic divorcée. She divided her cabinet appointments evenly: ten men and ten women. As already noted, a half dozen countries have elected women presidents, yet politics remains largely a male preserve. Women tend to be appointed primarily to "women's" ministries (social welfare, health, education), although three ministers of defense, including Bachelet, have been women. Bachelet was returned to office by a strong majority in 2014 and pledged to lead the attack on inequality in Chile.

The percentages of women in Latin American legislatures has risen from around 10 percent to an average of 20 percent, which is in fact above the world average.[4] One reason for that improvement is that twelve Latin American countries passed laws setting a minimum level of 20 to 40 percent of women candidates. The results are affected by the system of proportional representation: representatives are not elected on a winner-take-all system, as in the United States, but rather on the basis of slates of candidates per state or province; the seats are apportioned in terms of the number of votes for the party, starting with the top candidates. The high proportion in Argentina is an indication of the effectiveness of its legislation. Even though Brazil enacted similar legislation, its proportion remains low.

Domestic violence. In 1983, Maria da Penha was a thirty-eight-year-old Brazilian pharmacist when her husband, a university professor, shot her and left her a paraplegic. When she returned from the hospital, he attempted to electrocute her. He was found guilty but managed to file appeals and was still free of prison fifteen years later, showing how lightly the justice system treated domestic violence. At that point, activists took the case to the Inter-American Court of Human Rights, which in 2001 found the Brazilian government guilty of negligence. In 2006, the legislature enacted a new law, called the "Maria da Penha Law," which took a number of steps to give greater priority to domestic violence.

Maria da Penha is simply an egregious example of domestic violence: until recently, perpetrators acted with impunity. In a 2000 report, Human Rights Watch stated that of two thousand cases of aggression against women reported to police in Rio de Janeiro, not one perpetrator was punished, and of four thousand in the state of Maranhão, only two were punished (Piovesan 2009, 115). Soledad Larraín draws some figures from studies of violence:

TABLE 8.2. Proportion of Seats Held by Women in National Parliaments, 2006

COUNTRY	PERCENTAGE
Cuba	49
Costa Rica	39
Ecuador	42
Nicaragua	40
Mexico	37
Argentina	37
El Salvador	26
Honduras	26
Bolivia	25
Peru	22
Dominican Republic	21
[United States]	[18]
Chile	16
Paraguay	15
Uruguay	13
Guatemala	13
Colombia	12
Brazil	9
Panama	9
Haiti	4

Source: World Bank (2014). United States (in brackets) is for purposes of comparison.

Fifty-two percent of women in Managua experienced psychological, physical and/or sexual violence in the 12 months preceding the survey; in Santiago, the figure was over 40 percent, while it was 22.7 for women in Montevideo and Canelones in Uruguay. Thirty-five percent of the women in Costa Rica stated that they frequently experienced this type of aggression, while in Lima 88 percent of women suffered from some type of aggression by their partner. In Colombia, 20 percent of women were physically abused, while 33 percent were psychologically abused. (Larraín 1999, 109)

These figures should not be used comparatively, because the definitions of violence varied (e.g., physical and/or psychological), as did the time periods and wording of questions. What they illustrate is that domestic violence is pervasive and until recently was not regarded as a crime.

The underlying source of this violence is machismo or patriarchy. It might be a combination of a man's assumed right to control his household or punish his partner for her behavior, the effects of alcohol, or perhaps the venting of his own frustration or anger. The form found in Latin American societies can be traced to the domination brought by the Iberian conquerors, the Mediterranean world from which they came, and patriarchal patterns and assumptions dating back millennia. Even in North America and Europe until recent decades it was assumed that what went on inside the household was not of public concern.[5]

Insofar as domestic disputes might reach the legal system, they were treated in family court. What has changed is the realization and acknowledgment that domestic violence is a crime. By the mid-1990s, virtually all Latin American governments had passed laws criminalizing domestic violence. However, legislation has little effect if it is not enforced, if police are poorly trained or corrupt, or if the legal system is ineffective. Male police may be disinclined to enforce the law.[6] One initiative has been to open special police stations specifically for domestic violence and staffed by women officers, pioneered in São Paulo in the 1980s. Staff are trained to assist the victims on the various aspects of the law and to provide counseling. They have special units for investigating, counseling, and preventing rape. These units have been aided by networks of volunteers. Other countries have devised similar programs. In Colombia, the first unit was set up in 1989 and soon there were hundreds throughout the country. NGOs have set up hotlines and shelters where battered women can take refuge, together with their children.[7]

Violence against women may be the result of decades or centuries of conditioning of men, but it can be reversed. Caroline Moser found that Ecuadoreans who had emigrated to Barcelona were learning to deal with different standards and expectations. A woman said that her present partner would not dare to strike her because he knows she would go to the police, as opposed to her previous experience in Ecuador where her husband routinely insulted and beat her. It illustrates that much depends on the messages men receive from the environment. In recent years, campaigns against domestic violence on billboards and television have become common in Latin America, with slogans like "Domestic violence is a crime" and "Say No to Machismo," sometimes featuring well-known male singers or actors.

Reproductive matters. Women's organizations have understandably turned toward reproductive issues. As noted, contraception is widely available, as is shown in the dramatic decline in birthrates in recent decades.

That abortion remains controversial and disputed should be no surprise: forty years after *Roe v. Wade* it remains contested terrain in the United States. Abortion is absolutely prohibited in Chile, the Dominican Republic, El Salvador, Haiti, Honduras, and Nicaragua, and is permitted under limited conditions in other countries. Only in Cuba (and Puerto Rico) is it permitted without restriction.

Yet abortion is common. In 2008, an estimated 4.4 million abortions were

Say "NO" to Machismo: sign at a bus stop in Lago Agrio, Ecuador. © Phillip Berryman.

performed in Latin America. Ninety-five percent of these abortions are regarded as unsafe by World Health Organization (WHO) standards: they are performed either by a person without the necessary skills or in an environment that does not conform to minimum medical standards or both. In Argentina, an estimated 40 percent of pregnancies end in abortion; figures for Peru are 37 percent, and Chile, 35 percent, while most other countries are near the US rate of 20 percent.

A Bolivian feminist points to the hypocrisy: women with the means to pay $400 can get a safe abortion; clinics advertising gynecological services on a crowded street in downtown La Paz provide abortions. Wealthy women might simply fly to a country where abortion is legal.[8] Most abortions are performed by traditional practitioners, and that is the source of the large number of unsafe abortions. About one million women a year in Latin America are hospitalized for complications from abortion.

Thus it is not surprising that feminist groups in Latin America advocate for expanding access to legal abortion and, more generally, to reproductive services. In fact, abortion rates tend to be higher where the procedure is criminalized than where it is permitted and regulated. In the United States, for example, there are nineteen abortions per year per one thousand women (as opposed to thirty-two in Latin America). To the extent that women have control over reproduction, they will have fewer unwanted pregnancies and thus less need for abortion. Internationally, access to reproductive services is considered a human right, and Latin American governments are signatories to agreements that assure such rights.

However, those challenging law and practice encounter resistance. Although women of all classes were involved in the struggles to overthrow dictatorships in Chile, Brazil, Argentina, and elsewhere, feminists find few allies on reproductive issues. Center-left governments in Chile beginning in 1990 were unwilling to offend or confront the Catholic hierarchy, which had played an important role in resistance to the Pinochet regime and in the struggle for democracy. Under President Daniel Ortega, Nicaraguan legislation became even more restrictive.

Sometimes these conflicts became public dramas. In Brazil in 2009, a nine-year-old girl had been raped by her stepfather and was pregnant with twins. Her mother and her doctors wished her to have an abortion. Archbishop Sobrino of Recife appealed to have a judge halt the procedure; when the judge refused, he excommunicated the mother and the doctors. He was supported by the Vatican. President Lula said that as a Catholic, he deeply regretted the action and said that the doctors were right. The archbishop was unrepentant: asked why the rapist-stepfather was not excommunicated, he said that abortion is an even worse crime than rape. Similar public incidents have occurred in other countries, illustrating the existence of an increasing culture war

Gynecology clinic where abortions are said to be performed, La Paz, Bolivia. © Phillip Berryman.

around such issues. When Mexico City lifted restrictions on first-trimester abortion in 2007, states elsewhere in the country moved to make it more restrictive.[9]

CLOSET OPENING

Strawberry and Chocolate, a 1993 Cuban film by Tomás Alea Gutiérrez, was noteworthy for two reasons: it carried some criticism of the regime for its repression of expression, and one of the main characters was gay. It perhaps represented a step toward broader acceptance of gays and lesbians in Latin America, at least among artistic and intellectual elites.

In the 1990s and continuing into the 2000s, various steps were taken legislatively. Some countries passed laws or initiated programs to eliminate homophobia and discrimination. Same-sex relationships were being de-criminalized in at least some parts of some countries. Legislatures were considering laws to allow social security and inheritance rights to same-sex partners.

Yet populations seemed to be divided over these matters. Large cities were becoming increasingly gay friendly. An openly gay columnist wrote regularly in the Colombian daily *El Tiempo*. By the late 2000s, the São Paulo Gay Pride March was claiming to be the largest (or the best) in the world.[10] It enjoys the support of the city, state, and federal governments and has corporate sponsorship. Mexico City and Buenos Aires have had much smaller events. On the other hand, the International Lesbian and Gay Association reported that in 2005 a gay man was killed in Latin America every two days, solely because of his sexual identity.

At the personal and household level, situations vary considerably. Gays and lesbians often never come out to their families, who may guess at the sexual orientation but do not inquire. Differences are largely generational: younger people routinely invite same-sex couples to parties, perhaps to the dismay of older generations. In explaining the progress made, Javier Corrales points to the smart tactics of the region's LGBT movements: they have made alliances with feminists, worked with governments on health campaigns, promoted gay tourism in their countries, and avoided being identified with the antiglobalization ideologies of some sectors of the left. Nevertheless, the public remains divided. Corrales (2009) notes that when polled, 58 percent of Brazilians say homosexuality is a sin, and 41 percent say it is an illness that should be treated.

FUTURE DIRECTIONS

The common thread running through this chapter has been customary machismo and challenges to it in both private and public life. We have noted that attitudes and behaviors vary from country to country and with significant differences by social class. We close with some observations by the Chilean anthropologist Loreto Rebolledo on the emergence of new attitudes toward fatherhood in contemporary Chile. Based on in-depth interviews with upper-, middle-, and lower-class fathers, she proposes a typology of these emerging patterns. Starting with the assumption that fathers have traditionally been distant from their children, she distinguishes three models: 1. Fathers who are "present and close to" the children; 2. "Neo-patriarchal" fathers, typical of middle and upper classes who are present in terms of providing for their family, usually alongside working spouses, but leave the actual details to the mother (and domestic help); 3. "Peripheral-communicative" fathers, who are involved with their work and not especially present, but who wish to have good communication with their children when they are with them.[11] Despite the differences of model, a great value is placed on being communicative with one's children. This is reinforced in television programming: whereas advertising used to display images of fathers with young children, there is now a trend toward showing fathers engaged in activities with their older children. Rebolledo concludes:

> Given the advances of feminism, legislative changes, conceptions of childhood, the massive entry of women into labor markets, and so forth, men and women have had to renegotiate the ways of organizing family and assuming parental roles. (Rebolledo 2008, 138)

We began by noting that machismo is deep-seated in Latin American societies and culture, and in some forms is still defended by conservative forces in society. One factor for change has been women's activism in society, both in courageously confronting repressive governments and also at the neighborhood level, especially in the early stages of barrio formation. A key development has been women's expanded participation in the workforce. Women are measurably at least as represented in formal politics as they are in the United States (six have been elected heads of state). Feminist organizations, local and national, have sought to deal with domestic violence, political representation, and reproductive rights. Advances in legislation may signal a generational change; for example, younger people are increasingly accepting of same-sex relationships because they see them in their friends and acquaintances.

Rebolledo's findings in the Chilean case perhaps suggest a future direction. Insofar as Latin American societies become more middle class (more "Chilean"), a less patriarchal and more companionate type of marriage and family may develop. Both men and women might find it increasingly desirable to have dual careers with comparable goals and ambitions. That would entail a deeper type of communication between spouses and with children. Such a model might spread through society—or it could remain class-specific, especially if societies remain highly unequal and exclusionary.

FURTHER READING

On women under dictatorships, see Fisher (1993). Menjívar (2011) is valuable precisely for its emphasis on invisible internalized violence. For country studies on women in politics, see Jaquette (2009); for women in business, Maxfield (2005); and on abortion, Mollmann (2012).

A Changing Religious Landscape

Signs of religion in Latin America are not hard to find. The traditional center of virtually any capital city is a plaza flanked on one side by the cathedral and on another by the legislature or the presidency. That same pattern of plaza and church is reproduced in smaller cities and even rural villages. On any given evening in a poor neighborhood, small evangelical churches resound with boisterous singing and amplified preaching. Indigenous towns hold annual festivals to celebrate their patron saint. A significant segment of television programming is devoted to Protestant televangelists and conservative Catholic talk shows. Brazil is the world's largest "Catholic" country, and Latin America is said to hold 40 percent of the world's Catholics. In 2013, the Argentine cardinal Jorge Bergoglio was elected pope and began to shake up Roman Catholicism, influenced by his own life experience in his troubled homeland.

In Latin America, relatively few Catholics—perhaps 5 percent—attend Mass on any given weekend, and in some countries half of the Catholic clergy and sisters are nonnative. The significance of traditional expressions of religiosity is an open question as the Facebook generation in cities loses contact with the religious observances of rural towns and villages.

It is well to keep in mind that the very notion of "religion" is elusive. Is "religion" primarily a set of beliefs or a worldview? Is it a moral code, and if so, of the community or the individual? Is it expressed most clearly in community worship or in individual contemplation?[1] "Religion" obviously means various things and has varied expressions.

This chapter explores the role of religion in Latin American life by examining the legacy of five centuries of Catholicism, the role of religion in resistance to dictatorships and struggles for justice and human rights, the rapid rise of Pentecostal churches and charismatic Catholicism, and the recent emergence of religious pluralism.

PARADOXES OF TRADITIONAL CATHOLICISM

Upon going ashore on the island of Hispaniola in 1492, Christopher Columbus planted a cross in the ground to claim the land. Franciscan friars accompanied him on his second voyage, and Roman Catholicism thereafter enjoyed a religious quasi-monopoly until the second half of the twentieth century. That monopoly is the source of Catholicism's paradoxical strength and weakness in Latin America.

The Iberian conquerors arrived at the very moment when the unity of medieval Christendom[2] was being disrupted. While they were overthrowing the Aztec and Inca Empires and founding cities, the Protestant Reformation erupted in Northern Europe, and Catholics responded with their own Counter-Reformation. Catholics and Protestants disputed—and princes went to war over—religion, ending in a peace settlement in the mid-seventeenth century. Those very wars discredited religious fervor at least among the intelligentsia, where the movement known as the Enlightenment argued for "tolerance" and in favor of a more benign form of deistic belief. The French Revolution assaulted the bishops and clergy as the embodiment of the "old regime." Astronomy, geology, Darwinian evolution, and historical research dealt further blows to literal belief in the biblical stories. By the nineteenth century, it was not only the intelligentsia but also the industrial working class that was lost to the Catholic Church. By the twentieth century, much of Europe had become secularized. That five-century struggle over religion that is central to modernity in the West was largely bypassed in Latin America. The upshot was that Catholicism was taken for granted: until a few decades ago, most Mexicans, Brazilians, or Peruvians might never encounter a non-Catholic, and Catholicism was assumed to be part of their identity.

In fact, however, Latin American Catholicism existed in two different forms, official and popular. Official Catholicism, centered on the Mass and the sacraments and "saving one's soul," was influential where the clergy was well established.[3] Popular Catholicism functioned primarily to serve the immediate needs of the poor (weather, crops, illness of a child) through the intercession of the saints and the Blessed Virgin Mary.

The story of Our Lady of Guadalupe illustrates this popular side of Catholicism. According to legend, in 1531 a Mexican peasant named Juan Diego had a vision of a young woman, the Blessed Virgin Mary, who asked that a church be built in her honor at that site. When he took the request to Archbishop Juan de Zumárraga, he was told to request a miracle as proof. He returned, and the Virgin told him to pick flowers at the top of Tepeyac Hill. Although it was December, he found roses, a non-native flower, and wrapped them in his cloak. When he opened the cloak to show the bishop, it was imprinted with an image of the Virgin. That image of a mestizo woman combined with elements from the book of Revelation has been venerated since then by Mexicans and others.[4] Millions visit the shrine annually, some walking on their knees over concrete and asphalt. Copies of the Guadalupe image were carried by peasant troops in the early battles for Mexican independence, by Emiliano Zapata in the Mexican Revolution, and by farmworkers in the United States in the 1960s and 1970s under the leadership of Cesar Chavez.

Similar stories and images are found in all Latin American countries. The shrine of Our Lady of Aparecida (a black Virgin found miraculously in the eighteenth century)

Our Lady of Guadalupe: photograph of image in the Basilica of Our Lady of Guadalupe, Mexico City.

draws thousands of Brazilian pilgrims a year, as does the Black Christ of Esquipulas in Guatemala. Ecuador has Jesús del Gran Poder (Jesus of Great Power), and Peru has El Señor de los Milagros (Lord of Miracles). Each of these has annual feast days typically celebrated with processions, as do many other venerated national and local figures.[5] The activities themselves (bands, firecrackers, drinking, playing pranks) may not look especially "religious" to outsiders. People have shrines or altars to the Virgin or saints in their houses; bus drivers may have images on their dashboards or they may be painted on the buses themselves. Such popular religion is focused on immediate needs rather than on salvation after death; the saints or the Virgin are intercessors for recovery from illness or rain for crops. Individuals may make a *manda*, or a promise to God; for example, if my child recovers from this illness (or if I get this job), I will make a pilgrimage to the shrine. When the favor is granted, the person is obligated to "pay back" the promise.[6]

One sign of weakness in Catholicism during the colonial period was the continuing need for clergy and religious personnel to be supplied from the mother countries, Spain and Portugal. Those who became priests or sisters tended to be from the European colonial elites; very few indigenous or black candidates were admitted. In fact, popular religious traditions were largely passed on not by clergy but by family and village tradition, such as through annual saints feasts.

The Church was further weakened institutionally by the independence struggle (1810–1824) and its aftermath in the nineteenth century. Although some priests were sympathetic to independence, and it was a priest who issued the first call for independence in Mexico, the bishops and most of the clergy were identified with Spain, and hence many left or were expelled in the aftermath of independence. The Vatican, still reeling from the effects of the French Revolution, was not sympathetic to revolutions and did not recognize the new governments until 1831. Weakened by its loss of personnel and its difficulty in recruiting new candidates to the priesthood and religious life, the Catholic Church was chronically understaffed. In 1940 in Guatemala, there was only one priest for every thirty thousand people, almost all of them in the cities; rural indigenous Guatemalans rarely saw a priest.

In the decades after independence, Latin American politics was typically a struggle between a Liberal and a Conservative party, and a key point of contention was the role and privileges of the Catholic Church. The Liberals saw the Church as an obstacle to progress (which they identified with European industrialization and urbanization). They sought to end or cut subsidies to the Church, to allow or require civil marriage (as opposed to ecclesiastical marriage), and to weaken religious orders by taking away their extensive landholdings (and making them available for export crops). In resistance to these efforts, the bishops were allied with Conservative parties. In the later nineteenth century, the Liberals generally prevailed, and thus the Church lost ground institutionally.

In the first half of the twentieth century, institutional Catholicism slowly recovered as new waves of priests and sisters came from Spain and elsewhere in Europe, and as the hierarchy made peace with Liberal political parties. The exception was Mexico, where the revolution that began in 1910 took an anticlerical turn and was aggravated by the peasant Cristero Rebellion of the 1920s under the slogan Viva Cristo Rey! (Long Live Christ the King!). The Mexican government actively persecuted the Church, and for decades priests and sisters could not wear distinctive clothing or vote in elections.

The institutional weakness of the Church was especially noteworthy in the countryside, where priests came around only for ritual occasions. Likewise, the Church was unable to keep pace with rapid urbanization, so that by the second half of the twentieth century a parish priest might have tens of thousands of parishioners under his care. This institutional weakness did not immediately affect the Catholic identity of most people, however, because Catholicism was largely transmitted through family and community, prayers and processions, statues and rosaries, which did not require the presence of a priest.

Another impact of the post-independence period was a growing distance between artists and intellectuals and the Church. The pattern is traceable at least to the independence leader Simón Bolívar, who was a freethinker, and it grew over the course of the nineteenth century and into the early twentieth century. The Mexican muralists like Diego Rivera and David Siqueiros in the 1920s painted friars and priests as exploiters of the common people. Virtually none of the major intellectual and artistic figures in the two centuries since independence were conventional practicing Catholics. Political figures tended to see the Catholic Church as part of the political landscape. Conservatives regarded the Church as a bulwark of "order" in society, while those in the Liberal tradition might see it as an enemy of "progress." These attitudes were characteristic of the elites, not the masses. However, among the poor and even the middle classes, adult males tended to regard attending church as a women's activity. When the priest came to the village for Mass, men commonly stood by the doors, often outside, while women occupied the pews.

By the mid-twentieth century, Catholic religious orders had established schools, which served significant portions of the middle classes, who in turn were more inclined to be practicing Catholics. By that time Catholicism was a paradoxical combination of strength and weakness. It enjoyed a quasi-monopoly, and almost everyone was baptized and identified as Catholic, yet church attendance was low and the parishes and schools were often staffed by foreign priests and sisters.

THE MEDELLÍN GENERATION

In March 1980, as Archbishop Óscar Romero of San Salvador reached the end of a sermon that had begun with the texts of the day, he mentioned some recent events in which government troops had killed unarmed peasants. He said that soldiers should not obey orders against God's will, and pleaded with the military and government to stop the repression. As was customary, his words were being broadcast by radio across the country. The next evening, as he was saying Mass for a small congregation, a sharpshooter entered the chapel and shot him through the heart. The outdoor funeral Mass the following Sunday was interrupted by bomb blasts, and the terrified crowd of 70,000 or more sought shelter in the cathedral or the adjoining streets as snipers fired and at least twenty people were killed in the melee.

The killing of Romero was not an isolated event. Later that year, three US nuns and a lay volunteer were stopped by Salvadoran National Guard troops and were raped and murdered. In 1989, after a decade of civil war, troops entered the Catholic university by night; took out six Jesuits, a housekeeper, and her daughter; and murdered them all. In numerous Latin American countries, priests, nuns, pastors, and lay people were murdered in the 1970s and 1980s for their involvement in movements for social change. They believed they were carrying out their pastoral mission; their killers regarded them as legitimate targets.[7]

These events grew out of the renewal in Latin American Catholicism in the wake of the Second Vatican Council (Vatican II, 1962–1965). Unlike in Europe and North America, where the challenge was widespread unbelief, in Latin America the crucial issue was poverty. In August 1968, bishops from Latin American countries gathered in Medellín, Colombia, to apply Vatican II to their continent and produced a set of documents on topics ranging from justice, peace, education, and family to pastoral matters such as liturgy. Taken together, the Medellín documents were a kind of pastoral road map, which called for "sweeping, bold, urgent, and profound renovating changes"; they described economic and social development as the "transition from less human to more human conditions for each and every person," and compared it

Archbishop Óscar Romero with small farmers, San Salvador, late 1970s. © Central American Jesuits.

to the biblical exodus; they freely used the term "liberation" and called for a kind of education in which people become "agents of their own development"; as a pastoral methodology they encouraged the formation of "Christian Base Communities," small lay-led discussions of the Gospel and people's lives.

Throughout Latin America, priests and sisters were recognizing that Church personnel were disproportionately serving urban middle classes in schools and parishes, and they were taking steps to move closer to the poor, sometimes living in the midst of them and sharing their conditions. They met with small groups in people's homes, discussed the connection between the scriptures and everyday life, and developed leadership among poor people in the countryside and the expanding urban shantytowns. This model of work was by no means that of the majority; around 10 percent of parishes used this approach, but it was qualitatively important.

This pastoral movement drew on "liberation theology," a term first used by the Peruvian theologian Gustavo Gutiérrez in 1968.[8] Its proponents typically worked not in classrooms but with bishops, priests, and sisters in pastoral work. The term "liberation" assumed that Christians were to be engaged in the struggle for emancipation, for more human conditions for all, starting with the poorest. The traditional notion that "salvation" refers primarily to an afterlife needed to be challenged: the "kingdom of God" must begin in the here and now.

Liberation theology was a rationale for the new kind of pastoral work being undertaken, sharing the life of the poor, helping them recognize their inherent dignity as children of God and learn to assert their rights. It represented a rediscovery of aspects of the scripture, such as the message of justice of the prophets of Israel, and particularly the life of Jesus, such as the moment when he begins his ministry in the synagogue by reading a passage in which the prophet is sent by God to bring glad tidings to the poor, proclaim liberty to captives, and free the oppressed (Luke 4:18), or the parable of the last judgment where Jesus says, "I was hungry and you gave me to eat, thirsty and you gave me to drink, in prison and you visited me" (Matthew 25:35). That is, Christian faith is more fundamentally about practice than adherence to doctrine. The conflictive side of the present shed light on conflicts in the life of Jesus and vice versa. In early 1977, the Salvadoran government arrested some priests, roughed some up, and deported some. In a sermon, the Jesuit Rutilio Grande said that if Jesus returned to El Salvador, he would be deported as a "subversive." In March he himself was gunned down while driving to say Mass, together with an old man and a youth traveling with him.[9]

These events should be seen as part of the broader Latin American context.[10] In the aftermath of the Cuban Revolution, many activists and intellectuals became radicalized and assumed that the region's development problems were systemic: a just society could not be achieved under capitalism, and some form of socialism—not a carbon copy of the Soviet Union or even Cuba, but a "Latin American socialism"— was required. Although many understood "liberation" as implying a different model of society, Church activists generally avoided speaking of socialism.[11]

The brutal September 1973 coup in Chile made it clear that if there was any new model of society on the horizon, it was not socialism but military dictatorship. By the mid-1970s, Brazil, Argentina, Uruguay, and Chile were under regimes that practiced abduction, torture, imprisonment, "disappearance," and murder, and Church people felt impelled to respond. In Chile, some sisters and priests had to flee into exile; those who stayed helped tens of thousands of Chileans and foreigners escape the country. As the congress and political parties were suppressed, unions broken, the press muzzled, and universities occupied, the Catholic Church became the sole space of resistance. The Vicariate of Solidarity established by the archdiocese of Santiago became a place where people came to report the disappearance of family members. Vicariate lawyers filed habeas corpus cases in courts; it was a formality, but it provided a record of arrests and disappearances. In poor neighborhoods, parish communities opened soup kitchens and self-employment projects. During the Brazilian military dictatorship (1964–1985), the bishops acted as a voice of conscience, criticizing the use of torture and the model of development that was aggravating inequality and poverty.

In Argentina, the Catholic hierarchy remained silent as at least nine thousand people were killed or "disappeared" in the "dirty war" waged by the military, primarily against unarmed civilians, which reached its apogee in the 1976–1978 period, even though the victims included priests and at least one bishop. Some bishops even defended the military and consorted with the masterminds of torture and "disappearance."[12]

In Central America, the Sandinista revolutionary movement overthrew the Somoza dictatorship and took power in Nicaragua in 1979, and similar outcomes seemed possible in El Salvador and Guatemala. This revolution resembled the movement that had taken power in Cuba in 1959, but in this case many Sandinistas had been participants in Church movements in the university or in parishes. Priests and sisters began working with the new government, including four priests in cabinet positions, and the bishops gave cautious support. Less than a year later, however, businesspeople went into opposition, as did the Nicaraguan bishops led by Archbishop Miguel Obando y Bravo. For the next decade, the polarization of Nicaraguan society was reflected in a division in the Church. On a visit in 1983, Pope John Paul II, whose worldview was shaped by his life under communism in Poland, reprimanded the priest, poet, and Minister of Culture Ernesto Cardenal on the tarmac when he landed. An outdoor Mass turned into a shouting match between Sandinista supporters and opponents. The Vatican and the Nicaraguan bishops pressured the priests to leave their posts; they did not submit but did not function publicly as priests.

In 1984, the Vatican issued a wide-ranging attack on liberation theology written by Cardinal Josef Ratzinger (the future Pope Benedict XVI). The Brazilian theologian Leonardo Boff was silenced, despite support from important Brazilian bishops. Nevertheless, some elements from liberation theology were adopted into official Catholic teaching, such as that the Church should make a "preferential option for the poor."

Church figures played significant roles in resolving the conflicts of the 1980s. In Chile, Cardinal Juan Francisco Fresno served as a broker in assisting the opposition parties to form a united front against the Pinochet dictatorship. In Nicaragua, El

Salvador, and Guatemala, Catholic bishops and evangelical pastors were actively involved in peace and reconciliation processes.[13] In those countries that did not fit the pattern of either right-wing dictatorship or revolutionary struggle to take power, such as Mexico, Colombia, Venezuela, and Panama, the involvement of church people in defense of human rights tended to be more local.

Changes in the surrounding society after 1990 affected such religiously inspired political involvement. The most obvious reason was the change in the political landscape: the dictatorships were replaced by elected governments, and the conflicts in Central America wound down. The end of the Cold War rendered any noncapitalist form of society implausible. For the next two decades, the Vatican consistently appointed bishops based on their doctrinal loyalty rather than their pastoral sensitivity.

DRIVEN BY THE SPIRIT

Until around 1990, "the Church" in Latin America meant Roman Catholicism; Protestants were assumed to be statistically negligible. It was thus surprising to find that Pentecostal Protestantism was challenging Catholicism: Pentecostals, who were 2 percent of Latin America in 1960, were 15 percent by 1990—roughly doubling each decade. In 1992, five new evangelical churches a week were opening in Rio de Janeiro. Such exponential growth takes place as new converts feel called to invite others, starting with their own family members, but also work colleagues and friends. Joining such a church is very often an emotional experience in which one breaks with the past: perhaps with alcoholism, or marital infidelity, or simply with Catholic "idolatry" (veneration of Mary and saints).

Some dismissed these new churches as alien, as "imports" from the United States. In fact, the history of Latin American Protestantism can be traced back to itinerant Bible salesmen, and then to the establishment of congregations of Presbyterians, Baptists, Lutherans, and others in the late nineteenth century. In Brazil, the Assemblies of God and the Christian Congregation, both Pentecostal, were started a century ago, and a second wave of churches (Brazil for Christ and God Is Love) arose in the 1950s. Chilean Pentecostalism also traces its history back a century.

Pentecostal worship services follow a common pattern, with considerable variation. People assemble and sing several songs with many verses, backed up by an electronic band and drums. The pastor operates as a kind of master of ceremonies with a microphone, even in small congregations of only a few people. At various moments, individuals lead prayers, and sometimes all are invited to pray aloud, and do so by closing their eyes, raising their arms, and praying, sometimes in tongues (nonsense syllables). Individuals give testimonies; some churches practice exorcism (calling it "liberation"). Toward the end, the leader delivers a sermon, with interjections of "Amen!" and "Alleluia!," and at some point a collection is taken. The ceremony, which may last two hours, ends with more singing. That framework is common to Pentecostal churches around the world. Worship is held not only on Sunday or Saturday, but

Pentecostal worship, National Youth Congress of the Assemblies of God, Cancún, Quintana Roo, Mexico (2010). © Rayttc.

other nights of the week. The Brazilian-originated Universal Church of the Kingdom of God typically holds four services a day, seven days a week, inviting people to come in off the street.

Some churches clearly cater to middle-class people or those who aspire to the middle class; in others, all those attending are poor. Some are megachurches, with a very large space holding perhaps a thousand or more people, but they also have networks of house churches. While some churches have many ministries to help congregants, in others the primary activity is worship itself. Such variety means that individual churches occupy particular niches in the overall religious ecology.

Numerous explanations have been offered for the rapid evangelical expansion: the shortage of Catholic priests and sisters and an inability to communicate with people; the liveliness of Pentecostal worship; the sense of community and mutual assistance for believers; the powerful effect of conversion manifested in overcoming drinking or other vices; the joy and relief found after conversion; the sense of self-worth that comes with embracing a new life in a new community.

Catholicism has its own version, the Charismatic Renewal, which arose in US Catholic universities in the late 1960s and rapidly spread around the world, including

Latin America in the early 1970s. Its worship is similar to Pentecostalism, but its practitioners emphasize specifically Catholic elements, such as devotion to Mary and loyalty to the pope. Although some Catholics experience a conversion, becoming charismatic typically does not entail a break with one's past, as does Pentecostal conversion. In most countries it began in middle-class circles and only slowly made inroads among the poor.

In the 1990s, a Brazilian Catholic priest, Fr. Marcelo Rossi, rose to fame for his charismatic preaching, his CDs of religious songs, and his massive religious celebrations. One such celebration in 2008 at the race track in São Paulo is said to have brought out three million people. Noted pop stars sometimes sing with him on videos.

AFRICAN SPIRITS

In Brazil, Cuba, and Haiti, the religious field includes variants of African-originated religion. The anthropologist Lindsay Hale offers an account of his encounters with one of these religions, Umbanda. He begins by describing how one afternoon, under the guidance of Dona Luciana, a veteran Umbanda medium, he places a tiny paper boat carrying his own personal concerns into the surf at Copacabana beach as an offering to Iemanjá, goddess of the sea. When the boat drifts a few feet and is sunk by a wave, Dona Luciana interprets it as a sign of the goddess accepting the offer. Umbanda is a fusion of African religion, which for centuries had been largely clandestine and even persecuted, and nineteenth-century spiritism coming from Europe—a religion created in Brazil.

Two key two aspects of Umbanda are a system of spirits and the mediums through whom they communicate, like Dona Luciana. The highest spirits are a number of African deities called *orixás*, including Iemanjá, whom they honored with the paper boat ritual. The spirits whom mediums channel fall into three groups: *caboclos*, native Americans (even with feathered headdresses); *pretos velhos* ("old blacks," i.e., slaves), regarded as repositories of wisdom; and *exus*, morally ambiguous trickster-like figures. When they enter a trance, mediums become possessed by these figures, who are able to aid their clients through the mediums.

Dona Luciana's career as a medium began when she was in her mid-forties and came to an Umbanda session while suffering a crisis, including a failing marriage. There she went into a trance, which was recognized as a calling from the *orixás* to become a medium herself. Being a medium is a combination of one's own gift and further development and training.

One element in Umbanda's success in the twentieth century was that it seemed "whiter" than Candomblé or Xangô. (Dona Luciana was white and middle class.) By the 1970s, perhaps 10 percent of the Brazilian population practiced Umbanda. Its popularity has declined since then, as some former practitioners joined Pentecostal churches and now regard Umbanda as the work of the devil, and others moved toward more clearly African forms (Hale 2009).

In Cuba and Puerto Rico, African religions are called Santería, and in Haiti, Vodou. These religions occupy an ambiguous position. To scholars, they look like independent religions, because although they may borrow Catholic saints, they are clearly different in doctrine and cosmology. Those who have trained to be mediums may also view themselves as practitioners of a religion, superior to that of the Catholics they see around them. However, many adherents who may consult a medium from time to time, when asked, would identify themselves as Catholics.

ADVENT OF PLURALISM

Since the recognition of a significant proportion of Protestants, primarily Pentecostal, twenty years ago, it has been increasingly acknowledged that Latin America is now religiously pluralistic, after four and a half centuries of an assumed Catholic monopoly. Table 9.1 gives an indication of religious identity in seven countries. Religious identity indicates which label people will choose when surveyed; it says nothing of the intensity of commitment or the consequences of that identity. Those who replied "Protestant" are far more likely to be active churchgoers than Catholics.

As the statistics indicate, Jews are very small percentages of the overall population except in Argentina and Uruguay, where they are somewhere between 0.5 percent and 1 percent of the population. Although some *conversos* (Jews and their descendants who converted at least outwardly to Catholicism) were present in colonial times, little remains of their presence. A relatively large-scale arrival of Jews occurred in the 1880–1914 period (both Ashkenazi and Sephardic, i.e., from Europe, the Middle East, and North Africa) and then later from Germany in the 1930s. In the countries where they are most numerous, Argentina and Uruguay, Jews are generally secular, although synagogues can be found in virtually all Latin American countries. As cardinal of Buenos Aires, Pope Francis engaged in dialogue with his friend Rabbi Abraham

TABLE 9.1. Religious Identity in Latin America (in Percentages)

	ARGEN-TINA	BRAZIL	CHILE	COLOM-BIA	GUATE-MALA	MEXICO	PERU
Catholic	71	69	63	77	58	86	78
Protestant	8	19	15	10	33	3	12
Jewish	0.8	.06	.07	-	.42	-	.07
Afro-religious	0.4	9	.07	-	.08	.2	-
Other	2.5	2	4	5	2	4	4
Atheist/Agnostic	3	1	2	.6	2	1	1
Without Religion	14	6	15	7.5	6	5	4

Note: Some figures are rounded up or down.
Source: Valenzuela, Scully, and Somma (2009).

Skorka, and the two published their dialogue in book form. A concern among Latin American Jews is declining numbers, particularly due to marriage with non-Jews.

In the figures cited above, few Latin Americans claim to be atheistic or even agnostic, but a significant number, when polled, will say they are "without religion," meaning, it would seem, that they do not identify with any institutional form of religion. It should be noted that in Uruguay, which has a long secularist tradition and is composed largely of descendants of European immigrants, 40 percent claim to have no religion, and 17 percent say they are atheists.

The work of the Chilean sociologist Cristián Parker (2009) may be relevant for discerning emerging trends. Dissatisfied with survey categories in which respondents would either identify with a church or as nonbelievers, over time he developed categories such as *católico a mi manera* (Catholic in my own way), that is, people who do not disavow their Catholicism but do not necessarily follow the dictates of the official Church. In 2005, he found the breakdown indicated on table 9.2 among university students. Parker also found significant correlations along gender and socioeconomic lines: poorer people and women tend to be more evangelical; males and higher-income people tend to be more critical of Catholicism and institutional religion.

What is significant is that even among high school students the percentage of "Catholics in my own way" is almost on a par with those who simply identify as "Catholics," and that over 34 percent disavow organized religion: atheists, nonbelievers, and "believers without religion." Parker suggests that there is a general tendency for greater levels of education to produce people who seek a more rationalized form of religion and are correspondingly less likely to adhere to either evangelicalism or institutionalized Catholicism.

Parker proposes that rising levels of schooling will affect the religious future.

TABLE 9.2. Religious Affiliation of Chilean University Students, Ages 17–29, 2005

Catholic	30.1
Catholic "in my own way"	25.8
Evangelical	5.7
Protestant (historical churches)	1.0
Other religion	2.4
Jewish	0.7
Atheist	6.4
Nonbeliever	10.8
Believer without religion	17.1

Source: Parker (2009).

Whereas in 1950 in most Latin American countries, fewer than 4 percent of the population had any higher education, "by 2002–2003 the gross rate of enrollment of university and other post secondary students in fifteen selected countries had reached 30 percent" (Parker 2009, 162). As possible factors in changing religious adherence, Parker cites changes in the family (fewer grandparents in the home) and media expansion: older religious loyalties were transmitted through the family and local community.

Since the time of independence, there has been a small but significant strain of freethinking in Latin America. Some people in public life, such as former president Fernando Henrique Cardoso of Brazil and President Michelle Bachelet of Chile, say they are agnostics.[14] If Parker is right, as more people attend university, more may openly declare their distance from organized religion.

LOOKING AHEAD

Several decades ago, sociologists of religion had generally adopted some version of "secularization theory," assuming that modernization would take place along the lines of the West and especially Europe, with a reduction of the influence and public role of religion, which was destined to become at most a private affair. That assumption has been overturned by events, especially in light of the resurgence of Islam and the spread of Pentecostal religion, not only in Latin America and Africa but even in North America and Europe, as well as the persistence of the "religious right" in US politics. On the other hand, until the 1980s, Ireland appeared to be the most "Catholic" country in the world, unaffected by the turmoil elsewhere in Catholicism. Then many Irish rapidly became disenchanted with, or even angry at, the Church. The future will no doubt bring surprises, including in Latin America.

These various forms of religion—Roman Catholicism in its varieties (including popular religion), Pentecostalism, African-origin religions, and self-declared secularism—are jostling with one another in societies that are democratic (at least formally) and urban, more highly educated, entering the Information Age, and increasingly middle class. The public and private role of religion is inevitably being affected by these trends.

We close with observations on three contemporary developments: Pentecostal gang and prison ministry, new cults independent of the churches, and the Catholic Church's attempts to adjust to the new situation of religious pluralism, particularly in its public role.

In a year of observing youth on the outskirts of the city of El Progreso, Honduras, in the early 2000s, Jon Wolseth found surprising examples of outreach and successful evangelization of gang youth by Pentecostal churches, particularly the God Is Love Pentecostal Church. As elsewhere in Latin America, by that time gangs were present in poor neighborhoods, partly as a result of deportations of Central Americans from the United States. Young gang members who wished to leave gang life were finding the means to do so by converting to evangelical churches. The conversion itself occurs at the church, in the climax of a worship service when the preacher invites people to come forward to accept Christ.

In his account, Wolseth emphasizes two spatial metaphors. The church functions as a kind of "sanctuary": it is a refuge from the life of the "street" outside, and it offers a church community that marks one off from those outside. The second metaphor is that of taking the "path of God" in how one conducts one's life: avoiding drugs, alcohol, improper sexual relations, and, of course, violence.

Perhaps surprisingly, the gangs themselves generally respect the decision of members to become Christian. If a young man tries to leave the gang on his own, he may be killed; if he becomes a believer and behaves accordingly, his decision will be respected. Gang members fear that God will punish them if they do violence to a believer. Wolseth notes that "currently involved gang members, ex-gang members, and others in the community told me on numerous occasions that the only way for a young man to leave a gang, once involved, was to convert to an evangelical religion" (Wolseth 2011, 112).

Catholic youth groups in the same area have a different approach. They do not see their group as a "sanctuary" from dangers in the street; they regard it as their mission to be open to everyone in the neighborhood, even those in gangs.[15] Following a Base Community approach, they discuss community problems and the underlying reasons for them, and engage collectively in actions on behalf of the community, such as picking trash out of the ravine or raising funds for community projects. In accounting for gangs and violence, they place the blame on social factors such as unemployment, lack of educational opportunities, inequality, or capitalism—but not the responsibility of the individual. The Pentecostal insistence that gang members make a clean break with the past—leaving the gang and its way of life and joining the church—is more effective than the gradualist Catholic approach. This seems similar to the effectiveness of Pentecostals with alcoholics by requiring total abstention as a requirement and mark of conversion.[16] Although Catholic youth groups can provide an alternative community for nongang youth, they cannot offer actual gang members a way out.

Similarly, in his fieldwork, which included living as an inmate in a Rio prison for two weeks, Andrew Johnson found that Pentecostalism is the dominant faith in prisons. In prisons in Rio and elsewhere in Brazil, inmates form their own autonomous Pentecostal churches behind bars. They elect their own pastors, deacons, and other officers and conduct services. Often evangelicals are allowed to live together in the same cellblock as a community. The gangs that dominate prisons respect these churches and even allow their members to leave the gang and join them, provided their motivation is judged to be genuine. In Johnson's observation, 90 percent of pastoral visits to prisons were Pentecostal. When visitors from the outside arrive, the other inmates change their behavior: they turn down radios, put on shirts, and stop smoking. Although prisons are dangerous places, these evangelical visitors feel that they are safe for them and may even bring their wives and children.

Johnson gives an account of a prison crisis in 2010 in the northern city of

Maranhão, when a fight broke out between rival groups, some inmates were killed, and some prison employees were taken hostage. One group was threatening to kill ten inmates if their demands were not met. Rather than call for a SWAT team, the head of the prisons for the state called for mediation by Pastor Marcos Pereira from the Rio area. Pereira boarded a plane for the north along with ten other members of the church and arrived at the prison at midnight. In the course of the next day, Pastor Pereira defused the situation, had the hostages released, and collected weapons. This was not an isolated instance; several pastors have achieved some fame through such interventions (Johnson 2015).

The churches that take up this ministry are those that live side by side with gangs in the favelas. More middle-class churches presumably reflect the attitude of the larger society and regard gangs as the work of the devil and might favor harsh measures against gang youth, even when they have not been convicted of a crime. Such work with gangs and in prisons demonstrates the continuing relevance of Pentecostal churches.

It seems plausible to expect that urbanization would affect the kind of popular Catholicism described earlier in the chapter, and perhaps hasten its overall decline as people lose their ties to the rural way of life in which it arose. That assumption, however, is challenged by three devotions in Mexico, each more distant from official Catholicism, which have spread rapidly in urban environments. Thousands of devotees of San Judas Tadeo (St. Jude Thaddeus) come to the shrine of a reputedly miraculous image of him in the Tepito neighborhood of Mexico City on the twenty-eighth of every month, when sixteen masses are celebrated one after another. The crowds are so large that police have to cordon off traffic. Drug traffickers are known to be devoted to St. Jude, and some transactions apparently take place on these occasions.[17]

Unlike St. Jude, who is recognized as a Catholic saint, Jesús Malverde is a cult figure whose legend grew up in mysterious circumstances, possibly in connection with a thief with a "Robin Hood" reputation who was executed in Sinaloa in 1909. In the 1980s, a devotee hired an artisan to make a bust of him, with instructions to make him resemble the mid-twentieth-century movie star Pedro Infante. He is a favorite of drug traffickers, to the point where police in the United States are trained to recognize his image as an indication of possible trafficking activity.

The most bizarre figure of all is Santa Muerte (Holy Death or Saint Death), the origins of which are obscure. The representation is of a skeleton in a cape, a kind of Grim Reaper. People go to her shrine or have images of her on their own altar or are tattooed with "Santa Muerte." Catholic Church officials have issued warnings that Santa Muerte is not a legitimate object of worship, but to little effect, since the devotees are not regular churchgoers. Santa Muerte is especially popular among prisoners. Devotees are convinced that Santa Muerte protects them.

These three phenomena—rooted in traditional Catholicism associated with the poor, and flourishing especially in the urban underworld of Mexico and northern Central America—offer a counterpoint to the projections of Cristián Parker based on research among university students.

At the official level, Roman Catholicism is still attempting to adjust to its new context in which it no longer enjoys a monopoly in democratic and increasingly middle-class societies where traditional deference is fading. In a number of countries, the bishops have spent their political capital lobbying against legislative measures to loosen abortion restrictions or recognize same-sex marriage. Bishops have publicly opposed abortion even in high-profile extreme cases. Although the Church as an institution enjoys a high reputation, at least in comparison to other institutions (legislatures, the press), and governments are loath to challenge bishops directly, how much weight their pronouncements carry is questionable. Abortion rates in Latin America are actually among the highest in the world, even though the procedure is largely illegal. The practice occurs underground and is rarely prosecuted, and politicians have been unwilling to consider legalizing it. That began to change in the 2000s as the issue began to be debated in the press and legislation legalizing it was proposed.

The tradition represented by advocacy for the poor persists. Catholic-inspired groups, and especially some bishops, have been outspoken in denouncing mining projects that threaten the traditional way of life of indigenous peoples. For example, Bishop Álvaro Ramazzini of San Marcos, Guatemala, along with the clergy of the area, has been a consistent opponent of mining, and particularly of the Marlin gold mine in his diocese. Priests in Colombia have worked heroically and nonviolently in areas where the people were subject to violence from left-wing guerrillas, right-wing paramilitaries, and the Colombian armed forces and police. Church groups have formed organizations to assist Central Americans migrating north through Mexico to the United States, in a situation in which they are ready prey to being shaken down by gangs. In El Salvador, Bishop Fabio Colindres played a major role in brokering a gang truce in 2012.

In 2007 the Catholic bishops conference (CELAM, or Consejo Episcopal Latinoamericano; Latin American Episcopal Council) met at Aparecida, Brazil, to reflect on the situation of the Church, the third such meeting since the 1968 Medellín conference.[18] A major thrust of their book-length reflections and conclusions is that the Church must become "missionary" and engage in outreach. Seven years later, however, there were few signs that either priests or parishioners, let alone bishops, were in fact going door-to-door. Unlike evangelicals who often have a life-changing conversion, lifelong Catholics do not feel an urgency to share their faith. For three and a half decades the Vatican has made doctrinal loyalty to Rome rather than pastoral effectiveness the key to being made a bishop. Such company men are not a likely source of innovation.

The head of the drafting committee at Aparecida was Cardinal Jorge Bergoglio of Buenos Aires, who had evidently earned the admiration of his fellow Latin American bishops. In hindsight, it is possible to find in the Aparecida documents characteristic concerns of Pope Francis for the poor, immigrants, and the young and the elderly. The document notes that "Jesus went out to meet people in very different situations"; "We cannot passively and calmly wait in our church buildings . . ."; "We are asked to devote time to the poor, provide them kind attention, listen to them with interest, stand by them in the most difficult moments, choosing to spend hours, weeks, or years of our lives with them, and striving to transform their situation from within their midst."[19]

In his first year as pope, the Argentine Jorge Bergoglio, now Pope Francis, surprised almost all observers with his contrast in manner to his predecessors. He shunned some accoutrements of papal finery, sat down with other bishops as equals, and tended to put aside his prepared remarks and speak spontaneously. By all accounts, he was doctrinally conservative, but he seemed to bring a new spirit to Catholicism. It was often remarked that as archbishop of Buenos Aires he had traveled on public transport rather than being chauffeured. He seemed to have learned some lessons through years of contact with ordinary Argentineans in informal settings, especially in the wake of the financial collapse of the early 2000s. Perhaps his example could help Latin American Catholicism adjust to its new context. However, Catholicism now shares the religious field with Pentecostals and other Protestants, small but sometimes significant numbers of Jews and Muslims, and a growing number of Latin Americans who do not identify with any religion.

FURTHER READING

The most comprehensive recent view of religion in Latin America is Levine (2012), based on decades of research and thorough study of the literature. Chestnut (2003) provides a broad-strokes history to explain the emerging religious situation. For the churches in Central America, see Berryman (1994). Steigenga and Cleary (2007) shows the varieties of conversion. The studies in Hagopian (2009a) examine the implications of pluralism for Catholicism.

PART II

History

CHAPTER 10

Conquest and Colonial Order

This and the following two chapters consider Latin American history in three broad periods: from the peopling of the hemisphere until independence; through the nineteenth century to 1960; and the last half century of contemporary history. The aim is to shed further light on the topics considered in previous chapters and to provide a background for the final section of the book, which considers economics, politics and governance, and international relations. The purpose of the necessarily broadbrush treatment that follows is to gain insight into, and appreciation of, the Latin American past.[1]

ACHIEVEMENTS OF EARLY AMERICANS

Until recently, archaeologists believed that the Americas were populated by migrants who came across the Bering Strait around 13,000 BCE when Eurasia and the Americas were connected by a "land bridge." That date has now been pushed back, among other reasons because of solid evidence of human habitation in Chile and elsewhere from 10,000 BCE or earlier. The peopling of the hemisphere is now believed to have taken place over thousands of years and over more than one route, possibly including migration by coastal people who used boats. At some point migration stopped and the peoples of the Americas were separated from those of Eurasia until the arrival of Columbus.[2] It is striking that the early Americans evolved along lines similar to those occurring in Eurasia; indeed, two of humankind's original six civilizations arose in what is now Mexico and the Andean region.[3] Archaeological evidence shows the emergence of increasingly complex types of societies:

- Nomadic: small groups living from hunting, fishing, and foraging
- Semisedentary: practicing limited slash-and-burn agriculture
- Sedentary: permanently settled groups domesticating some crops and animals
- Chiefdoms: larger, more complex societies

- Cities and empires: monumental architecture (temples), complex social structure with noble elites, artisans, armies, markets, division of labor, elaborate mythologies, and priesthoods

Evidence for development comes from foods. Some coastal peoples made seafood an important part of their diet. Nomadic peoples discovered that seeds deposited in the ground grew into usable plants, and they began to encourage the traits they desired. The characteristic core diets (still eaten to this day) of the three major regions were developed: corn (augmented by beans, squash, and chiles) in Mesoamerica, potatoes in the Andes, and manioc in the Caribbean and South American coastal lowlands.

Fully sedentary communities existed by 3000 BCE. Pottery began to be made, first as containers but then for ritual purposes, and household objects were adorned with art. Compared to Eurasia, few animals were domesticated, and none were used for carrying heavy burdens or human passengers. None of these societies developed the wheel, and all labor and transport was by human power.[4]

The emergence of more complex societies and civilizations took place over millennia. The site of Caral in the Supe Valley (125 miles north of Lima on the dry coastal Peruvian plain) shows what is regarded as the first city or set of cities in the Americas, dated at 3000 BCE (Norte Chico civilization, contemporaneous with pyramids in Egypt). Its pyramids are evidence that it had an agricultural surplus and that it could compel or persuade labor, by force or religious belief. Caral and the approximately

TABLE 10.1. Early Achievements of Peoples of the Americas

DATE (ALL BCE)	PLACE	ACHIEVEMENT
As early as 30,000		First crossings of humans from Asia (continue until approx. 15,000 BCE)
10,000–8000	Mesoamerica	Domestication of gourds (as containers)
7500	Pacific South America	Evidence of fish and shellfish consumption
4000	South America	Cotton domesticated
3800	Peru	Potato domesticated
3450	Mesoamerica	Corn domesticated
3350	Colombia	Pottery
3000–2000	Ecuador	First human figurines (in stone, then ceramic)
2700–2000	Peru	Caral—first "city"
2000	Andes	Domestication of llamas and alpacas

Caral: remains of a city near coast of Peru, occupied from 2600 to 2000 BCE. © Tommie Sue Montgomery.

twenty other nearby urban centers evidence trade with distant regions, but there is no indication of ceramics, art, or warfare.

The Olmec sites near the Gulf of Mexico were ceremonial centers more than residential cities. The Olmecs[5] are best known for their remarkable large stone sculptures and the fact that they transported stones weighing many tons for these sculptures and other uses from many miles away. Characteristic features of subsequent Mesoamerican civilizations—a calendar and hence mathematics, incipient writing, and the ball game[6]—all began and developed under the Olmecs.

At roughly the same period, a center for ritual observances and sacrifice was also created in the Andean highlands at Chavín de Huántar in Peru. Chavín art shows images of lowland jungle animals and plants, and the remains of products from hundreds of miles away indicate long-distance trading.

True cities appeared in the following period. Teotihuacán, located about 30 miles northeast of modern Mexico City, was built between 100 BCE and 250 CE, and by 500 CE was one of the largest cities in the world, housing perhaps 150,000 people. Its most striking feature is the grandeur of its design, especially the Avenue of the Dead with the monumental Pyramid of the Sun and Pyramid of the Moon. Teotihuacán was a center of trade and artisan work whose influence can be seen in surrounding societies. To what extent that was the result of military conquest or imitation is not settled.[7]

Mayan civilization, exemplified in well-known sites like Tikal and Copán, expanded in the lowlands of northern Guatemala and southern Mexico in the Classic period (200–900 CE). Rather than a centralized empire, Mayan civilization was a network of city-states frequently at war with one another. Mayan writings, deciphered in the 1980s, are largely occupied with war and the doings of kings.

The question of the "collapse" of Mayan civilization has attracted a great deal of attention and discussion. Around 900 CE something drastic occurred: construction and writing stopped in the Mayan sites of Guatemala. Most explanations involve the environment: droughts or expanding population and failing soil, perhaps combined with internal or external warfare. It should be noted, however, that what collapsed was the organization of some city-states. People continued to live and work in the same area, reverting back to village or chiefdom-type societies. Moreover, some cities such as Mitla in Oaxaca and Mayapán in Yucatán continued to flourish. The city of Tihuanaku (Bolivia) also apparently "collapsed" during this same period due to drought and the inability to collect tribute.

The city of Tenochtitlán (modern Mexico City) was originally founded in 1325 CE by Mexica peoples on an island in the middle of a lake. When the Nahuatl-speaking

Pyramid structures in Teotihuacán, which flourished for several centuries after its founding around 100 BCE. © Tommie Sue Montgomery.

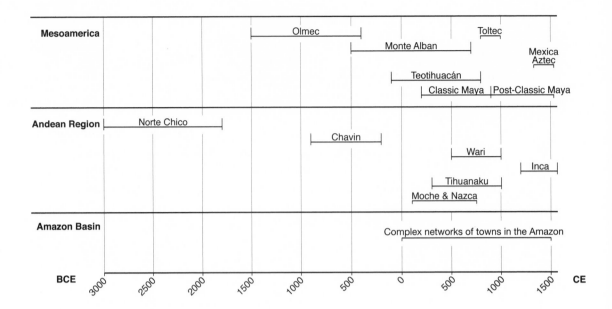

GRAPH 10.1. *Precolonial civilizations and societies.*

Aztecs invaded from the north, they took it over and constructed great public works such as causeways connecting the island to the surrounding areas. Under several emperors, starting with Itzcoatl, the Aztecs conquered neighboring peoples and created an expanding empire, compelling other peoples to pay tribute. By 1500, Tenochtitlán had an estimated 200,000 inhabitants, making it the largest city in the Americas. Similarly, by the fourteenth century, the Quechua-speaking peoples had begun conquering neighboring peoples and had gone on to create an "Inca" empire that reached from Ecuador to northern Chile.

As the chronology indicates, both the Aztecs and the Incas rose to power little more than a century before the arrival of the Spanish. Both civilizations drew on the achievements of the previous centuries. Both were theocracies investing great power in the ruler; both practiced human sacrifice and slavery. Their style of governing was different, insofar as the Incas sought to govern the lands they controlled directly, while the Mexica left the local nobles in place, ruling and exacting tribute through them.

Growing evidence indicates that the Amazon basin was the site of a third set of complex human societies, perhaps comparable in sophistication to those of Mesoamerica and the Andes. Sixteenth-century Spanish explorers reported seeing well-populated towns and villages along the Amazon River, but their reports were dismissed as fanciful because later travelers found forests that seemed almost uninhabited.

When the anthropologist Michael Heckenberger went to do fieldwork with the Kuikuro people along the Xingu River in Brazil in the 1990s, he was taken to see evidence of an ancient ditch 2 kilometers long, 2 or 3 meters deep and more than 10 meters wide. Working with the local people, he discovered roads, refuse heaps with

Machu Picchu: Inca city built on mountaintop in Peru. © Tommie Sue Montgomery.

Artist's rendition of a pre-Columbian town in Brazilian Amazon. © Luigi Marini.

pottery in them, the ruins of ancient buildings, and, notably, areas of dark earth, which had been improved by human management. Radiocarbon dating indicates that the area was settled fifteen hundred or more years ago. It was organized into clusters of large walled settlements over an area the size of the state of Vermont. Heckenberger proposes that the ancestral towns, villages, and roads once supported a population perhaps twenty times as dense as the present one. Some of the patterns can be detected from the air or by satellite imaging (Heckenberger 2009). Because these peoples did not erect stone monuments, even their large settlements mostly decayed.[8]

As the Genoese entrepreneur Christopher Columbus set sail to the west, the Americas were populated by perhaps fifty million[9] or more people, whose societies varied from the Aztec and Inca Empires that contained dozens of peoples, to smaller societies and nomadic peoples. One indication of their variety is that they spoke an estimated two thousand languages.[10] Even though these original peoples were decimated by the Iberian conquerors, their accomplishments are part of the larger story of humankind.

CONQUEST AND SETTLEMENT

As noted in chapter 7, native Americans throughout the hemisphere have objected to celebrating the "discovery" of the Americas, as it was commonly called in textbooks; it was a "conquest" or an "invasion." Some have proposed calling it the "encounter" of different peoples, thereby placing Europeans and Amerindians on the same level. "Re-encounter" might be even better: two portions of humanity were coming together again after fifteen thousand years of separation.

That re-encounter, however, was a violent conquest, and it took place in four stages: the first three (Caribbean, Mexico, Peru) lasted only about forty years (1490s–1530s), but the full subjugation of all the native peoples lasted decades or even centuries. In spirit, the process was a continuation of the centuries-long process of "reconquest" of Spain and Portugal from Muslim control, which was completed with the fall of Granada in 1492—the very year in which Columbus set sail. The Spanish conquerors brought with them much of the combative mind-set and intolerance of those wars.

The basic pattern was set in Hispaniola (present-day Dominican Republic and Haiti) by the colony established in 1493 on Columbus's second voyage. Although they were outnumbered by the native peoples, the Spaniards had cannons, firearms, steel swords, horses, large attack dogs, and, most devastatingly, diseases to which the natives were not immune. As they made their way across Hispaniola, they defeated the demoralized natives, often killing their chief, or cacique. They then moved to Puerto Rico and Cuba, which became their Caribbean headquarters. Meanwhile, other explorations were bringing reports of larger lands to the north, west, and south.

In 1519, Hernán Cortés landed on the shore of eastern Mexico and began preparing to move toward Tenochtitlán, the seat of the Aztec Empire. After making alliances with other peoples chafing under Aztec rule, Cortés and his men entered Tenochtitlán as guests of Moctezuma II, its ruler. At one point they audaciously took him hostage.

The story is full of intrigue and mysterious events, including a bloody Spanish retreat and the death of Moctezuma (possibly stoned by his own people). In 1521, Cortés and his army and allies captured the city. The Spaniards, numbering no more than a thousand, had defeated the empire and taken it over. In addition to the advantages mentioned, Cortés had the help of a young Mexica woman of noble birth, Marina or La Malinche, who became his partner for several years and was crucial to his success. Since she spoke Nahuatl and other languages, she could explain to Cortés what was happening.[11] The Aztecs on the other hand, could not understand who these men were, and possibly took them to be divine beings.

Francisco Pizarro, a distant relative of Cortés, applied a similar formula to the Inca Empire, first traveling from Panama down the Pacific coast to what is now Ecuador. He had only 160 troops but came upon the Incas at a time of a civil war between factions in Peru. (The Spanish forces were also at war with one another.) At one point, he took the Inca Atahualpa captive and demanded as ransom a room full of gold and silver objects; after Atahualpa complied, he was nevertheless killed. By 1532, the Spanish had taken Cuzco, the seat of the empire. In both instances, the Spanish had decapitated empires, literally killing the emperors, and confusing and demoralizing their subjects.

The settling of Brazil took a different course after its "discovery" by Pedro Álvares Cabral in 1500. The early explorers found no civilizations or precious minerals and did not establish major settlements until later in the sixteenth century, when they set up sugar plantations in what is now northeast Brazil. Settlements in Rio de Janeiro and São Paulo remained minor until the discovery of gold inland in Ouro Preto in the late seventeenth century.

The conquest did not end with the military defeat of the Aztec and Inca Empires. Gold artworks were melted down to be turned into gold bars and shipped to Spain. In the ensuing years, the colonists systematically sought to destroy the native religions, which the clergy regarded as idolatrous. Temples were demolished and used as quarries for building churches. Mayan writings on bark paper were burned, and thus knowledge of their society was irretrievably lost. Most devastating was the effect of smallpox and other diseases to which the indigenous people had no resistance.[12] Whole communities perished, and the population declined drastically, reaching a low point in the mid-seventeenth century. Demographers debate just how many people died, but a figure of 85 or 90 percent is not unreasonable.

COLONIAL SOCIETY: ECONOMY, GOVERNANCE, RELIGION

The new colonies that arose out of the conquest proved to be stable for three hundred years, lasting until the outbreak of the wars of independence in the early nineteenth century. Economically, they revolved around mining and agriculture; they were governed by an administrative structure that reached from Iberia down to local towns; and their formal spirituality and worldview were provided by Counter-Reformation Catholicism.

The Iberians, starting with Columbus himself, were driven by a desire for precious metals. After melting readily available gold art items, the conquerors went looking for rumored cities of gold. The greatest source of wealth, however, proved to be in silver, first discovered in a hill above Potosí (Bolivia) in 1545. Indigenous people and Africans were forced to work in the mine, where four out of five died within a year. Within a few decades, this 12,000-foot-high city came to rival Paris and London in size.

The silver was processed into bars and carried by pack trains through the Andes to Lima, and then by sea to Panama and on to Spain. The Spanish Crown monopolized trade and required a fifth of the gold and silver for itself. Gold and silver from the Americas were used extravagantly in baroque churches in Europe and the Americas. More importantly, they increased the world supply of precious metals eightfold, making it possible for coins to become the common means of exchange and thus paving the way for a worldwide trading economy.

The other source of wealth was agriculture, particularly sugar plantations, established in Brazil and the Caribbean. Sugar was made from crushed cane liquid, which was boiled and processed and shaped into uniform pieces of hard sugar. Sugar mills were industrial operations, requiring significant investment. Other plantation-like farms were haciendas devoted to ranching for meat and hides and other goods for local consumption rather than to export crops.

As noted in chapter 3, Latin American economic history into the twentieth century has revolved around control over land and labor. Both the Spanish and Portuguese monarchies granted tracts of land in the Americas to the conquerors and explorers, taking it for granted that they were entitled to do so, and the Spanish Crown granted rights to indigenous labor. The names and legal forms of land tenure and compulsory labor changed, but the principle and practice remained the same. It was Spanish policy to gather indigenous people in *pueblos de indios* (Indian towns) to facilitate control over them, collect tributes, and "Christianize" them. The survivors of this treatment sought to carry on their inherited way of life as best they could.

Black slaves were present in the colonies from the first settlements, but their numbers increased rapidly after the 1570s, with the establishment of sugar plantations in Brazil, and later in the Caribbean. The slave trade then continued into the nineteenth century. An estimated 12 to 15 million slaves were brought to the Americas, primarily from West Africa, two males for every female. Half went to the Caribbean, about a third to Brazil, a tenth to the rest of Spanish America, and the remainder (6%) to the future United States (Eakin 2007, 103).

Because African people from different places were brought together, they lost their original languages and much of their culture—or rather, they were forced to forge new cultures under conditions of oppression. Some slaves escaped, fled, and managed to establish communities beyond white control. In Brazil, these were called *quilombos*, the most famous of which was Palmares, where a large group of blacks set up a self-governing society. Palmares withstood attacks through most of the seventeenth century, until it was finally conquered in 1694. Groups of free blacks formed communities elsewhere, notably along the Pacific coast of Colombia.

TABLE 10.2. Colonial Timeline

1492	Caribbean	Columbus lands in Hispaniola
1494		Treaty of Tordesillas—Pope divides newly discovered lands between Spanish and Portuguese Crowns
1500	Brazil	Cabral lands on coast
1513	Panama	Balboa discovers Pacific Ocean
1519–1521	Mexico	Cortés conquers Tenochtitlán and Aztec Empire
1519–1522	Spain, South America, India	Circumnavigation of world sponsored by Spanish king, initially led by Ferdinand Magellan
1524	Spain	Creation of the Council of the Indies to govern colonies
1532–1535	Peru	Conquest of Inca Empire by Francisco Pizarro
1532	Brazil	First permanent settlement
1537		Pope declares indigenous are humans
1538	Brazil	First African slaves brought to northeast Brazil
1542	Spain	New Laws of the Indies
1545–1546	Bolivia	Silver discovered at Potosí, Bolivia, and Zacatecas, Mexico
1550	Valladolid, Spain	Debate between Las Casas and Sepúlveda on treatment of Indians
1550s	Lima, Mexico City, Santo Domingo	Universities founded
1605–1694	Brazil	Slaves escape and form *quilombo* called Palmares, which resists until finally destroyed
1690s	Minas Gerais, Brazil	Gold discovered
1700s	Spain	Bourbon reforms—tighter administration of colonies
1780–1781	Peru	Uprising led by Tupac Amaru II
1791–1804	Haiti	Uprising and establishment of black-led republic

To govern the colonies, the Spanish Crown worked through viceroys, representatives of the king, located in Lima and Mexico City. The primary issues for governance were assuring control over the colonists themselves, overseeing revenue for the Crown, organizing public works, providing defense, protecting the natives from oppressive colonists, and managing relations with the Church. One problem was

Slave market in Rio de Janeiro.

obviously distance: voyages from Spain to Havana took weeks, and the travel time was even greater to Mexico City, Lima, Bogotá, or Potosí. The governing structure was top down: from the Council of the Indies, a bureaucracy in Spain; to the viceroys in Lima and Mexico City; to ten lower-level districts called *audiencias*; and finally to local municipalities (including a town and its surrounding countryside).[13] At upper levels these administrative positions were filled by *peninsulares* (those born in Spain); at lower levels, by *criollos* (native-born men of European ancestry). The municipalities had town councils made up of local notables.

This system had no division of powers: at all levels, these bodies and individuals performed legislative, executive, and judicial functions. Local officials, who had sometimes had to purchase their position, understandably saw office as a source of revenue and operated with considerable discretion. Because no precious metals were found in Brazil for almost two centuries, the Portuguese Crown showed less interest in its colonies, and administration was more in the hands of native-born officials.

Colonial government was concentrated in the cities and towns, which were built to resemble those in Spain and Portugal. The vast majority of people lived in the countryside, tilling their own farms or working on the plantations and haciendas, and had only occasional contact with this administrative structure. Even after the colonial governing structure was set up, some lands remained out of Spanish control. Major campaigns against indigenous peoples took place in Venezuela in the eighteenth century, and in Chile the Mapuches held out even after independence and were subdued only in the 1880s.

How thoroughly Catholicism was part of the colonial order can be seen in the architectural remains in major cities, such as the well-preserved center of Quito. The most impressive site is the plaza of San Francisco with its (Franciscan) church; within a few blocks one finds the churches of the Compañía de Jesús (Jesuits), Santo Domingo (Dominicans), La Merced (Mercedarians), and others. As cities were built, each religious order sought to build its own church, which served as a basis from which to evangelize and baptize. They carried out missionary work in the countryside, sometimes on the far frontier. Decades later, as the colonies became settled, Catholicism set up its territorial structure of dioceses and parishes. Religious orders of women also arrived, but they were typically contemplative orders, whose entire life took place in a round of work and prayer within convent walls. Religious orders also set up schools, hospitals, and universities.

Examining the inside of a colonial church, one can see an entire world represented: God in his heaven, with Jesus and the Holy Spirit, the Virgin Mary, and legions of saints and angels, and down below, devils and sometimes portrayals of the agonies of hell, in imitation of churches in Spain and Portugal. The Catholicism of colonial Latin America now looks hard-edged and militant. One of the constant figures in colonial art is St. Michael the Archangel, defeating Satan with a spear or sword.

It should be pointed out, however, that the sole defenders of the native peoples in colonial times were friars, notably the Dominican Fray Bartolomé de Las Casas. Las Casas was part of the early wave of settlers to Hispaniola and initially held slaves himself, even after being ordained a priest. After a religious conversion triggered by a sermon questioning abuse of Indians, he gave up his slaves and lands and began to campaign on behalf of the indigenous people. Las Casas wrote extensively, traveled back and forth to Spain, and served as bishop in Guatemala and southern Mexico. He was instrumental in persuading the Spanish Crown to issue the New Laws of the Indies in 1542. A number of other church figures also defended the dignity and rights of the native peoples, notably the Jesuit António Vieira in Brazil.

In the early seventeenth century, the Jesuits in what is now Paraguay agreed to take a new approach to the indigenous Guaraní in the region, who at that time were sedentary and had not been converted or brought under colonial control. They designed a model of communities gathered into a central town surrounded by cultivated fields called "reductions." Life in the reductions was regulated, starting with Mass and prayers in the morning, breakfast, work in the fields, lunch, siesta, more work, prayers, a meal, and sleep—all rather like the scheduled life of a religious order. They had their own governing structure, although the Jesuits themselves were no doubt the final authority. Residents learned crafts and even fine arts, including making and playing violins and other musical instruments. For the indigenous people, the greatest benefit was that they were protected from predatory colonists seeking

Bartolomé de Las Casas, Dominican friar who devoted his life to denouncing the crimes against native people. Sixteenth-century portrait, artist unknown, General Archive of the Indies, Seville, Spain.

slaves, and in fact they organized militias for self-defense. In Paraguay, there were around thirty reductions, which lasted a century and a half until the expulsion of the Jesuits in the 1760s.[14] Similar schemes of self-contained indigenous communities run by religious orders existed elsewhere, including the missions in California and the American Southwest. Given the context of the time, they may have been a humane endeavor; from the standpoint of today, however, they were part of an overall pacification in which indigenous ways of life were destroyed and lost.

The Catholic Church, in both religious orders and diocesan structures, became the largest landholder in most of the colonies. One reason was that clergy and religious personnel had no heirs, and hence wealth accumulated in the hands of religious orders and dioceses, which also became moneylenders and bankers. The Church enjoyed a monopoly over education, marriage, and cemeteries. A regular source of income was tithing, providing a portion (in principle, one-tenth) of harvests or earnings to the Church.

"PROTOGLOBALIZATION" (THE COLUMBIAN EXCHANGE)

The "re-encounter" of the peoples of Eurasia with those of the Americas was itself part of a larger movement that began with the voyages of Portuguese explorers down the west coast of Africa, around the Cape of Good Hope, and then to India, roughly at the same time as the voyages of Columbus and Cabral. The "discovery" of the Pacific in Panama by Vasco Núñez de Balboa (1513) was followed by the voyage led by Ferdinand Magellan (1519–1522) around Tierra del Fuego, across the Pacific to the Philippines, and then to India. In 1565, the Spanish conquered the Philippines and established regular trade routes to Mexico. Explorers from other nations, such as Holland, England, and France, joined the pursuit.

This "protoglobalization" soon led to a vast expansion in trade, now by sea rather than the overland Silk Route, and with commodities like sugar, tobacco, tea, and coffee rather than the luxury goods of previous trade routes. One result was the "Columbian Exchange,"[15] the rapid introduction of new products (corn, potatoes, tomatoes) from the Americas into Europe and the rest of the world, and the introduction into the Americas of domesticated animals and crops from Eurasia. Among the latter were horses, cattle, pigs, and chickens. Wheat and grapes introduced into Chile made it possible to duplicate Mediterranean-like diets. In diseases, the exchange was quite unequal: besides smallpox, the Europeans brought about a dozen diseases to which the native Americans had no resistance. Syphilis broke out in Europe shortly after the return of Columbus's ships, and hence it is believed to be one disease that traveled the other way.

LATER COLONIAL PERIOD

As previously noted, the societies established in the sixteenth century proved remarkably durable, lasting for about three centuries (1500–1800). During the seventeenth century, the Spanish Crown was largely absorbed in rivalries and alliances with other rising European powers and, despite the flow of silver from the New World, was increasingly weakened. That situation changed in the eighteenth century as the Bourbon and Braganza monarchies in Spain and Portugal sought to reassert themselves, particularly in the face of the rising power of the English and French monarchies. In the Spanish colonies, the reforms took the form of expanding the small armies, enhancing administrative systems, increasing tax revenues, stimulating economic activity, and seeking to rein in the power of the Church. Since the founding of the colonies, the Spanish Crown had sought to strictly control trade, mandating that it had to flow through designated ports in annual flotillas that gathered in Havana to travel to Cádiz. The Crown now relaxed these restrictions while still keeping trade

TABLE 10.3. The Columbian Exchange

	EURASIA/AFRICA TO AMERICAS	AMERICAS TO EURASIA/ AFRICA
Domesticated animals	Horses Cows Pigs Sheep and goats Chickens Honeybees	Turkeys
Vegetables and fruits	Rice Wheat Barley Cabbage, broccoli, etc. Citrus Coffee Grapes Onions Turnips Beets Apples Bananas Sugar	Maize (corn) Potatoes Beans Tomatoes Peppers (sweet & hot) Manioc Chocolate Peanuts Cashews Cotton Pineapple Avocado
Diseases	Smallpox Cholera Malaria Measles Typhoid Yellow Fever Chicken Pox Bubonic Plague Diphtheria Influenza Leprosy	Syphilis Chagas disease

under royal control. Goods now came down from Bolivia and elsewhere to the port of Buenos Aires. As part of its reforms, the Bourbon monarchy placed more *peninsular* (Spanish-born) officials in positions of power in the state and even in the Church. That had the unintended effect of sharpening the resentment of the *criollo* (native-born) elites, who regarded themselves as the equals of those sent from Spain.

The seeds of what became the independence movement were already being sown in the later eighteenth century, first through the circulation of writings by Enlightenment authors (even though they were on the Church's Index of Prohibited Books), and then with the examples of the American (1776), French (1789), and Haitian (1891)

Revolutions. The local elites did not necessarily want to emulate these revolutions: the Haitian Revolution, with the specter of poor black people overthrowing the social order and burning down plantations, was seen more as a sign of potential dangerous outcomes, as was the French Revolution in its later phases. The later colonial period saw various internal uprisings, most notably that of Tupac Amaru II, a descendant of the Incas, in Peru (1780–1781).

Some have sought in the colonial (or even precolonial) period a cultural explanation for Latin American underdevelopment, contrasting Iberian culture to the more dynamic cultures of northern Europe. Although such facile explanations deserve skepticism, we can discern some features of this early history that leave traces to this day, several of which were discussed in previous chapters (the organization of the colonial economy around mining and plantation exports; racial and ethnic relations; gender and family patterns; official and popular Roman Catholicism). The top-down pyramid of colonial authority led to a society in which those on the lower rungs were expected to show deference to those higher up, vestiges of which remain to this day.

FURTHER READINGS

Representative one-volume histories include Herring (1972), Burns (1994), Chasteen (2007), Martin and Wasserman (2005), and Eakin (2007). Selections of primary source materials are found in Keen (1986) and Dawson (2011). On ordinary life, see Bauer (2001).

The Galeano trilogy (1985–1988) is not traditional history but a collection of many hundreds of short vignettes in strict chronological order, which vividly portray individual moments within the sweep of the history of the hemisphere. On slavery, see Klein and Vinson (2007).

CHAPTER 11

Forging New Nations

Most Latin American nations became independent in the decade and a half after 1810, about forty years after the United States did. Although a nation formally begins to exist at independence, its institutions must then be constructed over a long process. Many of the noble sentiments in the US Declaration of Independence were not achieved until much later: the ending of slavery in the Civil War, the vote for women in 1920, and the vote for African Americans in the South in the 1960s. The history of Latin American nations from independence to the present is likewise a story of confronting problems of development and of their own identity. This chapter outlines events of the first century and a half of independent life in Latin America.

As noted at the end of the previous chapter, the native-born elites had been chafing at control by the Spanish-born officials sent to administer the colonies, and were inspired by the examples of the American, French, and Haitian Revolutions. The immediate trigger for independence was the overthrow of both the Spanish and Portuguese monarchies by the emperor Napoleon in 1808. Refusing to recognize French rule, local elites began to conspire and attack Spanish forces with militias. Even after the Iberian monarchies were restored by 1814, these movements had gathered momentum that would prove difficult to stop. The independence struggle unfolded over the better part of a generation. Schematically, the various processes can be summarized as follows:

- *Mexico and Central America.* In September 1810, the freethinking priest Miguel Hidalgo issued a call for independence that included ideals of social justice. He gathered a large peasant army but was defeated and executed in 1811. Another priest who took up the struggle, José María Morelos, met a similar fate. Alarmed by the possibility of genuine social revolution, the elites ceased agitating for independence, but when the restored Spanish monarchy proclaimed liberal reforms, a conservative independence movement installed Agustín de Iturbide as emperor in 1821. Guatemala soon pulled away, and then itself was dismembered into the present-day Central American countries over the course of several years.

- *South America*. Separate independence movements began in northern and southern South America also in 1810. The leader in the north was the Venezuelan Simón Bolívar, who had a vision of a united Spanish-speaking America. After some initial struggles, Bolívar was forced into exile. Upon his return, he enlisted the help of rural *llaneros* (cowboys) and advanced militarily from Venezuela to Colombia. The Argentinean José de San Martín began in Buenos Aires, moved west and led his armies over the Andes, and joined forces with Chileans to defeat the Spanish. Over the next few years, he moved north to Lima. Bolívar and San Martín and their armies converged in Guayaquil, Ecuador. The Battle of Ayacucho (1824) in Peru marked the final defeat of Spain.
- *Brazil*. In 1808, with British help, the entire Portuguese court fled Portugal and sailed to Rio de Janeiro, where it continued until 1821. After Napoleon's defeat, King João returned to Portugal, leaving his son Pedro in charge in Brazil. When Pedro was ordered to return in 1822, he sided with the native elites and was crowned emperor of Brazil in a nearly bloodless process.
- *Caribbean*. Cuba and Puerto Rico remained in Spanish hands for the rest of the century; after a brief declaration of independence in 1821, the Dominican Republic was invaded by Haiti, from which it won back its independence in 1844.

By 1825, most of today's Latin American nations had achieved independence.

In the early nineteenth century, monarchy was still the prevailing form of government in the world, but it had been challenged by the United States, which was operating as a republic. Brazil maintained a monarchy through most of the century (as shown today in streets named after "barons" and "counts"). In Mexico, the initial empire was shortly replaced by a republic, but the ideal of a monarchical form of government remained in the minds of conservatives for decades.

Although emancipatory ideals can be found in the proclamations of Miguel Hidalgo and José María Morelos and in some writings of Simón Bolívar and other heroes of independence, for the vast majority of the people, small farmers and plantation or hacienda workers, independence meant primarily a shift from Spanish to native overlords. However, independence offered opportunities for new leaders to emerge, especially if they were supported by loyal troops.

SEEKING ORDER AND PROGRESS

Contrary to Bolívar's dream of a united Spanish-speaking America, the new nations were fractured, primarily over disputes between former soldiers. Out of the chaos there eventually emerged caudillos, military leaders who had loyal followers and who dominated politics in most countries. In Mexico it was Antonio López de Santa Anna, whose career lasted about five decades, starting in 1810; he was president more

Monument of Simón Bolívar and José de San Martín in Guayaquil, Ecuador. © Tommie Sue Montgomery.

than once. From the 1830s to the 1850s, Argentina was dominated by Juan Manuel de Rosas, twice governor of Buenos Aires, an authoritarian leader who attracted a mass following. Caudillos in Central America include Francisco Morazán in Honduras and Rafael Carrera in Guatemala. Perhaps the most striking figure is that of "Dr. Francia" (José Gaspar Rodríguez de Francia), who governed Paraguay as a benevolent dictator from 1814 until his death in 1840. Not surprisingly, in a climate of civil war, strongman leaders rose to impose order. Although this particular form of one-man rule eventually gave way to institutions, the figure of the caudillo long remained in the Latin American mind.[1]

Brazil followed a different course. After the proclamation of independence in 1822, Pedro I, the son of the Portuguese king João, ruled as emperor of Brazil until 1831 when he returned to Portugal. His son, Pedro II, took the throne while still a child, and after a regency period, he ruled Brazil as emperor until 1889, when he was finally deposed. At the local level, power was largely in the hand of landholders and regional power brokers. Brazil remained united and enjoyed relative stability into the twentieth century.

Throughout the nineteenth century, the new Latin American nations were in pursuit of "order and progress," the words enshrined on the Brazilian flag in the late nineteenth century. "Order" meant a minimum of stability, particularly after decades of rival caudillos fighting for power. "Progress" was assumed to be modernity, identified with what the elites could see in Europe and later in the United States.

Formally, the new nations were constitutional republics, in contrast to Europe where the prevailing form of governance remained monarchy. The constitutions were generally modeled after that of the United States; some lasted for decades, but most were periodically replaced. It was taken for granted that the constitutions were ground rules for disputes among elites. Politics was divided along liberal and conservative lines; in fact, in many countries the major political parties bore those names. Liberals stood for "progress," implementing Enlightenment ideas, especially for developing trade and exports, and placed strong emphasis on individual achievement and merit. Conservatives defended established tradition and privilege, including that of the Catholic Church, and tended to observe more Spanish models. The heroes of the independence era were largely liberals like Bolívar, but into the mid-nineteenth century, the caudillo age, most governments were conservative.

In their pursuit of "progress," liberals saw the Catholic Church, with its wealth and cultural power, as an obstacle. They advocated the creation of public schools, civil marriage, and secular cemeteries. Because Catholic religious orders and dioceses had acquired large landholdings, the liberals sought to have them expropriated and put to more "productive" use. In practice, both liberals and conservatives tended to be authoritarian, and neither had much to offer the vast majority of people who lived in the countryside. In Brazil, although Pedro II presided over an empire, he sought to implant liberal ideas.[2]

At the time of independence, half of Brazil's population of three million was enslaved. Slavery was ended in most Spanish-speaking lands in the years after independence, but it continued in Brazil, Cuba, and Puerto Rico. The slave trade was ended in midcentury under outside pressure, and children born of slaves were allowed their freedom, but slavery itself was abolished in Cuba as late as 1886 and in Brazil in 1888.

Writing in the 1840s, Domingo Sarmiento, the Argentine intellectual and educator who later became president, described his society around two poles: city and countryside, which he equated with "civilization" and "barbarism." The main character of his novel *Facundo* is portrayed as a gaucho caudillo. The book revolves around dichotomies: countryside and city, southern and northern Europe, ignorance and enlightenment, tyranny and peace. Sarmiento's widely read work typifies the elite attitude at the time. It is reflected in architecture that copied European design, painters trained in European academies, and composers sounding Viennese.

COMMODITY ECONOMIES

One of the aims of the independence movement was to be able to trade freely, unconstrained by Iberian control. British merchants and traders began to arrive in the 1830s, but the new nations were slow to engage in foreign trade due to political upheaval. Some of the more stable countries began to accelerate trade by the 1840s (coffee in Brazil and Costa Rica). In the decades after 1870, export increased from a trickle to a torrent, driven by demand from Europe and, over time, from the United States. Exports per capita from Latin America almost quadrupled from 1850 to 1912, from $5.4 to $20.4 (Bulmer-Thomas 1994, 69).

Individual countries specialized in producing a small number of products, sometimes to the point where it was primarily one product (monoculture). Such was the case with Bolivia (tin); Chile (nitrates); Cuba (sugar); El Salvador, Guatemala, and Haiti (coffee); and Panama (bananas). For most countries, three-fourths or more of their commodity exports were concentrated in only two products. Shipments of beef and lamb from Argentina and Uruguay accelerated with the development of refrigeration in the late nineteenth century.

As exports expanded in response to demand, a country's whole economy came to be shaped around its key exports. Railway tracks were laid from the mines or fields to the ports, not for transporting passengers or goods for the domestic economy but for expediting the movement of products out of the country. Fluctuations in the market price for a commodity brought alternating booms and busts. The extreme case was the rubber boom in the Amazon basin. Rubber had been known about since Columbus's time, but it became a desired good for industry around 1880. The rubber boom spurred the growth of the cities of Manaus in the middle of the Amazon and Belém at the mouth of the Amazon River. Fortunes were made, symbolized by the construction of an opera house in Manaus, to which Italian opera companies were brought to perform in the sweltering tropical heat. Around 1912, rubber from Malaysian plantations, the seeds for which had been brought from Brazil, came on the market at a lower price, and the Amazon rubber boom came to an abrupt halt. Manaus went

TABLE 11.1. Export Commodity Concentration in Latin America, ca. 1913

COUNTRY	FIRST PRODUCT	PERCENTAGE OF EXPORTS	SECOND PRODUCT	PERCENTAGE	TOTAL
Argentina	Maize	22.5	Wheat	20.7	43.2
Bolivia	Tin	72.3	Silver	4.3	76.6
Brazil	Coffee	62.3	Rubber	15.9	78.2
Chile	Nitrates	71.3	Copper	7.0	78.3
Colombia	Coffee	37.2	Gold	20.4	57.6
Costa Rica	Bananas	50.9	Coffee	35.2	86.1
Cuba	Sugar	72.0	Tobacco	19.5	91.5
Dominican Republic	Cacao	39.2	Sugar	34.8	74.0
Ecuador	Cacao	64.1	Coffee	5.4	69.5
El Salvador	Coffee	79.6	Precious metals	15.9	95.5
Guatemala	Coffee	84.8	Bananas	5.7	90.5
Haiti	Coffee	64.0	Cacao	6.8	70.8
Honduras	Bananas	50.1	Precious metals	25.9	76.0
Mexico	Silver	30.3	Copper	10.3	40.6
Nicaragua	Coffee	64.9	Precious metals	13.8	78.7
Panama	Bananas	65.0	Coconuts	7.0	72.0
Paraguay	Yerba mate	32.1	Tobacco	15.8	47.9
Peru	Copper	22.0	Sugar	15.4	37.4
Puerto Rico	Sugar	47.0	Coffee	19.0	66.0
Uruguay	Wool	42.0	Meat	24.0	66.0
Venezuela	Coffee	52.0	Cacao	21.4	73.4

Source: Bulmer-Thomas (1994, 59).

into several decades of decline, and Brazilian finances were severely affected. Less dramatic boom-and-bust cycles affected other countries.

Bananas were a particular case. In the late nineteenth century, several American entrepreneurs recognized an opportunity and set up integrated operations from their plantations to US ports, particularly New Orleans. The plantations on the north coast of Honduras, for example, had little contact with the rest of the Honduran economy. The Caribbean port San Pedro Sula became at least as important as the inland capital, Tegucigalpa. Three American companies, United Fruit, Standard Brands, and Cuyamel, controlled banana production, getting favorable deals from the governments of Honduras and other countries (Panama, Guatemala, Costa Rica).[3]

Latin American elites accepted their assigned role in the "international division of labor": their economies were to specialize in certain agricultural and mining commodities, and with the proceeds they could import manufactured goods, both machinery and household consumption items. Thus they could enjoy the fruits of "progress" as they were developed: Mexico City, Buenos Aires, and Rio de Janeiro had electric street lights, indoor plumbing, trolley cars, automobiles, movies, and other amenities shortly after they became common in London or New York. Major avenues in Buenos Aires emulated what the elites saw in Paris. Most Latin Americans, particularly farmers in the countryside, enjoyed little of this kind of development, however. The elites had little incentive to extend the benefits of "progress." They needed only their land and a sufficient workforce, including managers and office workers, who formed part of the beginnings of a middle class. Such industries as existed tended to be related to export, such as meatpacking in Argentina. Despite some incipient manufacturing (food processing, textiles, and clothing) in some of the larger countries, notably Mexico, Latin America did not undergo a true industrial revolution.

The elites imported the products of the industrializing world, including automobiles, but they did not participate in devising or improving the new technologies. As an illustrative example, consider the Brazilian Alberto Santos-Dumont, the son of a successful coffee farmer, who was an aviation pioneer. He won a prize for developing the first practically navigable airship in 1901. Later he developed the first heavier-than-air production aircraft in 1908. However, he did all of this in France, where he was in contact with dozens of other aircraft inventors. Had he remained in Brazil, he would not have had the context in which his inventiveness could flourish.[4]

Not surprisingly, the governments of the era tended to serve the landholding and merchant classes. In some countries, presidents and parliaments were generally elected (Costa Rica, Uruguay, Chile), while elsewhere political succession often took place through coups.

In the late nineteenth and early twentieth centuries, new waves of immigrants came especially to the Southern Cone (Argentina, Uruguay, and southern Brazil). Over four million Italians and three million Spaniards came during the same period that immigrants from southern Europe were also going to the United States. The influence was most marked in Argentina, where in 1914, 30 percent of the population was foreign-born. Starting in 1908, Japanese began arriving by the shipload in Brazil and came to have a distinct presence, especially in São Paulo. Significant numbers of Jews emigrated to Argentina and southern Brazil. The first generations of these new arrivals were often small farmers or peddlers; their children often went into the professions or became successful industrialists.

WARS AND ARMIES

Asked to give a quick overview of their own history, many Americans would instinctively structure it around wars: War of Independence, War of 1812, Civil War, World Wars I and II, Korean War, Vietnam War, Afghanistan and Iraq Wars. They might not offer accounts of military campaigns, but the wars provide a framework for ordering events (e.g., "post–World War II prosperity"). European history seems even more bound up with war, culminating in the two great conflagrations of the first half of the twentieth century, followed by an unprecedented long "European peace."

TABLE 11.2. Major Wars between Latin American Countries

1836–1839: War of the Peruvian-Bolivian Confederation	Confederation of Peru and Bolivia defeated by forces of Chile and Peruvian dissidents.
1865–1870: War of the Triple Alliance	Brazil, Argentina, and Uruguay go to war against Paraguay, which by one estimate loses 60% of its population.
1879–1884: War of the Pacific	Fought over guano resources; Chile gains territory in north, Bolivia and Peru lose territory, and Bolivia loses access to the sea.
1932–1935: Chaco War	Paraguay and Bolivia go to war over barren Chaco land, reputed to have oil. Paraguay gains territory; no oil is found.

War between Latin American countries has played a relatively small part in post-independence history, but significant exceptions are shown in table 11.2. In the war of the Triple Alliance, Paraguay lost an estimated 300,000 of its total population of 550,000, making it apparently the most destructive war in history in per capita terms. The depopulation and destruction left a mark on Paraguay for decades. To this day, Bolivians lament their status as a landlocked nation, which dates back a hundred and thirty years to the War of the Pacific.

Latin American countries have disputed borders and their adjoining territories. From early independence until the end of the twentieth century, Ecuador and Peru disputed the Amazon portion of the boundaries between the countries. That dispute erupted into armed conflict at various times, until a comprehensive peace treaty was signed in 1998. Tensions have arisen over borders between southern Chile and Argentina, and between Chile and Peru. These disagreements have sometimes led to skirmishes but not outright war.

Some countries have had prolonged internal conflicts. In the Uruguayan civil war of the 1850s, Montevideo was under siege for nine years, and other countries were involved. Disputes in Colombia between the Liberal and Conservative forces led to the War of a Thousand Days (1899–1902), which ended with a treaty signed on an American battleship.

In the second half of the nineteenth century, armies became more institutionalized, often with the assistance of trainers from Europe, especially Germany. Serving in the army officer corps was a career option for some members of the elite. Even though most Latin American countries have not been threatened by hostile foreign nations, they have had the full range of military institutions and have sought to have up-to-date weapons. Their primary function has been that of maintaining internal order, identified with protecting the interests of landholding and merchant classes.

YANKEE INTERFERENCE

In 1904, the Nicaraguan poet Rubén Darío published "To Roosevelt," a sarcastic ode that addresses President Theodore Roosevelt, calling him "primitive and modern, simple and complex." The poet's indignation was prompted by Roosevelt's action of sending US warships to enable Panama to break away from Colombia. The United States wanted to build a canal across Panama, but the Colombian senate balked. Panamanian leaders declared independence in November 1903, and three weeks later US representatives signed a treaty in New York with a French engineer involved in previous canal attempts; no Panamanians were present. The treaty gave the United States rights to a 10-mile-wide strip of land from the Caribbean to the Pacific (the Canal Zone) "as though it were sovereign."[5]

Darío had in mind a series of US interventions dating back to the 1846–1848 war, in which the United States took half of Mexico's territory.[6] In 1898, President William McKinley declared war on Spain after an explosion on the USS *Maine* in the harbor of Havana. In this "splendid little war," Teddy Roosevelt became a hero and the United States took control of Puerto Rico and Cuba (frustrating the independence movement in the latter), the Philippines, and other Spanish possessions. The outcome signaled the rise of the United States to world-power status and demonstrated its territorial ambitions.

In his poem, Darío continued:

> You are the United States,
> you are the future invader
> of naïve America whose blood is indigenous,
> which still prays to Jesus Christ and prays in Spanish.
> (Fernández 1986; translation mine)

As Darío foresaw, further instances of intervention followed. In 1909, the United States conspired to overthrow the president of Honduras, who was not sufficiently amenable to the banana companies. In 1912, a US Marine detachment went to Nicaragua, installed the employee of a US mining company as president, and remained in the country for over two decades. In the 1920s, the US Marines became involved in a guerrilla war with Augusto César Sandino, whom they called a "bandit" but whom many Nicaraguans viewed as a patriotic hero. The Marines left in the early 1930s, after training a National Guard, which was left in the hands of Anastasio Somoza, who then used it as the basis for a family dynasty that lasted until 1979. In 1914 and 1917, US troops entered Mexico, in the midst of that country's revolution. US troops also occupied both Haiti (1915–1934) and the Dominican Republic (1916–1924), in both cases to restore or maintain order and to assure payment of obligations. US occupation of the Dominican Republic led to the dictatorship of Rafael Trujillo, who ran the country either as president or the power behind the throne from 1930 to 1961.

In his 1904 poem, Darío, regarded as a pivotal figure in Spanish-language poetry,

TABLE 11.3. US Military Interventions in Latin America, Nineteenth and Early Twentieth Centuries (Partial List)

1823	Monroe Doctrine—US president warns European nations not to intervene in the hemisphere.
1847–1848	United States goes to war with Mexico over southern boundary of Texas (previously wrested away by US settlers). Forty percent of territory ceded to the United States.
1850s	William Walker, adventurer from Tennessee, becomes involved in Central American politics, briefly becoming president of Nicaragua. Captured and executed in Honduras in 1860.
1898	Spanish-American War—United States takes control of Puerto Rico, Cuba, and the Philippines.
1903	United States sends gunboats to enable Panama to declare independence from Colombia, and allow United States to build an interoceanic canal.
1912–1919	US Marines occupy Nicaragua, become involved in a guerrilla war with Augusto César Sandino.
1914	US troops occupy Veracruz, Mexico.
1915–1934	Occupation of Haiti to safeguard US business interests.
1916–1924	Occupation of Dominican Republic to restore order and assure revenue collection—guerrilla war in part of the country.
1917	US troops cross border into Mexico in pursuit of Pancho Villa.

pits the power of the United States (which he compares to earthquakes and volcanoes) against "our America," which had poets in pre-Columbian times, and whose ancestors had built civilizations that were the equals of Greece and Rome. This America "lives from light, from fire, from fragrance, from love." He warns the "men of Saxon eyes and barbaric soul" that this America "lives. And dreams. And loves, and trembles, and is the daughter of the Sun." He ends grandiloquently, "You have everything, but one thing is lacking: God!"[7]

Darío had spent most of his adult life away from Nicaragua, in Europe and other Latin American countries, and felt in solidarity with people in the continent. His defiance of the United States reflects a sentiment common among such intellectuals and artists at the time, that despite the material inequality between the new power in the north and the southern countries, Latin Americans had some spiritual quality lacking in the north. In his essay *Ariel* (1900), the Uruguayan writer José Enrique Rodó urged Latin American youth to cultivate the values of the spirit, which he identified with the Western classical tradition stretching back to Greece and Rome, rather

Rubén Darío (1867–1916), Nicaraguan poet and diplomat.

than the utilitarian spirit that he identified with the emergent United States. Another nationalist and less aristocratic intellectual was the Cuban poet, journalist, and essayist José Martí, who devoted his life to Cuban independence from Spain, primarily from exile in Mexico, Guatemala, the United States, and elsewhere. Although he died in combat with Spanish troops in 1895, his writings inspired generations of Cubans and other Latin Americans.

Although Latin American intellectuals as distant as Uruguay or Chile resented

US assertions of power, the United States intervened in what it regarded as its sphere of influence (the Caribbean, Mexico, and Central America). The list above is only partial: there were numerous instances of smaller actions in Panama, Honduras, and elsewhere. Starting in the early 1930s, US presidents consciously turned away from direct interventions and pursued what they called the Good Neighbor Policy, which lasted until the onset of the Cold War.

A REVOLUTION AND THE RISE OF NATIONALISM

In 1910 a revolution broke out in Mexico whose effects lasted through the century, and to some extent continue even today. Its roots reach back into the mid-nineteenth century when the liberals had finally triumphed and installed as president Benito Juárez, a lawyer of indigenous extraction. In the early 1860s, Emperor Napoleon III of France sent troops to occupy Mexico in alliance with Mexican conservatives, who had never relinquished their preference for monarchy. The liberals fought back and defeated the French and then fell into conflicts among themselves, which were ended by the rise of Porfirio Díaz, who ran the country as a dictatorship from 1876 until 1910. Under the Porfiriato, as it is called, the country grew economically, as evidenced in the spread of a national railway network, but the rural poor were increasingly marginalized by large landholders who amassed more property.

What detonated the revolution was an election announced for 1910 by Díaz, then eighty years old. When Francisco Madero was mounting a credible opposition, Díaz had him jailed and won the election. Madero escaped from jail, and opposition forces arose in various parts of the country. Díaz fled in 1911, and Madero took office, but by then more radical currents were at work. Peasants led by Emiliano Zapata in the south and Francisco (Pancho) Villa in the north were demanding land and, in some instances, taking it. A third force was organized labor in the larger cities. The US government meddled in the process at various points. An estimated one million people (out of a population of fifteen million) lost their lives in the violent phase of the revolution.

A key moment was the drafting of the 1917 constitution, which declared land reform, imposed constraints on the Catholic Church, established labor rights, asserted Mexican ownership of natural resources, prohibited reelection, and enacted other reforms. In the 1920s, Presidents Álvaro Obregón and Plutarco Elías Calles created the institutions of modern Mexico. In 1929, Calles merged the elites representing different interests and regions into a single political party (after 1946 called the Partido Revolucionario Institucional, or PRI; Institutional Revolutionary Party), which thereafter extended its power throughout the country down to the local level. Under President Lázaro Cárdenas (1934–1940), land reform was accelerated; large estates were broken up and the land distributed to peasants. It was often poor land, however, and the peasants were not given sufficient assistance. Industrial laborers were given labor rights, but they had to belong to PRI-sponsored unions. When Cárdenas nationalized Mexican oil fields in 1938, President Roosevelt, who might have been expected to take military action—particularly since the Mexican Revolution was sometimes portrayed in US public opinion as a "Bolshevik" revolution—opted to negotiate a solution.

The revolutionary phase ended after 1940, as the PRI turned away from social reform and toward economic growth, making alliances with business and industry. Through monopolistic control of politics, coercion, corruption, and co-optation, the PRI came to hold sway over the political life of the country at all levels, expanding state bureaucracies in the process. New large landholders appeared who were engaged in more modern commercial agriculture, especially in the northern states with access to US markets.

The Mexican Revolution led to an upsurge of nationalism that was manifested in the arts and institutionalized in the culture itself. Perhaps the most noteworthy example is seen in the work of the mural painters Diego Rivera, José Clemente Orozco, Alfredo Zalce, and David Siqueiros. Many of their works portray the panorama of Mexican history, showing an exploitative past from the conquest through the Porfirian dictatorship, and then people engaged in the tasks of building a new kind of society. Figures in the paintings with European features are the exploiters or at least arrogant bourgeoisie; those with Indian features are noble, often linked to their Aztec ancestors.

The educator and philosopher José Vasconcelos coined the phrase *la raza cósmica* (the cosmic race) to express his notion that in Mexico and Latin America the various "races" of humankind were being brought together in a higher synthesis. While rector of the National Autonomous University, he sought to define the role of the university as serving the people rather than simply preparing young people for professional careers. As minister of education, Vasconcelos promoted the expansion of schooling to all and portrayed teachers as apostles with a mission. The ministry published many books cheaply and set up a network of two thousand libraries around the country.

Composers like Carlos Chávez, Silvestre Revueltas, and Manuel Ponce moved away from late-Romantic styles and incorporated indigenous sounds and rhythms in their compositions, as well as twentieth-century dissonance and irregular rhythms (e.g., Chávez's *Sinfonía india*). Similar nationalist strains appeared elsewhere. For example, Heitor Villa-Lobos combined Brazilian rhythms and melodies with classical musical forms. A generation of Brazilian painters combined modern forms with subjects of ordinary life. A watershed event was the Modern Art Week, an arts festival held in São Paulo in 1922, at which artists were seeking to be both modern and Brazilian.

Artists and intellectuals were moving away from the stance of those like Sarmiento who sought to distance themselves from the "barbarians" of their rural hinterlands by looking toward Europe, or those like Rodó and Darío who invoked Latin "spiritual" qualities to set themselves off from the "barbarians" to the north. Artists and writers were now finding their subject matter in the ordinary people around them. Through much of the twentieth century, artists and writers would struggle with a tension between being Latin American and cosmopolitan, and between making their art relevant to their societies and asserting their own unique individuality.

Mural by Alfredo Zalce depicting Mexican independence struggle. © Tommie Sue Montgomery.

Films and popular music of the 1930s–1950s attested to the changes taking place. Film industries developed in Mexico, Brazil, and Argentina not long after the Hollywood studio system was created. Genres included musical comedies and the equivalent of cowboy films. Mexican films were popular throughout the Spanish-speaking countries. Urban audiences enjoyed the idealized depiction of the countryside that they had left, and also tales of poor but honest heroes and heroines who triumph over their foes and get the girl (or guy). A recording industry likewise grew up throughout the continent. The tango, which had arisen in bars and bordellos (at the same time as jazz in New Orleans), was both a dance and a song form, and spread beyond Argentina in records and films. The Cuban Ernesto Lecuona, like George Gershwin, composed popular songs and Latin-inflected classical music, and bolero songs from composers like the Mexican songwriter Agustín Lara as performed by Trío Los Panchos became sentimental favorites. Commercial popular culture thus helped forge national identity in an urbanizing continent.

STATE-LED DEVELOPMENT AND POPULIST POLITICS

Three outside shocks revealed the weaknesses of economies based on export of commodities. World War I cut off trade with most European countries, although by this time the United States had replaced Great Britain as Latin America's primary trading partner. Even more serious was the onset of the Great Depression (1930), which caused demand and prices for commodity exports to plummet. Brazil in particular took to stockpiling coffee in an attempt to constrict supply and so sustain prices, but the beans were almost worthless. An immediate effect of the drop in demand for exports was a social crisis in most countries. In El Salvador, rural unemployment and discontent fueled a Marxist-led peasant uprising in 1932, which was foiled in the early stages. The government of Maximiliano Hernández Martínez nevertheless went on to slaughter at least ten thousand peasants.[8] World War II interrupted the supply of manufactured goods from both Europe and the United States, even as it increased demand for war-related commodities.

Latin American leaders and analysts concluded that they had to expand their industries and manufacture goods that they had been importing, a process called "import-substitution industrialization" (ISI). ISI represented a shift inward, toward making domestic demand the economic mainspring. It fit with the increasing nationalism that came to the fore in the twentieth century. It also entailed a strategic alliance between the state, domestic business and industry, and organized labor. ISI meant developing basic industry, such as steel production and increased energy generation from hydropower or petroleum. In principle, one would start with simpler goods and move toward the more complex, toward mass consumer durables, such as household appliances. For example, a Mexican company called Mabe, formed in 1947, began by manufacturing kitchen stoves, while importing some parts. It was soon able to manufacture those parts in Mexico, and by 1964 it was manufacturing refrigerators. Its operations, which went beyond Mexico, totaled $20 million in worth, and it employed a thousand workers at several plants in Mexico.

In the mid-twentieth century, Mexico, Brazil, and Argentina opted to develop auto industries. They invited existing European and American auto companies to build plants, and raised tariffs on imported cars, thus assuring a market for domestically manufactured vehicles. The industries might begin by importing many components, but over time incentives were given to develop auto parts industries, so that eventually the car would be 100 percent manufactured in Mexico or Brazil. ISI worked best in the larger countries, where a significant market for such goods existed. It worked less well in medium-sized countries, and scarcely at all in the small Central American and Caribbean nations, whose economies continued to revolve around commodity export.

Characteristic of this period was the emergence of a new type of populist leader, best exemplified in Juan Domingo Perón in Argentina. Perón was an Argentine army officer who had been minister of labor. He was a gifted speaker, adept at addressing large crowds or a radio audience, consistently pitting himself and his followers—*el pueblo*, "the people"—against the "oligarchy." His wife, Evita Duarte de Perón, could also address crowds, but her characteristic feature was maintaining charities with public funds from which she provided assistance like a "mother of the nation."

Similar figures appeared elsewhere in the middle of the twentieth century. The Colombian Liberal Party leader Jorge Eliécer Gaitán built up a following among the

Juan Domingo Perón and his wife Evita (Eva Duarte de Perón).

country's poor. In 1948, he was murdered under mysterious circumstances that were never clarified.[9] Getúlio Vargas was first made president of Brazil in 1930 after a coup, and he eventually ruled as a dictator until 1945, and later as an elected president from 1951 to 1954. Under his government, industries developed under state protection. His social policies earned him the title "Father of the Poor." Faced with a rebellion among the officers of the armed forces, he took his own life in 1954.[10]

The primary electoral constituencies of populists were the urban poor and labor. Labor unions were allowed to form, but they were under the control of political parties. The effect was a three-way partnership: the state fostered industrial development, workers were paid relatively well and received benefits, and the nascent industries were protected from competition. Populism helped weaken the power of the older landholding oligarchy and represented the new urban masses. Populist leaders generally did little for the rural poor, with the exception of President Lázaro Cárdenas of Mexico, who accelerated land redistribution. Price controls on basic foods like rice, beans, and corn favored the urban masses at the expense of the poor farmers who produced them.

Populists made a direct appeal to "the people" as opposed to exploitative wealthy elites. Like Perón, they addressed large audiences using mass media. José María Velasco Ibarra of Ecuador boasted: "Give me a balcony and I will be president." Populists skillfully used ordinary speech, appealing to the common people for their electoral support and promising to deliver the benefits to which they were entitled. Classic populists demanded personal loyalty in a kind of with-me-or-against-me dynamic.

Latin American populists showed some affinity with fascist regimes in Europe, but in World War II they joined the Allies. Perón was deposed by the army in 1955, returned to power briefly in the mid-1970s, and died in office; to this day, Argentine politics remains divided into Peronists and anti-Peronists (and contesting factions of *peronismo*). Populism has continually recurred as a style in Latin American politics.[11]

On December 1, 1948, President José Figueres of Costa Rica abolished the country's army, symbolically smashing a portion of the country's main military headquarters. He had come to power after leading a rebellion against a government imposed by electoral fraud after a two-month civil war that cost two thousand lives. The next year, Costa Rica's lack of an army was enshrined in the country's constitution. Freed of a military budget, Costa Rican governments have spent the savings on education and health care, and later on environmental protection. As a result, Costa Rica had all of its school-age children in school decades before most other Latin American countries, and the health-care system was serving virtually all Costa Ricans at a time when the poor in Guatemala, for example, were still relying on folk remedies.

The course taken by Costa Rica was to some extent the outgrowth of its previous history. The country did not have precious metals, and the original settlers were largely farmers who worked the land themselves rather than running plantations and haciendas that used African or indigenous labor. When coffee production began in the nineteenth century, it was primarily in the hands of family farmers, and that helped set the stage for a relatively egalitarian ethos as their descendants moved to the city. The wealthy and powerful are not inclined to conspicuous display of wealth. The absence of an army and the emphasis on schooling, health care, and the environment have become part of the national identity of Costa Rica. Despite different historical circumstances, other countries in the region might yet emulate that experience.[12]

Although prior to World War II fascism gained some sympathy in Latin America, after Pearl Harbor all Latin American countries to one degree or another joined the Allied cause. Brazil sent troops to Europe, and a squadron of the Mexican Air Force participated in combat in the Pacific. The war in Europe and the shift from civilian to military manufacturing in the United States offered favorable opportunities for Latin American industry to grow. The war increased demand for some commodities, notably Amazonian rubber.

Eighteen of the approximately fifty countries that founded the United Nations in 1945 were Latin American, and their diplomats were active in the deliberations, especially in drafting the UN Universal Declaration of Human Rights (1948). Thus, although Latin America has often been categorized as part of an underdeveloped "Third World" of new nations (like those in Africa and Asia) emerging from colonialism, Latin American nations were no longer "new"—they had existed for well over a century.

Populations continued a rise that had begun around the turn of the century. Women were still having as many children as they had in the countryside, but with lower childhood mortality more were surviving. Modernization in the form of roads, schools, and electricity was bringing more people out of rural isolation.

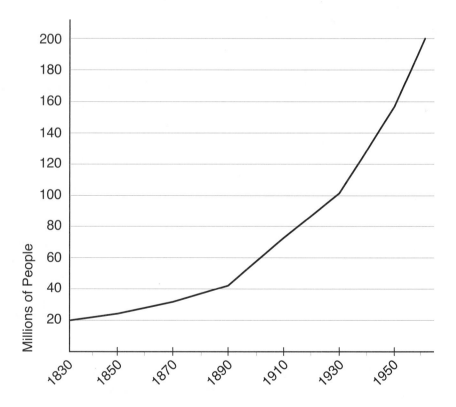

GRAPH 11.1. *Population Growth.*

At midcentury, as Latin American countries approached the anniversary of a century and a half of independence in 1960, the political panorama was somewhat mixed. Broadly speaking, it could be said that the trend was away from dictatorships and toward democracy—or perhaps more accurately toward elected civilian governments. In Mexico, the PRI continued to dominate what was in effect a one-party state. Brazil enjoyed a twenty-year period of civilian governments. Chile, Uruguay, and Costa Rica continued their long-standing traditions of electoral democracy. Some smaller countries were still under old-style personal dictatorships: Nicaragua (Anastasio Somoza), the Dominican Republic (Rafael Trujillo), and Paraguay (Alfredo Stroessner). In 1958, the political elites in both Colombia and Venezuela made agreements assuring orderly alternation of power by civilian governments, which provided a kind of political stability for three decades.

A disputed election in 1951 in Bolivia triggered a revolution led by the Revolutionary Nationalist Movement (Movimiento Nacionalista Revolucionario; MNR), with backing from organized miners and the military. The revolutionary government carried out some land reform, nationalized mines, and, perhaps most importantly, gave some recognition and dignity to the traditionally oppressed Quechua and Aymara peoples. By the 1960s, the revolution was spent, and Bolivia then went through two decades of frequent coups and abrupt changes of governments (right and left, civilian and military).

An ominous event occurred in Guatemala. After decades of dictatorship, a popular uprising in 1944 had led to democratically elected, moderately left governments. In the early 1950s, however, the Eisenhower administration became hostile to the government of Jacobo Arbenz (1951–1954) over two issues: applying the land reform to United Fruit, the largest landholder in the country,[13] and tolerating small numbers of communists in the country. The CIA orchestrated a coup, organizing a guerrilla army in neighboring Honduras and even strafing Guatemala City. The Guatemalan army abandoned Arbenz, who fled into exile. The new president, Col. Carlos Castillo Armas, was flown into the capital on a US embassy plane. The army then executed an estimated two hundred labor leaders and others, using lists prepared by the CIA. The army thereafter assumed the position of arbiter of Guatemala for decades.[14]

Latin American countries were already being viewed through a Cold War lens. In the Pact of Rio de Janeiro (Inter-American Treaty of Reciprocal Assistance, 1947), the militaries of the United States and Latin America pledged to combat communism. The United States began training tens of thousands of Latin American military officers over the next several decades. Those officers also imbibed the Cold War vision of the time and believed their mission was to combat "subversion," primarily among their own citizens, in what they came to view as a true war.

The aspirations of the post–World War II period were symbolized in the project of Brasília. In 1956, President Juscelino Kubitschek announced plans to move the capital from Rio de Janeiro on the coast to the interior of the country. The idea was to advance "fifty years in five," he said. Lúcio Costa (planner), Oscar Niemeyer (architect), and Roberto Burle Marx (landscape architect) produced elegant highly

Brasília's legislature building. © Mario Roberto Duran Ortiz.

modern designs. The construction was completed in forty-one months, on time for the dedication in 1960. The moment of Brazil, and by extension, of Latin America, seemed to have arrived.

FURTHER READING

Halperin Donghi (1993) surveys post-independence history with attention to individual countries. For economic history since independence, see Bulmer-Thomas (1994), and for the twentieth century, Thorp (1998). Krauze (1997) traces modern Mexican history through the prism of successive presidencies.

The Zigzag Path to Democracy and Development

With its rationalistic layout and ultramodern buildings, Brasília symbolized the hopes for development a half century ago. After the relatively quick rebuilding of Europe and Japan in the wake of World War II, a similar effort could and should be undertaken to speed the development of those countries that were now being called "underdeveloped." The rich countries, and particularly the United States, could assist with aid programs and know-how. The rapid construction of Brasília suggested that great strides could be made.

Flaws soon appeared in the sleek new city, however. The planners had assumed that the residents would be government employees and would travel by private auto, and had therefore not made provision for sidewalks. Nor had they planned for poor people, many thousands of whom were soon living in satellite cities of favelas. The rationalistic design of the planners, segregating residential from business areas and assigning different businesses to different areas, was another miscalculation.[1]

By the mid- to late 1960s, many Latin Americans, particularly intellectuals, were disillusioned with the prospects for development. Despite signs of progress—roads and dams, schools and clinics, transistor radios and television sets—the benefits seemed to flow to a narrow group of elites. Small farmers in the countryside languished; shantytowns multiplied in the cities faster than they could be supplied with urban services. Economic growth was insufficient to provide jobs for an ever-growing workforce. The sign of the future might not be Brasília but Havana.

Cuba, where a socialist revolution had taken power, seemed to offer an alternative: the island was organized around meeting the basic needs of all Cubans, and within a few years it seemed to be showing impressive results in improving people's welfare. Socialism as a system had a plausibility in the 1960s that is difficult to imagine today. Roughly half the earth's population was under some form of state socialism, not only the Soviet Union and Eastern Europe but also China, India, and various other Asian and African countries. Socialism seemed especially effective in launching basic industries like steel and cement, and in providing schooling and health care on a massive scale, even though it did not produce attractive consumer goods.[2]

Radical critics claimed that the capitalist economic system was controlled by the wealthy nations of North America and Europe, which kept the Third World, including Latin America, in a situation of subservience, assigned to providing raw materials in an unjust international division of labor. Domestically, the local elites, large landholders or owners of large businesses, were able to live in luxury while most people remained poor. Their criticism was fueled by an element of nationalism. "Development," as conventionally conceived, seemed to suggest pursuing a mirage, a poorer version of the "American way of life," which was in fact unattainable. Third World nations had no chance of "catching up" with the First World under capitalism. If they needed to forge a new kind of egalitarian society, nothing short of revolution would suffice. Latin American economic elites, governments, and the military, along with the US government, interpreted the critique and grassroots organizing as a threat to the present order and reacted accordingly; by the mid-1970s, two-thirds of Latin Americans were under repressive authoritarian rule. This chapter outlines how Latin American nations have pursued development in the course of the last half century.

CUBA IN THE 1960s

Cuba had remained a Spanish colony through the nineteenth century after other countries gained independence. The US war against Spain (1898) had thwarted the existing independence movement and had made Cuba a protectorate of the United States. The economy revolved around sugar plantations, many of which were in American hands. By the 1950s, Cuba was also a playground for American celebrities and gangsters, under the dictatorship of Fulgencio Batista. In 1953, a young lawyer named Fidel Castro was jailed for a failed attempt at revolution; upon his release, he went to Mexico where he gathered others around him, including the young Argentine physician Ernesto "Che" Guevara. In 1956, with several dozen rebels, they sailed from Mexico and landed in Cuba but were attacked by the army; only about twenty survived. They forged ties with peasants and with resistance movements in the cities, added recruits, and began to engage Batista's army. Although they were never numerous, the rebels grew bolder; support for Batista dried up; and in early January 1959, Castro and his troops entered Havana.

The revolution quickly became radicalized both in Cuba and in relation to other countries, particularly toward the United States. Hundreds of figures from the Batista regime were given summary trials, and many were executed by firing squad. Lands and businesses were nationalized, especially those that were foreign owned. The island was now being governed by people in their thirties, wearing fatigues rather than business suits. Former government officials, the wealthy, and professionals soon fled the island.[3]

In 1961, a CIA-organized invasion by a Cuban exile army failed disastrously at the Bay of Pigs. The next year, when Soviet missiles were discovered in Cuba, President John F. Kennedy and Premier Nikita Khrushchev engaged in a nuclear showdown, until the USSR agreed to withdraw the missiles in return for certain conditions,

Fidel Castro and crowd on the way to Havana, 1959. © Burt Glinn, Magnum Photos.

including a pledge from the United States not to invade Cuba. The Kennedy administration isolated Cuba with an economic boycott (prohibiting US trade) and had Cuba expelled from the Organization of American States (OAS). Under US pressure, most Latin American governments broke diplomatic relations with Cuba; the major exception was Mexico, which maintained relations out of nationalism, the principle of nonintervention, and concerns for its own domestic left. Cuba entered into closer, albeit not always harmonious, ties with the Soviet Union.

Ordinary poor Cubans soon enjoyed significant benefits. In the 1960 literacy campaign, schools closed for several months, and young people went to the countryside to teach peasants to read and write. Illiteracy was drastically reduced, and, just as significantly, the young volunteers encountered rural poverty firsthand. Schools were built in the countryside, and by the end of the decade, virtually all Cuban children were attending them. Likewise, hospitals and clinics were built and doctors were educated, even as large numbers of existing physicians went into exile. Although wages were low, all Cuban households were guaranteed a monthly supply of basic rations. Soon Cuban longevity approached that of developing countries, while it lagged in most of the rest of Latin America, where children still commonly died of preventable diseases.

In an effort to move away from sugar dependency, the country sought to diversify agriculture and to attempt rapid import-substitution industrialization under

Minister of the Economy Ernesto Guevara (who had no training in economics). After rising trade imbalances demonstrated the failure of that course, the strategy switched back to sugar exportation in 1964. The Soviet Union agreed to buy sugar and supply petroleum on preferential terms.

The fact that Cuba had come into the Soviet orbit did not prevent the Cuban government and the USSR from having disagreements. Under the influence of Che Guevara, the revolution proposed the ideal of a socialist "New Man," for whom moral incentives were more important than the material incentives of pay, and hence great emphasis was placed on volunteer campaigns to build houses or cut sugarcane. The Cuban leadership also encouraged further revolutions in Latin America, while the Soviets did not believe they would succeed.

Given the crucial role of sugar in the island's economic strategy, Castro set a target of producing 10 million tons in the 1970 harvest. Despite massive mobilization, the harvest only yielded 8.5 million tons, a record figure but far below what had been attempted. Several reasons for the failure could be cited: sugar equipment had not been maintained, the country had lost experienced managers, sugar-refining capacity had declined, and many of the field workers were unskilled volunteers from the civilian population and the armed forces. Appearing before a mass audience in the Plaza of the Revolution, Fidel Castro accepted responsibility for the failure and theatrically offered to resign, but the crowd urged him to continue.

After the 1970 failure, a chastened Fidel Castro found himself moving closer to the Soviets, with whom he entered into a grand bargain: Cuba would supply sugar to the USSR, which for its part would pay guaranteed above-market prices and would supply petroleum and other goods, thereby making it possible to make long-term development plans. For the next twenty years, the Cuban Revolution became institutionalized along Soviet lines, and with subsidies from the USSR, seemed to make steady progress in meeting the basic needs of Cubans. In the 1970s, Cuba became more cautious about supporting guerrilla movements, and one by one other Latin American countries reestablished diplomatic relations with and allowed travel to Cuba.

From the standpoint of the present, it may be difficult to understand why the Cuban model seemed attractive to other Latin Americans: What was the appeal of a dictatorship within the Soviet orbit that jailed or exiled its critics and was obviously an economic failure?

The most obvious reason was the benefits brought to ordinary Cubans in terms of economic security, education, and health care, in comparison to the situation of the poor elsewhere. To illustrate the point, in the mid-1970s, Brazil's per capita GDP was double that of Cuba; skyscrapers were rising in its cities, and it manufactured automobiles, buses, and aircraft. Nevertheless, if one had to choose between being reborn randomly as an infant in Brazil or Cuba, the latter would be the more rational choice in terms of survival and meeting basic needs.

That Cuba was a dictatorship with crucial decision-making power in the hands of one man was undeniable. However, "democracy" elsewhere was limited to periodic elections of governments that seemed to serve elite interests, and by the 1970s, other countries were increasingly in the hands of murderous dictatorships. If Fidel Castro was a dictator, he was not along the lines of the traditional kleptocrat like Anastasio Somoza in Nicaragua. Castro's notorious four-hour speeches were often lessons in history or economic development, and he exemplified some features of the classic

TABLE 12.1. Course of the Cuban Revolution

1953	Fidel Castro jailed after failed attempt at insurrection; later released; goes to Mexico to continue plotting
1956	Boatload of revolutionaries arrive from Mexico, almost wiped out, but survivors establish ties with peasantry and urban opposition
1959	Batista flees and revolutionaries take power; early tensions with existing elites and US government
1960	Literacy campaign
1961	Bay of Pigs invasion
1962	Missile Crisis—United States and USSR come close to nuclear war
1964	Cuba expelled from OAS
1960s	Economy nationalized—Cuba encourages revolution elsewhere, contrary to views of USSR
1967	Che Guevara killed in Bolivia
1970	Attempt at 10-million-ton sugar harvest fails
1970s	Revolution institutionalized—relationship with USSR more solid
1980	Mariel Boatlift—Castro allows tens of thousands to leave Cuba
1989–1991	End of communism in Eastern Europe and USSR—Cuba unexpectedly forced to survive without Soviet subsidies; Castro declares a "Special Period in Time of Peace"; living standards fall
2000s	Alliance formed with Venezuela
2006	Castro in failing health; presidency passed to Raúl Castro in 2008
2010s	Reforms promised but are enacted very timidly
2014	After secret negotiations fostered by Vatican diplomacy, Presidents Obama and Castro declare intention to end embargo and renew diplomatic relations
2014–2015	Presidents Obama and Castro take steps toward intensifying contacts, ending the embargo, and renewing diplomatic relations between the United States and Cuba

populist. A further attractive feature was nationalism: Cuba seemed to have broken free of US domination and to be charting its own course.[4]

For a time Cuba seemed to be a center of artistic creation. Asked about the role of art in Cuba, Castro replied, "Within the revolution, anything; against the revolution, nothing": writers and artists were free to pursue their inspiration, provided it did not become counterrevolutionary. The Casa de las Américas awarded prizes for fiction and poetry from Latin American countries. Some of that luster was lost with the imprisonment of the poet Heberto Padilla in 1971, which prompted international protests and signaled a tightening of restrictions on expression. Nevertheless, some artists, like filmmaker Tomás Alea Gutiérrez and composer Leo Brouwer, continued to do significant work. Ordinary Cubans had access to art and music lessons and performances.

Guerrilla movements attempting to follow the Cuban model arose in a number of countries in the 1960s. Most were quickly suppressed, but serious rural guerrilla movements continued in Colombia, Venezuela, Guatemala, and Peru; all were Marxist in orientation but were not led by orthodox communist parties connected to the USSR. For some years, the prevailing strategy was to establish a guerrilla *foco* (focal point) in the countryside, win the loyalty of the peasantry, and encircle the cities, as it was believed had been done in Cuba (and previously in China). In late 1966, Che Guevara and a band of revolutionaries clandestinely entered Bolivia, hoping to ignite a revolution that would spread through South America. However, they failed to secure the adherence of local peasants or the Bolivian Communist Party. With CIA and US Army Ranger assistance, the Bolivian army surrounded them, and Guevara was wounded, captured, and executed in August 1967. Urban guerrilla groups arose in Brazil, Argentina, and Uruguay in the late 1960s and early 1970s, but they were ruthlessly crushed. US-led efforts to prevent "another Cuba" had apparently succeeded.

UNDER THE MILITARY BOOT

For a brief period, Chile seemed to offer a promise that the kinds of changes revolutionaries sought could be won peacefully, through the ballot box.[5] In the 1970 election, a socialist coalition headed by Salvador Allende won a narrow victory over two other parties. Because the opposition parties had a majority in the legislature, Allende could act only through existing legislation, such as speeding up the pace of land reform already on the books. Minimum wages were raised, and health care and schooling received more funding. The arts flourished, and it was a time of street demonstrations and protest music, when change seemed possible.

The Nixon administration opposed Allende from the beginning, pressuring international agencies to cut off loans to Chile. The CIA poured millions of dollars into opposition activities, particularly strikes and other actions intended to destabilize the country. By 1972, inflation was rising and middle-class women were organizing marches while banging pots and pans. Nevertheless, Allende's Popular Unity coalition received even more votes in elections.

Bombing of the presidential palace, La Moneda, by the Chilean Air Force, September 11, 1973, Santiago, Chile. © AP Images.

On September 11, 1973, the Chilean armed forces carried out a coup (stunning many Chileans who thought their long democratic tradition would make that impossible). President Allende and some close advisors were in the presidential palace when it was strafed and bombed; Allende then took his own life.[6] Troops immediately set about rounding up thousands of Allende supporters. Well over a thousand people were tortured and killed in the first few months, and the practice continued for well over a decade. The media were muzzled, congress was closed, tens of thousands went into exile. The military dictatorship, led by Gen. Augusto Pinochet, crushed spirits not only in Chile but throughout Latin America.

Brazil had already been under dictatorship since a coup in 1964. Argentina had oscillated between civilian and military governments since the ouster of Perón in 1955. Perón returned in 1973 and became president in 1974, but he died in office in less than a year, and was replaced by his wife, the vice president, who governed by relying on her advisors. In 1976, on the grounds that the country was threatened by subversion, the military overthrew her, took direct control, and stepped up its "dirty war" against opposition forces, especially young activists. Its distinguishing feature was forced "disappearance": after being abducted and tortured, the victim was buried or dropped in the sea, leaving loved ones in a state of uncertainty for years. At least nine thousand people disappeared, and some estimates go much higher.

The following military regimes were in control during the twenty-five-year period of 1964–1989:

- Brazil (1964–1985)
- Bolivia (1964–1980; military governments alternating with unstable civilian administrations)
- Peru (1968–1980)
- Panama (1968–1989)
- Ecuador (1972–1979)
- Chile (1973–1989)
- Uruguay (1973–1984)
- Argentina (1976–1983)

In the 1970s, more and more Latin Americans came under direct military rule. Although most of these were right-wing regimes, Peru and Panama were under left-wing populist military governments, as was Bolivia for a short period. At one point, Uruguay, a democratic middle-class country with a welfare state for many decades, had the highest ratio of political prisoners in the world. In some countries, the mechanisms of elections and legislatures were retained, but the real power was in the hands of the military (Guatemala, El Salvador, Honduras). Nicaragua and Paraguay were under old-fashioned personal dictatorships. By 1975, only four Latin American countries (Mexico, Colombia, Venezuela, and Costa Rica) were under elected civilian governments. Brutal military regimes that abducted, tortured, and killed with impunity had become the norm.

These regimes were unlike the classic dictatorships run by a caudillo or strongman; they were institutional in the sense that it was the army or the armed forces as a whole that was the basic arbiter in society, and they typically had mechanisms for transferring power in an orderly way. Thus Brazil was headed by a series of five generals over twenty-one years, each of whom was designated by the officer corps and duly presented for election against acquiescent civilian political parties.

In each case, the military decided to take power when the civilian government seemed to be losing its grip and the nation was descending into chaos. The coups enjoyed support from the upper and middle classes and others who longed for order; the "chaos" was typically massive street protests by the militant left: students, workers, slum dwellers, and small farmers. Upon taking power, the military could claim to be "saving" the nation and defending "western Christian civilization." Brazilian military ideologues elaborated a National Security Doctrine, according to which Latin America stood on the front lines of a worldwide war against Marxist subversion. The armed forces had the key role in maintaining internal security and defeating enemies, who were seen to be everywhere. Technocrats were brought into governments to achieve development conceived of in terms of national security.

These military regimes could rely on support from successive US administrations, which viewed Latin America in terms of its own Cold War with the Soviet Union. As early as the Rio Pact (1947), the militaries pledged to defend the hemisphere against communism; that urgency intensified after the Cuban Revolution. Tens of thousands of officers and troops were trained by the US military at the School of the Americas in the Panama Canal Zone and elsewhere. In addition to what they learned about military doctrines and strategies, procedures, and equipment, Latin American officers imbibed a grandiose sense of mission. The "enemy" was not a foreign army—in the two centuries since independence, Latin American nations have rarely gone to war with one another—but domestic "subversives" and their ideas. In the hour of crisis, they felt called to step in to save the nation.

By the mid-1970s, the armed forces of Argentina, Bolivia, Brazil, Chile, Paraguay, and Uruguay were coordinating their actions against what they regarded as international communist subversion, particularly sharing information on exiles in each others' countries in what was called Operation Condor. US military and intelligence agencies assisted with technical information, and the State Department was cognizant of what was happening. In September 1976, the Chilean exile Orlando Letelier, a former ambassador to the United States and foreign minister, and his American colleague Ronni Moffitt, were killed by a car bomb in downtown Washington, DC, in an action that was traced to the Chilean intelligence agency. The outrageous nature of that attack gradually caused the US government to pull back from its support of the Pinochet regime and military governments generally. Under President Jimmy Carter, human rights concerns began to influence US policy in Latin America, but the Reagan administration explicitly reversed that thrust in the name of security.

These regimes systematically practiced abduction, torture, murder, and "disappearance" with impunity. During the worst periods of repression, the Catholic Church was the only institution that could offer some space of resistance. In Chile, the Vicariate of Solidarity gathered testimonies on deaths and disappearances and filed them in the Chilean courts, fully aware that no action would be taken. Under Church sponsorship, soup kitchens were started to help families deal with increased unemployment and poverty. As noted in chapter 8, the Mothers of the Plaza de Mayo were the only group to publicly oppose the "dirty war" by the Argentine military at its height.

Many tens of thousands were forced into exile from Brazil, Chile, Argentina, Uruguay, and elsewhere. Careers were ruined, and spirits were crushed. Torture victims continued to suffer psychologically for years afterward.[7] It is no exaggeration to say that a generation of young Latin Americans was lost in various countries.

Not all countries followed the path of military rule. After 1940, Mexico ceased to be revolutionary as the PRI managed the nation under state-sponsored industrialization. The problem of political succession was "solved" through a system whereby each president picked his successor, and the country went from six-year term to six-year term, as the PRI always defeated the conservative Partido Acción Nacional (PAN; National Action Party). After the 1968 massacre of an estimated three hundred student demonstrators in the plaza of Tlatelolco in Mexico City, PRI rule began to lose its luster, but it held on to power for three more decades.

In Venezuela, two parties, the Acción Democrática (AD; Democratic Action) and the Comité de Organización Política Electoral Independiente (COPEI; Christian Democratic), alternated peacefully in power. Politics was lubricated by abundant petroleum revenues. Venezuela (along with Argentina and Panama) had a per capita income considerably above the Latin American average, but unequal distribution meant that many lived in rural or urban poverty.

In Colombia, the armed struggle between Liberals and Conservatives (La Violencia) unleashed by the assassination of Gaitán in 1948 ended in 1958 with an agreement (called the Frente Nacional/National Front) between the two parties to alternate in the presidency and equally divide cabinet positions for the next sixteen years. In the 1960s, new Marxist guerrilla groups arose, two of which (FARC, Fuerzas Armadas Revolucionarias de Colombia, and ELN, Ejército de Liberación Nacional) were still active fifty years later. In the 1970s and 1980s, Colombian drug organizations set up networks between coca growers in Peru and Bolivia, processors in Colombia, and distributors in the United States and elsewhere. Right-wing paramilitary groups were organized with military connivance, starting in the 1980s, ostensibly to combat leftist guerrillas, but the victims were largely labor leaders and other civilians. The upshot was a war between various armed actors: Colombian military and police, left-wing guerrillas, right-wing paramilitaries, and drug traffickers—with various ties among them. The losers were the civilian population. By 1990 in Medellín and elsewhere, young assassins (*sicarios*) would kill for $50, unafraid of government forces but fearing fellow assassins. An estimated four million Colombians were forced to flee from their homes and lands.

In 1968, a military coup overthrew the elected president of Peru and installed Gen. Juan Velasco Alvarado, who led an attempt at top-down authoritarian reform. Land reform ended the power of large landholders on the Pacific coast but did little for the indigenous people of the highlands. Rather than simply combat new urban invasions, the government tried to assist them, labeling them *pueblos jóvenes* (young towns). Many industries, especially in natural resource extraction, were nationalized. Velasco was unseated by another military coup in 1975, which led the way back to civilian rule in 1980. Ecuador and Bolivia likewise seesawed between civilian and military governments after the mid-1960s, some of them highly repressive.

CENTRAL AMERICAN AGONY

In July 1979, a revolution led by the Sandinista National Liberation Front overthrew the Somoza dictatorship in Nicaragua. As had happened in Cuba twenty years earlier, young revolutionaries in fatigues cruised the capital city in vehicles abandoned by the dictator's fleeing army. Similar revolutionary movements seemed poised to take power in El Salvador and possibly Guatemala. Struggles for power and US involvement in them continued in Central America for a decade.[8]

These countries had several features in common: they were small (Guatemala, the largest, had seven million people at the time), their economies were built around the export of tropical crops, and all were situated in what the United States regarded as its sphere of influence. All had been under oppressive regimes: the Somoza dictatorship in Nicaragua and de facto military rule in Guatemala and El Salvador.

The Somozas had ruled Nicaragua directly or indirectly since the 1930s, when Anastasio Somoza was placed in charge of the National Guard created by US Marines before they ended their occupation. The Sandinistas were founded in the 1960s, but they remained small and clandestine and had little impact until the 1970s, when the public began to object to Somoza's large-scale profiteering in the reconstruction after the 1972 earthquake that leveled downtown Managua. An uprising in 1977 was put down with tanks and bombing, thereby stirring up more opposition and escalating confrontation; in mid-1979, Somoza fled the country and his National Guard fell apart.

Vowing not to repeat Cuba's mistakes, the Sandinistas sought to maintain a mixed (private and state) economy, to have cordial relations with many countries rather than ally with the USSR, and to avoid one-man rule. However, the honeymoon was short: in less than a year, business groups, political parties, and the Catholic hierarchy began to oppose the Sandinistas. Although some went into exile, most opponents of the Sandinistas remained in Nicaragua and maintained open opposition in political parties, business associations, and the press. The CIA and the Reagan administration organized and funded a counterrevolutionary army (the *contras*), which carried out raids in Nicaragua from bases in Honduras and Costa Rica. The Sandinistas themselves alienated some of their potential constituency, particularly the Miskito Indians on the Atlantic coast and many small farmers. By 1983, the country was highly polarized, and the government was spending revenue primarily on defense rather than development.

The Reagan administration viewed the situation as a threat to US security,[9] as irrational as it was to think that a country with one-eightieth of the US population and one-thousandth of its GDP could be a "threat." The US government funded the *contra* army and sought to isolate Nicaragua. Mines laid by the CIA in the Nicaraguan port of Corinto damaged several vessels, leading to a 1986 ruling against the United States in the World Court. By contrast, European and Latin American governments maintained normal relations with the Sandinista government.

In El Salvador, mass opposition movements of peasants, workers, slum dwellers, and students had been marching in the streets since 1975 and had been met by violence from official forces and from death squads operating with impunity. In October 1979, a group of reformist military officers carried out a coup and promised revolutionary changes, clearly hoping to stave off a Nicaragua-style revolution. In fact, violent repression increased to the point where hundreds of people were being killed each month. The civilian reformers resigned from the junta and joined the opposition. In March 1980, after he appealed to soldiers not to kill their unarmed peasant brothers and sisters, Archbishop Óscar Romero was murdered while saying Mass.

The country slid toward civil war, which broke out formally in January 1981. The Reagan administration backed the Salvadoran military and government with what became billions of dollars and was thoroughly involved in the country's internal politics, pressing for elections and rebuffing proposals for a negotiated settlement. Over the next decade, the Frente Farabundo Martí para la Liberación Nacional (FMLN; Farabundo Martí National Liberation Front) guerrillas occupied territory along the Honduran border and fought the military to a stalemate. Meanwhile, civilians were killed by the tens of thousands.

In Guatemala, after several years of grassroots militancy and a growing guerrilla movement, in 1981 the army launched a systematic offensive, first against urban opposition networks and then in the countryside against indigenous areas where the guerrillas had carried out attacks against the army. By one count, the army carried out 440 massacres of Indian populations, in some instances of hundreds of people. The army forced all males in these areas to take part in "civilian patrols," in effect forcing them to act as a buffer between itself and the guerrillas. In 1982, the Guatemalan Catholic bishops estimated that a million people—mostly indigenous—had been uprooted from their homes. The brutal tactics worked: by 1983, the guerrillas had lost civilian support and were on the defensive, although peace processes only began years later.

Throughout the 1980s, various peace initiatives were proposed for individual countries and for Central America as a whole, by other governments and by church groups, but they were all thwarted by the Reagan administration. What brought an end to the conflicts, besides fatigue, was a change in the context, the collapse of communism in Eastern Europe and thus the Cold War justification. The November 1989 murder of six Jesuits, their housekeeper, and her daughter by the elite US-trained Atlacatl Battalion in El Salvador in the midst of a guerrilla offensive showed the bankruptcy of US support for the Salvadoran military. In March 1990, the Sandinistas were voted out of office.

The human cost had been high. A UN commission estimated that 75,000 Salvadorans had lost their lives in the civil war, 85 percent at the hands of official forces, 10 percent from the death squads, and 5 percent from the left. The figure often cited for Guatemala over its three decades and more of conflict was 200,000, although precise figures are impossible to obtain. An estimate for Nicaragua in both the anti-Somoza struggle and the 1980s is 50,000 dead.

One legacy of the wars of the 1980s is the large-scale migration of Central Americans to the United States; they now number around 2.9 million people, two-thirds of them from El Salvador and Guatemala. Unfortunately, in the two decades since the end of hostilities, some problems in their homelands, far from being resolved, have been compounded, especially by ineffective and corrupt governments in Nicaragua, Honduras, and Guatemala. Poor governance and a failure to develop economic opportunities help account for the expansion of criminal organizations in the region and for the flow of migrants northward.[10]

Jesuits murdered by US-trained Salvadoran troops, El Salvador, November 1989. © Central American Jesuits.

RETURN OF CIVILIAN RULE

In 1982, the Argentine armed forces launched an attack on the Malvinas (Falkland) Islands, in the south Atlantic over 300 miles from Patagonia, inhabited by a few thousand British-descended sheepherders, which the country had long claimed as its territory. The attack was partly motivated by a desire to stoke nationalism and distract the public from domestic economic problems. To their surprise, the British sent troops and delivered a resounding defeat.[11] Thus humiliated, the military scheduled elections with civilian parties the next year and retired from direct rule, after first issuing an amnesty that would have the effect of protecting them from prosecution for crimes committed during the "dirty war" against the left.

Although it was not clear at the time, that was one in a series of steps whereby the military ceded control of politics to civilians in country after country. Civilian control returned in Peru and Bolivia in 1980. After a constitution proposed by the Uruguayan military was rejected in a 1980 referendum, elections were scheduled for 1984, and civilian government returned. In a carefully calibrated process lasting over a decade, the Brazilian military relinquished control by allowing the indirect election of a civilian president in 1985. In 1988, the Pinochet government held a simple "yes" or "no" plebiscite over whether the military government should continue; the "no" voters won and in 1989 an anti-Pinochet coalition won the presidency and congress (and remained in power until 2010). In 1989, an army coup ended the thirty-five-year rule of Gen. Alfredo Stroessner in Paraguay, leading to the election of a civilian president in 1993.

In the 1988 presidential election in Mexico, when a left-wing coalition seemed to be on the verge of victory, the government claimed a computer crash, and then engineered a narrow PRI victory. Around that time, opposition parties began to be allowed to win some governorships and mayoral posts. After electoral reforms in the 1990s, the PAN (National Action Party) candidate, Vicente Fox, won the presidency in 2000, marking the end of seven decades of PRI rule.

Initially, many Latin Americans suspected that these changes would be another fluctuation in the long-standing seesawing between civilian and military governments in their region. Over time, however, it has become clear that procedural democracy—change of political power through fair elections with agreed-upon rules—has taken firm hold. The actual circumstances of the end of military or authoritarian rule varied from country to country, but taken together, they formed part of a larger movement.[12] The economic difficulties resulting from the debt crisis of the 1980s made the armed forces more willing to relinquish direct governance.

Grassroots movements played a role in the return to civilian rule, but they cannot be said to have been the primary factor. In Argentina, there had been virtually no public opposition until the Malvinas War—the Mothers of the Plaza de Mayo were an important moral voice, but they were not a political force. In Chile, opposition to the Pinochet regime began to emerge publicly in the wake of the severe economic crisis of 1982, but even opponents of Pinochet were not confident of their strength at the start of the 1988 "No" campaign.[13]

One issue was what to do about the crimes committed under the authoritarian regimes. The armed forces believed that they had been defending "civilization," and that even the excesses of the "dirty wars" were justified. In Argentina, a government-appointed committee led by the novelist Ernesto Sábato examined human rights violations and published its findings in a book titled *Nunca Más* (Never Again). A book by the same title in Brazil was drawn from army reports of torture of individual victims discovered by human rights lawyers who came upon the files while pursuing legal action. With the backing of Church authorities, for several years they removed the papers overnight and photocopied them clandestinely.[14] In Chile, the civilian government formed a commission to gather information, which it then published in two massive volumes, taking each case of a murder or disappearance name by name, briefly describing the event, organized chronologically and tabulated. Similar "truth and reconciliation" commissions were formed in Uruguay, El Salvador, Guatemala, and Peru under various auspices. The resulting reports were courageous because the militaries and their supporters regarded criticism of the armed forces as traitorous.[15] Particularly in the early years before democracy took hold, many feared that, if provoked, the military could return to power.

Although such commissions might be able to tell the truth that had been suppressed, they did not bring justice: with very few exceptions, the perpetrators of the atrocities were not brought to trial. In Argentina, a few top officers were arrested in the 1990s but were later pardoned by President Carlos Menem. Virtually no one was brought to justice in Guatemala or El Salvador.

In 1998, the British government arrested Gen. Pinochet in London in response to a request from the Spanish government to extradite him to stand trial for crimes against Spanish citizens. Pinochet was eventually allowed to return to Chile, but the event stirred the Chilean justice system to begin to consider complaints filed there for human rights crimes during the dictatorship. The general pattern, however, is that the crimes were committed with an impunity that lasted for decades, thereby having a corrupting influence on the practice of justice in these societies.

In many instances, the subsequent performance of civilian governments served to tarnish the idea of democracy. In Brazil, the administration of Fernando Collor de Mello, an obscure but flamboyant provincial governor elected president in 1989, became a soap opera of corruption, excess, and sex scandals that ended in his impeachment in 1992. The next year, Venezuelan president Carlos Andrés Pérez was forced to step down; the immediate reason was accusations of corruption, but the deeper reason was frustration over the inability of either of the country's main parties to make oil wealth benefit ordinary people. In 1992, Peruvian president Alberto Fujimori engineered a "self-coup," suspending congress and ruling by decree for the better part of a decade. He won reelection and remained popular until tapes showing his top aide, Vladimiro Montesinos, paying bribes were made public. In opinion polls, popular support for democracy waxed and waned, and a significant portion of the population said it would be willing to accept an authoritarian nondemocratic government if it could establish order and produce results.

During the process of returning to democracy, many spoke of the emergence of "civil society," referring to grassroots social movements and NGOs (nongovernmental organizations), which were proliferating.[16] To some extent, civil society arose during the state repression of the 1970s and 1980s (the Mothers of the Disappeared; soup kitchens in poor neighborhoods during hard economic times). Movements were often the outgrowth of grassroots church work or idealistic and radicalized university students or young people. Community members would express their needs, a program would be devised, and funding sought, perhaps from a church organization or from a European development agency.[17] Over time, the project could become independent, with its own staffing and funding. Outside organizers typically saw individual projects as part of what they hoped was a larger movement toward fundamental change. The aim was not simply to solve a local problem, such as to help small farmers get better yields, but to forge links between organizations so as to create mass popular movements. By the same token, intelligence agencies often branded such work as "subversive."

These NGOs evolved over time in response to changing circumstances. In El Salvador, people who had devoted themselves to the revolution in the 1980s expanded their work in the 1990s.[18] Likewise, when the Sandinistas surprisingly lost the 1990 election, many Nicaraguans who had devoted a decade of their life to the revolution hastened to create NGOs in health, education, development, agriculture, or the environment, and wrote funding proposals to continue their work. In Oaxaca, Mexico, when a progressive bishop retired and his replacement systematically went about dismantling work that had been done under Church aegis, the activists likewise sought to continue what they had been doing in the form of secular NGOs. In Brazil and Chile, left-wing governments often hired activists from NGOs.

In short, the Latin American NGO movement had its origins in opposition movements and culture. Individual projects such as improving agricultural techniques or building houses were seen as means to the larger aim of grassroots mobilization, and that itself was regarded as a step toward a qualitatively different kind of society.

Popular movements networked among themselves. The World Social Forum (WSF), which first met in Porto Alegre, Brazil, in 2001, consciously saw itself as a kind of worldwide civil society, in opposition to the annual meeting of the World Economic Forum, a meeting of elites by invitation, held annually in January in Davos, Switzerland. The Brazilian Partido dos Trabalhadores (PT; Workers' Party) was a sponsor of the first meeting, and it was held in a city governed by the PT, which was experimenting with "participatory budgets." From its inception, the WSF has avoided enforcing a single line of thought or action, and it is thus a meeting ground for many social movements (agricultural, environmental, indigenous) in opposition to "neoliberalism"; it was often branded as "antiglobalization," but its participants would say that they are in favor of "globalization from below."

DEBT CRISIS AND GLOBALIZATION

In August 1982, the Mexican government surprised the world by announcing that it could not meet its debt payments and would suspend them for ninety days. As it became clear that a number of countries were overindebted and that the banks themselves were dangerously exposed, the "Latin American debt crisis" was believed to be threatening the international financial system. For the next decade and beyond, governments, banks, and international lending agencies struggled to deal with the crisis, focusing first on the banks, not on the human consequences. What ensued was a "lost decade" of falling growth and greater poverty.

Governments had been borrowing for decades, particularly from international agencies and donor governments (foreign aid was often in the form of loans with favorable terms). A typical case was lending at lower than market rates for infrastructure projects like roads or a dam—it is analogous to a household taking out a loan to finance a car. However, with sharp oil price hikes in 1973 and 1979, Middle Eastern oil countries enjoyed a windfall of dollars, which they deposited in commercial banks, particularly in the United States. Eager to lend this money, these banks found willing borrowers in governments, especially in Latin America, since loans to governments are regarded as safe. Some governments spent the money on worthwhile long-term projects, but others used it to pay current expenses.

Even by 1980 banks were seeing danger signs and becoming less willing to lend. When the US Federal Reserve sharply raised interest rates to reduce inflation domestically, the cost of servicing the debt rose. Governments could no longer obtain loans, and large-scale capital flight began. In the worldwide recession of the early 1980s, demand for Latin American exports fell. Mexico was the first to declare that it could not meet its obligations.

Three parties to the crisis—the banks, international lending agencies, and the debtor countries—then engaged in negotiations for the better part of the decade. The International Monetary Fund (IMF) came to play a key role. As conditions for further loans, Latin American governments were told that they had to bring spending into line with revenues. To do that, governments had to reduce payroll, cut services, and privatize state-owned enterprises. The justification for the latter was that the sale would produce immediate one-time revenues, which could be used for debt reduction, and that often these enterprises were overstaffed, inefficient, and losing money. Understandably, privatization was opposed by nationalists and especially by the employees of state companies.

Opponents often used the debt crisis to criticize the international financial system and its agents (US government, World Bank, Inter-American Development Bank, and so forth) on moral grounds: governments were paying off billions in loans when basic services to the poor were being cut. Why should the poor be forced to pay for loans acquired by unrepresentative governments for projects that did not benefit them? President Alan García of Peru (1985–1990) vowed that his country would pay no more than 10 percent of its GDP to service its debt. For a short time there was talk of a "debtors' cartel": if Third World countries stood together, they could force the banks to cancel their debts.

Seen from Latin America, it seemed as though the IMF and World Bank, under the aegis of the United States, were dictating to their governments. It is true that at particular junctures, different governments were forced to make important policy changes in order to obtain crucially needed loans. Critics spoke of a neoliberal economic model being forced upon Latin America. A convenient target was the "Washington Consensus," a list of ten policies drawn up by the British economist John Williamson in 1989. The economic disaster of the "lost decade" was taken as proof that the model did not work.

However, that may be a shortsighted way of understanding events. Consider the cases of China and India, the two largest economies in the world, one governed by the Communist Party, the other the world's largest democracy. For decades, each had pursued internal development with a state-directed economy. In 1978, after the death of Mao Zedong, the Chinese Communist Party opted to open to international trade, motivated in part by the examples of Korea, Taiwan, Singapore, and other Asian countries, which were enjoying sustained rapid growth. The result has been the most dramatic rise from poverty in history. In the early 1990s, India made a similar shift toward a market-based economy. When taken together with the shift in the former Soviet Union and Eastern Europe after 1989–1991 and numerous other countries, it is clear that what Latin Americans call "neoliberalism" is part of a worldwide shift toward economic models that are market-based domestically and seek to be competitive internationally.[19]

One expression of the new economic situation has been trade agreements: NAFTA (1994—between the United States, Mexico, and Canada), MERCOSUR (1990s—Brazil, Argentina, Uruguay, and Paraguay), and many others.[20] The larger challenge facing Latin American economies was not which trade agreements to make or sign, but how to produce globally competitive goods and services.

Countries continued to find themselves in economic crisis: Mexico in 1995, Brazil in 1998, and Argentina from 1998 to 2002. In Mexico's "tequila crisis," the currency dropped in value against the dollar by 50 percent in six months. The country fell into recession, banks failed, and some Mexicans defaulted on their loans as a result of higher interest rates. Even so, the country soon returned to growth. In 1999, Brazil likewise suffered a financial crisis, partly as a reflection of a severe financial crisis in Asia in 1998, which prompted investors to withdraw capital from emerging economies.

A more serious financial crisis occurred in Argentina, which had enjoyed relative prosperity in the 1990s after overcoming hyperinflation, in part by establishing a fixed exchange rate with the dollar. As recession hit in the late 1990s, the government was forced to establish severe austerity measures as a condition for further borrowing. As additional measures were instituted, an angry public began withdrawing money from bank accounts, prompting the government to freeze them for a year. People went to the streets in protest in late 2001 and 2002, and the country saw five presidents within a two-week period. At the end of 2001, the government defaulted on most of its public debt, $132 billion. Unemployment rose to nearly 25 percent. In 2002 and into 2003, over half of Argentineans were below the official poverty rate, and a quarter were estimated to be at extreme poverty level (meaning not having enough to eat properly). This was an astonishing development in a largely middle-class urban country that had once been the wealthiest in Latin America. In some instances, workers took over factories that had been closed by their owners. After 2003, the economy rebounded, driven especially by demand for soy and other agricultural products.

LATIN AMERICA AT TWO HUNDRED

By the time Latin American countries began their bicentennials, reasons for optimism were not hard to find: the region had enjoyed a decade of growth; poverty rates were modestly declining; new middle classes were emerging; and all major political actors, including the military, seemed to agree that the procedures of democracy had to be observed. Analysts had been slow to recognize these developments,[21] but some observers were predicting that the 2010s would be the "decade of Latin America." In that vein, the Chilean businessman Raúl Rivera Andueza entitled his book on the region *Nuestra Hora* (Our Moment) (2011), to indicate that Latin America was finally taking its rightful place on the world stage.

Some of these developments have been traced elsewhere in this book, but they may seem surprising in light of Latin American history, the recent experience of dictatorship and repression, and the debt crisis of the 1980s. To some extent, such positive developments are the result of steady incremental processes such as urbanization: at the very least, the urban poor are generally better off than subsistence farmers. What began as shantytowns became neighborhoods; the children of those who came to the cities did better than their parents in schooling and employment; and their children advanced even further. As the pace of urbanization slowed, municipalities were able to extend urban services, such as sewer lines. By the end of the twentieth century, elementary school was virtually universal, and rates of secondary school and university attendance were rising.

A second perhaps technocratic but important achievement was the halting of inflation. Consider Brazil, where by the 1990s, inflation was ingrained in people's expectations through "indexation" (regular adjustments of prices and wages) so that the value of the currency declined significantly, making it difficult for households and businesses to plan for the future. Various plans to halt it had failed. In 1994, the finance minister Fernando Henrique Cardoso announced a plan with a new currency and an end to indexation. Inflation fell to almost negligible rates; businesses could now plan, and people's earnings no longer lost value. Other countries had also had high inflation and even hyperinflation. In the 1980s and 1990s, inflation in Latin American countries averaged 400 percent, but by the 2000s it was in single digits. Control of inflation was a reflection of better overall financial management in Latin America. One result was that Latin American countries were little affected by the financial crisis that affected North America and Europe starting in 2008.

Yet another reason was an export boom for Latin American products (agricultural, mining, and hydrocarbons), which began in the early 2000s, driven by rising demand from China and elsewhere. Those revenues helped Argentina recover from its 2001–2002 financial and political crisis. Brazil became a major agricultural exporter, rivaling the United States. Mining companies were increasing operations in almost all countries in the region (generally over the protests of indigenous people and environmentalists). The exports translated into revenues for governments and employment for their citizens, with the corresponding multiplier effect. By 2015, a slowing world economy, especially in China, was forcing Latin American countries to look beyond high commodity prices as a source of growth.

Latin American governments, whether they called themselves left or right, tended to act pragmatically. One example is the conditional cash transfers, mentioned elsewhere in this book. Some improvements came from initiatives on the state or municipal level, and governments increasingly emulated innovations that seemed to be successful elsewhere.

The next five chapters examine developments in economics, politics, governance, health and education, and international relations, and attempt to summarize lessons learned.

FURTHER READING

Jorge Castañeda (1993) presents a window into the Latin American left and argues that the collapse of communism left open the question of just what kind of capitalism was appropriate. Chapters 9–11 of Chasteen (2007) provide a tight narrative. Guillermoprieto (1994) and (2001) are vivid journalistic accounts of various countries at particular junctures in the 1980s and 1990s. LeoGrande (1998) surveys the conflicts of Central America and US involvement there; Brands (2010) sets Latin America in the Cold War context. On Cuba, see Pérez-Stable (1999). Constable and Valenzuela (1991) and the oral histories in Politzer (1989) capture well the feel of Chile in the 1980s. Preston and Dillon (2004) present a fascinating account of Mexico in the last three decades of the twentieth century, including power struggles within the ruling PRI.

PART III

Economic and Political Challenges of the Present

Toward Twenty-First-Century Economies

As noted at the end of the last chapter, by the second decade of the twenty-first century, most Latin American countries had enjoyed a decade or more of growth, inequality was modestly declining, and the middle classes were growing. Chile seemed to be on its way toward reaching the living standards of Portugal or Spain, and it had become anachronistic to think of Brazil as "underdeveloped." This period of growth may turn out to be temporary, driven largely by high prices for commodity exports, yet it is plausible that Latin American countries are finding their way toward sustained growth, as happened with smaller Asian countries several decades ago and more recently with China and India.

That possibility is the starting point of this chapter. The assumption is that nations can learn from one another, but that they must do so by taking into account their own situation: in the expression of the development economist Dani Rodrik (2007): "One economics, many recipes." We begin with some observations on the economic directions taken by various countries, and then attempt to distill lessons for the path ahead.

DIFFERENT APPROACHES

Economically, societies and nations have to start from the hand they have been dealt. Giant countries like Brazil (200 million) and Mexico (110 million) have internal markets large enough to sustain industries in automobiles or some consumer durables driven by domestic demand, a possibility denied in countries of only a few million people (e.g., Honduras or Paraguay). Most Latin American economies have been shaped historically by their insertion into an international trading system in which they supplied mining and agricultural products and imported manufactured goods. As noted in chapter 11, Latin American countries industrialized in the mid-twentieth century, albeit unevenly. But geography and history are not destiny—or need not be. Elements of economic success can be drawn from three different experiences: Chile, Brazil, and Costa Rica.

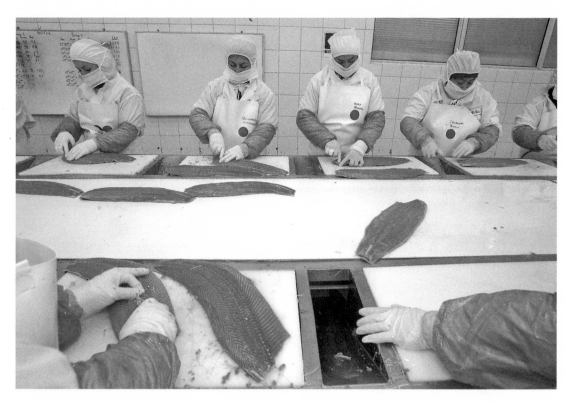

Workers preparing farm-grown salmon for sale as steaks, sushi, and filets on the world market, Puerto Montt, Chile. © Noah Friedman-Rudovsky.

Chile has been far more successful in diminishing poverty than the rest of Latin America. Over the 1975–2006 period, Chilean per capita income rose from 25 percent to 40 percent of that of the United States. That growth was driven by high prices for copper, which provides 20 percent of GDP and 60 percent of exports. Furthermore, because its central valley is similar to that of California but is in the southern hemisphere, Chile supplies California-type products to North America and Europe during the northern hemisphere winter, and does so using sophisticated technology from the field to the market. Salmon, wine, and timber products are also significant exports.

It is true that the "Chilean miracle" began during the Pinochet dictatorship and was proposed by the "Chicago Boys," Chilean economists who had imbibed Milton Friedman's extreme free-market doctrines. That is enough to condemn it in the eyes of the left, whereas some on the right celebrate Chile for pioneering the shift away from statism even before the Reagan-Thatcher revolution. The reality is more nuanced, however. The immediate effect of the first application of Chicago Boys medicine in 1975 (dropping of tariffs, privatization of state enterprises and health insurance and pensions) was a severe recession, as factories and businesses closed and many thousands lost their jobs. A recovery in the late 1970s was followed by another harsh recession in the early 1980s, at which point the government became more pragmatic. When a center-left coalition took power in 1990, it did not reverse the policies of the

Pinochet era, but it began to address the needs of the poor more directly with new social programs.

Chile is the most economically successful country in Latin America, aided unquestionably by high copper prices, but it has been Chilean businesspeople and their employees who seized the opportunities to supply world markets. They have been aided by sound policies. For example, when copper prices are high, governments are limited by a legislatively mandated formula in what they can spend; the rest must be invested in sovereign wealth funds, to be drawn on when conditions demand. The government drew on these funds during the post-2007 recession and for recovery from the 2010 earthquake. Chile has not resolved all its economic problems, however; approximately 15 percent of Chileans still live below the official poverty line.

For over a decade, **Brazil** has been recognized as one of the four "BRICs" (along with Russia, India, and China), that is, as an emerging powerhouse (by some reckonings, the sixth-largest economy in the world) and a favored spot for investment. In 2009, it had sufficient foreign reserves to offer the IMF credits; two decades previously it had required IMF assistance. It is the fourth-largest creditor of the United States. Brazil has the largest number of beef cattle in the world, double that of the United States. In earlier chapters, we have already noted some of the strengths of the Brazilian economy: the transformation of the *cerrado* region into a breadbasket rivaling the US Midwest; large *multilatinas* like Petrobras, Embraer, and AmBev; and an expanding middle class of consumers.

A key moment came in 1994 when inflation was finally tamed after decades in which it had been taken for granted and built into expectations and behavior. The stabilization of the currency made it possible for credit to be unleashed, both for businesses and for consumers. Starting in the 1990s, the economy turned outward to freer trade, and businesses and industries were forced to compete, although Brazil still has relatively high tariffs. According to the journalist Larry Rohter (2012), as a late starter in industrialization, Brazil has strategically sought to identify niches that it can fill. Much of the success has been built on a partnership between government and business; for example, as noted in chapter 4, the agricultural research agency EMBRAPA developed varieties of soy suited for the tropics.[1] Brazilian companies are developing intellectual property in biotechnology, and not simply importing it. Norman Borlaug, the "father of the green revolution," said that EMBRAPA scientists deserve credit for "one of the great achievements of agricultural science in the twentieth century" (Rohter 2012, 155).

Costa Rica demonstrates that even a small Latin American country can achieve a good standard of living for its citizens. Given its geography, size, and history, Costa Rica should be similar to its Central American neighbors, but the country's GDP per capita is twice that of El Salvador, and six times that of next-door-neighbor Nicaragua. Forrest Colburn (2006) points out that in the 1960s Costa Rica and Nicaragua both had 17 percent of the region's exports. By 1989, Costa Rica had risen to 28 percent and Nicaragua had fallen to 9 percent. The country expanded tourism, especially ecotourism, and in doing so has developed an extensive system of parks and protected areas.

In 1996, Intel opted to set up operations in Costa Rica (over Brazil, Chile, Mexico, Thailand, Indonesia, and the Philippines) and invested $400 million. Other high-tech companies then followed. A hundred software companies and over a dozen medical device manufacturing companies have operations in the country. Significant pharmaceutical research is being done as foreign firms partner with universities. By 2014, Intel operations in Costa Rica were worth $2 billion and constituted 20 percent of the country's exports. Hence, when Intel decided to move most of its operations to Asia and eliminate 1,500 jobs (out of 2,500), it was a sharp blow to the economy. Newly elected president Luis Guillermo Solís nevertheless vowed that the country would continue policies intended to make Costa Rica favorable for technology investment.

Costa Rica's relative economic and social success is rooted in its history. The early colonists did not have forced labor from either indigenous or African slaves and so worked the land themselves. When coffee was introduced in the nineteenth century, much of it was produced on small family farms. Their prosperity helped prepare the way for the middle-class ethos of the country.[2] Most importantly, after abolishing the army in 1949, the government developed a welfare state, particularly in schooling and health care.

Forrest Colburn summarizes the reason for Costa Rica's success:

> strategic location, long-standing investments in public welfare, education in particular, political stability, strong institutions, a private sector with incentives to respond to a new model of economic development, foreign guidance and assistance, a gradual, pragmatic—and even incomplete—embracing of economic liberalism—and the advantage of being "first" in many economic endeavors—and getting a boost from those attracted to the country's many charms. (2006, 354)

Moving beyond these three examples, it may be helpful to broadly categorize Latin American countries in terms of the core of their economies (see table 13.1). These categories obviously combine various elements and are not airtight: copper export is certainly central to the Chilean economy, and interesting examples of the use of human capital are found in Colombia. The point is to draw attention to both the conditioning factors and the differences in the overall economic strategy of Latin American countries. Mexico and Brazil are two and four times the size of the next largest countries, and thus have far more of a domestic market. They also have large and increasingly sophisticated industries. However, Mexico is very tightly integrated with the United States and Canada, while Brazil has more diversified trading relationships: one-fourth European Union, one-fourth Latin America, one-fourth Asia (primarily China), 12 percent United States, and the remainder other regions.

Structurally, the small countries of Central America plus the Dominican Republic and Paraguay resemble one another insofar as the mainspring of their economies remained the export of agricultural products rather than ISI (import-substitution industrialization) through the twentieth century.[3] Most receive very significant

TABLE 13.1. Characteristics of National Economies

CHARACTERISTICS	COUNTRIES
Large population: manufacturing, commercial agriculture, large internal markets	Brazil, Mexico
Medium-sized: commodity based	Colombia, Argentina, Peru
Small population: tropical agroexport, free trade zones, remittances	Guatemala, El Salvador, Honduras, Nicaragua, Dominican Republic, Paraguay
State-led: commodity export	Cuba, Venezuela, Bolivia, Ecuador
Human-capital based	Chile, Uruguay, Costa Rica, Panama

TABLE 13.2. GDP per capita of Latin American Countries in US dollars, 2010–2014

Uruguay	16,350	Ecuador	6,003
Chile	15,732	Dominican Republic	5,879
Argentina	14,715	El Salvador	3,826
Venezuela	14,414	Paraguay	4,264
Mexico	10,307	Guatemala	3,477
Brazil	11,208	Bolivia	2,867
Panama	11,036	Honduras	2,290
Costa Rica	10,184	Nicaragua	1,851
Colombia	7,831	Haiti	819
Peru	6,661		

Source: World Bank (2015).

inputs from remittances, money sent from abroad (in some cases it is close to 10% of GDP).[4] In the economic strategies of Venezuela, Bolivia, and Ecuador, it is assumed that the wealth of the country lies in natural resources (primarily petroleum and natural gas) and that the key to development is state control over those resources in order to maximize their benefit for the population. Cuba is attempting to find its way after having had a fully statist economy for over a half century.

Chile, Uruguay, and Costa Rica have sought to move away from the traditional export of commodities toward more value-added products, that is, to move toward economies that depend primarily on human capital. We have already noted that

Uruguay has provided laptops for all students up to sixth grade. Panama can be grouped with these countries insofar as its economy is built around the Panama Canal and its status as a banking and financial services center. Colombia, Argentina, and Peru are medium-sized countries (from 30 to 50 million people) that export commodities (mining and agriculture).

The economic experience of Argentina is unique. It resembles Canada, Australia, and New Zealand in that it lies in the temperate zone, has abundant farming and grazing land, and was settled relatively late by European immigrants. As late as 1920, its level of development was similar to those countries and even the United States, but since then its economic development has lagged behind theirs. The underlying explanation would have to be attributed to poor economic management and dysfunctional politics (battles between Peronism and anti-Peronism, coups, and military governments).

Latin American countries differ considerably in their level of development as indicated by GDP per capita (see table 13.2). The dollar figure for Chile and Argentina is five times that of Nicaragua.[5]

LESSONS LEARNED AND FUTURE DIRECTIONS

The remainder of this chapter offers a number of observations indicating directions for Latin American economies, based not so much on economic theory as on pragmatic experience. Most have something to do with government policy, but rather than policy prescriptions they are primarily conclusions drawn from what has worked in recent decades. Some aspects will be discussed further in succeeding chapters (e.g., combating crime and corruption). The aim is to summarize some of the primary ingredients in economic growth that work for all, based on observation of recent history.

Maintain Macroeconomic Stability

The inflation and hyperinflation that once plagued Latin America have been largely tamed. From an average rate of over 440 percent in 1990, rates had dropped to under 5 percent by 2002. Inflation affects everyone, but it hits the poor especially hard. Inflation was tamed in various ways, including switching to the dollar in El Salvador and Ecuador,[6] but a crucial element was bringing government spending in line with revenue collection. That often meant reducing government payroll, including the privatization of state-owned enterprises, many of which were money-losing operations. The immediate effect was higher unemployment and sometimes reduced government services. The aim is not really a smaller state for its own sake: revenues in Latin American countries average less than 15 percent of GDP, as opposed to the 23 percent in industrialized countries (Franko 2007, 136–137).[7]

Part of the reason why Latin American countries were less affected by the post-2007 recession was that they had put their fiscal house in order. Looking toward the future, it is important to maintain stability, which is indispensable for sustained growth.[8]

Make Conditional Cash Transfers (and Carry Out Other Pro-poor Policies)

In the 1990s, both Brazil and Mexico pioneered programs in which poor families were given monthly cash stipends, provided the families met certain conditions, typically having infants inoculated or keeping their children in school. Over time, these initial programs have expanded to the point where they extend to twelve million families in Brazil and five million in Mexico (in each case, somewhere around a quarter or more of the population). Most Latin American countries have adopted some version of conditional cash transfers (CCTs), as have many other countries around the world. Brazilian families in extreme poverty receive the equivalent of $40 a month with no conditions and may receive an additional $13 for each child in school. Families have been means tested; it is usually the mother who picks up the monthly allowance from an ATM.

As small as these sums may seem, they may double the cash income of poor families. Considered together at the level of a village or town, they are a stimulus for local businesses and hence the local economy. Some of their effects have been measured: child labor has been reduced, children have remained longer in school, sometimes to the point of graduating from high school (for which the Mexican program provides a one-time bonus of $330). In short, these programs provide relief for poor families

Woman showing card used in conditional cash transfer program, Dominican Republic. © Inter-American Development Bank.

and improve social outcomes, and they stimulate the local economy, especially in rural areas, and have helped reduce poverty rates. They are not a panacea: spending more years in classrooms and even graduating in itself will do little if the quality of teaching is poor.

In more traditional government efforts at poverty alleviation, much money inevitably went into the expenses of the program, especially salaries. Cash transfers go directly to people. Although they could be criticized from the left as treating symptoms rather than root causes, and from the right as lessening incentives for poor people to better their condition, in view of the results, there is in fact little opposition to them.

The growing purchasing power of lower-income people has forced businesspeople to see them more as consumers. Years ago, a Peruvian economist explained, "If I'm in business, I'd rather have one person with $200 than two hundred people with a dollar each." It was a crude simplification, but it made the point: merchants selling major consumer items in a highly unequal society have little incentive to favor better income distribution. More recently, however, businesses have been discovering the buying power of the poor and are pursuing it, looking for ways to serve that market. As mentioned in chapter 4, poorer people have increasingly gone to supermarkets and malls. The relevance here is that programs that directly help the poor can be part of a larger effort to help more people enter the market, and that can create a virtuous circle: more money in people's hands generates more consumption and the creation of small businesses and jobs, which in turn puts more money in people's hands. Pro-poor policies can benefit other sectors of society as well.

Move toward Diversified Economies Based on Human Talent

Latin Americans have often pointed to the apparent paradox: "How can we be poor if we're so rich in natural resources?" However, in a study of ninety-seven countries, Jeffrey Sachs and Andrew Warner (1995) found empirical evidence that countries whose development is based on natural resources grow more slowly than those that are not so endowed.[9] At first glance this seems counterintuitive: all things being equal, if country A is well endowed with minerals or good agricultural land and country B is not, country A should be wealthier. Specific examples, however, may begin to suggest the reasons for the findings of Sachs and Warner: Saudi Arabia and South Korea have similar per capita incomes, but few would say Saudi Arabia is as developed as Korea, which rose from poverty to prosperity in three or four decades through industrialization. Saudis are wealthy because of something lying under the ground; the wealth of Koreans derives from their skills and the efficiency with which those skills are utilized to supply goods and services.

Economic historians have identified a "natural resources curse": the possession of natural resources does not translate into human development for all. Commodity prices tend to be subject to a boom-and-bust cycle. Countries with commodities like oil and minerals tend to have overvalued currencies, making other exports less competitive. Government revenues tend to come primarily from commodity export rather than from taxing the citizenry, and hence government officials are less accountable. Corruption is more common in commodity export countries, and their governments often have bloated, inefficient bureaucracies.

For almost a century, Venezuela has exemplified these trends. During the boom decades starting in the 1950s, Venezuelan two-party democracy seemed stable as the two major parties alternated in power and both used oil money for social programs and to provide public employment. With those revenues the country could import foreign goods, and hence there was little incentive for industrialization. The country has long been a net importer of food. Only a tiny percentage of the population works directly in oil production—1–2 percent in 2015—but everyone feels that "the oil is ours." Gasoline prices are highly subsidized. While the rest of the world was paying well over three and a half dollars a gallon for gasoline in 2010, Venezuelans were paying ten cents. Although the country's per capita GDP once rivaled that of Argentina as Latin America's highest, wealth and income were distributed unequally, as evidenced by the highly visible slums in the hills above Caracas. Venezuela enjoyed the oil price boom of the 1970s, but then suffered the slump in prices in the 1980s, leading to falling living standards and political crisis through the 1990s.

Michael Reid notes that government social spending in Venezuela was higher than in other countries but that "in 1988 infant mortality was three times higher than in Chile, which spent only a third as much. Vaccination rates were half the regional average. Every few years, hospitals had to be re-equipped because of theft or neglect." The system depended on rising oil incomes, but government revenues fell from a peak of $1,540 per person in 1974 to $315 in 1998. In 1989, "53 per cent of Venezuelans lived in poverty, and income per head had receded to its level of 1973" (Reid 2007, 163).

Since the 1930s, Venezuelan intellectuals had said that the country had to *sembrar el petróleo* (sow the oil), that is, use oil revenues to develop other types of production to free the country from oil dependence. The fact that petroleum constitutes 90 percent of Venezuelan exports, and that the country is still a net importer of food, underlines how difficult that is. Dependence on oil is a decades-old structural problem. Booming oil prices enabled President Hugo Chávez to use the state-owned oil company PDVSA as a cash cow for social projects, such as hospitals served by Cuban doctors and free access to universities for the poor, but Venezuela's structural economic problems were only aggravated.

For decades many Venezuelans and other Latin Americans believed that they were poor because they had been despoiled by foreign companies and their own rapacious elites of the natural resource wealth that was rightfully theirs. If so, the remedy would be state control over natural resources and channeling the proceeds to the people. Such is the logic behind Bolivia's mandate that foreign oil and gas companies must renegotiate their contracts. Ecuador and Bolivia in particular have shaped their development strategies around state capture of natural resource revenues and distribution for the satisfaction of social needs. Doing so, however, seems to fall into the natural resources trap.[10]

The alternative would be to deliberately focus on higher value-added sectors of the economy. For example, although Uruguay exports beef, wool, dairy products, and rice, and has beach tourism, it has also served as an international banking center and with its well-educated workforce is a major player in software development, including partnerships with firms in India.

The example of Costa Rica earlier in the chapter exemplifies the general direction. As recently as the 1980s, 60 percent of exports had been perishable goods (coffee, fruit, etc.). In 1996, Intel set up a $300 million plant for chip assembly and testing, and within a few years Intel constituted 20 percent of the country's exports, and agricultural exports were down to 25 percent. Intel had been attracted by Costa Rica's stability, good business climate, and particular incentives. Intel's "seal of approval" on the country served as an attraction for other technology companies, pharmaceuticals, and others, including Procter & Gamble, which decided to set up its western hemisphere headquarters in the country. Even as Intel downsized its Costa Rica operations, the government vowed to keep striving to make the country attractive for investment in technology operations.

As these examples indicate, the primary wealth of Latin America lies not in the soil but in the human capital of Latin Americans. A key aim of economic strategy is to allow that talent to flourish and be rewarded.

Making It Easy to Start and Run Businesses

Chapter 4 considered the work of the Peruvian economist Hernando de Soto, who with his colleagues created a mock company and then documented the many bureaucratic steps and time needed to register the business. Before long, similar investigations were taking place elsewhere, and an Ease of Starting a Business Index had been devised, that is, countries could be ranked on how easy or hard it was to start a business. From there it was a logical step to studying how hard it was to operate an ongoing business, and so criteria were devised (getting permits, registering property, obtaining credit, paying/collecting taxes, contract enforcement, and so forth). For years now the World Bank has periodically updated the index. The point of such comparisons can be seen in the results: the highest-ranking countries are in northern Europe but include some from Asia and the Middle East; the lowest quarter of countries are almost all in sub-Saharan Africa. Only three Latin American countries are in the first quarter, and over half are below the midpoint; Bolivia and Venezuela are in the bottom quarter.

Publishing this list gives governments a more or less objective look at how businesspeople perceive them. Since those governments desire investment, both foreign and domestic, they can seek to remove some of the obstacles to starting and running a business. No automatic correlation exists between the Ease of Doing Business rating and growth; China is only at the midpoint. However, all things being equal, a country where it is easier to start and run a business will generate more economic activity and hence employment, and thus a better standard of living.[11] De Soto oversold his

Pharmaceutical plant, El Alto, Bolivia. © Noah Friedman-Rudovsky.

argument in claiming that removing government red tape would be the key to ending poverty. Rather it should be seen pragmatically as a useful ingredient but not in itself the single key to development.

Some of what business regards as obstacles and costs organized labor would regard as legal protection of workers' rights. Workers in Brazil and elsewhere are entitled to severance pay when they are fired, typically one month's wages per year worked. Thus after a dozen years, a dismissed worker would be entitled to a year's wages. This no doubt helps workers manage while they seek new employment, and it gives them considerable job security. By the same token, it makes employers wary of hiring new permanent employees and thus may increase unemployment, at least in the formal sector.

The Ease of Doing Business Index is heavily based on regulations and paperwork. If governments streamline procedures, their score will rise on the index, but that does not necessarily mean it would be easier for real entrepreneurs to start and run a business. It should also be noted that the individual data are gathered from experts in each country and hence it is inevitably somewhat subjective. If businesspeople think that government is hostile to them, it may affect their rankings. The aim should not be to be ranked higher on comparative indexes but to create a climate in which entrepreneurs can open and develop small, medium, and large enterprises that provide quality goods and services and generate solid employment.

TABLE 13.3. Ease of Doing Business Rankings (2015)

[Singapore]	[1]	[China]	[90]
[United States]	[7]		
		Paraguay	92
Colombia	34	Honduras	104
Peru	35	El Salvador	109
		Ecuador	115
Mexico	39	Nicaragua	119
		Brazil	120
[Israel]	[40]	Argentina	124
Chile	41	Bolivia	157
Panama	52		
		Venezuela	182
Guatemala	73		
Uruguay	82	[Afghanistan]	[183]
Costa Rica	83	[Eritrea]	[189]
Dominican Republic	84		

Note: Total of 189 countries. Countries in brackets are for comparison purposes.

Source: World Bank Group (2015).

Expand the Formal Sector of the Economy

A large portion of the economy in Latin American countries is informal (not regis-tered with the government and not paying taxes or benefits), although the rate varies widely, from an estimated 70 percent in Bolivia to around 20 percent in Chile (similar to the rate in some European countries). The formal sector grew in the mid-twentieth century in the form of employment in large companies and in the state, and then declined in the 1990s as the advent of goods imported under globalization forced uncompetitive industries to close and as government employment declined or stag-nated. Since the 1990s, the formal sector has grown somewhat in Brazil and elsewhere.

In principle, moving toward a more formal economy makes sense: workers would receive benefits (unemployment insurance, retirement pensions, perhaps health care), and the state would receive revenues from taxes. As will be discussed in the next section, overall productivity should improve. However, any approach to increasing the formal-sector share of the economy must be based on an understanding of the informal sector.

Although the term "informal sector" tends to conjure up images of street vendors, it applies to many people: a car mechanic who operates in the street; a domestic worker who is paid in cash; a builder who hires a small crew to construct a house; the adolescent at the counter of a family store. The vast majority of workers in the informal sector are in enterprises of fewer than five workers. A World Bank report notes that "in Brazil, 76 percent of microfirms do not have an operating license and 94 percent do not pay taxes. Those rates fall to 33 and 23 percent, respectively, among firms with five paid workers" (Perry et al. 2007, 9). As the number of workers rises, businesses become more visible and harder to hide from inspectors or tax officials.

To consider how a transition might take place, let us consider an auto mechanic named Carlos who repairs vehicles for clients who come to him when they have a problem. After diagnosing the problem, he locates and buys parts as needed, and does the repair in the street or near his house, perhaps with the aid of an assistant hired by the job. Carlos is a freelance mechanic by choice; he feels that he earns more than he would at any job available to him, since he did not graduate from high school. Although he could register his business and begin to make payments, he does not believe any benefit would be worth paying taxes and benefits and the costs of accounting.

Suppose, however, that over time Carlos has more customers and he expands: he gets a shop, and more workers, and now wants to buy a tow truck and some testing equipment. For that he needs credit, so he registers his business, hires a bookkeeper, takes out loans from a bank, and pays social security for his workers. Whereas he began doing two or three jobs a week, he now has twenty-five or thirty and he spends much of his time dealing with customers and overseeing the work of his employees. He has gone from being a street mechanic to the proprietor of a car-repair business. Carlos and his workers are now covered by government social security and pension plans, and the state now receives taxes from the business. Carlos and his employees are more productive than he was by himself, and his expensive equipment enables him to diagnose problems and do more sophisticated work. However, his rates are correspondingly higher and some vehicle owners prefer to take their chances with other street mechanics. Carlos did not decide to move to the formal sector for its own sake; rather, he found himself expanding and eventually registered his business. In countries where a larger portion of the economy is informal, he might have expanded his business without registering it.

Even larger businesses are often only partially formal. They may underreport sales so as to avoid taxes, or pay social security for only some employees, or utilize temporary workers, or outsource some operations to the informal sector (e.g., pay someone for office cleaning services, similar to off-the-books domestic service, or have their vehicles serviced by street mechanics). Reducing informality entails not only inducing smaller firms to become formal but correcting the informality of larger firms.

The willingness of businesspeople to operate in the formal economy is affected by their view of the state. Societies with a high degree of formality, such as Chile or Costa Rica, are also societies in which citizens believe that government officials and agencies perform relatively well and are fair and evenhanded. Conversely, where it is assumed that government officials and agencies serve the public poorly, or play favorites or expect bribes, or are ineffective at enforcement, it is more rational to evade taxes or underreport sales or employees. As one study states:

> Achieving a deeper change in incentives also requires actions to change the pervasive culture of noncompliance that we observe in most countries in the region. Because such social norms are, in part, the result of a lack of trust in the effectiveness of the state and the equity of its actions, overcoming the culture of informality probably requires major improvements in the quality and fairness of state institutions and policies. In short, it requires building an effective and inclusive social contract in which the great majority of individuals feel compelled to participate and comply with state mandates. (Perry et al. 2007, 14)

Increase Productivity

Businesses in Latin America are less productive than in more advanced countries. To take an obvious example, a family-operated US commercial farm produces far more than a farm in highland Guatemala. One has hundreds of acres and is farmed by machinery, while the other has at most a few acres and is farmed with a hoe and a machete. That helps account for the fact that in the United States farming is done by only 1–2 percent of the population, while in Latin America it averages 20 percent. Something similar is true of industry and services.

Not only are Latin American economies less productive, but productivity itself has been growing more slowly, as shown in table 13.4, drawn from a 2010 report prepared by the Inter-American Development Bank.[12] Latin American productivity grew more slowly when compared with the developed countries, that is, not only did it not "catch up" but it fell further behind. That is even truer in comparison to East Asian economies. In 1960, Latin American per capita income was almost a quarter that of the United States, but a half century later it had fallen to a sixth. If Venezuela and Uruguay had grown at the average rate for the rest of the world, by 2006 they would have had per capita incomes similar to Israel and Spain respectively, triple (Venezuela) and double (Uruguay) their current incomes. With variations, the same is true of other countries.

As indicated in the table, the sector that did the best in Latin America was agriculture, that is, productivity grew fastest in that sector. To some extent, that finding may reflect Brazilian commercial agriculture. Productivity was more disappointing in industry, where it was very low or sometimes even negative. It was even lower in services, where for a half century productivity has grown very little.

The authors note that unlike the developed nations, where increased productivity

TABLE 13.4. Average Annual Productivity Growth in Agriculture, Industry, and Services, 1951–2005 (Percentage)

	AGRICULTURE			INDUSTRY			SERVICES		
	1951–1975	1975–1990	1990–2005	1951–1975	1975–1990	1990–2005	1951–1975	1975–1990	1990–2005
Latin America	2.8%	1.8%	3.51%	1.8%	-0.9%	2.0%	1.3%	-1.8%	0.1%
East Asia		3.8%	2.5%		3.2%	3.5%		2.4%	2.5%
High-income Countries		5.0%	3.6%		2.6%	2.2%		1.3%	1.4%

Source: Inter-American Development Bank (2010).

went hand in hand with decades of industrialization before evolving to an economy centered on services, Latin America has already arrived at that third stage: 60 percent of the workforce is in services (with 20% each in agriculture and industry). They then draw the conclusion that it is the service sector where productivity should be most improved for two reasons: that is where productivity growth has been lowest and where well over half of the workforce is employed.

Their seemingly simple explanation is that the economy is "allocated to too many small low-productivity companies." They add that "a Latin American company with more than 100 employees can generate, on average, double the output with the same resources of a company with only 10 to 19 employees" (Pagés 2010, 4).[13] Indeed, Chile, the country where formalization is highest, is also the country where productivity has grown most. In fact, it is the only Latin American country where productivity growth has more or less kept pace with that of the rest of the world.

Thus, the issue of productivity connects with that of formalization and with policies designed to foster business creation. Not only should policies make it easier to formalize a business (e.g., reducing red tape), but insofar as possible formalization should not bring excessive penalties. One route is simply enforcement: require businesses to register and enforce those requirements. Formalization should make it easier to obtain credit and perhaps technical assistance so that those who start a business can grow. Correspondingly, if some small businesses succeed and expand to become medium-sized enterprises, less productive businesses may find it hard to compete and be driven out of business or forced to devise other services or products.[14]

Reduce the Economic Costs of Corruption and Crime

Chapter 15 is devoted to a discussion of efforts to reduce corruption and crime and what more can and should be done. This section considers the extent to which these two factors hinder development, and hence how reducing them is crucial for development.

Corruption takes multiple forms: a "tip" to an official to expedite red tape; a kickback from a contractor who wins a large construction bid; criminal gangs that extort monthly protection payments from merchants; police who make an arrest to extort money, a portion of which they send up the line to their superiors. A 2005 survey of economic literature[15] found that corruption is associated with lower GDP growth, lower investment, less foreign investment, higher inflation, a lower quality of infrastructure (e.g., roads and electricity), higher infant mortality, weakened institutions (e.g., a poorly functioning court system), and higher pollution. These findings are roughly borne out in the Corruption Perceptions Index (table 13.5), which is published periodically by Transparency International, an NGO headquartered in Berlin.

Information for the 2011 report was gathered from thirteen different sources, and by assigning numerical values, each country could be assigned a value from 1 to 10. Of 183 countries on the list, the highest-scoring was New Zealand (9.5) and the lowest, Somalia (1.0), tied with North Korea for last place. Corruption in this instance is defined as the "misuse of public power for private profit," and hence it has to do with what takes place in government, not, for example, kickbacks in a transaction involving private parties. It is a measure of *perceptions* of corruption, since corruption is generally secret and cannot be investigated directly. If corruption were in fact equal between country A and country B, but the citizens in country A thought it was greater in their country, country A would score lower on the scale.

As table 13.5 indicates, there is also a strong correlation between poverty and corruption, that is, the countries toward the bottom are generally among the poorest in the world, and the top ten countries are all prosperous. (Given its per capita income, Venezuela should be closer to the middle of the pack.) Interestingly, Chile scores slightly higher than the United States, and Uruguay is close to it. As with the other indexes, many Latin American countries score in the middle of the 183 countries on the list, and Paraguay and Venezuela score near the bottom on a world scale. Why did Venezuela score so low? It may be because oil wealth is associated with corruption; it may also be that citizens opposed to Hugo Chávez subjectively believed that corruption was more prevalent than it was.

Does association or correlation prove causality, in other words, does corruption cause poverty or does poverty encourage corruption? Causality may in fact be circular. In a country where corruption is common, it is not surprising that infrastructure deteriorates more quickly (contractors may win bids through bribery or use inferior materials or bribe inspectors). When corruption becomes prevalent, it is taken for granted as the way things are done, especially if detection, let alone sanction, is unlikely. Excessive red tape increases corruption, and people will be willing to pay to "expedite" permits. Poverty makes graft more "rational," and a high level of graft weakens development.

Common crime, ranging from theft and robbery to murder, obviously has costs to the victims. Does it also affect economic growth and welfare? A simple example may suggest that it does. If an executive feels he needs private security services to guard the company premises, has to move his family to a gated community to feel safe, and

TABLE 13.5. Corruption Perceptions Index—2014

COUNTRY	RANK	SCORE
[Denmark]	[1]	[91]
[United States]	[17]	[74]
Chile	21	73
Uruguay	21	73
Puerto Rico	31	63
Costa Rica	47	54
Cuba	63	46
Brazil	69	43
El Salvador	80	39
Peru	85	38
Colombia	94	37
Panama	94	37
[China]	[100]	[36]
Bolivia	103	35
Mexico	103	35
Argentina	107	34
Ecuador	110	33
Dominican Republic	115	32
Guatemala	115	32
Honduras	126	29
Nicaragua	133	28
Paraguay	150	24
Haiti	161	19
Venezuela	161	19
[South Sudan, Afghanistan, Sudan, North Korea, Somalia]	[171–175]	[15–8]

Note: Countries in brackets are for purposes of comparison.
Source: Transparency International (2014).

has to hire bodyguards for protection against kidnapping, he and his company are incurring extra expenses that would not be necessary in a country with lower crime levels and effective policing. Although a perceived need for security generates some economic activity, including jobs, it does not enhance anyone's welfare, but simply protects against losses.

TABLE 13.6. Economic Costs of Crime and Violence in Central America

COUNTRY	BILLION DOLLARS	PERCENTAGE OF GDP
Guatemala	2.3	7.7
El Salvador	2	10.8
Honduras	.9	9.6
Nicaragua	.5	10
Costa Rica	.8	3.6

Source: World Bank—LAC (2011).

A 2011 World Bank report seeks to calculate the economic costs of crime and violence in Central America in terms of health costs (medical attention, lost production, emotional damage), institutional costs (public security, administration of justice), private security costs for households and businesses, and finally material costs, and reaches the estimates in table 13.6. In four of the five countries, the costs are significant. When researchers asked businesspeople about priorities for improving productivity, all five countries listed reducing crime among the top three (along with factors like improved infrastructure, regulation environment, and corporate governance). The same study showed that if homicide rates were reduced by 10 percent, productivity would rise significantly (1.0% in El Salvador and 0.7% in Guatemala; World Bank 2011).

CONCLUSION: IMPORTANCE OF INSTITUTIONS

This chapter has drawn attention to similarities in different countries in keeping with Dani Rodrik's observation that different "recipes" may be applied even based on similar understandings of economics. The title of a 2006 book by the Spanish economist Javier Santiso captured a shift taking place in economic thinking in Latin America: *Latin America's Political Economy of the Possible: Beyond Good Revolutionaries and Free-Marketeers*. The book consisted primarily of case studies of the political economies of Chile, Brazil, Mexico, Argentina, and Venezuela, and was dedicated to Albert Hirschman, whose work on development economics spanned more than a half century, much of it devoted to Latin America.[16] At the time he was writing, Santiso discerned a shift from grand schemes, whether state-directed economies or the market-solves-all mantras, toward pragmatic stances.

In addition to skepticism toward grand theories, development economists are increasingly paying attention to the importance of *institutions*. The term sounds fuzzy, but an illustration may help. Suppose a mutual fund manager is considering investment possibilities in two countries: in country A, there is a great deal of red tape and bureaucracy (but matters can be expedited with "tips" or having the right contacts);

courts are slow and arbitrary and outcomes are unpredictable; robbery, kidnapping, and murder rates are high; it is well to be suspicious and not take what people say at face value. In country B, procedures are clear, the legal system works well, the police are effective and trusted, and most people can be taken at their word. All things being equal, he or she would pick country B, where the "rules of the game" are clear and are fairly applied.[17]

That example is abstract, but in practice Latin American countries may vary considerably along these lines. It is no accident that in the various indexes (ease of doing business, corruption, competitiveness), Chile, Costa Rica, and Uruguay tend to score high for Latin America, near the 25 percent point on a world scale, whereas other countries score toward the 50 percent mark and some well into the bottom half. In terms of economic theory, the considerations put forth in this chapter mesh well with what is called the "new institutional economics," associated with the economist and economic historian Douglass C. North,[18] who has drawn attention to the importance of reliable institutions for economic development.

After considering some of the major ingredients for successful twenty-first-century economies, we now turn to the role of the state, similarly seeking to draw on the lessons of recent decades.

FURTHER READING

A thorough overview of economic issues in Latin America from various angles is Franko (2007), although it cannot take into account developments of the past decade. For basic contemporary development economics, see Rodrik (2007), and for political economy, see Santiso (2006). On issues of formality and informality, see Perry et al. (2007). Pagés (2010) considers productivity. Helwege (2011) raises questions about what is needed for long-range growth. Rohter (2012) and Reid (2014) consider recent economic developments in Brazil journalistically; Castañeda (2011) does the same for Mexico.

Making Democracy Work

Politics and the State

In 1975, most of Latin America was under one form or another of authoritarian rule. Only four countries were electoral democracies in which power was really in the hands of civilians, and one of those (Mexico) was thoroughly dominated by one party. By the early 1990s, all countries in the region except Cuba were democracies—at least in the sense that political transition took place through reasonably fair elections. Today most have been democracies for twenty-five or thirty years.

This chapter considers various aspects of contemporary democratic politics, moving from conceptual issues to electoral politics to governance. The discussion continues in chapter 15 (corruption, crime, and establishing the rule of law), and chapter 16 (education and health care). No attempt is made to present the specific features of each country; instead, broad trends and developments are illustrated with examples drawn from recent experience.

DEMOCRACY AND PAST LEGACIES

This move to democracy is part of a larger movement in history. In 1900, no country on earth could be regarded as a full democracy in the contemporary sense, because they did not have full suffrage (women could not vote). The number of democratic countries grew until World War I, and then after World War II, by which time 20 or 30 countries were democracies. What is called a "Third Wave" of democratization began in Europe (Portugal and Spain) in the 1970s, and has included Latin America, Eastern Europe, and portions of Asia and Africa. Now around 120 countries can be regarded as democratic.

In the nineteenth century, most Latin American countries had the trappings of constitutional republican government modeled to some extent on the United States[1] (although Brazil was a monarchy until 1889). Political parties were formed and presidents and congresses were elected, but politics was essentially a struggle between factions of the elite, especially large landholders. In the twentieth century, voting was gradually extended so that by the 1950s, most countries had a form of electoral democracy, even if it was frequently interrupted with coups. In some smaller countries, dictators like Anastasio Somoza (Nicaragua), Rafael Trujillo (Dominican Republic), Alfredo Stroessner (Paraguay), and Fulgencio Batista (Cuba) held power for decades. Some countries had orderly democracies in which parties alternated in power (Venezuela, Colombia, Costa Rica, Chile, Uruguay). Even during the period of repressive military rule, some countries retained the formalities of democracy with elections and parties (Brazil, Guatemala, El Salvador) even though real power was in the hands of the military. Thus the recent wave of democracy did not start from zero.

Political scientists and philosophers discuss just what democracy means. One approach can be called *formal democracy* and emphasizes procedures for election and transfer of power: thus the focus is on transparency, access to information, pluralistic media, and fair vote counting. Formal democracy is certainly an advance over a situation in which power can be taken through military coup, or in which an individual dictator or an authoritarian regime can control political power with no consent from society, but by itself it may seem irrelevant. One can imagine a country in which elections are held, candidates make promises, legislatures convene, and laws are passed, but it all means little to most people. Thus formal or procedural democracy is sometimes contrasted to *substantive democracy*, in which people's real interests are represented and governments are accountable to citizens and serve their needs.

People everywhere complain of government, but they also rely on it for police protection; schooling and health care; civil and criminal courts; providing (or regulating) electricity, water, and gas; trash disposal; highways and bridges; monitoring health, safety, and environmental conditions; responding to emergencies; zoning regulations; and economic development. These ongoing functions take place at local, regional, and national levels and often do not depend directly on which party is in the presidency or the legislature. Latin Americans complain about their governments, notably about corruption and bureaucracy. A common complaint is that politicians make promises during election campaigns but then ignore them once in office. In some countries, corruption has been taken for granted, and it is assumed that matters are settled through an inner circle of people with connections.[2] Polls find that Latin Americans generally favor democracy but that their support is often lukewarm. A significant minority would be willing to accept an authoritarian government if it could be more effective at getting things done.

The legacy of the past, when populists dispensed favors to the populace, has remained. Consider a minor but perhaps revealing example from Panama. Gen. Omar Torrijos had come to power after a 1968 military coup in Panama. He abolished the previous political parties and legislature and ruled by decree (eventually creating a docile assembly where he had an overwhelming majority). He helicoptered around the country to visit rural communities and invoked nationalism, especially around recovering the Panama Canal and the Canal Zone from the United States. Torrijos was drawing on the kind of personalistic politics exemplified by Perón in Argentina and other figures in the mid-twentieth century.[3] In the mid-1970s, a community group in an overcrowded downtown slum of Panama City, after exploring alternatives, had decided that it wanted to build a new community on undeveloped land it had located. The organization had support from architects and international development agencies; the sticking point was the Torrijos government, which suspected that the people opposed his government. Torrijos finally met with them on the land, accepted their proposal, and then said, "Guys, it's hot here. Let's take a swim," and jumped into the nearby stream in his clothes, with some of his aides and the people following him.[4]

In a mature democracy, a decision to undertake a large housing development would be made on its own merits as part of the larger strategy of the ministry of housing or urban development; it would not be the result of an on-the-spot decision by one man for a group of people. This example illustrates the classic pattern of what political scientists call "clientelism," a pattern of behavior in which those with power dispense favors to those under them in return for their loyalty.[5]

A traditional outlet for clientelism is government hiring. Upon winning an election, a party dispenses jobs at all levels of government, and people are hired through their connections. The upshot is a large turnover with each change of administration, positions filled on the basis of connections rather than competence, and a general assumption that the state exists primarily as a source of patronage. The origins of clientelism can be traced at least to ancient Rome, where wealthy men spent a portion of their day receiving "clients" who came to ask their help in return for loyalty. The patrons themselves typically were clients to even more powerful men above them.[6]

Clientelism helps explain why Latin American political parties and politicians often do not seem to be clear in terms of ideology and principles.[7] The state itself is regarded as a kind of "patrimony" that is fought over ("patrimonialism").[8] Even in modern democracies it helps to have access and to "network"; nevertheless, the ideal should be a society in which citizens are treated equally and do not need to find patrons, one in which agreed-upon fair rules apply to all, especially in politics. Temptations of falling into the interrelated patterns of populism, clientelism, and patrimonialism remain.

ELECTORAL POLITICS: PARTIES, PRESIDENTS, LEGISLATURES, AND OTHER ACTORS

Procedurally, Latin American democracies resemble politics in the United States. Elections are held on a regular basis, parties propose candidates for president and the legislature, votes are counted, and a new government takes office on the designated day. Like the United States, these are presidential democracies, in which the president is elected directly, as opposed to parliamentary democracies in Europe, Canada, Israel, and elsewhere, where the prime minister is chosen by the majority party in parliament, and governments can fall after a vote of no confidence. The overall framework is set by constitutions, which are not accorded the quasi-scriptural status of the US constitution. Most countries have had several constitutions since independence, and often the current one was written within people's living memory: Chile (1980), Brazil (1988), Colombia (1991), Venezuela (1999), Ecuador (2008), and Bolivia (2009).

Some differences with the United States are also worth noting. One is simply that of scale: about half of Latin American countries are small, with ten million or fewer people. Thus although they have a national government with its various ministries, the magnitude is closer to that of a major US city. The 2010 budget for the city of Philadelphia ($4 billion) was twice as large as that of Nicaragua. Brazil, Mexico, Argentina, and Colombia have federal systems, in which states, provinces, or departments have their own legislatures. Brazil is the country that is most truly federal, in the sense that state governors and legislatures have real power and are able to generate their own revenues and budgets.[9]

In the United States a two-party system is taken for granted, even though the Constitution does not mention parties (which the founders called "factions" and regarded as divisive). Nevertheless, parties arose almost immediately, and the United States soon evolved into a two-party system (with occasional third and fourth parties). In political theory, parties are said to channel the interests of citizens and to provide an orderly way for those interests to be represented, advocated, and translated into policies and programs.

Some Latin American countries have (or have had) a two-party system with a left and a right wing, particularly Chile, where since 1990 center-left and center-right coalitions have alternated in office.[10] Mexico has three main parties, the right-wing (pro-business and pro–Catholic Church) PAN (National Action Party), the left-wing PRD (Party of the Democratic Revolution), and the PRI (Institutional Revolutionary Party), which ideologically can be situated in between them.[11]

Voting center in San Salvador; poll watchers are wearing vests. © Edgar Romero.

However, many countries are far from a two-party system. In the 2011 Guatemalan election, eleven parties competed for the presidency and fourteen had candidates for congress. None of the parties had a long-standing tradition, and most were vehicles for individual politicians. Guatemala might be an extreme case, but other countries, most notably Brazil, have similar systems with a multiplicity of parties. The primary reason for that multiplicity is the way the electoral rules function, particularly the system of proportional representation. Unlike winner-take-all systems, such as that of the United States where candidates vie to represent single districts, in a proportional-representation system, each party proposes a slate of candidates. If, for example, a province or department has fifteen seats in congress, each party proposes a slate of fifteen candidates with its preferred candidates at the top of the list. Citizens cast their vote for the party slate; the fifteen seats are then apportioned according to a formula; the parties with the most votes win the largest numbers of representatives, but above a threshold, for example, 5 percent, a party will be given one representative (the top name on the slate).[12]

In that 2011 election in Guatemala, the leading presidential candidate, Otto Pérez Molina, received 36 percent of the vote; the candidate next in line received 23 percent; the third, 16 percent; and all others, under 10 percent. Pérez Molina won the runoff election between the two top candidates. However, since his own party held only 26 percent of the seats in congress, he and the party needed to forge alliances with other parties. That situation is common in Latin American governments. One study covering eighteen Latin American countries during the 1990–2004 period found that in only 20 percent of presidential-congressional periods did a single party occupy the presidency and also have a majority in congress (the figure rose to 36 percent if the party had a near majority) (Stein 2006, 38). In some cases, a stable coalition government was formed, but others were like the one described for Guatemala, a president whose own party was far from a majority. Presidents who do not have a working majority in congress must form coalitions. Thus, in 2012, eight of Brazilian president Dilma Rousseff's twenty-six cabinet ministers were from allied parties.

This fragmentation is privileged by the rules of the electoral game: if by achieving a minimum percentage, parties can win at least one congressional seat, the incentives favor forming new small parties. Such parties tend to be built around personalities and to be relatively short-lived. They may not embody clear principles or clearly represent distinct sectors of society. In Guatemala in 2011, the campaign posters all showed broadly smiling candidates offering vacuous platitudes.[13]

The role of Latin American legislatures in making laws and budgeting is less than that of the US Congress. One recent study notes that "scholars had tended to consider legislatures in Latin American countries to be largely irrelevant throughout much of the twentieth century and not worthy of study in and of themselves" (Stein 2006, 42).[14] Presidents are often able to rule by decree or executive order, bypassing congress, sometimes declaring periods of emergency. When President Alberto Fujimori closed congress in Peru in 1992, he initially enjoyed the support of the public.

More recently, observers are seeing a larger role for legislatures, even if it is often

Vote in Bolivian Congress, La Paz. © Noah Friedman-Rudovsky.

negative, as in refusing to pass legislation proposed by the executive. In a survey of business executives on the effectiveness of congress in their countries, on a rating of 1 to 7 the only country above the midpoint was Chile with 3.7; Brazil had 3.1; ten countries scored 2 or lower, meaning their legislatures were regarded as performing poorly (Stein 2006, 44). The constitutional powers of presidents and congresses vary considerably. About half the countries have unicameral legislatures, and half are bicameral (having an upper and a lower house). In some cases, presidents have powers to legislate independently of congress.

Given the proportional-representation system, members of congress do not have constituents in the same way that US representatives do. Moreover, it is through party loyalty that they are placed high enough on the slate to actually enter congress, and hence they are far more beholden to the party structure than to the electorate. In Mexico and Costa Rica, reelection is prohibited, and so as their term ends, politicians are looking for their next step, either returning to the private sector or seeking another job or position through the party.

As in the United States, legislators set up committees around common topics. However, congressional committees generally do not have sufficient staff. Budget committees in Brazil, Chile, and Colombia have professional staffs to assist them.

The comparative study of Latin American legislatures mentioned above classifies them into those that are "limited" (do not initiate much legislation or act as a check on the executive); "reactive obstructionist" (can veto presidential initiatives); "reactive constructive" (can shape and amend what comes from the executive); "proactive" (can take some initiatives). In three of the four categories they are thus regarded as subordinate to the presidency (Stein 2006).

The same study seeks to measure the competence of the legislators by assembling various indicators of capabilities (education, years of experience, committee membership, technical expertise, perception of effectiveness). By combining all of these, they derive a "Congress Capabilities Index," on which four countries rate high (Brazil, Chile, Colombia, and Uruguay); those rating lowest are Argentina, Dominican Republic, Guatemala, Honduras, and Peru (Stein 2006, 54–56).

CITIZEN VOICES

In a democracy, the primary way of influencing lawmakers is through the vote, particularly by replacing incumbents with challengers. However, even between elections lawmakers are sensitive to citizens' views, made known through polling and lobbying (as attested by over 12,000 lobbyists registered in Washington, reflecting interest groups, and a continual flow of citizens and interest groups presenting their cases in congressional and senate offices). The notion of "lobbying" is new in Latin America. In fact, in the early 1990s, as grassroots groups were playing more active roles in the newly restored democracies, there was no exact Spanish equivalent term.[15] In this section, we consider how influence is brought to bear on the governing process, by business, organized labor, grassroots groups, and NGOs, as well as the role of the media.

In Latin America, business is generally the best-organized sector of society, most able to get access to lawmakers. Trade associations of particular lines of business, especially large farmers, are linked in umbrella organizations, sometimes functioning as a spokesperson for the private sector. Individual businesses certainly use their access to members of the government through informal ties or by contacting the relevant officials. Business spokespersons also frequently seek to influence public opinion through the media.

Organized labor has far less power. Labor unions came to prominence in the mid-twentieth century during the period of state-led development. In Argentina, Mexico, and Brazil, most union membership came from the public sector and large industry, and hence they represented only a portion of the working population. Labor unions had ties to particular parties in Argentina, Brazil, Mexico, Peru, and Venezuela and were able to achieve favorable labor legislation with benefits for their members. Today they typically represent little more than 10 percent of the economically active population,[16] and they are disproportionately composed of public-sector employees, notably teachers. The decline in membership reflects both cutbacks in the public sector and an earlier decline of formal-sector employment. Labor unions understandably defend the interests of their members, but in some instances they join in coalitions for broader issues. In the 1990s, they fought to resist privatization and reforms in matters like pension programs. They have sought to make alliances with labor unions in North America and Europe, such as to resist free-trade agreements in Colombia and Central America.[17]

Earlier chapters noted the rise of organizations of urban slum dwellers, small farmers, women, indigenous people, Afro-descendants, environmentalists, and human rights defenders. Some are mass grassroots organizations and some are in the form of NGOs (nongovernmental organizations), typically with a small staff. These grew and spread during the period of authoritarian government, often with funding from overseas organizations, primarily in Europe. They have continued to march in street demonstrations and often represent a voice of conscience in society. Akin to them are research institutes or think tanks devoted to particular issues.

Sometimes the power of grassroots organizations goes beyond simply seeking to influence particular policies. In May 1993, Venezuela's president Carlos Andrés Pérez was impeached and forced out of office. Formally the reason was embezzlement, but he had largely lost legitimacy in 1989, when the austerity measures he imposed suddenly led to protests, which were put down with violence in which hundreds of people were killed. Brazilian president Fernando Collor de Mello had been impeached the previous year.[18] In each case the formalities were followed, but it was clear that the events were driven by angry organized demonstrators in the street. Over the next two decades, similar events occurred in other countries (see table 14.1).

Latin Americans have had a long tradition of taking to the streets, but these events seemed to signal a new kind of "people's power," particularly in the cases of Bolivia and Ecuador, where indigenous people, long marginalized, were major participants. They were part of the process that led to the presidencies of Evo Morales and Rafael Correa. These events were generally triggered by an economic or political crisis, and often signaled not only opposition to a particular president but disenchantment with the political class as a whole. In the Argentine crisis of 2001, protesters shouted, "Que se vayan todos!" (Get rid of them all!) and indeed the country saw five presidents in the space of two weeks. Massive university student protests in Chile and Colombia in 2011 forced conservative governments to take seriously student demands. In 2013, Brazilians took to the street in large numbers to protest poor public services while billions were being spent preparing for the 2014 World Cup and the 2016 Summer Olympics. What was new was that the protesters were largely middle class, suggesting that people were losing patience with traditional political practices and demanding more accountability from politicians.

Although these instances express a kind of democracy (in the root sense of people's power), they also indicate the institutional weakness of democratic institutions in these societies. Moreover, they are primarily the exercise of a kind of veto power, an ability of people to say "Enough!" Translating this same energy into a consensus on solutions, however, often proves elusive.

Two other instances of presidents forced out of office, although not by people in the street, should also be mentioned. In June 2009, Honduran president Manuel Zelaya was arrested and deported in his pajamas to Costa Rica by the military, ostensibly for calling for a referendum in coming elections to allow for a new constitution.

TABLE 14.1. Presidents Forced Out of Office by Popular Protest

COUNTRY	YEAR	PRESIDENT AND ACTION	REASONS
Brazil	1992	Fernando Collor de Mello—forced out of office	Corruption, economic crisis, personal scandals
Venezuela	1993	Carlos Andrés Pérez—impeached	Disenchantment with parties, economic crisis, corruption
Guatemala	1993	Jorge Serrano Elías—forced out	Disbanding congress in attempting a "self-coup"
Ecuador	1997	Abdalá Bucaram Ortiz—impeached	Economic crisis, unpopular economic measures
Paraguay	1999	Raúl Cubas Grau—impeached	Misuse of power; alleged involvement in murder of vice president
Peru	2000	Alberto Fujimori—forced into exile	Authoritarian rule, corruption, human rights violations
Argentina	2001	Fernando de la Rúa—forced to resign	Economic collapse
Bolivia	2003	Gonzalo Sánchez de Lozada—forced out of office	Proposal to export natural gas, economic crisis, demands of indigenous people
Bolivia	2005	Carlos Mesa—forced to resign	Protests over export of natural gas

Zelaya, a wealthy rancher, turned leftward and populist while in office and allied himself with President Chávez of Venezuela. He lost the support of the middle classes, congress, the supreme court, his own party, and the army, although he had many supporters among the poor. Other Latin American countries refused to recognize the new government and were slow to recognize the legitimacy of the elections held in 2010, which installed President Porfirio Lobo.

In June 2012, Paraguayan president Fernando Lugo was quickly impeached. A former Catholic bishop who had spent years championing the poor and especially indigenous people, he successfully ran for president in 2007. In 2012, a land dispute led to violence in which seven police and nine farmers were killed. Congress accused Lugo of mismanagement and impeached him, with the backing of the supreme court and the electoral commission. Again, other Latin American countries were loath to admit the legitimacy of the proceedings, and Paraguay was ejected from the trade group MERCOSUR. In both cases, the president lost the support of congress. Whether these were technically coups could be debated, but they showed the fragility of institutions in these countries. Elsewhere in Latin America, the unseating of elected presidents in Honduras and Paraguay, regardless of their shortcomings, was regarded as a cautionary tale about the importance of remaining within the bounds of the existing democratic framework.

Not surprisingly, the media play a large role in Latin American politics, and politicians need to be media savvy and telegenic. Some differences from the media landscape in the United States should be noted, however. For one thing, print journalism is thriving. Even small countries typically have several national daily newspapers. Most countries have at least one national weekly magazine (akin to *Time* or *The Economist*) covering national news, but also including stories on municipal politics and issues.

Regular television news coverage tends to follow a format similar to that in the United States, short accounts of leading national and international stories, crime, sports, celebrities, weather, and traffic. However, serious political journalism manages to find a place among the telenovelas, game shows, televangelism, old movies, reality shows, and talent contests. Some programs featuring interviews and discussions with politicians and analysts may be an hour long in prime time. Their tone is generally civil, and they do not feature clashes of incompatible worldviews. Even more surprising is that such programs are often popular.

Media, and television in particular, tend to be concentrated, most notably Globo in Brazil, the world's fourth-largest television network. Thus, on the whole, the media represent their owners and business interests more generally. The relationship between media and politics has been conflictive, particularly where a populist government portrays itself as defending the "people" against wealthy elites. The powers of government, including lawsuits before a pliant judiciary and controlling the paper supply, have been used against opposition media in Venezuela, Argentina, and Ecuador.

LEFT(S) IN POWER

In the 1960s, those who advocated a Cuba-style revolution generally dismissed electoral politics as "bourgeois democracy." Marx's description of the state as the "executive committee of the ruling class" seemed plausible in a situation where landholders could shape or veto legislation. That sense was initially reinforced by the military dictatorships in South America and the murderous regimes in Central America: the very violence unleashed seemed to validate the worldview of the left. Nevertheless, over time, Brazilian, Chilean, Central American, and other leftists, many in exile in Europe and elsewhere, reconsidered their disdain for procedural democracy. With the end of communism in 1989–1991, it became clear that the only legitimate way to win political power would be through the ballot.

It seemed logical that given a free choice, the vast majority of the population, which was poor, should vote for the left, which was on their side rather than for right-wing parties aligned with big business, but left-wing parties did poorly in national elections in the 1990s. The one exception was Chile, where a center-left coalition won the 1989 election and remained in power for twenty years. In Brazil, Lula ran for president unsuccessfully in 1989, 1994, and 1998; Mexico's PRD trailed in elections in 1994 and 2000; the Sandinistas in Nicaragua, the FMLN in El Salvador, and the Unidad Revolucionaria Nacional Guatemalteca (URNG; Guatemalan National Revolutionary Unity) in Guatemala ran presidential candidates in the 1990s and lost to nonleft parties (although some left-wing parties won mayorships, governorships, and seats in parliament). It was especially frustrating for many Salvadorans to see the right-wing party Alianza Republicana Nacionalista (ARENA; Nationalist Republican Alliance), whose founders had sponsored death squads, win four presidential elections, until they were finally unseated in 2007.

To answer why left-wing parties had difficulty mustering electoral victory in countries with large populations of the poor would require examining nations on a case-by-case basis, but some general observations may be made. People vote based on more than the material interests of their class, and their identities are complex. Some people, particularly fundamentalist Christians, might respond to appeals for strict morality. Some voters might respond to personalities more than ideology. Candidates promising to get tough with crime could persuade voters, even if that meant arresting large numbers of adolescent males from poor neighborhoods.

Eventually, however, leftist parties won elections, notably in Brazil and Venezuela, but also in Uruguay, the Dominican Republic, Argentina, Ecuador, Bolivia, El Salvador, Nicaragua, and Paraguay. By 2010, most Latin American presidents were of the left. What being of the left meant, however, varied considerably, as can be shown by first comparing two of the most well-known examples, Hugo Chávez and Luiz Inácio Lula da Silva.

US media tended to portray Chávez, who governed Venezuela from 1999 until his death in early 2013, in terms of his hostility to the United States and his associations with Fidel Castro and President Ahmadinejad of Iran. Here, however, we focus on Chávez from the standpoint of Venezuelans. Chávez first came to attention in the 1990s when the traditional two-party system had imploded. He was imprisoned after leading a failed coup attempt in 1992 but was then released and became something of a folk hero. With his populist skills, he won the 1999 election and immediately convoked a convention to write a new constitution, with the aim of "refounding" the country on new principles. The resulting constitution was ratified in elections, and Chávez ran for president again. He claimed to be leading a "Bolivarian revolution," invoking Simón Bolívar, the Venezuelan liberator, in order to build "twenty-first-century socialism." In classic leftist fashion, he denounced US imperialism and took various initiatives to form alliances of Latin American nations, using oil revenues to do so. Venezuelan oil has been a lifeline to Cuba, and in return Cuba has sent thousands of physicians and other specialists to assist Venezuela.

In Chávez's analysis, the key was to bring oil under the control of the state and to use oil revenues for the benefit of poor Venezuelans. Between 2003 and 2009, the Venezuelan GDP doubled, primarily as a result of higher oil prices. Clinics and hospitals were built and staffed in poor areas; educational programs reduced illiteracy, and school enrollment expanded, including in universities. Cooperatives were created in the countryside, as well as "communes" in urban areas. The poverty rate dropped from over 59 percent to 30 percent by 2006, and extreme poverty dropped from 21.7 percent to 9.9 percent in the same period.

Chávez operated like a classic populist, tapping into the long-standing resentment of poor people, who could identify with him, even with his mulatto face. On his weekly television call-in program, he spoke for hours, denouncing the oligarchy and calling on people to unite. With a majority in congress and a subservient judiciary, Chávez could run the country by his own orders. A characteristic feature of the Chávez presidency was that of "missions": upon seeing a need not being met (illiteracy, medical attention, basic food items), Chávez devised, equipped, and staffed a "mission." One of the most prominent was Barrio Adentro (Into the Neighborhood), through which many clinics were built and staffed in poor neighborhoods. At one point, 30,000 people were working on it (half of them Cuban physicians and other health workers). The emphasis was on primary care, including prevention. Another mission was Mercal, a system of state-run stores selling basic food items at low cost. Although the "missions" approach had the advantage of bringing assistance directly to the poor, it bypassed existing structures, such as the ministries of health and education, with consequent duplication and waste. The missions were also politicized: one mission had the purpose of mobilizing people for the 2004 election, and another involved setting up civilian "militias" supposedly to resist a US invasion, but clearly constituted as a set of pro-Chávez groups that might unleash violence against fellow Venezuelans.

Chávez also politicized PDVSA, the Venezuelan national oil company, which although state-owned had generally operated on sound business criteria. In 2002–2003, when many company workers sided with the anti-Chávez opposition, 19,000 employees were fired, taking their expertise with them,[19] and were replaced by Chávez loyalists. Since then, large percentages of company revenues have been taken by the state to use for social programs, leading to disinvestment and declining production. The "natural resource curse" discussed in the previous chapter certainly applies to Venezuela. It antedated Chávez by decades, but his administration aggravated its worst features (Rosenberg 2007).

Venezuela was highly polarized long before Chávez, but he skillfully harnessed that polarization, enjoying enough popularity to win various elections, although he narrowly lost a referendum in 2009. That the poor have benefited through lavish use of oil profits is undeniable. What is less clear is whether any solid economic development was taking place. Independent reports put inflation at figures higher than the official ones, and there were persistent reports of food shortages, even in government stores, suggesting that prices were being kept too low for farmers to produce. The murder rate in Venezuela rose to be considerably higher than that of Colombia or Mexico, by some accounts 75 per 100,000 people. That fact would suggest that the "Bolivarian" revolution may be irrelevant for many Venezuelans.[20] After Chávez died of cancer in early 2013, his hand-picked successor, Nicolás Maduro, succeeded for some time in holding the Chávez coalition together and in maintaining his basis

Presidents Morales, Lula, and Chávez at a presidential summit, Rio de Janeiro, 2007. © Noah Friedman-Rudovsky.

of support, but accumulating problems, especially inflation, suggested that its days were numbered.

The aim here is not to reach a definitive judgment about Hugo Chávez but to outline some features of his style of government: a focus on funneling resources, primarily from petroleum, to the poor; bypassing much of the existing state structure; and invoking nationalism to maintain a working electoral majority.

Many activists in the Brazilian Workers' Party (Partido dos Trabalhadores, PT) shared the worldview of people like Chávez: that capitalism is inherently unjust and must be overthrown and that the "Third World," as it was then called, needed to chart its own socialist course. Lula, who was one of the founders of the party in 1980, sometimes reflected this kind of rhetoric, although by personal inclination he was more of a pragmatist. By the time of his fourth run for the presidency, the party had won elections in dozens of cities, and so had gained experience in the practicalities of governing, such as in participatory budgets. Under the guidance of campaign consultants, for the 2002 campaign Lula modified his image (wearing more suits) and lowered his rhetorical tone, to the point where some derided this shift as "Lula lite." With a larger share of the middle-class vote, he won the election. His cabinet included social-movement veterans, but his economic appointments were orthodox. For example, Henrique Meirelles, former chief operating officer of BankBoston, was made Central Bank president, and he assured investors that macroeconomic stability would be maintained and that Brazil would not repudiate debts owed to the IMF, as some factions of the PT advocated. The more radical tendencies in the PT were disappointed in the moderate nature of Lula's approach.

Lula retained much of what had begun under President Fernando Henrique Cardoso (1995–2002), contrary to the common practice of repudiating previous programs. He renamed and expanded the Family Allowance program; land reform continued, but the government also continued to support large commercial agriculture. Although some activists from grassroots social movements worked in the government, the movements themselves felt that they were being kept at arm's length. Early in his administration Lula attempted to tackle a reform of the government pension system (75% of the benefits were going to 15% of government employees), but the labor unions (a core PT constituency) resisted, and he had to back off.

The biggest disappointment came in 2005 when it was revealed that the PT, which had maintained a reputation for honesty, was making large monthly payments through various mechanisms to legislators in other parties to secure their votes. Over thirty legislators were indicted, and the scandal touched people high in the PT, but Lula claimed that he had been unaware of the payments. The scandal was evidence of how, once in power, the PT felt compelled to practice traditional political maneuvers, particularly deal making with regional political power brokers. Lula nevertheless won reelection in 2006, this time drawing more support from the poor in the northeast who were receiving the benefits of the Bolsa Familia (Family Allowance) program than from the more highly educated middle-class voters in the south who had become disenchanted. Yet when he left office, Lula enjoyed an 80 percent approval rating. His success is largely due to continued economic growth and initiatives to assure that the benefits were widely shared. His handpicked successor, Dilma Rousseff, won the 2010 election handily and was reelected more narrowly in 2014. The PT was further tarnished as a corruption scandal involving Petrobras unfolded in 2015. The courts indicted dozens of businesspeople and politicians. Although initially no charges were brought against President Rousseff, she had chaired the oil company for seven years when the kickbacks and payoffs occurred.

Chávez and Lula serve to exemplify the different styles of the left. The governments of Evo Morales (Bolivia), Rafael Correa (Ecuador), Daniel Ortega (Nicaragua), and Cristina Fernández de Kirchner (Argentina) can be said to have some of the features of the populist left. Each case needs to be examined on its own, however: none is as personalistic as Chávez's was, and Argentina's economy is not primarily based on natural resources. The administrations of the Dominican Republic (Leonel Fernández), Chile (four presidents until 2010), El Salvador (Mauricio Funes and Salvador Sánchez Cerén), and Uruguay (Tabaré Vázquez and José Mujica), can be said to belong to the pragmatic left. Table 14.2 indicates some of the contrasts between these two models of leftist governments in power. Presidents Chávez, Morales, and Correa all oversaw conventions to write new constitutions, based on the conviction that nothing less than "refounding" the nation would provide the basis for the kind of society they

TABLE 14.2. Comparison of Left-wing Governments

POPULIST	PRAGMATIC
Economic strategy based on natural resources	Broad economic strategy, including agroexport and developing human capital
Anti-imperialist vision—United States is the enemy	Cooperative relationships with other countries; readiness to pursue their country's interest, even in opposition to the United States
Mobilize the "people" against the oligarchy	Accept the constraints of a pluralist society, seek a pragmatic consensus
New constitution; attempt to establish the "revolution" permanently	Accept the conventions of multiparty democracy, including being voted out of power
The state is leading actor in the economy	An effective, efficient state is needed, in conjunction with private sector and nonprofit sector

envisioned. They saw their presidencies as transformational; Chávez intended to be president indefinitely before he developed cancer.

Many activists and academics in Latin America and elsewhere sympathize with the populist left, which they see as committed to a revolutionary vision, and they regard what is here being called a pragmatic left as too accommodating to capitalism. The crucial question, however, is what will work in the long run to shape societies in which all citizens have a decent life and opportunity for themselves and their children.

Perhaps the very meaning of "left" and "right" in Latin America is changing. In Chile, the center-left Concertación governments did not overturn the economic thrust of the Pinochet period, but they made significant changes so that the country enjoyed twenty years of growth, poverty was reduced, and the country achieved Latin America's highest standard of living. When the center-right won the 2010 election, it did not reverse what had been done, or even argue for "downsizing" the state, which is a mantra of US conservatives. At the national level, Colombia has had conservative governments for several presidential periods and never a truly "left" administration. Nevertheless, some aspects taken for granted in Colombia would be regarded as "left" elsewhere. For example, all households in the country are classified into six economic strata, and those in poorer strata pay less for utilities and medical care. Moreover, preschool daycare is available to all families. Right-wing Colombian governments treat as normal what would be ridiculed as "unaffordable" and labeled "socialism" if proposed in the United States.

RESHAPING THE STATE

In the 1980s, under the pressure of the debt crisis, a process of reform began in the Latin American state. At first, it seemed to be largely a matter of cutting payroll and selling off state enterprises (as a condition of the IMF before further loans would be made to meet debt servicing), but it soon became clear that the aim was to redefine the role of the state. For a half century, particularly in the larger countries, it had been taken for granted that the state played a lead role in promoting development, including building roads, hydroelectric plants, bridges, and other infrastructure items. In a number of countries, governments ran large enterprises, not only the utilities (water, electricity, gas, telephones) but major banks, mines, oil companies, cement and steel plants, railways, and airlines. In the early 1980s, state-owned companies made up around 12 percent of GDP in Latin America.

A key argument for privatization was that these companies were often poorly managed and even ran at a loss. Government companies were used by clientelistic politicians to provide jobs for their supporters. The upshot was that state-run companies typically had more employees than they would have had under private management, where the incentives are stronger to cut costs and be efficient. Rather than generating revenues, many of these companies had to be subsidized by general government funds. A further reason for privatizing was that the revenue from sales could be used to bring down government debt, which was a heavy burden in the 1980s and 1990s. Opposition to privatization came from employees, who understandably feared that privatization might jeopardize their jobs. A further argument was based on national sovereignty, especially if the companies might be sold to foreign investors.

Nevertheless, privatization moved ahead in Latin America more rapidly than in any other region of the world. Companies were typically sold in a public sealed-bid auction. In some cases, employees were able to acquire shares. One form of privatization was by shifting to contracting: instead of maintaining departments of permanent workers devoted to highway maintenance, for example, governments could contract specific jobs to private-sector companies. Chile was where privatization took place the earliest and most dramatically: state enterprises dropped from 40 percent of GDP to 16 percent. The figure would have been 6.6 percent had the government copper company Codelco been sold, but that was a cash cow for both the government and the military and was retained. In Mexico between 1982 and 1994, the number of state enterprises (in areas such as petroleum, gas, water, electricity, highway, railways, and ports) dropped from 1,155 to 219. Most of the money raised ($23 billion) from their sale went to retiring government debt. When privatized, these enterprises typically reduced the workforce; for example, the number of railway employees was cut in half from 46,000 to 23,000. The percentage of the labor force in state-owned enterprises dropped from 4.4 to 2 percent. In a very different situation, in the 1990s the post-Sandinista governments in Nicaragua sold off 343 government enterprises. One place where ordinary Latin Americans noticed the effects of privatization was in telephone service. Prior to privatization, a household often had to wait years for a phone line or pay a high installation fee that priced out the poor. Privatization coincided with the rise of cell phones, which are now in the hands of even poor rural Latin Americans.

Privatization did not always turn out well. In some cases, procedures were not transparent and assets were bought cheaply by insiders. The Chilean government had to renationalize much of the banking system in the crisis of the early 1980s. What had been state monopolies could become private monopolies or oligopolies. The Mexican billionaire Carlos Slim acquired the Mexican government phone system, and came to control 90 percent of landlines and 80 percent of mobile phones. Mexicans paid among the highest rates in the world, due to lack of competition, which Slim resisted, using his economic clout. In 2013, however, the government finally moved to end his monopoly, but his power was unlikely to be curtailed.

A well-known case of a failed privatization was that of water service in Cochabamba, Bolivia, in 2000. The city is the third largest in the country and had been growing rapidly. Over half the people did not have access to piped water. The World Bank had been pressuring Bolivia to privatize water companies. A consortium was formed, with heavy foreign participation, especially by Bechtel Corporation, with a proposal to extend coverage. However, as a first step it added a 35 percent rate hike, typically bringing costs to $20 per month, prohibitively high for the poor. Demonstrations were organized that brought people together across class lines, with support from movements elsewhere in the country. The standoff escalated into what became known as the "water wars": to the protesters, it was clear that a plan was being forced on Bolivians by the World Bank and corporations like Bechtel that would cost the poor more. The demonstrations spread to other parts of the country, and the president declared a state of siege.

Many organizers were arrested and beaten, and several participants were killed. The government was forced to back down. Bechtel attempted to sue the government for $25 million for breach of contract but eventually desisted. Some Bolivians and those combating "neoliberalism" at the World Social Forum and elsewhere regarded it as victory, but over a decade later, the needed water improvements had not been made. Poor people were still getting their water from trucks and paying ten times as much as those with connections in the city.

As elsewhere, Latin Americans are debating the proper role of the state in the age of globalization. However, there are few voices arguing that government should be "downsized," as is proposed by conservatives in the United States. One reason is that the state is already small in comparison to developed countries. Tax revenue averages 20 percent of GDP in Latin America, while it is 35 percent in OECD countries (Arnson, Bergman, and Fairfield 2012). In Guatemala in 2010 it was a little over 11 percent, and in Paraguay it was 14 percent.[21]

There are two major problems with taxes: the design of the tax system itself and tax evasion. Until around 1980, 27.7 percent of taxes came from imports and exports. With the opening to the global market, these taxes have been brought down to 5 percent of tax revenue. Unlike in the United States, where all households file income taxes, in Latin American countries only people in upper-income brackets file personal tax returns, and the rates they pay are low.[22] Only a small proportion of total tax comes from income tax, 1.5 percent of GDP as opposed to 9 percent in OECD countries.

A large portion (36.2%) of taxes is in the form of the VAT (value-added tax), which is a sales tax applied at various stages of the production and sale of a good (from raw materials to manufacture to wholesale to final retail sale). At each of these stages a percentage of the VAT is to be paid and recorded, and each buyer verifies that it has been done. Thus, the system is self-policing, and that is part of its attraction to governments. However, it applies only to the formal sector of the economy, and thus in some countries, half or more of the economy is not taxed.

Policy analysts generally believe that Latin American countries need to increase total taxes in order to provide the services expected in twenty-first-century nations. In principle, people should be required to pay more taxes, including income taxes. Tax-paying citizens are more likely to hold their governments accountable and are understandably angry when they believe that their governments do not provide services properly. A government regarded as honest and competent may give citizens the sense that their taxes are well spent; when a government is regarded as crooked or ineffective, people will feel justified in resisting new taxes and evading existing ones.

TOWARD CIVIL SERVICE

Stereotypes of dealing with Latin American governments include long waiting lines, excessive paperwork, repeated stamping of documents in different offices, and government workers who brandish their own authority rather than providing efficient service to citizens. In chapter 4 we noted the number of bureaucratic steps needed to register a business.

In modern societies, citizens expect government agencies to give prompt, effective, and competent service. Advanced countries typically have a civil service, that is, a system whereby government employees are recruited and promoted by merit and enjoy job security, meaning they will not be fired after a change of administration. Hiring is not a matter of political patronage, although the positions at the top of major agencies are reserved for political appointments by the current administration. Some people are satisfied to spend a career as professional government employees.

All Latin American countries have civil service systems on the books, but with some exceptions they remain largely on paper. Patronage is still the primary way public sector jobs are filled.[23] As noted earlier, patronage has been taken for granted in Latin America, and many view politics primarily in terms of political power to be utilized for oneself and one's allies (patrimonialism).

Merilee Grindle (2010) observes that the key element in establishing a modern civil service in Latin America is not in the legislation but in its implementation. In a civil service system, most positions are filled through credentialing based on education or testing; employees advance up the career ladder based on merit and have job security; the system runs on clear rules. Civil servants are working for the state or the particular agency, not for the party or patron through whom they were hired.

Only three countries, Costa Rica, Chile, and Brazil, "recruited significant numbers of public sector workers through a structured career civil service system" (Grindle 2010, 8). In some countries (all of Central America except Costa Rica, Paraguay, Peru, Ecuador, Dominican Republic, Bolivia), few appointments are merit based. Grindle summarizes how civil service laws are bypassed: exceptions are given to particular agencies not to observe the rules or funding is cut for examinations.

In Brazil, the first efforts to establish a civil service system date back to the Vargas administration in the 1930s and 1940s. In Argentina, a reform in 1991 set up a new system intended to apply to 30,000 positions in the government, but through temporary (180-day) contracts, administrations bypassed the program. In Mexico, under the PRI one-party rule, the lower levels of the government had stability through unions, which ran a patronage system, while the upper layers were political appointees who rotated with each new administration. Some portions of this system, such as the foreign service, the statistics agency, and the office of the attorney general, became enclaves of professional career employees. In the 1980s and 1990s, with the cooperation of the other parties and the legislature, a new career civil service was developed, which was intended to apply to 43,000 middle and upper positions. However, due to resistance from politicians, by 2007 only 8,300 public servants were in the new system.

In Chile, elements of a civil service existed for decades, alongside large elements of discretionary hiring. The military government used those discretionary mechanisms after 1973, and the postdictatorship government likewise used them to place pro-democracy appointees after 1990. After a 2003 political scandal, a new system was devised, establishing rules to assure that high-level government positions were chosen from pools of candidates who had passed competitive examinations, but this system encountered resistance.

After surveying progress toward and resistance to civil service reform, Grindle concludes that "patronage systems will eventually be supplanted by career civil service systems—slowly, incrementally, and adaptively" (2010, 23).

TOWARD MATURE DEMOCRACY

Older Latin American activists cherish memories of heady days of political excitement: Chileans during the Allende government in the early 1970s, and then in the street demonstrations and the campaign to vote against General Pinochet in 1988 and 1989; grassroots Venezuelans, Ecuadoreans, and Bolivians whose demonstrations forced presidents out in the 1990s and 2000s; Mexicans protesting the electoral fraud of 1988 and marching in solidarity with the Zapatistas; Central Americans in the popular movements of the 1970s and the rallies of the Sandinista revolution; Argentineans protesting against the whole political class in the economic collapse of 2001. Under both repressive military governments and civilian governments, political life has often been vigorous.

As noted earlier, procedural democracy is now well established in most of Latin

America. The task is to assure that government works efficiently and equitably. Occasions arise when people go to the streets even in well-functioning democracies, such as the mass movements of students in Chile in 2012. And some groups will have to serve as the conscience of society itself, not simply defenders of their own rights, for example, drawing attention to violence against women or the threats to the environment from mining and fossil fuels. The spontaneous street protests in Brazil in 2013 and 2015 were triggered by specific issues like urban transportation and extravagant spending in preparation for the World Cup, but they were driven by a sense among the middle classes that the nation deserved better from its government. The abduction and disappearance in 2014 of forty-three Mexican students by local police in conjunction with the mayor and organized criminal gangs triggered nationwide demonstrations against the government's inability to confront rampant violence and corruption.

The next two chapters take up further challenges facing society and governments: citizen security and the rule of law (chapter 15) and health and education (chapter 16).

FURTHER READING

Two case-study collections examine democracy: Levine and Molina (2011) primarily from the standpoint of procedural democracy, and Mainwaring and Scully (2010) with a focus on governance. Ignacio Walker (2013) presents wide-ranging essays grounded in his own experience in Chile. Hellinger (2011) is an overview sympathetic to the Latin American left. De la Torre and Arnson (2013) collects a number of country studies of populism. On the reform of the state, see Lora (2006).

Toward Rule of Law

Combating Crime and Corruption

After over a decade of war in Guatemala, El Salvador, and Nicaragua, which spilled over into neighboring countries, Central Americans hoped they could reap the blessings of peace. Instead, they have had to confront expanding crime in its varying forms, starting in the 1990s and worsening into the 2000s. By 2012, Honduras, which had not endured a civil war, had the highest murder rate in the world, and government forces were beating, jailing, and occasionally killing opposition leaders with impunity in the wake of the army's removal of President Zelaya in 2009. Market vendors in San Salvador were paying monthly protection fees to gangs. Wealthy and middle-class neighborhoods in Guatemala City were gated communities, and even more modest neighborhoods had retrofitted themselves with checkpoints. Officials at all levels in Guatemala, from rural mayors to all political parties, were said to be on the take from drug traffickers, and that seemed to be true of all countries in the region (except perhaps Costa Rica). People would no longer go to certain parts of cities, out of fear of being mugged.

The six small countries of Central America should not be considered a microcosm of the whole region. However, these related and self-reinforcing conditions—common crime, gangs, drug trafficking, low- and high-level corruption, ineffective and corrupt police and courts, human rights violations—are found throughout Latin America. This chapter examines various forms of crime and corruption, the reasons for them, and suitable responses to them, on the basis of initiatives already under way. The common thread is the need for an effective rule of law applied for all citizens, which is certainly a key function of a well-functioning state.

COMMON CRIME

Fear of crime is common in many parts of Latin America. A study in the late 1990s found that in Peru, Ecuador, Mexico, Venezuela, El Salvador, and Guatemala, 40 percent or more of respondents said that at least one family member had been victimized in the previous year. Examples of crime are pick-pocketing and variations on it, robbery with a weapon, breaking into a home or office when it is unoccupied, and car theft. Kidnapping for ransom has been a business for decades in some countries. One version is the "express kidnapping" in which the victim is taken at gunpoint to a bank machine and forced to withdraw the limit.[1] Between mid-2008 and mid-2009, forty-six kidnappings a day took place in Venezuela (Casas-Zamora 2012).

The longitudinal studies in Rio de Janeiro (Perlman 2010) and Guayaquil (Moser 2009) cited in chapter 2 describe how people look back fondly on an era decades ago when their community seemed to be united and peaceful. They contrast it with the present, when their material situation has improved but gun violence makes them afraid to go out at night. That is a common impression of people who experienced Latin American cities decades ago. Two anthropologists trace the evolution of Guatemala City neighborhoods in recent decades through ethnographic studies (Camus 2011, Levenson 2011): people who once felt some sense of achievement as aspiring lower middle class now feel that they are at the mercy of youth gangs. Collective frustration is vented in beatings or even lynching of thieves or rapists. Neither the neighborhood nor downtown Guatemala City offers places for youth to hang out. Many young people join evangelical churches as a way to escape the pressure to join gangs.

The move to the city perhaps removes some of the inhibitions restraining behavior in rural villages where people knew one another. That does not happen overnight; the first generation retains some internal restraints, which, however, may be lost in the next generation or the one after that. Young people are far more attuned to youth popular culture than to the life of the village from which their parents or grandparents came. In the aftermath of the wars of the 1980s, Central America was full of weapons and people who knew how to use them. However, it should be noted that crime and murder rates are significantly lower in Nicaragua than in neighboring countries, possibly because the Sandinista police are better trained and more honest than those in neighboring countries. Police are widely viewed as ineffective or even as criminals themselves. In Mexico, only one crime in ten is reported, and only a tenth of these is prosecuted. Criminals can thus operate with considerable assurance that they will not be caught and punished.

Latin American tabloids every day carry stories and photos of grisly murders. Murder rates in some countries (El Salvador, Guatemala, Honduras, Venezuela) are among the highest in the world. A 2012 worldwide study found that the world average of homicides was 6.9 people per 100,000. Some countries had only a fraction of that amount, while others have many multiples. Only three Latin American countries were below the world average (Chile, Argentina, Cuba), and many were far above it. Rates in Brazil and Mexico were triple the world average, and those of El Salvador and Honduras were ten times as high. The study did not provide a breakdown of types of homicides. The high rates in Central America, Mexico, Venezuela, Colombia, and Brazil are no doubt partly drug- and gang-related. Central America was the most violent subregion in the world.

TABLE 15.1. Comparative Murder Rates of Selected
Latin American Countries

COUNTRY	HOMICIDES PER 100,000
[Canada]	[1.6]
Chile	3.1
[United States]	[4.7]
Argentina	5.5
Costa Rica	8.5
Peru	9.6
Bolivia	12.1
Mexico	21.5
Brazil	25.2
El Salvador	41.2
Venezuela	53.7
Honduras	90.4

Source: United Nations Office on Drugs and Crime (2014, 128–129).
Countries in brackets are for purposes of comparison.

One factor in murder rates is domestic violence, men killing their wives or partners for alleged infidelity, or killing a rival. These are frequently called "crimes of passion," and in court the defendant and his lawyers will invoke this defense, seeking leniency on the basis of the presumed offended honor. Starting in 1993, a pattern of abduction and murder of young women took place in Ciudad Juárez, across the border from El Paso, Texas. Ten years later, the number of victims was estimated to be 370. The victims were young poor women, typically working in assembly plants. At least a third of the victims showed signs of rape and sexual violence. Many had their hands tied. Police and other authorities were slow to come to the scene and conducted poor investigations when they did; in fact, virtually no one was brought to justice for the crimes. The police generally assumed, with no evidence, that the young women were involved in prostitution or gangs or that they had been killed by their partners; in both instances they were blaming the victim. Eventually, activists organized around the issue of "femicide"—the murder of women as women. A somewhat similar pattern was discerned in Guatemala. The authorities were eventually shamed into recognizing the existence of the problem, but a decade later some women were still being murdered with impunity (Beltrán and Freeman 2007).

CENTRAL AMERICAN *MARAS* AND OTHER YOUTH GANGS

The incidence of gangs in Central America has often been attributed to youth deported from the United States in the 1990s, who are said to have brought with them the gangs that they had joined there. The *maras*, as they are called, are regarded as little different from the organized crime organizations responsible for drug trafficking and its associated violence. Although that theory has some elements of truth, it is seriously misleading.

It is true that the children of Central American refugees, especially in Los Angeles, often grew up poor and were obliged to fend for themselves while feeling threatened by Latino and African American gangs (Mexican Mafia, Crips, and Bloods). Partly in perceived self-defense, two Salvadoran gangs were formed, Mara Salvatrucha and 18th Street. Large-scale deportation began in the 1990s, and so eventually, thousands of young people were deported to situations of even greater poverty than they had experienced in the United States. Sonja Wolf observes:

> Returning youths often felt disoriented in a country that they had few memories of, and they felt alienated by the humble surroundings they encountered. Although many of them hoped to make a fresh start, weak family ties and continued marginalization prompted some to carry on with the gang life they knew best. Their comparatively smarter dress, money, and romanticized tales of gang life held a fascination that local adolescents found hard to resist. (2011, 49)

Research showed, however, that the gangs in El Salvador were overwhelmingly made up of local youth, not deportees. The police, the politicians, and the media tended to attribute most murders to these youth gangs, although studies suggested that three-quarters were not gang-related. In response to (media-fostered) public pressure, in the 2000s the Salvadoran government adopted a get-tough (*mano dura*, "tough fist") policy, which, for example, made gang membership itself (proven by appearance, e.g., tattoos) a crime. In the first year, 19,275 arrests were made (including repeated arrests), but 95 percent of the cases were dismissed in the courts (Wolf 2011, 59). The main result of *mano dura* was that gang members spent time in prison learning from one another and forming alliances, and they emerged hardened, with attitudes and behavior more like those of professional criminals. One indication of this was that gang members dropped tattoos and other distinguishing marks.

One feature of gang life is initiation. Initiates are sometimes beaten or forced to commit acts of violence, even murder. Young women are initiated through sex, sometimes with multiple partners determined by lot. Violence and drug consumption are features of gang life. The most common crime of Central American gangs is extortion, forcing businesses to pay a "protection" tax. They are also increasingly brought in to perform tasks for international drug trafficking operations (moving packages and "enforcement," even to the point of murder).

While youth gangs may operate in conjunction with organized crime, the two are not identical; indeed, gangs are common around the world where youth are alienated and feel they have few options.[2] Youth gangs also exist in cities like Guayaquil and Cali, where there is no connection to US gangs.

DRUG TRAFFICKING AND ORGANIZED CRIME

Levels of crime and violence in Latin America are closely related to drug trafficking, both internationally and domestically. Indeed, for over two decades Latin America has largely been viewed through the lens of drug trafficking by US policy makers and by the general public. We here examine the evolution of drug trafficking in broad strokes, with some effort to see it from the standpoint of Latin Americans.

Andean indigenous people have cultivated the coca leaf for many centuries, holding wads of it in their mouths for the relief it provides in bearing the cold, high altitude, and harsh working conditions. In the nineteenth century, German scientists discovered how to concentrate cocaine and began to experiment with it.[3] Likewise, marihuana was cultivated in western Mexico and sold in the United States in the mid-twentieth century. The roots of contemporary trafficking can be traced back to that period, driven after the 1960s by rising demand in the United States and Europe.

In the 1970s, Colombian traffickers set up a system whereby the leaf was grown in remote parts of Peru and Bolivia, concentrated into a paste through chemical processing, and then transported to laboratories in Colombia, where it was turned into powder. That powder could then be transported to the United States primarily through the Caribbean, by boat, plane, or individuals ("mules") transporting small quantities on their person. In the United States, it was distributed by networks to individual dealers. In the 1980s, a particularly addictive form of cocaine called crack was developed in the United States and marketed to the poor. During this same period, Brazil became a transit area for cocaine making its way to Europe, especially through ports near Rio and São Paulo. As internal consumption increased, the favelas of Rio were taken over by drug gangs, which by the late 1980s controlled some favelas, to the point where police rarely ventured in.

Thus the features of the drug production and distribution system have been in place for several decades. The chain goes from the field, to the lab, and then over land or sea into the consumer country, where it is distributed down to the retail level.[4] For small farmers, coca is an attractive crop: it can grow in poor soil and needs little tending, it can be harvested more than once a year, and it pays far better than legal crops, especially in remote areas. Under pressure or inducement from the United States, Peruvian, Bolivian, and later Colombian armies carried out eradication operations, pulling up crops and spraying pesticides from the air, which also hit legitimate crops and affected children and livestock. Critics pointed to the "balloon effect": impair production at one point and it will expand somewhere else; as long as a demand exists, someone will grow the crop. They also noted that those profiting the most (cartels in Colombia,[5] drug lords in the United States, or banks facilitating money-laundering) were less vulnerable than peasant growers or street sellers.

Those who were supposed to do the enforcing, police or army, might go through the motions, but they were likely to be receiving payoffs from traffickers, as were local and national politicians. If the supply were really being constricted, prices should go up, but on the whole the street price of cocaine has been little affected.

From a Latin American standpoint, it was hypocritical of the United States to blame their countries when the entire system was driven by demand, especially in the United States. Surveys of Americans over twelve who admitted to using cocaine "in the past month" rose from 2.6 percent in 1979 to a high of 3 percent in 1985, and then declined. Since 1990, the rate has fluctuated between 0.7 percent and 1 percent. (The same figure for marihuana was 13 percent, and since 1990 has fluctuated between 4.7 percent and 6 percent.)

The story of the Medellín drug lord Pablo Escobar embodies the emergence of the drug-trafficking system. Escobar rose from a life of petty crime to preside over an empire, using both payoffs and violence. At its height his organization was smuggling fifteen tons of cocaine a day into the United States and he was on the Forbes list of the wealthiest people in the world. In 1982, he was elected to the Colombian congress. Escobar was responsible for the deaths of hundreds (if not thousands) of people, including the bombing of a civilian airliner. Escobar had become a legend by cultivating a "Robin Hood" image, putting some of his money into housing developments, sports fields, and the like. Eventually the Colombian government pursued him, and after receiving assurances that he would not be extradited to the United States, he surrendered and was held at a luxury prison built especially for him, from which he continued to direct criminal operations. When he escaped, a special Colombian army unit, assisted by US Drug Enforcement Administration (DEA) and military specialists, hunted him down and killed him in a firefight in Medellín in December 1993. The "Cali cartel" briefly took leadership, but in the mid-1990s, the Colombian government arrested its major leaders and extradited some of them to the United States. Colombian drug organizations then splintered into dozens or even hundreds of smaller operations.[6]

For decades, many Latin Americans preferred to think that their countries were simply transit routes, not markets for drug consumption. Statistically, rates of use and addiction were far lower than in the United States and Europe, but they were not insignificant. Decades ago, Colombia had *bazuko*, a cheap version of cocaine similar to crack, and a drug trade existed in other countries. Brazil is a transit point to Europe, but its drug trade is driven primarily by internal demand: Brazil is the second-largest consumer of cocaine in the world—after the United States.

In the early 1970s, a group of common criminals in the Ilha Grande prison, on an island off the coast of Rio de Janeiro, formed a military-style organization[7] called the Red Command (Comando Vermelho), first in order to control the prison itself. After they were released, they engaged in bank robberies and kidnappings and decided to go into the drug trade, which had been growing in Rio since the late 1970s. By the end of the 1980s, the Red Command controlled an estimated 70 percent of the sale points in Rio. Other rival gangs disputed territory with them.

Bolivian soldiers destroying clandestine drug lab. © Noah Friedman-Rudovsky.

Like the Medellín organizations, the Rio drug gangs formed structures in the favelas, with a *dono* (lit. "owner") at the top and many under him providing protection, distributing, and selling—even reaching down to children serving as lookouts. They also provided some community services and sometimes meted out rough "justice." The police, who had never provided much protection in favelas, were now afraid to enter. The gangs moved to take over the traditional neighborhood organizations, placing their own loyalists into leadership positions through threats and violence.[8]

In the 1990s, as US interdiction efforts in the Caribbean had some success, Colombian drug lords shifted to overland routes, partnering with Mexican organizations and increasingly making their payments not in cash but in cocaine, which the Mexican dealers used for selling in the United States and in the internal Mexican market. The huge increase in cross-border traffic with NAFTA made it easier to transfer drugs. Mexican drug traffickers seized the initiative from Colombians and soon controlled international traffic. Several cartels based around cities and areas (Sinaloa, Tijuana, Ciudad Juárez, Gulf of Mexico, state of Michoacán) were involved in alliances and turf disputes. A further development was the emergence of a new group, the Zetas, originally formed by veterans of an elite army unit (many US-trained) who took their skills to the Gulf cartel initially as "enforcers," using violence (mass killings, decapitation) to instill fear. They then decided to run their own operations and to challenge the other organizations. They recruited others, including former Guatemalan army Kaibiles, also trained in counterinsurgency.

At the start of his term in 2006, after an extremely narrow and contested electoral victory, Mexican president Felipe Calderón declared a war against drug traffickers. Because the corruption of the various police forces and local politicians made them unreliable, he sent the Mexican army first into the state of Michoacán in central Mexico and then elsewhere. As Enrique Krauze (2012) summarizes, "A complicated gang war broke out, involving various cartels (linked to different local police contingents), as well as the Federal Police, navy assault forces, and units of the Mexican military." Calderón's initiative had unintended consequences, notably the rise in the murder rate, which had been declining in Mexico. By 2012, at least 60,000 people had been killed, many of them young men involved in drug trafficking but also many bystanders.

The Zetas in particular began to move into other forms of organized crime. One example was massive theft of oil from Pemex, the state oil company, which estimates that it is losing $750 million a year to theft. Kidnapping for ransom increased, as did extortion against Central American refugees making their way north. The mass killing of seventy-two Central American refugees in Mexico in August 2010 was a message to other refugees and a signal that the Zetas were more ruthless than other criminal organizations. To avoid leaving a paper or electronic trail, organizations

Vigil to protest violence in state of Guerrero, Mexico. © Noah Friedman-Rudovsky.

began doing money-laundering on a cash or barter basis through the informal economy. That of course brought many otherwise uninvolved citizens into their orbit. The cartels, and the Zetas in particular, expanded from their traditional areas of the north, west, and the eastern gulf to the point where they were present in most of Mexico's thirty-one states and the Federal District. Organized crime took advantage of government weakness after the 2000 election, which ended one-party centralized control at all levels of government, and worked particularly at the municipal level through either bribery or intimidation to assure that it could operate.

Starting in 2007, groups of Zetas moved into Guatemala and were soon judged to be responsible for various murders. In December 2010, a group of presumed Zetas forced their way into a radio station in Cobán, Guatemala, and accused President Álvaro Colom of having reneged on a promise to protect the Zetas and lift the state of siege (even though he had been given $11.5 million). In May 2011, twenty-seven people were decapitated in the relatively remote northern region of Guatemala; the killings were believed to have been ordered by a Zeta leader from his prison in Mexico. As murky as these incidents and details are in themselves, they indicate that organized crime had made major inroads into Guatemala, and that the government was unable or unwilling to halt it. Central America is a land bridge from Colombia to Mexico, and Panama is a banking haven, hence traffickers have used the isthmus for decades. Since the mid-1990s, this route has been used increasingly in preference to the Caribbean route.

Although the accent here has been on the evolution of cocaine traffic, the mix of products has varied over time. Marihuana is attractive to traffickers because it is a low-cost product that does not require chemical processing. Heroin is a relatively small percentage of traffic. A recent development is the expansion of methamphetamine, which is made entirely in laboratories, at one time from over-the-counter medicines in the rural United States. After restrictions were placed on precursor materials in the United States, production shifted to Mexico, where cartels have the advantage of being able to use those chemicals directly rather than extracting them from medications and thus can work on a larger scale. In February 2012, Mexican authorities found 15 tons of pure methamphetamine and a laboratory on the outskirts of Guadalajara. The lab was traced to Sinaloa cartel leader Joaquín (El Chapo) Guzmán. Meth was also being manufactured in Guatemala for delivery to Mexico, Europe, and the United States.

Despite the continuing references to the "cartels" (Sinaloa, Gulf) and the Zetas, the general trend seemed to be toward greater splintering into groups not under the control of a single capo. This was similar to what had happened in Colombia in the mid-1990s, after the Medellín and Cali cartels were broken up. The existing organizations tended to outsource operations, for example, using youth gangs in Central America for particular tasks. If caught, gang members would have no information about the inner workings of the organization itself.

In the late 1990s, the Colombian and US governments together devised "Plan Colombia." From the US side, aid was to be given for fighting drugs; from the angle of the Colombian military and government, drugs were part of a larger set of issues, particularly the fact that large areas of the countryside were controlled by left-wing guerrillas, not the Colombian state. Over the course of the next decade several billion dollars were spent from both US aid and Colombian resources. During those years, critics pointed to the deleterious effects of aerial spraying, human rights violations by the Colombian army and police, and collusion between the military and the paramilitaries. After the World Trade Center attack in 2001, the Colombian and US governments branded the left-wing guerrillas as "terrorists." From within Colombia, the key development was that the government reasserted its authority and presence in the countryside. It also dealt major blows against the guerrillas, especially the FARC. One result was that Colombians could now travel freely throughout their country. Combined with better security in major cities like Medellín and Bogotá and economic growth, the net effect was of a turnaround in the country. Nevertheless, Colombia remained the largest producer of cocaine and heroin in the hemisphere.

The long-term pattern is that international drug trafficking shifts and adapts. The trafficking routes shifted from the Caribbean to Central America and Mexico; turf wars then broke out all over Mexico, and then spilled down into Guatemala, and from there to Honduras, driving up murder rates. For decades Latin Americans have questioned attempts to attack drug trafficking "at the source" and insisted that as long as demand remained strong, supplies would be produced.

Critics have suggested a more radical solution: decriminalization of drug possession and treatment of addiction as a public health matter could eliminate the profits and hence the warfare from drug trafficking. At a 2012 summit of western hemisphere presidents, Presidents Otto Pérez Molina (Guatemala), Juan Manuel Santos (Colombia), and Laura Chinchilla (Costa Rica)—all three politically right-wing or center-right—stated that present policies focused on interdiction were not working and that alternatives, including some form of decriminalization, had to be explored.[9] President Obama and his entourage reiterated US objection to any form of legalization,[10] and no other presidents supported the notion, but a taboo had been broken. Tens of thousands of Latin Americans have died, and a significant portion of government revenues have gone into failed drug interdiction efforts, which are largely the result of foreign demand, especially in the United States. A further sign of shifting attitudes among the public and the region's elites was the 2013 "experiment" by the Uruguayan government to decriminalize possession and use of small quantities of marihuana and to control its production and sale, thereby eliminating the criminal dimension.

CORRUPTION

Drug trafficking brings with it corruption of public officials from the municipal level to congress, political parties, and presidencies. Latin Americans have often taken for granted that their politicians are corrupt, but it is only recently that the topic has gone beyond the anecdotal to be studied systematically. Research on the topic is driven by two questions: 1. whether and to what extent corruption undermines democracy, and 2. whether democracy itself can help end or curtail corruption.

Stephen D. Morris and Charles H. Blake (2010, 2–3) provide a useful list of types of corruption:

- *bribery*—an illegal payment made to a government worker as a condition for performing a particular act
- *kickback*—a payment made after the service is rendered, typically a portion of the government award
- *extortion*—a bribe made under threat by a public official
- *graft* and *embezzlement*—public funds appropriated for alternative uses (not involving exchange with citizens)
- *fraud*—schemes to appropriate public funds (e.g., fake companies, ghost workers on payroll, overcharging on contracts, false accounting)
- *nepotism, favoritism, conflict of interest*—jobs or contracts given to family members
- *state capture*—special interests take control of state institutions (e.g., organized crime with police and public officials)
- *illegal campaign contributions and expenditures, electoral fraud, vote buying*

The authors then make the distinction between upper-level corruption (high-level officials and large amounts of money) and lower-level corruption (ordinary citizens in their encounters with bureaucrats or police). Their focus is on political corruption, as in the examples listed above, but corruption can occur in the private sector, too, such as banks laundering money.

Although they cite definitions of corruption, Morris and Blake admit that the notion is "amorphous." The motive is not always the private gain of individuals; political parties may engage in corrupt practices for party purposes (e.g., the Brazilian PT giving cash to members of congress in other parties in return for crucial votes) or to get off-the-books money for campaign expenses. In concluding their conceptualization of corruption, the authors note that it "denotes a lack of congruence between the legitimate use of public power (as spelled out in the normative order) and self-interested behavior that violates the public trust" (Morris and Blake 2010, 4).

In a well-functioning society, public officials are respected, perform their jobs well, decide matters on merit, and observe clear rules; public-works contracts are awarded through a transparent bidding process; judges decide cases based on their merits; police pursue criminals and protect public order; and bribes are not even offered, let alone taken. That is a reasonable description of what happens most of the time in well-ordered societies, but it is true only by degrees in most Latin American countries, as indeed in the majority of countries in the world.

Although Latin Americans often assume that their politicians are corrupt, that generally cannot be known directly. Corruption is by its nature secret: if a driver pays a policeman to avoid getting a ticket, they are the only ones likely to know about it.

The same will be true of large-scale corruption; it may occasionally come to light, but normally it remains hidden. Nevertheless, since the 1990s, researchers have sought to measure corruption and to compare its prevalence in different countries.

We have already noted the rankings of Latin American countries on the Corruption Perceptions Index based on periodic surveys by Transparency International, headquartered in Berlin (see table 13.5). As noted there, while a few Latin American countries are ranked within the first quartile (Chile and Uruguay are close to the United States, which is itself in position number 27), most cluster around the midpoint, and Venezuela is in the bottom quartile.[11] Corruption in this instance is defined as the "misuse of public power for private profit," and hence it has to do with what takes place in government. What is being quantified is *perception* of corruption among those surveyed, not actual instances, since they are secret and cannot be investigated directly.

Another method of measuring corruption is to query ordinary citizens about their experience: Have they paid a bribe to police, court, customs, tax, health, education, or other government employees for services to which they were entitled as citizens? In this instance, the question is not about perception but about a fact, whether the individual has indeed paid for service. Although Latin American rates vary considerably among themselves, the region stands close to the world average—one-quarter of people worldwide report making such a payment in the past year.

That fact suggests that corruption has been endemic in the modern state, which in most countries of the world has emerged relatively recently from traditional autocracies. It is related to the clientelism discussed in the previous chapter, the notion that the state is a kind of booty to be seized and shared with one's allies. Part of the unfinished business of consolidating democracy is achieving accountability and transparency in government so that corruption will be recognized and denounced and those who practice it brought to justice.[12]

We now turn briefly to consider corruption in particular countries, starting with Mexico. Under the seven decades of PRI rule, corruption, both low level and high, was endemic. People paid to avoid paying traffic tickets or to avoid judgment in the criminal justice system. Stephen Morris notes that a "survey of 1,376 small and medium-sized businesses found that they spend US$43 billion annually on bribes and to cut through red tape" (Morris 2010, 139). A percentage of low-level bribes to state employees was passed on to superiors, who likewise paid up the line.

The democratization process of the past two decades has not brought an end to corruption and may have produced new forms of it. Privatization in the early 1990s allowed insiders engaging in crony capitalism to buy state companies and make them private monopolies and oligopolies. The ten-fold increase of cross-border traffic in the wake of NAFTA has allowed for more smuggling, contraband, and payoffs. We have already noted that the loss of the PRI monopoly has meant that drug traffickers now deal with a fragmented political system and thus focus on the corruption of local officials and police. Decentralization has meant that "state governors are now able to develop their own corrupt networks, utilize and misuse state resources, distort the rule of law, and operate in a virtually unaccountable fashion" (Morris 2010, 150).

Brazilians can find plenty of evidence of pervasive corruption; examples include the forced resignation of President Collor (1992) and the parliamentary bribery scandal (2005). Researchers combing newspapers spread around the country have found a rate of 3.5 new cases of corruption a day. One factor is the large state share in the economy, giving public officials discretion over contracts and jobs. Another is the cost of political campaigns: 70 percent of businesspeople surveyed felt compelled to contribute to political campaigns. To get around laws prohibiting nepotistic hiring, politicians practice "cross-hiring": agreements with other politicians to hire one's own supporters in return for a similar favor. Enforcement is weak because court cases can stretch out for years, and virtually no one ends up in jail for corruption. Of the twenty politicians involved in the 2005 bribery scandal, thirteen subsequently ran for election, and eight won (Taylor 2010).

With its statist economy, Cuba does not present opportunities for the same types of corruption. However, a study in the Morris and Blake volume (2010) finds three main types of corruption. The first is misuse of state goods, particularly diversion of goods to private use; for example, workers in a state-run cigar factory can smuggle out and sell some of what they produce. A second type is misuse of office, bureaucrats accepting a bribe to give favored treatment or simply favoring one's family or friends. The third form is what is practiced by high officials, such as having their children study abroad, or taking advantage of opportunities to enter into partnership with foreign investors. Although Fidel Castro and the leadership have sometimes meted out exemplary punishment for corruption, because the practices are so widespread and no independent deterrent mechanisms operate in the system, corruption, on a large and small scale, flourishes. These problems will become all the more relevant when the island integrates more fully into the international system (Díaz-Briquets and Pérez-López 2010).

CONTINUING IMPUNITY

As noted in chapter 12, massive human rights violations—abduction and detention, torture, murder, and "disappearance"—were committed by state agents in Chile and Argentina in the 1970s and 1980s; in Guatemala, El Salvador, and Peru primarily in the 1980s; and in Colombia well into the 2000s. The numbers were lower but still significant in Brazil, Mexico, Honduras, Ecuador, and elsewhere. Truth commissions have been set up in various countries and have issued reports, but due to the power of the perpetrators and their institutions even after civilian governments were established, virtually no one was brought to justice for these crimes.

It could be argued that such impunity is an affront to the rule of law. How can citizens believe in their justice systems when massive crimes have gone unpunished? Moreover, in places like Guatemala, impunity for the crimes of the civil-war period have provided a precedent for impunity for political murder to this day, even if the rates are far lower. Yet in postconflict situations, it is often argued that the most important thing is to avoid reopening wounds. Increasingly, only people aged forty or older have a living memory of the worst years of repression.

Human rights organizations have continued to press for justice for what was done in the past, partly to honor the victims and those whose lives were devastated by the violence, and partly out of principle. In Chile, particularly after Gen. Pinochet was charged in Spain and held in Great Britain, the invulnerability of the military began to be broken. Cases have been filed in more than three-quarters of the over three thousand documented killings and disappearances during the dictatorship, and over eight hundred former state agents have been charged or convicted. In Argentina, more than 250 former military and police have been convicted, including former president Jorge Rafael Videla (1976–1981), who died in prison in 2013. In Peru, President Fujimori and his chief of intelligence, Vladimir Montesinos, were sentenced to long prison terms, but no progress was made on other cases. Hesitant steps have been made in Brazil and Mexico.

In El Salvador and Guatemala, where the victims numbered at least in the tens of thousands, impunity has remained in place. In 2013, former president Efraín Ríos Montt (1982–1983) was found guilty of genocide, but the verdict was voided by the supreme court on a technicality. Virtually no member of the military has been brought to justice for human rights violations in either Guatemala or El Salvador.

Colombia illustrates the dangers of unpunished crimes leading to more impunity. Even in the 1990s there were reports of the army abducting peasants, dressing them up as guerrillas, murdering them, and presenting them as combat casualties. As astonishing as it may appear, this practice continued in the 2000s. The International Federation for Human Rights issued a report in 2012 showing evidence of possibly three thousand such "false positives," as they were called, between 2004 and 2008 (FIDH 2012). Although by Colombian law such cases should be handled in civilian courts, they were being processed in the military justice system, if at all, and were in effect covered up.

REDUCING CRIME AND CORRUPTION

High murder rates, muggings, kidnapping for ransom, international drug trafficking, the domestic drug trade, corruption of police and judges, bribe taking by officials, high-level embezzlement, impunity for crimes committed by the state—the issues are not only serious but interconnected. High murder rates, for example, are driven by competition between crime factions, but also by police and militias operating with impunity. The pervasiveness of crime and impunity could foster a sense of futility and cynicism.

The picture sketched in this chapter should be kept in perspective, however. Most Latin Americans go about their daily business taking reasonable precautions so as not to be crime victims, just as do residents of the United States. Rates for murder and other crimes have remained moderate in Mexico City even while rising along the US border and elsewhere. That may be because the police force of the Federal District is relatively well trained. In any case, it should be kept in mind that conditions vary considerably and that high crime rates, and especially violent confrontation, tend to be concentrated in particular areas.[13]

Other societies such as Italy and the United States have also faced well-entrenched organized crime engaging in turf battles, diversifying into legitimate businesses, and cultivating politicians and celebrities. Concerted efforts have succeeded in bringing mob bosses to justice and at least reducing their impact. From the standpoint of agencies like the FBI, the battle against organized crime is never-ending. Indeed, recent experience in the United States may be relevant. In the past two decades, US crime rates have declined; in New York City, murders declined from 2,245 (1992) to 471 (2007). In the country as a whole, property crimes declined, and the rate of violent crimes per 100,000 inhabitants dropped from 758 to 445 (Bratton and Andrews 2010). The reasons for the decline are debated, but one contributing element is smarter policing methods, including developing links to the community, tracking crime trends, and using the data to focus preventively on areas where crime is likely.

The rest of the chapter considers what needs to be done to reduce crime and corruption in their various forms. The discussion will draw on examples of at least incipient success that offer models for learning and replicating. The issues considered here are interconnected: success in investigating and arresting perpetrators of crimes will be of little use if cases are bottlenecked forever in the courts, or if prisons function as sites that return offenders to society more hardened and determined, or if both low- and high-level government officials can be bought off. At the very least, the experience of recent years should be utilized to avoid making matters worse.[14]

POLICING

Citizens of advanced countries expect police to be competent, professional, and honest. A police presence helps make public areas feel safe. Police are expected to take charge after auto accidents and to respond quickly to calls for help after a crime. Citizens expect police to be on their side, and to draw their weapons rarely if ever. That is not always the case even in rich countries. In urban minority communities, police are often regarded as using unnecessary force and accused of searching and frisking young males who have given no evidence of any criminal behavior; revelations of police corruption occur with regularity. Nevertheless, when police corruption is made public, it is punished; it is not taken for granted.

On the whole, police forces in Latin America are not suited to their task in the twenty-first century. They are typically divided into poorly trained, poorly paid, lower ranks, and a more educated and better-paid officer corps, devoted to administration. Moreover, different jurisdictions (national, state, municipal) may not work together. The hierarchical structure instills a mind-set of carrying out orders, with little room for taking initiative. Police have not been trained to solve crimes, and they enjoy little respect among ordinary people. These flaws reflect the fact that police forces were established primarily to maintain internal order, which in practice meant protecting the elites, not serving all citizens equally. In the authoritarian regimes of the 1970s and 1980s, these police were often directly involved in widespread torture, forced disappearance, and murder.[15] Not surprisingly, most crimes go unpunished. Only a fraction are reported, and few of those cases lead to arrest and conviction.

Since the early 1990s, efforts have been made in Latin America to find working models of policing, particularly through the use of community-oriented policing, an idea being implemented in the United States and elsewhere. A key notion is that police should do more than arrive after a crime has been committed; they must be proactive, using data to track crime, anticipate it, seek to reduce its causes. To do that they must work with the community in a variety of ways. An early such effort was made in the beachfront neighborhood of Copacabana in Rio de Janeiro. In 1995, a program was implemented with the support of local community organizations and businesspeople. Police came closer to the community through patrolling on foot and bicycles, even beach buggies, as well as cars. Special police booths were set up on the beach. Monthly meetings were held with community organizations. These led to getting better street lighting and training apartment doormen and security guards at businesses. Residents and businesspeople came to personally know individual officers. This pilot project was systematized into various components, such as a monthly breakfast with community leaders, community security councils, and community policing patrols.

It was not so easy to transfer these methods to the nearby favelas, however. For decades the police had largely left the favelas to themselves, and criminal gangs had established control. When the ordinary police entered, they did so with a military mind-set and often engaged in gun battles, leaving civilians dead. Understandably, the people of the favela did not trust the police. In 2000, a Special Areas Policing Group (GPAE) was set up to implement the new model of policing in one favela near the beach areas. The aim was to establish an ongoing police presence to protect the people of the favela themselves. One consequence was that police had to be involved in addressing community problems.

Before implementing the new model, a SWAT-type team called Special Operations Battalion (BOPE) went in to flush out the Red Command drug gang. In preparing the new force, Major Antonio Carlos Carballo of the Military Police fired a third of the officers for bribery, extortion, violence, and mistreating citizens. After some initial mistrust, the GPAE succeeded in establishing good relationships with the community and working with the residents association, schools, churches, and other groups. The number of violent deaths dropped significantly.

Not everyone was persuaded by community policing, however; most police continued to view the favelas as a war zone. In some instances, community policing apparently led to an increase in some types of crimes. That may be because previously the drug lords exercised a rough justice to punish instances of rape or theft; or it may be because people were more willing to report crimes than before. The new police might ignore drug trafficking, provided it was nonviolent. Finally, there were instances in which the new police also took bribes. In 2008, a model of policing called Pacifying Police Units (UPPs) was unveiled in the favela of Santa Marta. By 2012, twenty-eight favelas had this model and there were plans for it to continue. In part, the effort was driven by the need to increase security in the city in preparation for the 2014 soccer World Cup and the 2016 Summer Olympics.

On the basis of these and other experiences in Latin America and elsewhere, a set of principles for police reform, both for how they are organized and how they operate, can be drawn up:

- Police should not look like military; more importantly, they should not regard themselves as at war against an enemy, but as helping citizens live in security.
- All police should be professionals with an appropriate education level, and police forces should facilitate ongoing training and further education of officers. Pay should reflect professional status, and doing ordinary policing should be the path to leadership rank.
- Organization of police forces should be rationalized. That would typically mean decentralization, dividing of territories into manageable units and subunits (e.g., even small police posts in neighborhoods).
- Police should patrol on foot or bicycle and be assigned for long enough periods to form bonds with the community. Other innovations might be better street lighting, and even cameras, if desired by the community. Regular meetings between community and police are helpful.
- Crimes should be properly investigated, with evidence gathered and witnesses interviewed. Policies for use of force should be clear and enforced. Use of violence to obtain confessions should be prohibited and punished.
- Accountability mechanisms should be established within the police forces themselves.
- Gathering data, doing on-site investigation, and keeping good records that are analyzed at higher levels are part of developing a proactive approach, that is, studying trends and moving to prevent crime.
- Local officers should have sufficient discretionary power to make decisions. (Bratton and Andrews 2010)

As unrealistic as some of those practices might seem at first glance, they are simply a distillation of what has been found to work in practice in well-functioning police forces.

YOUTH GANGS

As noted earlier, it is a mistake to simply conflate youth gangs, like the Central American *maras*, with organized crime, even if in some instances they work with organized crime and some gangs have moved in that direction. Consider the approach of Nelsa

Gang members in prison in El Salvador during visit by rehabilitation specialists. © Edgar Romero.

Curbelo, a Uruguayan former nun in Guayaquil, Ecuador, who, after years as a teacher and human rights activist, turned to working with gangs. Before starting any projects, she spent two years getting to know young people and especially gang members in a neighborhood known as Zona Roja (Red Zone). Rather than dismiss the young people as delinquents, she recognized the positive values they sought in gangs. She believes that part of what drives gang culture is a need for recognition and respect that young people do not receive elsewhere. Out of these discussions she started a movement called Ser Paz (Being Peace) and set up Barrio de Paz (Neighborhood of Peace). The main mechanism is to help young people set up businesses (pizzeria, barber and beauty shop, bakery, print shop, T-shirt making, recording studio) with loans and support. As a condition for participation, however, the young people must give up crime and include members from rival gangs in their businesses. At one time, through Ser Paz, members turned in their guns, and in a symbolic ceremony sixty weapons in the neighborhood were crushed. Outside researchers documented that violent crime in this area had fallen to a fraction of what it was.

Although the work in Guayaquil no doubt derives partly from the leadership of an extraordinary woman, efforts along similar lines have been made elsewhere. Nicaragua, for example, has gangs, but the level of violence is far less than in neighboring countries. One reason may be that the Sandinista police are more professional; another may be that in the 1980s Nicaraguan exiles in the United States did not go primarily to the sites where the Salvadoran gangs originated. Most important, however, may be the starting point, namely that the gang member should be treated first as a person. Even in El Salvador, alongside the *mano dura* others were attempting approaches called Mano Extendida (Extended Hand). An effective approach was the use of former gang members as mentors. The emphasis was also on providing help in starting small businesses.

Some principles may be distilled from these experiences:

- pay attention to the specifics of gangs in a particular place;
- work on overcoming rivalries;
- distinguish between gang membership and criminal actions (beating, killing, extortion, drug trafficking);
- look for ways whereby gang members can be reinserted into society, by developing skills for becoming self-employed or starting small businesses.

CONTAINING ORGANIZED CRIME

The War on Drugs proclaimed by President Richard Nixon is now over forty years old and has passed through various stages, but it shows no signs of abating. The FBI, which took on bootleggers and bank robbers in the 1920s, still has thousands of agents combating organized crime (Russian mafias, cybercriminals) in the twenty-first century. Anything proposed about what can or should be done in Latin America to tackle organized crime should be suitably cautious. Yet history offers encouraging signs as well. Both Italy and the United States have reduced, albeit not ended, the power of La Cosa Nostra. Here the aim will be to point to some trends and draw some lessons from efforts against organized crime as it occurs in Latin America. Some of the story has been outlined earlier in this chapter.

It is useful to distinguish geographical areas. In Brazil, the focal point is Rio de Janeiro, and to a lesser extent São Paulo, and the key effort is being made by the state of Rio to wrest control back from drug gangs in the many favelas. The problem is primarily that of internal drug trafficking, not international transit. In the past decade, the Colombian state has wrested control back from drug gangs and left-wing guerrillas, albeit at the high price of displacing four million people, and with high rates of human rights violations by right-wing paramilitaries and official Colombian troops. The turnaround in Medellín and Bogotá (chapter 2) is often cited as a model from which others can learn.

In Mexico, President Felipe Calderón (2006–2012) began his term by sending the army into areas of organized crime in various parts of the country, especially the north. The most obvious effect was a spike in murder rates, leading by the end of his term to an estimated 60,000 deaths. His successor, Enrique Peña Nieto, vowed to shift the emphasis away from directly battling criminal organizations toward reducing violence and assuring citizen security. The abduction and disappearance of forty-three student activists in the state of Guerrero in 2014, in an operation involving police and drug gangs, led to national protests and seemed to reveal the incapability of the Mexican state to deal with organized crime.

Central America, especially Guatemala, Honduras, and El Salvador, seems to be the region least able to tackle increasing organized crime, due to its levels of corruption, weak state institutions, and lack of trust by the citizenry. This section will draw primarily on examples from these regions, although it must be noted that organized crime can be found elsewhere as well (Caribbean, Andean countries, Southern Cone); for decades, much of the Paraguayan economy was based on contraband, now augmented by drug trafficking.

It is important to be clear on the aims, which in fact may be in conflict. Is it to halt drug trafficking (as the United States might wish), to break up criminal organizations, or to reduce violence and promote citizen safety? In Tijuana, Mexico, murder rates dropped notably from 2010 to 2012, but the reason may be that the criminal organizations settled their rivalry over the *plaza*, as drug markets are called, through a truce. One organization may simply drive another out of its *plaza*, or they make a "pact" over how to operate. Indeed, Colombian and US forces were aided in the pursuit of Pablo Escobar by the Cali cartel, which supplied information, so there was at least a temporary "pact" between the government and a criminal organization.

In seeking immediate results, it is tempting to create or draw on special elite forces, who will have an attitude of professionals. That model was what Mexico did under Calderón and what was done in Rio; that is, special assault troops were sent in first, and then were replaced by specially trained police in the favelas. While that may be useful in some circumstances, it is no substitute for the transformation of all security and police forces into modern, competent bodies that enjoy the respect and confidence of the citizenry. In some instances, police chiefs or mayors have carried out wholesale purges of police forces, even using polygraphs to weed out corrupt officers.

In Guatemala, I have been told that corruption begins with the *alcalde*, the official who is the mayor of the main town but whose authority extends throughout the municipality or county. That makes sense because drug traffickers do not need to control the whole country, but they must have assured routes. It also suggests the difficulty of reform, because local officials can be faced with either the allure of payoffs or the threat of violence to themselves and their families.

In the more successful instances of a reversal of the power of organized crime, law enforcement has gone hand in hand with reestablishing the presence of the state, not simply in the form of police, but of clinics, schools, and improved access to the city, such as through cable cars to poor hillside neighborhoods in both Medellín and Rio de Janeiro. For durable results, it is important to have support from the local community. As a general principle, that seems obvious, but it may be hard to implement, particularly where local gangs have installed their own loyalists in leadership positions in residents associations and the like.

Since the experience of Colombia and Mexico shows that when high-profile capos are arrested, their place is quickly taken by their subordinates, perhaps accompanied by internecine war and splintering, it would be better to identify lower-level members and to make mass arrests of them in a sweep operation. Such approaches depend more on intelligence gathering than firepower, but they entail their own problems, such as the likelihood of information being leaked to organization members.

Finally, these considerations suggest a chicken-and-egg problem: how to reverse the hold of criminal organizations on society when many officials, high and low, have been bought off and intimidated, when ordinary citizens have become accustomed to accepting their presence or even paying them "taxes," and when, based on previous experience, it is rational to be cynical about any initiatives to change things.

For decades critics have argued that what drives profits and violence is the criminalization of drugs. The analogy is often made to the decade and a half of Prohibition in the United States: people continued to drink, and organized crime, mob wars, and corruption flourished. With the repeal of Prohibition in 1933, alcohol again became an item for sale, as it was in the rest of the world. The parallel is clearest in the case of marihuana, because it is plausible that marihuana might be used recreationally as alcohol is. It could be sold legally and used in moderation. Overuse or dependency would be treated as a medical or psychological problem, as is alcoholism. Cocaine, heroin, and methamphetamines are addictive and destructive and do not have legitimate recreational uses. Nevertheless, users could be enrolled in drug treatment programs, rather than having to risk their lives to supply their habit and fostering an international illicit trade that provides billions of dollars in profits to criminals.

JUSTICE SYSTEMS

Justice systems—courts, lawyers, judges, prosecutors—are not highly respected in Latin America. That is partly because they operate very slowly: cases may take years, so often over half of those incarcerated have not been found guilty but are simply awaiting trial. Legal systems follow the "civil law" tradition, which comes from nineteenth-century Napoleonic codes, and more remotely ancient Roman law. Court cases are argued in long written legal briefs, not orally in open public court as in the Anglo-American adversary system. The judge functions as an investigator, not an impartial arbiter, and there is no presumption of innocence. Procedures are opaque and cumbersome and take a long time. The courts acquiesced to the military governments of the 1970s and 1980s and were at best powerless or, more likely, in complicity. Judges have considerable discretion and may be susceptible to bribery.

As democracy returned, one area that needed attention was reform of the judiciary. European countries with a similar civil law tradition have also undertaken reform processes, and thus they offered experiences to be utilized. In the 1990s, Chile undertook legal reform to change the institutions inherited from the Pinochet period and moved from an inquisitorial toward a public, oral type of procedure. The whole process took over a decade to implement. According to one summary,

> considerable analysis and measurement of results were undertaken, with a large effort at training judges, prosecutors, public defenders, and judicial staff all along

the way. The government made a major investment in judicial infrastructure, including the construction of new, modern courthouses around the country, new jails, and a sophisticated upgrade in technology. When finally in place, the new system resulted in a vastly more efficient, transparent, and, almost certainly, fair administration of criminal justice, with far greater respect for the rights of the accused. (DeShazo and Vargas 2006, 7)

The effort had support from the administration and the legislature, the universities, business, and the bar association.

Efforts made in other countries have shown fewer results. These sometimes entailed writing new criminal codes, and some countries have attempted to move toward oral as opposed to written procedures. The reforms begun in the mid-1990s in Venezuela were subsequently vitiated by the control of the judiciary by the Chávez government (members of the Supreme Tribunal of Justice were appointed by a majority vote of the legislature, which was loyal to Chávez). The Supreme Tribunal has "purged" lower court judges for having ruled contrary to the administration. Thus the judiciary has no independence, and traditional corruption has not been corrected. In Latin America as a whole, some steps have been taken toward needed reform, but it has fallen short in most countries.

PRISON REFORM

Between 1990 and 2011, the number of prison inmates in Brazil rose from 90,000 to 515,000, leading to severe overcrowding. Other countries were also imprisoning more inmates without building new prisons. To deal with the numbers, authorities add bunk beds, sometimes several bunks high, and turn areas previously used for other purposes into sleeping quarters. Overcrowding means that prisoners live in squalor. Prisons are often run internally by gangs, and guards are limited to patrolling the perimeter of the cell area and have little effect inside. Rather than rehabilitating inmates, prisons draw them more deeply into gang life. Fires and uprisings have occurred in a number of prisons. In Venezuela, over 400 prisoners were killed each year between 2004 and 2008, and the figure for 2011 was 560.

Efforts to reverse these situations have been undertaken, particularly in Costa Rica and the Dominican Republic. In both cases the reform started by choosing and training staff from among candidates trained in criminology. Prisons traditionally have been run by the military or by civilians with no special training. Both countries refused offers to outsource prisons to private companies, because they determined that it would be more expensive and would not be replicable on a system-wide basis.

These new systems cost more than existing prisons: in the Dominican Republic, the cost is $12 per person per day, twice as much as the older prisons. They now provide educational programs: Roberto Santana, a former university rector who headed the program, required that prisoners learn to read. At a women's prison, some inmates are studying for university degrees. The new system helps prisoners find

Prisoners handcuffed together after a prison uprising, El Salvador. © Edgar Romero.

work upon release. A study found a very low rate of repeat offense, 3 percent after three years, as opposed to 50 percent under the old system. Another approach would be to find alternatives to incarceration for nonviolent offenders. One of the obstacles to prison reform is the lack of public sympathy for prisoners and their rights.[16]

CURBING CORRUPTION

In concluding their comparative study of corruption, Morris and Blake (2010) ask why, after two decades of democratization, all but three Latin American countries (Chile, Costa Rica, and Uruguay) retain medium to high perceived levels of corruption. Most countries showed little variation between 1996 and 2008. As indicated earlier in this chapter, Latin American countries cluster toward the middle of the countries of the world on the Transparency International indexes. Those indexes themselves range between the better-performing countries, typified by Western Europe, and the poorest countries, typified by sub-Saharan Africa and some Asian countries. The general conclusion is that corruption correlates with levels of development, hence no quick and easy solutions are likely. One sign of progress is that corruption, at least of the high-level variety, is more likely to be made public with competitive democracy and aggressive investigative journalism. One noteworthy advance was the Inter-American Convention against Corruption passed in 1996 and ratified by most governments.

As Morris and Blake summarize:

> ... Anti-corruption efforts in Latin America reached a scale that would have been unthinkable thirty years ago. Today corruption is held to be a more important problem by ordinary citizens than it was in prior decades; governments have created vast new institutions specifically pledged to fight corruption; and corruption scandals have proliferated in most Latin American countries, forcing numerous cabinet ministers and even a few presidents to resign amid public outrage. Such processes work over time to redefine the limits of acceptable behavior and strengthen institutional checks.

Nevertheless,

> very few public officials accused of corruption have been formally convicted of their alleged crimes. Instead, they have either kept their jobs or they have resigned, sometimes reappearing in a new political role once the scandal has died down . . . [M]oving from the detection of corruption toward its punishment is perhaps the central challenge of anticorruption efforts in Latin America in the 2010s. (Morris and Blake 2010, 213)

The topics considered here—common crime, youth gangs, organized crime, impunity, political corruption, reform of police, the judiciary, and prisons—are disparate. What draws them together is the need for the rule of law to be applied fairly and effectively, from crime prevention to apprehension of those who violate the law in crimes of property or violence, trafficking or embezzlement, and for the law to operate swiftly and impartially to achieve the security of all citizens. Likewise, as is clear from the examples cited, Latin Americans are taking initiative on all these fronts with some modest successes. Much of the change must take place at the local level, and municipalities, police forces, judiciaries, and prison systems can emulate initiatives taken elsewhere. The future of the region and its people greatly depends on whether they will have the political will and determination to succeed.

FURTHER READING

For an overview of organized crime, see Garzón (2008). On taking on urban violence, see WOLA (2011); on Central American youth gangs, Bruneau, Dammert, and Skinner (2011); on judicial reform, DeShazo and Vargas (2006).

InSight Crime, a network of researchers and journalists working on organized crime in Latin America, produces excellent reports on various Latin American countries: http://www.insightcrime.org/.

CHAPTER 16

Bodies and Minds

Achievements and Obstacles in Health and Education

Education and health care (sometimes shortened to "eds and meds") loom ever larger in the contemporary world. Both involve institutions like schools, clinics, and insurance programs, but they are not identified with institutions. Indeed, the healthier we are, the less need we have of health services, and what makes us "educated" is not the number of years we have spent in classrooms, but the use we have made of that schooling. Ideally, we are protagonists of our own health and education and not simply consumers of educational and health-care services. Both health and education involve specialization and expertise, such as technicians to run and interpret MRI tests, but all of us have our own expertise—or at least strong opinions—on health and education.

The modern state is expected to be involved in both realms, often in complex interactions between the public and the profit and nonprofit sectors of the economy. As will be apparent, Latin American societies have been striving to adapt their health-care and education systems to the twenty-first century. No country in the world has developed an ideal system for enabling all citizens to enjoy high-quality lifelong health care and educational opportunity.[1]

In 1960, people living in the United States and two dozen or so other countries could expect to live to around age seventy. Although one or two Latin American countries had comparable rates, most Latin Americans lived a decade or more less, and in the poorest countries it was common to die before one reached age fifty. Funerals of children were a common sight. The primary reasons for lower life expectancy were a lack of public health measures like safe drinking water and sanitation, and lack of access to the kinds of medicine common in the developed world.[2] In rural areas, many adults could not read and write, and only a small proportion of children were completing primary school. Poor health and lack of schooling were among the most prominent indicators of underdevelopment.

In Cuba, the revolutionary government set out to attack directly the lack of education and health care inherited from the Batista regime. In 1961, schools at all levels

TABLE 16.1. Life Expectancy at Birth in 1960

[Sweden]	[73.5]
[United States]	[70.0]
Uruguay	68.4
Argentina	65.5
Cuba	64.4
Costa Rica	63.0
Panama	62.0
Venezuela	61.0
Mexico	58.5
Colombia	57.9
Brazil	55.7
Nicaragua	48.6
Guatemala	47.0
Bolivia	43.5

Note: Countries in brackets are for purposes of comparison.
Source: UNCTAD

were suspended and 100,000 volunteers went to the countryside to end illiteracy. By the end of the year, literacy had reportedly risen from 75 percent to 96 percent. Contact with rural poverty served to motivate a generation of young Cubans to commit themselves to revolutionary change. Over the next few years, the revolution brought doctors, hospitals, and clinics to all Cubans, especially in the countryside. Cuban health care improved to the point where Cubans were living as long as people in developed countries. Even as many physicians fled the country, Cuba's medical schools produced a surplus of doctors. Schooling was extended and made universal. By 1970, Cuba had shown the world that dramatic progress could be made in health care and schooling. In 1999, Cuba had one doctor for every 170 people, the second-highest ratio in the world (after Italy), and had been exporting doctors to many countries, even though by most measures Cuba remained a poor country.

Other Latin American countries made no such concerted effort to assure that all citizens had access to health care and schooling. Nevertheless, over time they also made gains. This chapter traces those gains and efforts to address emerging challenges.

ADVANCING HEALTH

In the five decades since the start of the Cuban Revolution, a half dozen other countries have approached Cuba in longevity.[3] Even more remarkable, by 2010 all Latin American countries except Bolivia had life expectancies notably higher than that

TABLE 16.2. Life Expectancy at Birth in 2010

[Japan]	[83.69]
[United States]	[79.90]
Costa Rica	79.38
Cuba	79.14
Chile	79.10
Mexico	77.20
Uruguay	77.10
Panama	76.34
Ecuador	75.79
Venezuela	74.66
Nicaragua -	74.51
Colombia	73.94
Brazil	73.52
Guatemala	71.36
Bolivia	67.15

Note: Countries in brackets are for purposes of comparison.
Source: UNCTAD

of the United States in 1960.[4] Indeed, that was true of the whole world: today, in well over half the countries in the world, life expectancy is higher than it was in the United States in 1960.[5] Although some of this advance is due to improved health care and greater access to it, a good deal of the improvement must be attributed to public health measures, such as access to piped-in water and sewerage. By 2004, 91 percent of Latin Americans had access to water (96% in urban areas), and 77 percent had sewerage (86% in cities). Only 45 percent of people in rural areas had sanitation. Likewise, the improved life expectancy reflects decades of campaigns against childhood diseases and infectious diseases. Improved health is partly a by-product of the move to the city; it is easier to bring water and sewerage to an urban neighborhood, and for urban dwellers to reach a clinic or hospital.

GRASSROOTS HEALTH PROMOTERS

A generation or two ago, Latin Americans typically had a four-tiered health-care system:

- private clinics and hospitals serving the wealthy and upper middle classes who paid out-of-pocket;
- a system of hospitals and clinics for employees of large formal companies and governments, perhaps 10–15 percent of households, typically called the "social security" system;

- public health institutions (hospitals in larger cities, and clinics in some towns); and
- folk medicine.

People in the countryside might have to travel hours, even days, to reach a public health hospital or clinic. Even if they received a diagnosis at a public health facility, they might not be able to afford the medications prescribed. They might go to a traditional folk healer or describe their symptoms to a pharmacist who would sell them medications. Only the first two systems provided medical care comparable to that of developed countries.

One way to provide medical care for people not reached by the public health system was to train village-level health promoters. That was done in many rural areas, often by programs initiated by Catholic sisters. For two or three decades the manual *Donde No Hay Doctor* (*Where There Is No Doctor*), developed in Mexico by Dr. David Werner, helped bridge that gap. The manual and the training that went with it started with people's culture and understanding and gave them explanations and instructions with many illustrations.[6] The book went through many editions in Spanish and was translated into over twenty-five languages and used around the world.[7]

Village health promoters were typically trained and overseen by an outside NGO. They were not paid a salary, but sometimes they charged a modest fee for their consultations, thereby making their services more respected. Health promoters worked

Health educator in El Salvador. © Noah Friedman-Rudovsky.

to educate their communities on the importance of having latrines, boiling water for drinking, washing their hands, and other practices.

Physicians often opposed the idea of what they regarded as uneducated peasants administering antibiotics and other drugs and, in effect, practicing medicine. Over time, the ministries of health in some countries recognized their value and adopted similar programs.[8] Some advocates regarded this grassroots model as more than a second-best stopgap. It empowered people by educating them, as opposed to making them defer to health professionals, and it did more than serve the interests of profit-seeking drug companies. However, as existing health-care systems reached remote communities, this approach became less prominent.

HEALTH-CARE SYSTEMS AND REFORM

Since the 1980s, almost all Latin American countries have overhauled their health-care systems, seeking to extend coverage and make them work more efficiently. Reforms in Chile, Brazil, and Mexico are briefly compared below. Health care can be provided in various ways: private fee-for-service arrangements, government-provided services, private or public insurance, mandatory or voluntary enrollment, and so forth. Likewise, various actors are involved: patients, physicians and other health professionals, national and local governments, and drug and medical device companies. Any assessment should go beyond the design of a health-care system to its actual operation.

In *Chile*, the military dictatorship set out to dismantle the existing welfare state and foster private-sector solutions. In medicine, its key feature was the creation in 1981 of private health-care plans called ISAPREs (Instituciones de Salud Previsional; Health Insurance Institutions), which were insurance plans from which people could choose. In practice that meant only the upper 20–25 percent of the population. Meanwhile, the existing public health-care system was allowed to deteriorate (Edlin 2009).

In the 2000s, a new system was set up around an insurance plan called FONASA (Fondo Nacional de Salud; National Health Fund). Seven percent is deducted from the wages of all workers and then sent to either an ISAPRE or FONASA. Coverage is provided for a series of fifty-six defined conditions, according to a protocol. About 70 percent of people are enrolled in FONASA, and 16 percent in an ISAPRE. One criticism of ISAPREs is that premiums rise with age, so as people approach old age some opt to switch to FONASA, thereby placing strain on that system. Services are provided by both public and private facilities.

Health-care reform in *Brazil* can be traced to the 1988 constitution, which guarantees health care for all and makes it a government responsibility. The major step was the combination of the previous public and social-security systems into the Single Health System, which is administered by states and municipalities. It is free for all and is used by about 80 percent of the population. Providers are both public and private; a majority of hospitals are private, as are many specialist clinics and diagnostic centers (Paim et al. 2011).

Starting in 2003, **Mexico** implemented a reform called Seguro Popular (People's Insurance). The existing social-security systems (one for state employees and the other for formal private employers) remained in place. Part of the reason for establishing Seguro Popular was the recognition that out-of-pocket expenses for health care were high to the point of being unaffordable. The aim is to provide formal health insurance to 45 million Mexicans who previously could not afford it. Seguro Popular guarantees access to 255 defined health-care procedures, primarily for outpatient care, and 18 expensive procedures requiring hospitalization. The services are provided by existing hospitals. Seguro Popular assures that the services are provided free of charge. Funding for the system is set up to assure four types of spending: administration, community health services, noncatastrophic services, and high-cost procedures. The aim is to make sure that one type of health-care spending does not crowd out another (Jaff 2010).

Comparing the three reforms reveals similarities and differences:

- All three guarantee universal coverage, at least in principle: all citizens and residents are entitled to defined types of health care.
- All are segmented in some fashion; the wealthier can opt out of the system and pay for their own health care.
- Financing varies, particularly on whether it is based on payroll deductions.
- The Chilean and Mexican systems make use of insurance schemes; in Brazil, a portion of private health-care spending is based on voluntary insurance.

As an indication of the gap between design and practice, in Brazil, 60 percent of health-care spending is private.

Examination of worldwide per capita health-care spending shows that Latin American countries are clustered largely in the second quartile, with five countries well into the third quartile.[9] The figures cover *total* health-care spending (government and private). Both Brazil and Mexico are at the midpoint, at $920 dollars per year, with other countries ranging higher and lower. The highest-spending countries in Latin America (Argentina and Chile) spend about a sixth of what is spent in the United States. Their health-care spending in turn is six times what it is in Bolivia.

As a percentage of GDP, Cuba and Costa Rica rank highest, while Bolivia and Peru rank lowest. Most spend 7–9 percent of GDP on health care, which is typical of other societies in the world. (Health-care spending in the United States is obviously far higher in absolute terms and as a percentage of GDP than anywhere else in the world.)[10]

In 2000, the World Health Organization (WHO) attempted to rank the health-care systems of the world's countries based on the criteria of life expectancy, responsiveness (speed, quality), and fair financial cost. Most of the top twenty were European countries (the United States was number 38). Among the higher-scoring Latin American countries were Colombia (22), Costa Rica (37), Cuba (40), Dominican Republic (52), and Venezuela (55). The WHO has not updated this ranking, but in

TABLE 16.3. Total Health Expenditure Per Capita and as a Percentage of GDP (2010)

RANK AND COUNTRY	PER CAPITA HEALTH SPENDING (PPP)	AS % OF GDP
[1 United States]	[8,233]	[17.6]
[2 Luxembourg]	[6,712]	[7.9]
[8 Canada]	[4,433]	[11.4]
[10 Germany]	[4,342]	[11.5]
[16 UK]	[3,433]	[9.6]
[47 Poland]	[1,377]	[7.0]
48 Argentina	1,321	8.3
52 Panama	1,221	8.7
53 Costa Rica	1,197	10.3
54 Chile	1,191	7.4
59 Uruguay	1,132	8.1
62 Brazil	1,009	9.0
64 Mexico	962	6.3
81 Venezuela	642	5.3
82 Ecuador	635	7.9
84 Colombia	614	6.5
95 Dominican Republic	509	5.5
97 Paraguay	493	9.6
99 Peru	463	4.9
100 El Salvador	456	10.2
104 Cuba	414	6.9
[111 China]	[373]	[5.0]
115 Honduras	340	8.7
117 Guatemala	327	6.9
119 Nicaragua	276	9.9
121 Bolivia	264	5.5
169 Haiti	76	6.9
[191 Eritrea]	[17]	[2.9]

Note: Bracketed countries are for purposes of comparison.
Source: WHO (2010).

2014, Bloomberg Business made a similar effort with similar criteria.[11] The countries that ranked highest are those that have achieved good longevity and do not spend too much per capita on health care in either relative or absolute terms.

Brazil's remarkable success in dealing with HIV/AIDS should be noted. The first cases were discovered in the 1980s, and the disease began to spread, especially in

TABLE 16.4. Bloomberg Ranking on Health-Care Efficiency

[1. Hong Kong]	26. Venezuela
[2. Singapore]	28. Cuba
[3. Japan]	32. Argentina
[4. Israel]	35. Peru
13. Chile	42. Colombia
15. Mexico	[46. United States]
17. Canada	[47. Serbia]
20. Ecuador	48. Brazil

Note: Bracketed countries are for purposes of comparison.
Source: Bloomberg (2014).

metropolitan Rio de Janeiro and São Paulo. In the early 1990s, the World Bank predicted that 1.2 million Brazilians would contract the disease. At the urging of public health professionals, federal, state, and municipal authorities worked out a vigorous plan, using education (including media campaigns with celebrities) and condom promotion and distribution. A key ingredient was a decision to supply the "cocktail" of antiretroviral drugs free of charge, even though at the time that meant several thousand dollars per year per patient. Seven of the twenty-one drugs used are manufactured in Brazil. In bargaining with the pharmaceutical companies, which objected to generics on the grounds of protecting intellectual property, Brazil threatened to invoke provisions of international agreements allowing violation of such property rights in the event of a national emergency. As of 2012, drugs were being distributed to 217,000 people at $2,200 apiece per year. Brazil averted what could have been a far wider epidemic. In 2007, *The Economist* stated, "No developing country has had more success in tackling AIDS than Brazil."[12]

FROM ZERO HUNGER TO OBESITY

In his 2002 presidential campaign, Lula proposed a bold "Zero Hunger" program: if elected, he would mobilize the country to assure that no Brazilian would go hungry. The idea had an intuitive appeal to most Brazilians: we're a rich country, we export food, surely we can end hunger. It was taken for granted that a sizable number of Brazilians were hungry or malnourished, particularly in the parched rural areas of the northeast and in urban favelas. During the campaign, the means for achieving this goal were left undefined.

The path toward implementation proved bumpy. A key question was whether ending hunger was to be done by the government or by mobilizing civil society—or both. Did it mean getting food to people or enabling them to produce food? At one point it involved coordination between over forty government programs. Frei Betto, a well-known Dominican friar, who was appointed an unofficial advisor to the program,

Evidence of rising obesity, San José, Costa Rica. © Tommie Sue Montgomery.

resigned in frustration after a year. The program itself came to be embodied primarily in Bolsa Familia, the family allowance program. Eventually the term "Zero Hunger" fell into disuse.

Brazilians were surprised to find that "hunger" in the sense of insufficient caloric intake was not very common. The longevity of people in the very poor state of Piauí, who often appear lean as though hungry, is not far below the national average. In fact, in absolute numbers, more Brazilians are obese than hungry.[13] Obesity has also been growing elsewhere in the region. Seventy percent of Mexicans are overweight, and 32.8 percent of adults are obese, slightly above US rates. There are 400,000 new cases of diabetes a year, and 70,000 people die of the disease.

Today obesity and malnutrition are not opposites but can go hand in hand. The culprits in the obesity epidemic are changes in diets accompanied by a more sedentary way of life. Families have shifted from traditional to more processed foods, high in saturated fats, sugar, and additives, and they are consuming more snack foods and sugary soft drinks. Mexico has the largest per capita consumption of soft drinks in the world. As noted in chapter 4, fast-food chains have become part of the landscape. One of the perverse effects of family-allowance programs may be that some of the money is spent on junk food at local stores. In recent years, governments in Brazil, Mexico, and elsewhere have sought to combat these shifts (by making changes in school-lunch programs and taxing sugary drinks), but food merchandisers have fought back.

The hunger-obesity paradox serves as a signal of shifting health challenges. As communicable diseases have been tamed, and as populations live longer and the ratio of older people increases, societies will increasingly have to confront noncommunicable diseases common in developed countries, such as cancer and circulatory and respiratory conditions.

SCHOOLING AND EDUCATION

President Lula (2003–2010) had only about four years of schooling, as was common in the 1950s;[14] today a poor Brazilian boy or girl is very likely to finish elementary school. At least some primary schooling is now universal, even for indigenous girls in the Guatemalan highlands, who not long ago might not have attended school. University enrollment is increasing: in several countries, 30 percent or more of young people are enrolled in postsecondary education.

The present state of schooling and education reflects its history. Universities were established in the 1550s in Santo Domingo, Mexico City, and Lima, a century before Harvard. Schooling was in the hands of the Catholic religious orders and served urban elites. In the nineteenth century, reformers allied with liberal parties set forth at least the ideal of a widespread secular education available to all, embodied in the figure of the Argentine novelist, intellectual, and politician Domingo Faustino Sarmiento. He spent many years in exile in Chile and elsewhere in South America, and during a two-year period in the 1840s traveled to North America and Europe looking for models of schooling. He later founded the first teacher-training institution in South America. As president (1868–1874), he pressed for the expansion of schooling as part of a larger project of modernization, and even after his presidency he served as supervisor of schools for the ministry of education.

In the nineteenth century, some countries passed legislation providing for free and mandatory public education, but in practice, schools served the emergent urban middle classes. Starting in the 1920s, Mexican revolutionary governments sent teachers into the countryside imbued with a mission to overcome ignorance and modernize their country. In the first half of the twentieth century, Catholic religious orders set up schools, which served primarily those able to pay tuition. In Colombia, however, Catholic schools were extensive and served approximately half of the school-age population, thereby helping make Colombia the most "Catholic" society in the hemisphere.

CONCIENTIZAÇÃO AND NONFORMAL EDUCATION

Illiteracy was common in Latin America well beyond the mid-twentieth century, especially in the countryside where schools were scarce. Coffee pickers, sugarcane cutters, and subsistence farmers could do their work without reading. It was not clear how to overcome illiteracy without forcing adults to go back to elementary school.

In the early 1960s, Paulo Freire, an educator in the northeastern Brazilian city of Recife, developed a method by which peasants could learn to read and write in a matter of weeks. His pedagogical innovation was to stop treating the illiterate like first-graders and to assume that they had a great deal of knowledge acquired through life; what they lacked were the linguistic skills to "de-code" written symbols in order to read and write. His method entailed organizing meetings ("literacy circles") in which the starting point for discussion was an image of a scene from everyday life and the word for it, for example, a drawing of a house with the word *casa*. The session began with a question, "What do we see here?" Through probing questions, the group leader would draw from participants their experiences and ideas about what happens in a house, how it is built, what it means. After exploring their experiences of what "house" means, he or she would draw attention to the word *casa*, break it into its component syllables *ca-sa*. A further step would be to indicate how with a slight change it could spell *cosa* (= thing), or *cada* (= each). Each session was built around a "generating word," such as *casa*. It was "generating" in two senses: it could generate a discussion that was an exploration of people's culture and life, and it could generate further words, and together all the possibilities of the alphabet. Other generating words were related to work, land, family, markets, and so forth.

Implicit in the method was a conviction that generally no one asked peasants or poor people what they thought; their views were not taken seriously. They themselves had internalized that attitude to the point where they were deferential to authorities and to the rich and powerful. Freire described this as a "submerged consciousness": his proposed pedagogy was aimed at enabling that consciousness to "emerge" to the point of "critical consciousness." The process was called *concientização* ("concientization" or "consciousness-raising").

In early 1960s Brazil, *concientização* went hand in hand with organizing sugarcane workers and forming peasant leagues. Such activity was deemed subversive by the military who carried out the 1964 coup. Freire and his associates were jailed for some weeks, and he then went into exile, first in Chile for five years and then in Europe, before he was able to return to Brazil in 1980.

In the 1960s, his major works, *Education: The Practice of Freedom* and *Pedagogy*

Older woman learning to read in Bolivia. © *Noah Friedman-Rudovsky.*

ECONOMIC AND POLITICAL CHALLENGES OF THE PRESENT

of the Oppressed, were translated into many languages, and for a time his key ideas and philosophy were highly influential among educational reformers. The Freirean method, as it was called, was widely used throughout Latin America, not only for literacy but for grassroots education and organizing more broadly. It enabled many people, particularly those working with the Catholic Church, to enter into poor communities in both the city and the countryside, and to engage with people in a way that seemed to displace the traditional vertical teacher-student relationship with a more horizontal type of relationship. At its best, the Freire method offered a way to guide people toward claiming their rights and mobilizing to attain them.

One of Freire's best-known ideas is the critique of what he calls "banking education," the implicit assumption that the student is an empty receptacle that must be filled by the teacher. In opposition to that notion, Freire proposed that both teacher and students be engaged in examining the world together: the role of the teacher is to prod and press and provoke. Studying the world did not mean doing away with books or even lectures—Freire himself could give lectures for up to two hours—but it was a philosophical stance that should affect all education.[15] Freire likewise contrasted "liberating" education to "domesticating" education, which was the usual effect of conventional schooling. *Concientização* thus implied a critique of existing school systems.[16] Late in life, Freire headed the ministry of education for the city of São Paulo in the 1990s.

By the twenty-first century, the importance of *concientização* seemed to have waned, because literacy levels had been raised, even among adults in the countryside, and perhaps because even poor people were shedding their long-standing culture of deference.

SCHOOL SYSTEMS AND THEIR REFORM

By 2000, most Latin American countries were approaching universal coverage of elementary school: almost all school-age children were in school. Roughly half of adolescents were in secondary school. However, coverage varied widely by social class: high school completion was virtually universal for the top quintile, but only a little over 20 percent for the lowest quintile.

The key issue now, all observers agree, is the quality of the education being imparted. One measure is the PISA (Programme for International Student Assessment), a test administered every few years in dozens of countries around the world to randomly selected fifteen-year-olds. The 2009 test in mathematics, sciences, and reading was administered in seventy-four countries. The top ranks were occupied by European and Asian countries. In Latin America, Chile scored the highest ranking in all three categories: mathematics, 50; sciences, 44; and reading, 43. Costa Rica, Mexico, Uruguay, Argentina, Colombia, Brazil, and Panama were generally in the bottom third in all categories.[17] In short, the performance of even the best Latin American adolescents fares poorly when compared to other countries in the world.

The problems of public schools are manifest in infrastructure. For decades schools have operated on two shifts: mornings from 7:00 a.m. to noon, and afternoons from 1:00 to 6:00 p.m. Rural buildings sometimes lack running water or sewerage, and urban schools are often poorly maintained. Computers have only slowly been adopted. After almost a decade of efforts to bring computers to the classroom in Mexico, a study found that only 42 percent of the almost 200,000 public (primary and secondary) schools had computers and only 18 percent had Internet access. Access in indigenous areas was very low. Although in 2009 Uruguay took credit for being the first country in the world to supply all students up to the sixth grade with a laptop, a follow-up study found that often the machines were not working and were not incorporated into learning, particularly since teachers did not know how to do so. Schools have traditionally been managed with a top-down bureaucracy from the ministry of education down to the local school, where principals and teachers had little autonomy.

The crux of the educational process lies in what happens in the classroom, especially with the teacher. Teachers in lower grades often have only a secondary-school diploma themselves. Teaching is not a highly regarded or well-paid profession and has not attracted the most intelligent university graduates. Entering a typical school, a visitor is struck by the general level of noise emanating from classrooms. A key requirement for teachers is to be able to maintain a minimum of order and be heard above the din. Thus teachers are often rules-minded authoritarians, who dictate content that students are expected to copy into notebooks and then to answer on tests. Books, including textbooks, and school supplies are scarce.

Finally, teachers are often represented by strong national unions, whose bargaining power derives from their ability to shut down a national school system. The extreme case may have been Mexico, where two major teachers unions, not the ministry of education, controlled teaching assignments, which could be passed on to one's children or sold. President Enrique Peña Nieto sought to institute reform to break these practices and introduce merit evaluation into teacher selection. In 2013, the leader of the larger union, Elba Esther Gordillo, was jailed for embezzlement.[18] When teachers from the other union blockaded major areas of downtown Mexico City in 2013, they were cleared out by police. How far it would be possible to reform public schooling remained in doubt.

In most countries, the upper and middle classes have always sent their children to private, especially Catholic, schools. The new middle classes are also sending their children to private schools. In countries like Brazil and Colombia, where admittance to the best universities is through competitive examinations, private schooling is regarded as a necessity, because of the poor quality in public schools. Thus the "solution" to the problems of public education for a significant proportion of the population (including public school teachers themselves if they can afford it) is to opt out of the public school system.[19]

Various approaches have been taken to addressing the problem. One aspect is to repair or upgrade existing buildings and to build new ones. Another reform is decentralization of education systems from the national to the state or municipal level for

Teacher and student in the Dominican Republic. © Inter-American Development Bank.

budgeting and other decisions. At the school level, that means treating principals as more than simply the lowest level of bureaucracy, by making them responsible for the quality of teaching, even with the authority to hire or dismiss teachers. One favorable trend is the demographic shift under way: after decades in which schools had to expand to meet rising populations, falling fertility rates now mean that the number of children in schools is leveling out or even declining.

Implicit in the foregoing is that improving results in education depends on the quality of teachers. As Latin American countries consider how to improve public education they might consider the example of Finland, whose adolescents score near the top in the PISA tests. Forty years ago the Finnish school system was undistinguished. At that point the parliament decided to design a single comprehensive system for students from seven to sixteen years old. The key element is that all teachers must have completed a five-year master's program in theory and practice. Teachers thus have a prestige equal to that of doctors and lawyers. Curricula are in the form of broad guidelines that teachers can adapt and develop individually and in groups. A teacher follows his or her students through the various grades and thus comes to know them. Close attention to individual students is a key ingredient. Being a teacher is so prestigious that there are far more applicants than positions available. Virtually all Finnish children attend public schools, and achievement levels do not vary dramatically. Unlike Asian education systems, whose students are trained to be good test takers, Finnish education does not place much emphasis on testing. There are no standardized tests, except for a final test at the end of the senior year.

The aim in citing the Finnish example is not to propose that it could be copied literally. Rather it is to show that it is possible to successfully take a new direction in education and that the key may lie in the quality of teachers from the time they are trained and recruited. Even if they do not follow the Finnish model, Latin American school systems should focus more on upgrading teaching as a profession, and seek to attract bright, imaginative young people to serve as teachers. They then need to assure that the system itself fosters and rewards good teaching and learning rather than frustrating it.

For now, most countries—around the world, not only in Latin America—seem to be wedded to the model of mass schooling developed in the nineteenth century, with its lockstep system of cohorts marching through the ranks year after year. The introduction of new technologies may impel a breakthrough of some sort, but there are few signs of that on the horizon.

UNIVERSITIES

Decades ago, wealthy Latin Americans typically sent their children abroad for university. Capital cities often had two main universities, a highly politicized national university and a quieter Catholic university, regarded as more academically serious, and perhaps one or two more private institutions. Students studied primarily law, medicine, accounting, social sciences, and the like, with relatively few in the sciences or technical subjects. Only a tiny fraction of young people attended university, perhaps 2–5 percent, depending on the country. When many rural children were not even attending elementary school, university education seemed to be a luxury that disproportionately served the privileged.

In recent decades, though, the numbers of university students have expanded dramatically: in Brazil from 43,000 in 1945 to 6.5 million in 2010; in Chile from

250,000 in 1990 to 1,070,000 in 2011; and in Latin America as a whole from 7 to 13 million in a decade (1994–2003). Tiny Costa Rica, with under five million people, lists a hundred institutions of higher learning, half in the capital, San José. In Chile, half of young people of college age are studying; the rate is higher in Argentina and Panama; Mexico and Colombia are proposing to reach 50 percent.[20]

This expansion is driven by a recognition that a university degree is increasingly required for many kinds of employment. Despite efforts by governments to build new public university campuses, demand has exceeded supply, so much of the expansion is taken up by private universities, some of them for profit. The pioneer was Chile, where the Pinochet dictatorship actively promoted private universities for ideological reasons, but the example was swiftly followed almost everywhere.

Critics deride many of the private institutions as "garage universities," meaning that they lack basic facilities and are set up as businesses. The upshot is a divide in higher education: public universities where tuition is free or low-cost and private schools that charge tuition. As already noted, in countries like Brazil and Colombia, the need to pass stiff entrance examinations means that students in these institutions are often those whose parents could afford to send them to private elementary and secondary school. Thus, paradoxically, it is the less well-off students who have to attend private schools, working at the same time to pay their tuition.

Latin American universities differ from their US counterparts in several respects.

Colombian university students in protest march in Bogotá, 2012. © Julián García.

In the larger cities, most students commute from home. University life does not serve the function it does in the United States of a kind of four-year transition from home to "the world," in which young people spend freshman year in a dorm and move toward living in an apartment. The curriculum tends to be more like that of European universities, where most of one's courses are related to one's chosen field, as opposed to the US model, in which general education requirements may compose half the courses taken. Athletic programs play only a minor role, if any.

Some universities are of relatively high quality. In Bogotá, for example, the National University attracts many of the best students as a result of entrance examinations, the Universidad de los Andes is highly regarded for technical subjects and is expensive, and the Universidad Javeriana reflects Jesuit ideals of a humanistic education. However, quality of education is a serious problem in many universities. Many classes are taught by noncareer professors who do not have advanced degrees. By international standards, Latin American universities produce little research, and particularly research cited by others. In the 2013 QS World University Rankings,[21] no Latin American universities appear in the first hundred in the world. The University of São Paulo is number 127, UNAM (Mexico City) is 163, and the Catholic University of Chile is 165.[22] A further criticism is the mismatch between courses offered and the needs of the society: Latin American universities are still producing too many lawyers and social scientists and too few chemists and engineers. Similarly, there are too few partnerships between business and industry and universities.

Before considering attempts to address these shortcomings, it may be well to pause to consider what universities are for, especially in developing countries. Universities arose in medieval times as "communities of scholars" who came together around famous philosophers and theologians. For centuries, they were under the tutelage of the Church. In the early nineteenth century, Germany pioneered the modern research university, and later on, American universities added training in the professions. In the twentieth century, US universities were distinguished in "pure research" in fields like physics and biology with government and foundation money. At mid-century, much university research was driven by military needs, and then by corporate partnerships. Research in the humanities and social sciences has also benefited from foundation and government funding. The modern American university is a hydra-headed creature as complex as a large corporation, whose president is literally a CEO, paid hundreds of thousands of dollars a year. That is a long way from the arcades of medieval Bologna.

Latin American universities need not endeavor to emulate this pattern, at least in detail. Of course, a key part of their mission is to provide undergraduates an education suited to a future career and life. In addition to teaching, at least some professors should engage in research. Some of it might be "disinterested," but at least some of it may and should be relevant to the challenges of development. In short, the mission of the university is not simply to students but to the whole of society.

In several essays, the Jesuit philosopher and theologian Ignacio Ellacuría—the most well known of the Jesuits gunned down by Salvadoran troops in 1989—raised the question of the role of the university in a country like El Salvador (Ellacuría 1991). His answer was that it must serve the needs of the poor majority, but it must do so in a way proper to universities, that is, through research and teaching, not primarily through direct political activity. University activity should be focused on the "national reality," the overall situation of the country. Understanding the country, its problems, and possible solutions should be a guiding principle of research. In addition to scholarly work, the university should seek to communicate its findings to the national community. Finally, in teaching it should strive to develop a critical awareness of those problems in undergraduate students. These principles were embodied concretely in the books and journals published by the Jesuit university[23] where Ellacuría was rector (1979–1989).[24] The circumstances of today are not those of El Salvador in the 1970s and 1980s. Nevertheless, the example remains relevant: universities should not simply take for granted their traditional roles of preparing young people for professional careers or developing a workforce for existing employers, but should assist the quest for equitable and sustainable development.

The proliferation of private universities competing with one another, often as businesses, has fostered a situation in which teaching and degrees may be of little value. In various countries, accreditation agencies are being established, generally with the participation of the better and longer established universities. In Brazil, exit examinations are administered to graduating students; institutions whose students score too low are fined and the news is published, thereby pressuring them to maintain certain standards.

To strengthen the country's research capabilities, Brazil announced a plan to send 100,000 students to top-ranking world universities to earn advanced degrees in priority fields of science and engineering (75,000 with scholarships from government agencies and an expected 25,000 from the private sector); Chile announced a similar plan to send 25,000 students abroad for a similar purpose and with fewer conditions. Other countries announced similar if less ambitious plans. The general intention is to help universities leapfrog to becoming participants in the knowledge economy, ultimately as creators and not merely as transmitters of knowledge.

As university enrollment rises, questions of how to pay for it have increased. Traditionally, tuition at state institutions was free or nominal, and universities were guaranteed a percentage of the national budget. As enrollment and needs have expanded, free tuition has proved increasingly unworkable, and public universities have attempted to charge some tuition. Students understandably believe that a free university education is their right. However, it can be argued that they are receiving a significant subsidy from public funds and should be expected to pay it back, perhaps through student-loan formulas. That has proved difficult in practice because of shortcomings in the banking system and also the low pay earned by recent graduates.

In some institutions, efforts are being made to at least partly replace the traditional model of a lecturing professor. Student-centered learning and peer-instruction models have been tried, particularly that of assigning students to watch a video or read a text and come to class prepared to discuss it in groups.

LOOKING AHEAD

In the past half century, Latin American countries have made significant advances in both health and education. Childhood mortality has been reduced, people are living longer, virtually all school-age children are in class, secondary school has been expanding, and university is no longer the realm of a privileged few. In both health and education, today's problems are primarily those of quality. It is not enough to have declared that all citizens have a right to health care; existing systems must actually provide effective care. In the coming decades, as Latin Americans live longer, health care will encounter different sorts of challenges as the rates of cancer, heart disease, and diabetes increase. No one knows what the effect of new media will be on education in Latin America—or indeed, in the rest of the world.

However, how people regard improvements in health care and education may differ. When people live several years longer than their grandparents, everyone can be satisfied; no one's longevity affects anyone else's. However, insofar as schooling achievement affects employability, the expansion of schooling for some may devalue that of others. If jobs that once required only a high school diploma, such as accounting, now require a university degree, the value of secondary schooling has been devalued. Something similar happens as the number of university graduates rises. Individuals may respond by pursuing a master's degree, particularly from a prestigious foreign institution.

Society as a whole benefits, first because education should enhance anyone's life, regardless of its cash value for employment, and second because a more educated citizenry can be expected to demand a more accountable government. Nevertheless, individuals and households correctly understand that in an unequal society, education becomes a zero-sum game, at least in terms of credentialing for employment. Thus, it is likely that the better-off and particularly the middle classes, for whom schooling represents a great deal of sacrifice, will tolerate a system that in reality keeps many of the poor in schools that will not prepare them for the university, even if on some level they regret the impact on the poor.

FURTHER READING

Americas Quarterly: Education, Fall 2010; *ReVista: Universities*, Fall 2012a.
Americas Quarterly: Health Care, Summer 2010.

Goods and People Crossing Borders

Dimensions of Globalization

From time to time, we have noted global aspects of Latin America, such as the rise of *multilatinas* (chapter 4) and the shift away from protected inward-directed industrialization toward free trade (chapter 13). This chapter considers four aspects of Latin America in a globalized world: trade, including the presence of China; migration, including emigration into the United States; Latinos in the United States; and US-Latin American relations.

TRADE AND INTEGRATION IN A COMPETITIVE WORLD

In the 1980s, Latin American governments moved to open their economies, after a half century of inward-directed development. Critics denounced it as forced globalization under pressure from the IMF (International Monetary Fund) and the United States. However, virtually all countries in the world have embraced more open trade, notably China and India. We turn to consider trade agreements in their design and implementation, the rise of China, and the changing dynamics of Latin America in the world economy.

The general purpose of trade agreements is to remove trade barriers and establish clear rules of the game for all parties. Trade agreements proposed and established in the last two or three decades can be divided into those promoted by the United States (NAFTA and FTAA), those whose impetus comes from within Latin America (MERCOSUR and ALBA), and the comprehensive international framework of the WTO (World Trade Organization). Individual countries have also signed bilateral agreements with other countries.

NAFTA (North American Free Trade Agreement), which went into effect in 1994, unites Canada, the United States, and Mexico in a single free trade zone with a population of 465 million people (2012). At the time of its inception, proponents claimed that it would bring advantages to consumers and workers, and that, over time, Mexican living standards would converge toward those of the north. Critics charged that it would simply multiply the model of the assembly plants (maquiladoras) already existing along the US-Mexico border, which used cheap labor in manufacturing electronics, clothing, sports equipment, and the like with little impact on the rest of the Mexican economy. Opponents in the United States and Canada, especially labor unions, argued that companies would use it to "export jobs" to Mexico, further weakening workers and the middle class. Nationalists in Mexico viewed it as leading to a further takeover of the Mexican economy by foreign corporations.

MERCOSUR (Mercado Común del Sur; Common Market of the South), originally composed of Brazil, Argentina, Uruguay, and Paraguay, was consciously designed as an alternative to US-led globalization. The hope was that it could be the core of a South American trade bloc. At its most ambitious, it drew on the notion that through economic and political integration, South America could evolve toward something akin to the European Union. It functions as a customs union: the members establish a common tariff vis-à-vis outside countries, with no tariffs among members.

Meanwhile, starting with the Reagan and George H. W. Bush administrations, the United States had proposed a Free Trade Area of the Americas (FTAA), the aim of which would be a hemispheric free-trade organization, potentially the largest and richest in the world. Meanwhile, the World Trade Organization (WTO) had been pursuing negotiations (the Doha Round) that would include the entire world operating under a single set of rules in which tariffs and obstacles to trade would be removed and rules would be set for investment and protection of intellectual property.

NAFTA, the FTAA, and the WTO became the targets of protests against "globalization," which critics saw as being imposed by the United States through international agencies like the IMF and the World Bank to serve the interests of large corporations. At the 1999 WTO meeting in Seattle, protesters clashed repeatedly with police and six hundred people were arrested. The World Social Forum, which began meeting in Brazil in the early 2000s, was one venue of resistance to trade pacts. Some protesters insisted that they were not against globalization itself, but against corporate-led globalization that takes place without regard for workers' rights and the environment; they instead advocated a democratic "globalization from below."

In 2004, Venezuelan president Hugo Chávez proposed the Alianza Bolivariana para los Pueblos de Nuestra América (ALBA; Bolivarian Alliance for the Peoples of Our America),[1] which had expansive aims but initially was limited to Venezuela and Cuba, and was later joined by Nicaragua, Bolivia, and several small Caribbean nations. Designed to combat US-led globalization, ALBA was driven largely by President Chávez and his petroleum purse strings. ALBA invoked the language of Patria Grande (Great Homeland), which had inspired the Latin American left in the 1960s and whose origins can be traced to Simón Bolívar himself, who dreamed of Spanish-speaking America as a great confederation but who died watching it dissolve in disputes and territorial wars.

Latin American nations, notably Brazil, have played significant roles in slowing the rush to comprehensive trade agreements. In 2003, Brazil, joined by China, India, South Africa, and other "global South" nations, led opposition at the meeting of the WTO in Cancún, Mexico, standing up to the United States and Europe and halting

TABLE 17.1. Trade Agreements, 1981–2005

NAFTA (North American Free Trade Agreement)	United States-Mexico-Canada Implemented in 1994
MERCOSUR (Common Market of the South)	Brazil-Argentina-Uruguay-Paraguay (originally); Venezuela added; others with associate status Proposed in 1985, initiated in 1991, formalized in 1994
ALBA (Bolivarian Alliance of the Americas)	Venezuela, Cuba, Bolivia, Ecuador, Nicaragua, Suriname, and three Caribbean countries Proposed in 2004 by Venezuela as an alternative to the FTAA
FTAA (Free Trade Area of the Americas)	Proposed in 1994 by the United States, would extend NAFTA to all countries in western hemisphere Stalled since 2005
WTO (World Trade Organization)	Framework for trade negotiations: the Doha Round, aimed at establishing a set of rules applicable worldwide Stalled since 2003

any agreement. In 2005, the MERCOSUR countries led the way in blocking progress toward the FTAA. Both of these agreements foundered on two disputes. First, the United States and the northern countries were insisting on greater protection for patents and intellectual property. Brazil and other developing countries believed that the result would likely be higher prices, especially for pharmaceuticals. Second, the countries of the south were seeking a level playing field for their agricultural exports, and they objected to the farm subsidies provided in different forms by governments in Europe, North America, and Japan. Since the mid-2000s, large comprehensive schemes like the WTO and FTAA have been stalled.

Goods move more freely than two decades ago, but the grandiose promises of trade agreements have not been achieved. Two decades after NAFTA was launched, it had clearly not narrowed the gap between Mexican and US living standards. To be sure, it is difficult to isolate the effects of NAFTA from other developments, such as earlier steps toward trade liberalization, changes in Mexican domestic agricultural policy, and the severe currency crisis in 1995, which required a US bailout and a drastic devaluation of the peso. As the graph below indicates, during this period, US exports to Mexico more than doubled and Mexican exports to the United States more than tripled. In fifteen years, Mexico had gone from having a small trade deficit to a significant trade surplus with the United States.

The Mexican auto industry illustrates the effects of NAFTA. Prior to the agreement,

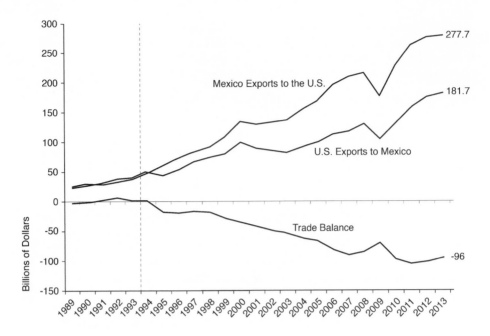

GRAPH 17.1. *US/Mexico Trade Before and After NAFTA, 1989–2010. Source: Berkeley Review of Latin American Studies.*

Mexican auto manufacturers produced solely for the domestic market. By 2011, 80 percent of the 1.5 million vehicles manufactured in the country were exported, and Mexico was assembling 20 percent of the vehicles made in North America. Mexico became the eighth-largest automotive manufacturer in the world (ahead of Spain, France, and Canada). In addition to assembly of finished vehicles, some parts were provided by Mexican auto parts manufacturers, and some of the latter also supplied automakers in the United States.

However, rather than conceiving of a "Mexican" auto industry, it is more accurate to see Mexican factories as links in a global auto industry chain. The research and development (R&D) and design and control of the process take place elsewhere. There is no "Mexican" automobile the way Hyundai is a Korean car and Tata is an Indian car. The fact that there are no Mexican-designed cars and none on the horizon indicates a major limitation of NAFTA-led industrialization.

Mexican agriculture has also been affected by NAFTA, although again it is difficult to isolate the effects of the trade agreements. Some small farmers have managed to sell their produce, such as tomatoes and onions, through NAFTA, particularly after they had upgraded their operations and learned to meet standards for quality and reliable delivery, so they might be said to be net winners under NAFTA. However, NAFTA's biggest losers may be small corn growers. Traditionally, the Mexican government had controlled corn prices, balancing the interests of urban consumers and farmers. With tariffs lifted under NAFTA, US farmers could sell their engineered corn cheaper than traditional Mexican corn.[2] Many small and subsistence farmers found that growing corn no longer made economic sense for them. That has undoubtedly contributed to the exodus from rural areas to cities and to the United States. By some estimates, as many as two million people have given up on farming. It should be noted, however, that most corn imported from the United States has gone to animal feed, and that Mexican corn production has actually shown a modest increase since NAFTA. The most likely interpretation is that NAFTA has accelerated a process already well under way: the extension of the commercial farm model to domestic food production, and the decline of subsistence farming.

In the 1990s, MERCOSUR was viewed as a rival to NAFTA, particularly because it offered a model of Latin American trade and integration independent of the United States. In practice, its success has been limited. One problem was the disparity between the member countries: both Paraguay and Uruguay are miniscule in comparison to Brazil or Argentina. (Venezuela was admitted in 2012.) Thus the most important effect was facilitating trade between Argentina and Brazil, but that was hindered by disputes between them. MERCOSUR operates as a customs union, that is, the member countries have adopted a uniform tariff to be applied to nonmember countries; hence, it is viewed as protectionist vis-à-vis non-MERCOSUR countries. Member countries are not permitted to establish free-trade agreements with non-member countries by themselves, but must negotiate through MERCOSUR. All in all, MERCOSUR has not lived up to the ambitious dreams of its founders.

Given the lack of comprehensive free-trade agreements, individual nations have pursued bilateral or regional agreements. Mexico and Chile each have a dozen or more agreements; the United States has made agreements with Central America and the Dominican Republic, Colombia, Chile, Peru, and Panama.

THE CHINA FACTOR

The advent of China in world markets has been as disruptive in Latin America as anywhere else in the world. Although Chinese economic power is now taken for granted, few in Latin America saw the implications as recently as 2000. One of the first such signs was the closing of many assembly plants along the Mexico-US border in the early 2000s, as companies transferred their operations to China. Soon Chinese goods were on sale in stores in Latin America, ranging from consumer electronics to tools and toys and clothing. Trade between China and Latin America rose from $10 billion in 2000 to $260 billion in 2012. In 2009, China overtook the United States as Brazil's largest trading partner.

The relationship is asymmetrical: Latin American countries are exporting commodities, such as soy, iron, copper, wood and pulp, and meat to China, which is exporting largely manufactured items, both consumer goods and machinery, to Latin America. The largest exporters to China are Brazil, Argentina, Chile, Venezuela, Peru, and Colombia. By contrast, Mexico and the countries of Central America and the Caribbean have significant trade deficits with China. Rising Chinese (and Indian) demand drove up prices for commodities worldwide, and was thus a major factor in Latin American growth starting in the early 2000s. Likewise, falling commodity prices in 2014, due to slackening demand in China, were slowing growth in the region.

Trade relations with China constitute a threefold challenge to Latin America:

- China may out-compete and displace Latin American manufacturers in world markets;
- China may likewise out-compete Latin American manufacturers in their domestic markets;
- with the demand for its commodities high, Latin America may find itself trapped in a division of labor, supplying minerals and agricultural goods in exchange for imported manufactured goods, echoing nineteenth-century trade patterns with Europe.

To take an example, consider the fact that all the bicycles for sale in a bike store in Cochabamba, Bolivia, are from China. Manufacturing bicycles would seem relatively simple: Why isn't a Bolivian company doing so? This is an instance of the "China Price": any manufacturer must be able to supply a product with a combination of price and quality to match what can be done by Chinese manufacturers at a given place (in this case, Cochabamba); otherwise, its business is not feasible.[3] The "China Price" is worldwide: many US manufacturers that could not meet it have been forced to close; sometimes the same company finds a supplier in China and becomes an import and sales operation. The same process has happened in Latin American countries to the point where it is now said that trade liberalization, particularly with the large-scale entrance of China, has led to de-industrialization.

Latin American countries are in danger of falling into the "middle-income trap": they cannot compete in world markets on the basis of cheap labor, and yet they cannot compete with the most advanced nations on the basis of technological innovation. Eva Paus cites declining clothing exports in Central America and Mexico: "The basis for global competitiveness in the field is moving toward the ability to provide the 'full package' all in one place: the purchase of inputs, cutting and assembly of cloth, attaching of accessories, finishing, packaging, and shipping. In contrast Central American and Mexican clothing sectors have remained in the 'cut and assemble' business" (Paus 2011, 74).

The challenge is not so much to confront China directly as to face the challenges of the present world environment, including the reality of China. The Miami-based Latin America business consultant John Price notes the dangers of the present situation of relying on the current model of "growth based on the export of commodities and expansion of domestic consumption—putting off needed political, judicial, educational and legal reforms." He cites a study listing ten promising areas of development for Latin America to pursue: 1. oil and gas; 2. semiprocessed agrifood/aquafood products; 3. mineral ores; 4. metals; 5. hides, textile inputs (e.g., wool); 6. agriculture/ aquaculture commodities; 7. tourism; 8. lumber, pulp, and paper products; 9. aviation;

Containers in port, Valparaíso, Chile. © Tommie Sue Montgomery.

10. chemicals and plastics. Latin American countries should start from where they are and try to advance into higher value-added sections. His recommendations are summarized in a closing paragraph:

> Fortunately, the region is blessed with certain competitive advantages, including abundant resources, cheap energy, market access, relatively open investment laws and reasonably high education levels, given their middle-income status. But Latin America will need to focus on the following: increasing access to long-term competitive debt or equity financing; improving R&D at leading schools to expand the number of well-trained scientists and engineers; creating a consistent regulatory climate; simplifying and streamlining the tax code and tax enforcement; and updating its woeful transportation infrastructure. (Price 2011, 14)

If that sounds like a reiteration of what was said in chapter 13, it is no accident. The implication is that rather than obsess about China, Latin American countries must find their own way in a globalized world and carry out needed reforms.

It might help to unpack the notion of "competitiveness." Strictly speaking, it is not nations that compete but firms. To return to bicycles, they are produced by individual companies, indeed hundreds of them. Chinese companies produce two-thirds of the world's bicycles, many of them inexpensive bikes for its internal consumption, but they export them worldwide. The key component of a bicycle is the frame, and hence the ability to manufacture adequate-quality frames is central to a bicycle industry. In fact, however, there are many variations and dozens of parts on any particular bicycle. Moreover, there is a wide range of bicycles, from cheap models, especially for children, to high-performance bikes, with a range of bikes in the middle, selling for hundreds of dollars.

Bicycle industries have existed in various Latin American countries, and there is no inherent reason why Latin American companies cannot produce bicycles on a par with Chinese firms. Indeed, Brazil is ranked the number-five manufacturer of bicycles in the world. A leading manufacturer, Caloi, produces over 750,000 bikes a year at a plant in the city of Manaus in the Amazon. The fact that companies like Caloi produce the key element of a bicycle, the frame, indicates that in principle Latin American countries can produce world-class products. In 2013, the Canadian company Dorel Industries bought a 70 percent share in Caloi in order to expand its own business in Brazil and South America.[4]

By 2012, surprising signs were coming from Mexico that it might be able to compete successfully with China. Chinese wages, which had once been one-fifth of Mexican wages, were now three-quarters as high. Truck transport to the United States is quicker and cheaper than shipping containers across the ocean. In a 2012 report, *The Economist* summarized: "The joint effect of pay, logistics and currency fluctuations had made Mexico the world's cheapest place to manufacture goods destined for the United States, undercutting China as well as countries such as India and Vietnam."

Brazil's growing presence in Africa is another example of globalization.[5] While in office, President Lula da Silva (2003–2011) made twelve trips to Africa and visited twenty-nine countries. Between 2000 and 2011, Brazil's trade with Africa rose from $4.2 billion to $27.6 billion. Like China and India, Brazil is interested in African commodities. Brazilian investment is focused on Portuguese-speaking countries, especially Angola and Mozambique. The Brazilian company Odebrecht is the largest private employer in Angola. To a degree, Brazil is competing with China, especially for contracts, but the Brazilians claim that they have more to offer African countries. Brazil is betting that rising prosperity in Africa will increase demand for Brazilian goods, including foods. Brazil presents its strategy as a South–South development partnership, not simply a business relationship. It can offer its technology as "tropicalized," and hence better suited for African conditions than US or European machinery. The research agencies Fiocruz (Fundação Oswaldo Cruz) and EMBRAPA are researching African agriculture and tropical disease.

EMBRAPA is working in fifteen African countries. Brazil is helping African family farmers to upgrade their techniques. Its health-care work includes assistance in combating HIV/AIDS, utilizing its own successful experience, with projects in Botswana, Burkina Faso, Congo, Ghana, Liberia, Kenya, Sierra Leone, Tanzania, Zambia, and Mozambique, where it has built a factory for antiretroviral drugs. In the field of energy, Brazil is assisting with rural electrification, transfer of biofuel technology, and deepwater oil exploration.

As indicated by Lula's visits, Brazil's initiatives in Africa have been led by the Brazilian government. The Brazilian private sector initially did not see opportunities, but companies large and small have now entered Africa. Chinese involvement in Africa, it may be noted, is also government led. Brazil's aim is to position itself as a leader in global development.[6]

These examples of China and Brazil illustrate a feature of globalization that must be kept in mind: the notion of a frictionless world of "free trade" is an illusion of economic theory; in the real world, governments and corporations bring their weight to bear. China penetrates markets around the world, but the domestic Chinese market is very difficult for outsiders to break into; they are forced to seek Chinese partners. Even with the move to freer trade, Brazil has continued to pursue an industrial policy. The government identifies promising sectors, which it then favors with financing and perhaps research. In opening up bidding for participation in its deepwater offshore oil, it has insisted that companies buy percentages of Brazilian goods and services, even if international sourcing would be cheaper.[7]

A clue to the future evolution of trade and integration may be offered by the Pacific Alliance formed by Chile, Peru, Colombia, and Mexico in 2012. These four nations, jointly representing 35 percent of Latin American GDP, reduced tariffs by 90 percent, with a pledge to eliminate the remaining 10 percent. They also integrated their stock markets, thereby offering investors and firms more options. The universities of these countries now recognize one another's degrees, thus facilitating movement of students and faculty. The lifting of visa requirements will ease travel between them. Besides fostering trade between the countries, in the long run the alliance is intended to facilitate trade with Asia, perhaps through an agreement with ASEAN (Association of Southeast Asian Nations). Costa Rica and Panama were seeking to join, and Canada, Australia, and New Zealand had observer status.[8]

PEOPLE ON THE MOVE

Until a few decades ago, Latin America was primarily *receiving* migrants, not sending them. During the same period when millions of Europeans were coming to Ellis Island and other ports of entry to the United States, others went to Latin America. Between 1870 and 1950, Argentina took in around six million immigrants from Europe, and Brazil received over five million. Tens of thousands of Jews arrived from Europe, especially in Argentina and Brazil.[9] Immigrants also came from the Middle East and Asia (especially Japanese to Brazil and Peru). Mexico and other countries received refugees from the Spanish Civil War and the Franco dictatorship. Oil wealth made Venezuela attractive to Spanish immigrants in the mid-twentieth century.

Since that time, this situation has reversed. Significant out-migration began, driven by a number of factors. Population was growing rapidly, and by the 1970s, employment was not keeping pace. People had already been moving massively from the countryside to cities, and that mobility could take people beyond their borders. A "push" factor was political repression in military dictatorships (Brazil, Chile,

Argentina, Uruguay) and Central America. Political refugees fleeing for their lives tended to go to other Latin American countries, especially Mexico but also Cuba, or to Europe. Economic crisis in particular countries (Brazil in the late 1980s, Ecuador in the late 1990s, Mexico in the 1980s and mid-1990s) spurred out-migration.

People have often migrated to nearby Latin American countries: Bolivians and Paraguayans to Argentina, Peruvians to Chile, Nicaraguans to Costa Rica (where they constitute 7 percent of the country's population), Guatemalans to southern Mexico, Haitians to the Dominican Republic, Dominicans to Puerto Rico—all are examples of cross-border migration in search of work. As a boy, President Evo Morales of Bolivia went with his father to work in Argentina. Male migrants often gravitate toward construction work, organized into crews of their own nationality; women work as domestics or in cleaning services. They begin as temporary workers but often stay for long periods of time.

Not all emigrants go for low-paying work. Increasingly, professionals and business executives accept jobs in other countries or are sent there by multinational companies. During the years of booming oil sales, Venezuela was a magnet for Colombians and other Latin Americans, skilled and unskilled; more recently, Venezuelan professionals have left to work elsewhere.

Today increasing migration is a worldwide phenomenon: an estimated 214 million people were living outside their native country in 2010, one out of every thirty-three people. Some have gone from one developing country to another, others from a developing to a developed country. Many countries have received immigrants: Americans who view the Statue of Liberty as a unique beacon might be surprised to learn that Canada has a considerably higher percentage of foreign-born residents (19.8%) than the United States (12.5%).

We may consider how migration works by looking at it first at the individual and household level, and then consider what patterns can be determined from a broader standpoint. Caroline Moser, whose work on a neighborhood of Guayaquil, Ecuador, was cited in chapter 2, also studied Ecuadoreans who migrated from that community to Barcelona (2009). In response to economic and political crises in the late 1990s, two million Ecuadoreans had gone overseas by 2004 (15% of the population), mainly to Spain. Moser cites the example of a seventeen-year-old named Douglas from Indio Guayas who emigrated immediately after secondary school. He first lived with a sister but soon had his own apartment, which then served as a first arrival point for dozens of other Ecuadoreans, who either came directly or from another point in Europe.

Moser points to the "community social capital" at work: migrants had a place to arrive and live temporarily, and contacts for getting jobs, and for borrowing money or getting a meal, if necessary. Working at first without work papers, they took low-level jobs. They tended to work in niches for foreign workers, such as construction, domestic care, or cleaning hotel rooms. Finding work was easier for women than for men. After getting residency papers, they found better jobs. Both men and women tended to find second jobs or work freelance, such as in apartment repair or cleaning. Over time, many managed to obtain a mortgage to buy an apartment. Spain's welcoming stance reversed after the economic crisis in the later 2000s.

The migrants had many adjustments to make, particularly at the household level. Men had to learn to cook and wash clothes, since there was no one to do it for them. Women experienced a greater sense of independence than they had had in Ecuador. They learned that domestic violence (hitting a spouse or child) would be treated as a crime by police and the courts.

Three out of four migrants whom Moser interviewed were sending remittances, at an average of $143 a month, back to Ecuador. Women were more reliable at sending money, and men tended to stop sending remittances when they found partners. Migrants also sent remittances for short-term crises. Moser tells of a woman named Carmen who had a live-in job taking care of an elderly woman with Alzheimer's disease. In four years, she managed to save $20,000, which she sent to rebuild her house in Guayaquil for her children. It was clear to the migrants that their children being raised in Barcelona would regard themselves not as Ecuadorean but as Spanish or Catalan of Ecuadorean descent.

Migrants typically go abroad not simply as individuals but as members of households and as part of a larger family economic strategy. The aim is to acquire assets, but doing so requires having some assets to start with, such as marketable skills or ability, as well as "social capital," particularly contacts. Research has shown that individuals are more likely to emigrate if they have contact with people who have successfully migrated and if they have family members or other contacts in the country of destination.

Latin Americans have arrived in the United States through several distinct waves of migration.

- Over a million Mexicans fled the violence of the revolution in 1910–1920, and others continued to come during the 1920s. During the Great Depression, however, the United States deported many Mexicans—estimates range from 500,000 to two million—some of them American citizens. Then during World War II, Mexicans were again encouraged to come as temporary laborers in the Bracero program, which lasted until 1965. By the 1950s, entire neighborhoods of Mexican Americans existed from California to Texas.
- Puerto Ricans, who are otherwise similar to Cubans, Dominicans, or Panamanians in speech, music, and culture, have been US citizens since 1917. Despite efforts at economic development in Puerto Rico in the 1950s, employment lagged and people began to emigrate to the mainland, especially New York. Today more Puerto Ricans live on the mainland (4.7 million) than on the island (3.6 million).
- A similar wave of migration from the Dominican Republic began in the 1960s, partly driven by the years of turmoil after the assassination of the dictator Rafael Trujillo.

- Like Puerto Ricans and Dominicans, some Cubans had migrated to the United States in the early twentieth century, but the Cuban American community was created in the aftermath of the Cuban Revolution (1959). The first wave was made up of those identified most closely with the previous regime, followed by those who feared losing property or power, and then by those who became disenchanted with the revolution. They settled primarily in Miami and south Florida. Another large wave came in 1980, when Fidel Castro encouraged discontents to leave. Cubans fleeing the island were welcomed by the US government and were given public assistance in obtaining housing and employment, and many have achieved remarkable economic success.
- Central Americans began to arrive in large numbers after 1980, primarily Salvadorans and Guatemalans fleeing violence.
- The 1990s witnessed increasing immigration from Mexico, Central America, and the Dominican Republic, driven by economic conditions and by a demand for labor in the United States. Migrants in this most recent wave have often settled in areas other than the traditional sites in the Southwest or northeast cities.
- In 2013–2014, over 60,000 youths from Honduras, El Salvador, and Guatemala entered the United States, fleeing gang violence and threats in their homeland.

These waves are interwoven with the history of US–Latin American relations and often driven by actions of the US government, starting with the US seizure of half of Mexico's territory in the Mexican-American War.[10] Some families in that region, especially in New Mexico, can trace their ancestors back to Spanish colonial times. The Spanish-American War left Puerto Rico as a colony and later a commonwealth. The Cuban independence movement was thwarted by that war, after which Cuba was held as a protectorate. United States' dominance of Cuba almost guaranteed that the revolution would be anti-American. US policy aggravated the wars in Central America, which sent people fleeing northward. The NAFTA-impelled changes in farming prompted many Mexicans to abandon their fields and head north.

Emigration to the United States can take place through various routes and at corresponding costs. Puerto Ricans can fly to the United States easily and at reasonable rates. Others will need a visa, which is easier to obtain if one can show proof of income and give assurance that he or she does not plan to stay beyond the visa period. That is unlikely for poorer people, hence they have traveled by land to the US-Mexico border. They then hired a local coyote, or smuggler, who took them across the border. In the mid-1980s, the Salvadoran newspapers ran classified ads offering to take people to the United States with a down payment in colones and final payment in dollars, totaling a few hundred dollars. Over time, the journey became far more dangerous, with the advent of criminal gangs and tighter border security on the US side. By the mid-2000s, fees for bringing people to the United States from Central or South America were typically several thousand dollars. Many immigrants were not smuggled but arrived with visas, which they then overstayed. In the 1980s and 1990s, undocumented immigrants occasionally returned to visit their hometowns, perhaps for holidays. As border enforcement was tightened, many decided not to make return visits, and their stays became longer. Undocumented immigrants live in continual fear of the immigration authorities and keep a low profile.

In the 2000s, many in the US public and Congress became convinced that the country had "lost control" of its borders. One response was to build new fences and barriers of various kinds along 700 miles of the almost 2,000-mile US-Mexico border. Since the fences were built near more populated areas, those seeking to cross were forced into more desolate areas. Since the early 2000s, the number of migrants who die each year attempting to cross the border has fluctuated in the 300–400 range. The number of Border Patrol agents increased from 15,000 in 2007 to 21,000 in 2013. Predator drones, cameras on towers, and ground-level sensors were being used to spot people attempting to cross. In 2013, the Border Patrol was costing $18 billion a year, more than all other federal law enforcement agencies combined.

By 2010, migration from Mexico to the United States had declined considerably and seemed to have reached a net zero rate. Arrests at the southwest border in 2011 fell to their lowest level since 1972. The reasons seemed to be the economic slowdown in the United States and the dangers from organized crime along the border. Mexicans continued to migrate but did so domestically. The *New York Times* reported that

Central American migrants hopping a train in Mexico. © Edgar Romero.

"nearly two million more Mexicans lived away from their hometowns in 2010 than was the case a decade earlier," and that similar movement was occurring elsewhere in Latin America. Migration was now looking "less like a compass pointing north and more like a hub with many spokes"[11] (Cave 2012b).

LATIN AMERICA IN THE UNITED STATES?

Hispanics or Latinos[12] are now the largest "minority" in the United States, almost one-sixth of the population (52 million people). According to the 2010 census, 37.6 million people in the United States speak Spanish at home; they also speak it in the streets, supermarkets, and subways. Major media markets have Spanish-speaking television and radio stations. Consumer products now routinely contain instructions in Spanish.

Although statistically the United States is the fifth-largest "Spanish-speaking" nation in the world, it would be misleading to imply that US Hispanics are somehow a twentieth Latin American nation. The basic insight can be gleaned from what Caroline Moser observed among Ecuadorean immigrants to Spain: children raised in Barcelona are growing up Spaniards (or Catalans). Broadly speaking, a similar process takes place in the United States with the second and third generations, and has been taking place for over a century of immigration from Mexico and elsewhere.

In *Who Are We? The Challenges to America's National Identity* (2004), the influential political scientist Samuel Huntington[13] argued otherwise. He believed that new immigrants, especially Mexicans, represent a fundamentally different reality from that of previous immigrants who assimilated into the nation's values, which he identifies with those of its original British Protestant settlers. Given their numbers, the contiguity of Mexico to the United States, the profound difference between Mexican culture and values and those of the United States' founders, and their tendency to continue to speak Spanish, the new immigrants represent a threat to the very identity of the United States. The importance of Huntington's contribution is perhaps not in the details (e.g., his stereotype of *mañana* Mexicans is quite the opposite of those who hire them for their work ethic), but in the fact that he articulated arguments that appeared in conservative publications and fueled anti-immigrant sentiments. Without responding directly, we can keep his position in mind as we consider the Latino presence in the United States.

Seventy-four percent of Hispanics are US citizens; many others are legal residents. Whether they originally intended to remain or not, many who come will ultimately remain and their children will be US citizens. Latinos thus form a kind of continuum from recent arrivals living in immigrant enclaves to fifth-generation citizens. Hispanics are geographically concentrated: 71 percent live in one hundred counties, and half of those counties are in California, Texas, and Florida. Nevertheless, the Latino populations have spread to areas other than their traditional communities. Mexicans and Mexican Americans constitute 65 percent of Latinos, and they are the largest group in fifty of the sixty metropolitan areas where they live.

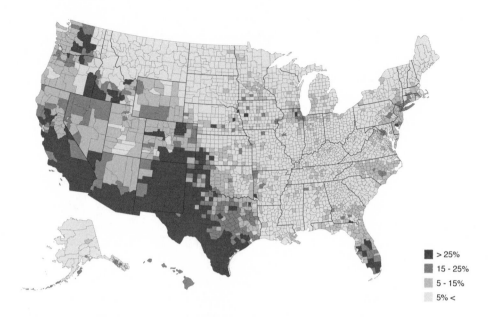

GRAPH 17.2. *The Distribution of the Nation's Hispanic Population, 2011 (Hispanic Share of Population by County). Source: "Mapping the Latino Population by State, County, and City." Pew Research Center, Washington, DC (August 29, 2013). http://pewrsr.ch/10700NY.*

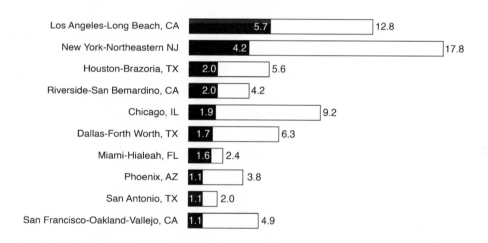

GRAPH 17.3. *Top Ten Metropolitan Areas by Hispanic Population, 2010 (in Millions). Source: "Mapping the Latino Population by State, County, and City." Pew Research Center, Washington, DC (August 29, 2013). http://pewrsr.ch/10700NY.*

As indicated in table 17.2, the two largest groups by national origin are Mexican and Puerto Rican; all other nationalities trail far behind. Again it should be kept in mind that Puerto Ricans are US citizens and can travel freely between the mainland and the island. They are concentrated heavily in New York City and New Jersey. Dominicans are largely in New York. Cuban Americans are concentrated in south Florida, with some presence in the Northeast, particularly New Jersey. Central

TABLE 17.2. Hispanic Population by Origin, 2011

ORIGIN	NUMBER (MILLIONS)	PERCENTAGE OF HISPANICS
Mexican	33.5	64.6
Puerto Rican	4.9	9.5
Salvadoran	1.9	3.8
Cuban	1.9	3.6
Dominican	1.5	2.9
Guatemalan	1.2	2.3
Colombian	.9	1.9
Honduran	.7	1.4
Ecuadorean	.6	1.2
Peruvian	.5	1.1
Nicaraguan	.4	0.8
Venezuelan	.2	0.5
Argentinean	.2	0.5

Note: Figures are rounded.
Source: Pew Research Center (2013a).

Americans have gravitated toward points where early immigrants had established a presence: Salvadorans in Los Angeles and Washington, DC; Guatemalans in Los Angeles, and some Guatemalan indigenous people in agricultural areas of central Florida; Hondurans in New Orleans.[14]

Latino political activism began in the mid-twentieth century in various places, primarily around issues like discriminatory treatment and police brutality. Discrimination and prejudice had a long prehistory, in particular the 1943 "Zoot Suit Riots" in Los Angeles, when for several days larger and larger gangs of marauding US servicemen went on a rampage beating up Mexican Americans. Influenced by the African American civil rights movement, in the late 1960s, Mexican Americans organized protests and formed political organizations. In East Los Angeles in 1968, students staged a walkout from schools to protest unequal conditions. The 1970 killing by a policeman of *Los Angeles Times* reporter Ruben Salazar, who had been covering a march protesting the high level of Latino casualties in the Vietnam War, led to further protests and arrests. For a brief period, the rhetoric reflected the revolutionary nationalist language of Third World solidarity, in which activists believed they were part of a worldwide movement for systemic change.

Despite that early radical rhetoric, in practice political organizing was directed at efforts to have people representing the community elected to school boards, city councils, state governments, and Congress. In the Southwest and Northeast, Latinos worked within the Democratic Party. In Florida, Cuban Americans gravitated toward the Republican Party, initially driven by anger at President Kennedy's "betrayal" in not sending air cover to the Bay of Pigs invasion, but also because they sympathized with the social conservatism and pro-business stance of the Republican Party.

From the 1960s to the 1980s, the struggle of the United Farm Workers (UFW) union was an inspiration that went beyond the immediate cause of the workers. Cesar Chavez and others, especially Dolores Huerta, led a nonviolent movement to organize farmworkers in California's Central Valley, using tactics of demonstrations, marches, and fasting. When the movement began, farmworkers often had to travel from region to region, picking crops in season at very low wages, and had no labor rights. The farmworker movement sought to establish a labor union to assure basic rights for those working in the fields, and in doing so, it used symbols such as a banner of Our Lady of Guadalupe and popular Mexican music. The movement cultivated allies and organized national boycotts of table grapes and Gallo wines. After years of struggle, the union won contracts. Chicano pride was expressed in the theater productions of El Teatro Campesino of playwright Luis Valdez and in art (murals taking inspiration from the Mexican muralists) in East Los Angeles and elsewhere in the Southwest. Similar initiatives were taking place in Puerto Rican communities in the East.

Based on demographic change, politicians and pundits have commented on the "Latino vote." The lopsided Democratic vote of Latinos in the 2012 presidential campaign was forcing the Republican Party to seek Latino faces and moderate its views, particularly on immigration reform. In actuality, there is no "Latino" vote, because Hispanics do not see themselves as having a single identity. According to a Pew Research Center survey, 69 percent of respondents say that Latinos "have many different cultures rather than a common culture." When asked about their identity, 51 percent say they use their family's country of origin—only 24 percent use "Hispanic or Latino"—and 21 percent say "American." About half say that they are like typical Americans, and half regard themselves as different (Taylor et al. 2012).

The crucial element is the second-generation, US-born children of immigrants. Not surprisingly, most of these Latinos believe that they are doing better economically than their parents. When asked whether with hard work one can succeed, they are more likely to agree (78%) than the US population as a whole (58%). Twenty-six percent of Hispanics marry non-Hispanics.

Eight in ten second-generation Hispanics say they speak Spanish fairly well. However, the proportion of Hispanics who speak Spanish well has been declining, from 78 percent in the 2000s to a projected two-thirds in 2020. Between 2010 and 2020, the number of Hispanics who speak only English at home is expected to rise from 25 percent to 34 percent. Spanish might thus reasonably be expected to decline generationally, as did Italian, German, Polish, and other languages a century ago. Counteracting that trend, however, might be a sense of the value of retaining Spanish in a globalized world, and the availability of media and ongoing contact with relatives in the ancestral homeland. Thus, it is plausible that along with English proficiency, the second and third generations may be more bilingual than the descendants of earlier waves of European immigrants.[15] Samuel Huntington notwithstanding, they will also be thoroughly American.

Although Hispanics have done relatively well when compared to their countries of origin, significant segments remain poor, as demonstrated in Pew Research Center reports in 2011 and 2013. The poverty rate among Hispanic children is 36 percent (as opposed to 15% among whites). Fifty-one percent of second-generation Hispanic women who recently gave birth were unmarried (as opposed to 36% in the US population as a whole). Median Hispanic household income is one-half that of white families ($37,000 vs. $72,000). The results can be seen in childhood diseases (e.g., asthma and obesity), cognitive development, and preparedness for school. Hispanic school achievement levels are lower, and Latino children attend schools with less experienced teachers and poorer course offerings. Hispanic adults age eighteen or over are 12 percent of the college population but 16 percent of the prison population. Hispanic homeowners were almost twice as likely to be affected by the housing crisis as white households: over a quarter who bought homes between 2004 and 2008 had lost their home or were in danger of losing it by 2011 (Brown and Patten 2014a, 2014b).

Hispanic poverty encompasses both that of recent immigrants whose children will probably emerge from poverty, and generational poverty, that of families in poor neighborhoods, where crime, drugs, poor schools, and single-parent families become self-reinforcing.

US–LATIN AMERICAN RELATIONS

Finally, we turn to official relations between Latin American countries and the United States. Such intergovernmental relations should be seen in the light of broader relationships between the peoples of Latin America and the United States. Those ties have been considered throughout this book and in this chapter, particularly in terms of the movement of goods and people. US exports to Latin America doubled between 2000 and 2012; the United States "exports more to Latin America than it does to Europe, twice as much to Mexico than it does to China, and more to Chile and Colombia than it does to Russia" (Inter-American Dialogue 2012, 12). As already noted, about one-sixth of the US population is Hispanic, particularly from Mexico. Immigrants and residents are now integral to the US labor force. They are in frequent contact with family members through Skype or the like.

Movement of people is not just one way. Between five and six million Americans visit Mexico each year; other millions go to the Caribbean and Central and South America. A growing trend is "medical tourism" to Mexico and elsewhere: people opt to have medical and dental procedures performed at a fraction of what it would cost them in the United States, even including the plane fare. Latin American cities are becoming tourist destinations similar to European cities. Several hundred thousand Americans have opted to live in Mexico, primarily retirees, but some have gone to open businesses. Costa Rica has attracted American retirees for decades, and more recently Panama has done so. Such retirees find that they can live a pleasant life and have what they require, including suitable medical care, at a fraction of what it would cost them in the United States. Portions of Latin America may come to play a role for retirees like that of Florida in the twentieth century.

In considering US–Latin American relations today, previous history (traced in chapters 11 and 12) should be kept in mind. Broadly speaking, US policy toward Latin America in the last century veered from active intervention (1898–1930), to a Good Neighbor Policy of cooperation until the 1950s, to a Cold War–driven policy of intervention from the 1950s to 1990 (preventing "another Cuba"). The end of the Cold War brought an abrupt shift in policy focus.[16] In the 1990s, trade was a major area of concern, along with the lingering effects of the debt crisis in a number of countries, as was drug trafficking. When he took office, President George W. Bush intended to improve relations with Latin America, and especially Mexico, but after the terrorist attacks of September 2001, Latin America fell off the foreign-policy map.[17]

From a Latin American standpoint, the fact that the United States government turned its attention elsewhere had its positive side. In the decade and a half since then, Latin American nations have become more self-confident and assertive. In the run-up to the Iraq War (2003), the Bush administration sought a UN Security Council resolution authorizing the invasion. Mexico and Chile were among the rotating council members at that point, and the Bush administration pressured them for their vote, even threatening retaliation in matters like trade. In both instances, these members voted against the resolution, in part because the Chilean and Mexican publics were overwhelmingly against the war.

US–Latin American governmental relations cannot follow a single template, as they might have during the Cold War. Each country must be approached considering its specific features. In that sense, Latin America will be increasingly like Europe: the United States has a "European" policy only in matters relating to European institutions. Certainly some matters might be treated on a regional (Central American, Caribbean, Andean) basis, if they are indeed regional, but dealing with countries in terms of an overarching "Latin American" policy makes less and less sense.

An important requirement is that US governments treat their Latin American counterparts with respect, particularly Mexico and Brazil, which are now among the ten largest economies in the world. Brazilians and Mexicans were angered (but not entirely surprised) at the revelations by the National Security Agency (NSA) employee Edward Snowden in 2013 that the United States had surveilled private e-mails and Internet use of Presidents Dilma Rousseff and Enrique Peña Nieto (even while a candidate), and had also hacked into the Brazilian state oil company, Petrobras. Brazilians were especially indignant, and President Rousseff canceled a state dinner at the White House, the only one that the Obama administration had prepared for a foreign leader in 2013, and which had been intended to cement US ties with Brazil.

US governments should respect Latin America's adherence to democratic standards, which Latin Americans see as failing in at least two instances in recent years. In 2002, when President Hugo Chávez was ousted by a military coup, the United

President Funes of El Salvador and President Obama at a presidential summit in Cartagena, Colombia, 2012.
© *Edgar Romero.*

States quickly welcomed the new government and offered support, even though no Latin American country did so. Chávez supporters rallied in the streets, and within two days another faction of the military restored him, leaving the Bush administration looking foolish. Chávez and his supporters were convinced that the United States had been involved in the coup itself. Other Latin American countries were not necessarily supporting Chávez and his policies, but rather the principle that democratically elected governments must not be terminated by military coups.

In 2009, Honduran president Manuel Zelaya was seized by the Honduran military and deported to Costa Rica. Again, Latin American governments unanimously refused to recognize the government installed by coup.[18] While not endorsing the coup, the Obama administration did not join other countries in the hemisphere in refusing to recognize the new government. It argued that the crisis should be resolved in future elections. Meanwhile, repression was unleashed against grassroots supporters of Zelaya and continued with impunity. It would have been wiser for the United States to follow the lead of other countries in the hemisphere.

An unresolved issue is the proper forum for dealing with hemispheric issues. The Organization of American States (OAS), which encompasses thirty-five nations, including a number of small Caribbean states, is headquartered in Washington and has historically been seen as a tool of Washington. CELAC (Community of Latin American and Caribbean States) is the outgrowth of presidential summits in the mid-2000s and includes most of the hemisphere, but excludes the United States and Canada. However, it has thus far served primarily as a venue for presidential summits.

Brief comments should be made on some recurring issues: Cuba, immigration reform, and drug policy.

Cuba

From 1959 onward, US-Cuba relations were caught in the Cold War, aggravated by powerful Cuban Americans in south Florida bent on regaining what they believed was rightfully theirs. The United States instituted a trade embargo and pressured other countries to do likewise in order to isolate Cuba. The two countries did not have embassies in each other's countries, and had to do business through third parties. Latin American countries, which, at the behest of the United States, had broken diplomatic ties in the 1960s, began to renew relations in the 1970s, and other countries in the world had more or less normal diplomatic relations with Havana. US efforts to isolate Cuba had left the United States isolated.

The sudden and unexpected end of communism in the Soviet Union and Eastern Europe in 1989–1991 might have been an opportunity for Cuba to reintegrate with the rest of the world, by initiating reforms internally and renewing relations with the United States. However, Fidel Castro defiantly proclaimed an emergency "Special Period in Time of Peace," evidently with the conviction that the collapse of socialism elsewhere made it all the more important to hold on to it in Cuba. He likewise identified that struggle with his own rule, meaning that he had to remain in power. Even after his illness and his transfer of power to his brother Raúl in 2008, internal reforms in Cuba were slow in coming.

Although the stranglehold on Cuba policy by hard-line Cuban Americans in Miami gradually loosened, US politicians and administrations showed no inclination to take new initiatives aimed at restoring US-Cuba relations. Even though actual attitudes softened among younger generations of Cuban Americans, hard-liners had a lock on official policy. Ironically, under the guise of family visits, many Cuban Americans were doing brisk trade with Cubans on the island, shipping large quantities of goods to Cubans running small businesses and sharing in the profits.

In April 2015, President Obama and President Raúl Castro met in Panama at the Summit of the Americas, the first meeting of Cuban and US presidents in over half a century. Later that year the two countries renewed diplomatic relations, but obstacles to full normalization remained. A crucial principle for US policy should be to favor an evolutionary process in which the key actors in determining their own fate are the eleven million Cubans on the island, not those bent on recovering property lost over a half century ago or settling scores. However, the road forward was unclear, particularly in light of US domestic politics.

Immigration Reform

Perhaps the most important step for the United States to take in improving relations with Latin America (at least Mexico and Central America) would be comprehensive immigration reform. Even if the flow has declined notably, an estimated eleven million unauthorized immigrants were in the United States in 2015. Eighty percent of farm labor is done by Mexicans, many of them undocumented. Immigrants are an essential part of the labor force, working in poultry processing, construction, manufacturing, restaurants, hotels, and elsewhere. Their children are in schools, even in universities.

The elements of immigration reform have been discussed and were present in legislation drawn up by a bipartisan group in the US Congress in 2013. They include programs for temporary work and residence permits, a "path to citizenship" for immigrants already in the country, a priority of family reunification, and rational border control. Opponents claim that immigrants are a drag on the economy, since they use social services (schools, hospitals), and some are guilty of criminal conduct. However, most economists argue that immigrants are a net economic plus, especially because by being part of the workforce and paying taxes, they will help keep Social Security viable. As consumers they help sustain the domestic economy.

However, anti-immigrant feelings were stoked by the notion that foreigners were taking American jobs, and that the country had lost control over its borders, thus giving rise to the militarization and heavy spending on border security mentioned earlier. As with Cuba policy, after the 2014 election, President Obama took executive action declaring that immigrants in the United States for five years who had children born in the United States and had no criminal record would not be deported. That step was short of comprehensive immigration reform, and its fate was uncertain under a Republican-controlled House and Senate.

Drug Policy

Chapter 15 traced the decades-long history of the "drug wars" and noted that Latin American leaders were questioning its premises and making other proposals. This is happening on several fronts, namely international forums, changing legislation, and specific initiatives. From their standpoint, the crux of the matter is not stopping drug production and trafficking in themselves, but reducing the violence associated with them. If consumption of marihuana were decriminalized, and if addiction to cocaine and other hard drugs were treated as a public health problem, the raison d'être of the entire drug trafficking network would collapse.

Taken together, these proposals can be seen as questioning the paradigm that has been in use for a half century, from the United Nations Single Convention on Narcotic Drugs (1961), and the "war on drugs" declared by President Nixon (1971), leading up to Plan Colombia (1999), and the Mérida Initiative (2008). For many years, Latin American publics and leaders tended to think that drug trafficking was a US problem for which they had been forced to pay the price. More recently, countries have recognized that their own domestic consumption is a facet of the problem.

Many analysts would contrast the rethinking in Latin America to the static drug policy of the United States. Since the institution of mandatory sentencing, US prisons have filled up with inmates charged with possession or low-level dealing. Public attitude also seems to be shifting as both Colorado and Washington, DC, have decriminalized use of marihuana and cultivation of a small number of plants for personal use.

In various places in Latin America, movements for decriminalization of marihuana use have been gaining ground. The most notable example is Uruguay, a small country that proposes its plan as an "experiment," but others had their eyes on it. A number of sitting presidents, notably in Guatemala and Colombia, have questioned the existing paradigm. The Obama administration did little more than listen politely. It has shown no sign of being open to considering revision, perhaps preferring to expend scarce political capital on battles it regards as more important. The issues will not go away and can be expected to return in dealings with Latin America.

As this chapter illustrates, Latin Americans live in the same globalized world as the rest of the world: their mobile phones are tracked by GPS, and they communicate online with relatives in other continents, including the United States. China is at once a major customer and a competitor. Their ties with the United States through trade and migration have deepened, but their governments have diversified their relationships, and US policymakers can no longer apply a one-size-fits-all policy to the region.

FURTHER READING

On competitiveness, see Haar and Price (2008); on China, Gallagher and Porzecanski (2010). For an evaluation of NAFTA, see Zepeda, Wise, and Gallagher (2009). On US Hispanics, see Pew Research Center (2013b) and Brown and Patten (2014a, 2014b); on US–Latin American relations today, Arnson (2013) and Inter-American Dialogue (2102). For drug policy, see Hakim and Covington (2012) and Latin American Commission on Drugs and Democracy (2009).

Hopes and Tasks of the Bicentennial Generation

The premise for this book is that the two-hundred-year anniversary of Latin American independence (2010 to 2025) offers an opportunity for taking a fresh look at the region. After examining a number of topics thematically (cities, agriculture, business, environment, inequality and class, race and ethnicity, gender, and religion), we surveyed Latin American history and then focused more specifically on current issues in economics, politics and governance, and globalization.

Some readers might be surprised by the resulting hopeful picture: most of the nineteen nations of Latin America may be on their way toward overcoming extreme poverty and underdevelopment. Until very recently, introductory books such as this one would have emphasized the impediments to development: the role of the region's elites, the United States, multinational corporations, or simply capitalism.

The hope being expressed here is modest, namely, that within a generation or two the great majority of Latin Americans could justifiably feel that their societies work reasonably well for them, that their lives are improving, and that their children's lives will be even better. Something like that is already true of an expanding circle of people, the emerging middle classes discussed from time to time in these pages. Such a society would not look exactly like the developed countries today: Latin American GDP per capita is a fraction of that of the United States and Europe; becoming "developed" will not mean equaling them in number of automobiles per capita or airline miles logged.

In this conclusion, I would like to expand on this possibility and indicate the grounds for it. I am not making a prediction, nor am I sketching a utopia that could exist under a different political or economic system, but rather a possibility rooted in present trends. One reason for hope is that today's generations are less ideological and more pragmatic than earlier ones, and they are more concerned about what works. Governing political parties and coalitions usually describe themselves as center-left or center-right. The left understands that occupying the power of the state does not in itself bring about successful development, and relatively few conservatives are so doctrinaire as to advocate simply downsizing the government. Both left and right agree that the issue is not the size of the state but its effectiveness.

One example is the "conditional cash transfers" mentioned at various points: government-provided modest allowances to poor households that meet certain requirements. Giving cash to people can be criticized as either a band-aid or as creating dependency, but practice has shown that it helps poor people eat better, keep their children in school, and perhaps start small businesses, and that it stimulates the local economy. Another example is the spread of bus rapid transit systems in major cities. Both innovations exemplify the adoption of "best practices" seen to be working elsewhere. Tech-savvy entrepreneurs are changing the way business is done.

Sustained growth and development involves "virtuous circles," examples of which we have considered. In 2009, President Lula announced a goal of building a million new homes: construction would be done by the private sector, but the government would assist with financing. Beneficiaries would include the construction industry, their suppliers, construction workers, and those providing the goods and services bought with their wages. Another possible virtuous circle comes from changing gender relations: now that women constitute half of university students, the expectations of young people may be inclining toward a companionate model of marriage in which partners are more equal in supporting the family, making decisions, and sharing housework. The larger role of women in the workplace means that their talents and insights are being harnessed in business and in public life.

Ideally, a virtuous circle operates between an effective government, a competitive private sector, and a vigorous nonprofit sector. One example cited in these pages is the work of the Brazilian research agency EMBRAPA in making the *cerrado* productive, and more recently in assisting African agriculture. In recent decades, NGOs have acted as a conscience in society, seeking to end impunity for state crimes and advocating for the rights of the powerless and on behalf of nature. "Corporate social responsibility," when it is not simply public relations or "greenwashing," is a practical embodiment of the sense that the stakeholders in a business include not only investors and employees, but the local community and the larger society as well.

These hopes could certainly be frustrated. According to the historic pattern of Latin America, the growth of the last decade or so should be followed by stagnation, resulting from either external or internal factors. By 2014, the higher prices for commodities driven by demand from China and India were declining, slowing the growth of countries that had been riding the commodities boom. A financial crisis could lead to reduced demand worldwide or even "vicious circle" behavior between nations. An ecological tipping point could be reached, unleashing unpredictable weather events worldwide.

Domestically, high levels of crime and violence or the power of organized crime could frustrate growth and put fearful and distrustful people into defensive zero-sum postures. Governments could continue to operate inefficiently, hiring more on patronage than merit. Citizens, and particularly the wealthy, could continue to resist paying higher taxes, and hence infrastructure (roads, ports, water and sewage systems) could remain inadequate. The middle classes could opt out of society, especially in the crucial realm of education.

Specifying the tasks of the bicentennial generation entails reminding the reader of points developed throughout the book but especially in chapters 13 to 17. Economically, it means moving away from dependence on commodity export toward producing competitive goods and services in the knowledge economy. They need not be automobiles or aircraft—or even bicycles—but the aim should be, even in small countries, to have world-class goods and services.

Economic growth must be sustainable. In 2013, a special report in *The Economist* was devoted to the positive links between economic prosperity and protection of the environment (Duncan 2013). It noted that in response to pressure from Brazilian urban consumers, large food retailers themselves refused to buy beef produced on illegally deforested lands. The effect was that ranchers hastened to make their practice conform to the law, and deforestation was slowed.

Democracy must be deepened: transferring political power through fair elections is not enough; governments and politicians must be held accountable and criminally liable when corruption is uncovered. A vigorous free press and an independent judiciary not subject to intimidation are essential ingredients. When citizens go to government agencies, they have a right to be met with honest, effective, and efficient responses. The norm should be a merit-based civil service managed by respected professionals.

Adequate health care must be extended to all, not only in principle, as with constitutional guarantees, but in delivery. A particular area of concern is that of providing preschool education for poor children. Adequate public schools should be expanded so that even the poor complete secondary school, and those schools should provide an education sufficient to enable graduates to pass university entrance examinations where they exist.

A national sense of solidarity should be fostered, especially where class divisions are deepened by race and ethnicity. We can hope that part of the legacy of the presidency of Evo Morales, whatever one may think of his performance, is that indigenous Bolivians will be regarded as full citizens.

Taken altogether, these projections are certainly a tall order, but it should be noted that on many fronts, Latin Americans are already taking steps along these lines, as indicated in chapters 13 to 16. Moreover, the various Latin American publics are increasingly demanding that their societies move in this direction. The spontaneous mass protests in Brazil in 2013 (as well as large-scale protests by students in Chile and Colombia in previous years) were driven by specific issues, but they are signs of a public that believes that it deserves better.

The year 2024 will mark the bicentennial celebration of the Battle of Ayacucho, when Spanish forces were defeated in Peru and most of Latin America formally became independent. We may hope that by that date, the bicentennial generation will have advanced toward achieving inclusive, prosperous societies.

Notes

INTRODUCTION

1. If readers prefer, however, they may opt to read chapters 10 to 12 first.

2. In 2012, the Mexican conglomerate Bimbo became the world's largest bakery company, with over one hundred brands (including Entenmann's and Sara Lee).

3. Galeano (1973). In 2009, President Hugo Chávez of Venezuela gave a copy to President Obama at a presidential summit. Before his death in 2015, Galeano admitted that he no longer held the views set forth in *Open Veins*, which he said reflected the period when it was written. His more durable legacy may be his trilogy, *Memory of Fire* (Galeano 1985, 1987, and 1988).

CHAPTER 1

1. *Central and North America*: Mexico, Guatemala, El Salvador, Honduras, Nicaragua, Costa Rica, Panama; *Caribbean*: Cuba and Dominican Republic; *South America*: Brazil, Venezuela, Colombia, Ecuador, Peru, Chile, Argentina, Uruguay, Paraguay, Bolivia. The Caribbean and northern South America have approximately ten dependencies of Britain, France, and the Netherlands. In population terms, however, all are small, and some of their populations number only in the few tens of thousands. The Organization of American States has thirty-five members, including the island nations of the Caribbean.

2. In 2012, in a restaurant in Lago Agrio at the western edge of the Ecuadorean Amazon, I observed patrons watching a large flat-screen television carrying the broadcast of a reality show of Jennifer Lopez and Marc Anthony traveling through various Latin American countries auditioning musicians and dance groups to bring the winners to Las Vegas.

3. The term "Latin America" may have been used first in France to designate *Amérique latine*. In any case, it was only in the later nineteenth century that intellectuals in the region began to speak of themselves as "*Latin* Americans," primarily to distinguish themselves from those of Anglo-Saxon America (United States and Canada). Latin Americans have sometimes been annoyed at the use of the term "Americans" to refer to people in the United States, ignoring the fact that the hemisphere has hundreds of millions of other "Americans." Thus they may refer to *norteamericanos* (North Americans) or, even more accurately, *estadounidenses* (people of the United States), but in everyday speech, *americanos* often means people of the United States.

4. The tropics is the area bounded by the Tropic of Capricorn in the south and the Tropic of Cancer in the north, each of which is the line farthest south or north at which the sun can stand overhead at noon on the solstice (Tropic of Cancer on June 21 and Tropic of Capricorn on December 21).

5. Mt. Aconcagua (23,000 feet) on the Argentine-Chilean border is the highest peak in the hemisphere, 3,000 feet higher than Mt. McKinley (Denali) in Alaska.

6. Tropical geography did not prevent pre-Columbian peoples from developing advanced civilizations.

7. Crossing the border from Guatemala to Mexico at Tapachula, one has the sensation that everything is on a larger scale, even though when seen from Mexico City, Tapachula seems to be the end of the world.

8. The HDI was devised to serve as a better measure of human welfare than per capita GDP (gross domestic product), which, though it generally measures wealth and poverty, can hide distortions. Some societies with modest means manage to improve the living standards of most people, while others with greater aggregate wealth and income can have greater poverty, due to inequality, poor management, or corruption.

9. The HDI is, of course, a rough measurement and should be used with caution. Rankings are dependent largely on government-supplied statistics; the methodologies used may vary, as may the accuracy of the data.

CHAPTER 2

1. For census purposes, governments establish a criterion for a settlement that counts as urban, typically a population of 2,000 to 5,000 people.

2. Cuba was the only country in Latin America that did not have an "urban bias." If anything, it had a "rural bias," as the revolutionary government built schools in the countryside and sent doctors there. Nevertheless, over time, many Cubans gravitated toward Havana and other cities.

3. Observed personally by the author.

4. The emblematic quality of photographs of the Rio favelas climbing hillsides and overlooking rich beachfront communities may obscure the fact that many favelas and other Latin American shantytowns sprawl for miles on land far from the city centers.

5. People distinguish between the *morro* (hill) and *asfalto* (pavement), meaning the favela and the rest of the city. The oral history *Lucia: Testimonies of a Brazilian Drug Dealer's Woman* by Robert Gay (2005) conveys well the stigma experienced by favela dwellers when they work and shop outside the favela.

6. Measurement of poverty is discussed in chapter 6.

7. Chapter 15 is devoted to crime, corruption, law enforcement, and achieving rule of law.

8. In 2005, Viva Rio helped sponsor a national referendum that would have prohibited gun ownership by civilians. Initially, a solid majority of the public was in favor, but after a slick advertising campaign assisted by the US National Rifle Association, 65 percent voted against it.

9. In 2012, automobile ownership in Ecuador was rising 8–9 percent per year, far above the 2–3 percent population increase.

10. Wealthy households get around the rules by buying extra vehicles.

11. See Peñalosa (2003) for a statement of his vision.

12. Francisco Carrión interview with the author, Quito, February 2012.

13. In his provocatively titled *If Mayors Ruled the World* (2013), Benjamin Barber goes so far as to contrast dysfunctional national politics—not only in the United States—to city-level politics. Mayors have to solve problems—potholes are neither liberal nor conservative. Barber presents many examples of cities around the world that are tackling problems that nation-states continue to evade, such as climate change.

CHAPTER 3

1. The US census lists 751,000 farmers and ranchers and 7.2 million teachers, out of a total labor force of 154.4 million. Adding the number of farm laborers to the number of farmers roughly doubles the number of those directly involved in agriculture.

2. Berdegué and Fuentealba (2011) examine various categories for classifying small farmers in eight Latin American countries, sometimes with different criteria, before proposing their own classification, here systematized in a grid.

3. Some US farmers have begun operations or invested in the *cerrado*.

4. On fair-trade coffee, see Haight (2011), Rice (2011), and Sherman (2012). For a very readable overview of the fair-trade movement, see Conroy (2007).

5. An early and excellent overview of the implications of supermarkets in Latin America is Reardon and Berdegué (2002).

6. The Guatemalan anthropologist Ricardo Falla remarked to me, "When young people have been to high school, they don't intend to make a living with an *azadón*" (the large hoe used by indigenous subsistence farmers).

7. In Central America in 2011, I was told that Walmart, which owns some supermarket chains, was sponsoring efforts to enable small producers to be part of the production chain.

CHAPTER 4

1. Industry employs less than 10 percent of US labor, and agriculture, 2 or 3 percent.

2. Even in the United States, the off-the-books sector of the economy is significant (8.6%), and it can be over 20 percent in some developed countries.

3. To demonstrate his point, he and his colleagues at the Institute for Liberty and Democracy set up a mock garment factory on the outskirts of Lima and began to go through the administrative procedures to register it formally. Obtaining the eleven permits required took 289 days of going from office to office, including ten requests for bribes. Had it been a genuine instance of people abiding by the rules, they would have lost ten months of revenue while waiting for legalization.

4. De Soto was celebrated in the United States because his argument bolstered the claim of free-market proponents that "government is the problem, not the solution." It was attractive to believe that the millions of people in the informal sector were protocapitalists who only needed to be freed of government shackles.

5. In a wonderful 1992 *New Yorker* article ("Mexico City, 1992" in Guillermoprieto 1994), Alma Guillermoprieto expressed dismay that on the eve of NAFTA Mexicans were about to surrender their own wonderful cuisine for overpriced US fast food.

6. These examples are primarily from Casanova and Fraser (2009).

7. By way of exception, the study uses a lower revenue threshold for "emerging" firms (such as Pollo Campero).

8. "Latin 500," 26–35.

9. *Latin Trade* publishes an annual list of the largest five hundred companies in Latin America.

10. Expanding auto ownership is not an unalloyed blessing; chapters 2 and 5 mention some initiatives to foster alternatives.

11. This section draws on Salamon (2010) and Casanova and Dumas (2010). See also Santiso (2013).

12. As recently as the mid-1990s, American university students did not necessarily use computers for assignments, did not do online research, and certainly did not have tablets or laptops. Within a few years, they were creating PowerPoint presentations and professors had to remind students not to text during class.

13. In 1994, Comandante Marcos, the visible spokesperson of the Zapatista revolutionary movement in Chiapas, Mexico, composed his messages from the Lacandon Jungle on a laptop (leading some to call the Zapatista movement the "first postmodern revolution").

14. Author observation of Parquesoft and interview with Orlando Rincón, Cali, Colombia, January 2012.

CHAPTER 5

1. The exact quote cannot be tracked down. I recall it being a general, but some sources speak of a politician. The expression became a commonplace reflecting the attitude of leaders in developing countries upon being lectured on their environmental responsibility.

2. World Commission on Environment and Development (1987; Bruntland Commission report).

3. Critics have charged these companies with "stealing" native knowledge.

4. The following paragraphs draw on Viana (2010).

5. When unlicensed logs are sold cheaply and with impunity, demand for legal logs drops; conversely, when the law is enforced, demand for licensed logs rises, and they can command a better price. The same is true of fish in the second measure taken.

6. See chapter 10 of this book.

7. Figures are imprecise because criteria for "protected" areas vary. Protected areas constitute 27 percent of the land area of the United States.

8. Territorio Indígena y Parque Nacional Isiboro Sécure—Isiboro Sécure Indigenous Territory and National Park.

9. In the wake of the post-2007 economic recession, the government could tap into $13 billion (6% of GDP) it had invested in sovereign wealth funds and thus offset some of the effects of the economic downturn.

10. In the end, the company suspended the project due to falling world prices for coal.

11. This section draws on the "Latin American Green City Index" study by The Economist Intelligence Unit (2010).

CHAPTER 6

1. In 2003, I was in the northeastern Brazilian city of João Pessoa, which when I had visited it decades previously, had exemplified utter poverty. Now I was surprised to see large areas of neat houses and even a modest freeway around the city. In beginning an interview with Brazilian nuns who work with the poor, I apologized for my question: "Is Brazil a poor country with some millionaires or a middle-class country that still has many poor people?" They replied that a similar question had recently been discussed on television. They said that appearances can be deceiving: poor-looking homes might have a surprising variety of electronic devices and consumer goods, and the people living in a decent house might have little furniture and be in real poverty.

2. Charles Booth, a British philanthropist, developed a measure for poverty in the late nineteenth century. However, it was Mollie Orshansky, a researcher for the US Social Security Administration, who in the 1960s proposed a poverty line for use by US government agencies. In the later twentieth century, governments around the world adopted poverty lines as a measuring stick for policy.

3. Subsequently it was raised to $1.25.

4. By way of comparison, consider the poverty line in the United States, which in 2013 was $23,550 per year for a family of four (which breaks down to $64.50 per day for the family or $16 per person). In the United States, only a third of this figure is assumed to be spent on food. In terms of cash incomes, almost all Nicaraguans would be poor in the United States, but in Nicaragua, a family of four receiving over $23,000 a year would live well.

5. Both major parties claim to be defending the middle class, and even the Democrats are reluctant to be perceived as advocating for the poor.

6. In Marxist theory, there are only two real classes, the bourgeoisie (owners of the means of production) and the proletariat (those who must sell their labor to the bourgeoisie). Underlying those categories was the sense that history was driven by the struggles of the proletariat to seize the means of production so that the wealth that is being produced socially (in large companies) but appropriated privately (by the owners of capital) would be appropriated socially in what would be a classless society.

7. Chile is already a member of the OECD, the thirty-four-member club of developed nations (as is Mexico).

CHAPTER 7

1. These are labels of convenience rather than strict geographical accuracy: the indigenous people in the low-lying Yucatán peninsula are descendants of the Maya and thus "highland"; over

twenty of the indigenous peoples of Colombia live in the highlands, but their relationship to Colombian society has been more like that of the "lowland" peoples described here.

2. The percentages are from national censuses. Other sources might give higher or lower figures.

3. In 2013, Gen. Efraín Ríos Montt, Guatemala's president in 1982–1983, was tried and found guilty of genocide and crimes against humanity and sentenced to eighty years in prison, but the verdict was voided by the Supreme Court on procedural grounds.

4. Discussed in chapter 2.

5. In the 1990s, microlending, which had been pioneered with women's groups in Bangladesh, spread among development agencies worldwide, with the notion that small loans could empower people, especially women, to start small businesses and work their way out of poverty.

6. Chevron sued the US lawyer, Stephen Donziger, who had pursued the case, and in 2014 a US judge barred any collection of damages in the United States, based on Donziger's alleged "wrongful actions" in Ecuador, including bribing a judge (Keefe 2012b).

7. See explanation in chapter 14.

8. Menchú's first-person account was influential in portraying repression against indigenous peoples (Menchú 1984). The anthropologist David Stoll (1999) aroused considerable controversy when he questioned some details of her account. Conservatives used Stoll to denounce Menchú as a liar and to criticize academics for widely assigning her book in their classes. That book was compiled by Elizabeth Burgos from eighteen hours of taped interviews in Paris. Menchú had been telling her story orally in many different settings. In acting as a spokesperson giving witness, she had recounted some incidents as though she were present when she was not. Most fair observers would say that Menchú's account was essentially true, even if not always literally so. For an informed and judicious assessment of Menchú, Stoll, and the controversy, see the review by Peter Canby (1999).

9. Identified by Mexican journalists as Rafael Sebastián Guillén Vicente.

10. See chapter 5.

11. Freyre did not coin the term, but he used it while also insisting that he did not deny the existence of racial discrimination in Brazil.

12. In 1976, the Brazilian Institute of Geography and Statistics (IBGE) asked people to identify their skin color and ended up with 134 terms, not all of which referred solely to skin (Levine and Crocitti 1999, 386–390).

13. Those who are not admitted to the federal universities can still attend private universities, whose enrollment is considerably larger than that of state universities.

CHAPTER 8

1. A related organization, the Grandmothers of the Plaza de Mayo, was formed to look for children who had been born while their mothers were in custody and later "disappeared." The children were then adopted and raised unaware of their biological families.

2. The journalist Liza Mundy (2012) argues that in the United States, Europe, and elsewhere, women are on their way to becoming the "richer sex." The number of households where the woman earns more than the man continues to rise. In part this is due to women's educational attainment; their refusal to be dependent on a male breadwinner; and the fact that in many of the growth sectors in the twenty-first-century economy, like education and health care, women have an edge, whereas traditionally "male" economic strongholds like manufacturing and construction have been hit hard by the recession or are in long-term decline. More controversially, Mundy says that surprising numbers of men are dropping out, either for the perhaps laudable reason to be available for home duties or simply because they remain psychological adolescents. The trends she notes are only incipient in Latin America but could become more prominent.

3. UN-sponsored World Conferences on Women were held in Mexico City (1975), Copenhagen (1980), Nairobi (1985), and Beijing (1995). Conventions on violence against women were formulated in 1979, 1993, 1994, and 1999. In 1993, the UN adopted the Declaration on the Elimination of Violence Against Women, and in 1994, appointed a Special Rapporteur on violence against women.

Also in 1994, the Inter-American Convention on the Prevention, Punishment and Eradication of Violence against Women (Convention of Belém do Pará) was adopted, with binding force on the countries of the hemisphere. Although such international agreements receive little attention in the United States, elsewhere in the world they are taken more seriously and have served to pressure governments to enact and enforce their own legislation on women's rights.

4. The exception by far is the Nordic countries, where an average of over 40 percent of parliamentarians are women.

5. The phrase "domestic violence" came into use only in the 1970s.

6. In Bolivia in 2012, I was told of an instance where police came upon a man severely beating a woman in a car. They halted the violence but advised the woman to wash off the blood and go home—they did not help her report the incident as a crime.

7. In 2012, I visited one such center in the frontier town of Lago Agrio, in the Ecuadorean Amazon region, attesting to how widespread such programs have become. This one had been initiated under the sponsorship of the Catholic Church.

8. Author interview with María Galindo, La Paz, February 2012.

9. This section draws on Guttmacher Institute (2012) and Mollmann (2012).

10. Estimates of the number of participants varied from several hundred thousand to two or three million.

11. Rebolledo includes as a subset male single-parent fathers, who are becoming more common as it becomes less stigmatizing for women to leave their family.

CHAPTER 9

1. Through decades of studying and writing about major religions, Karen Armstrong (2011) concluded that their core purpose was the cultivation of compassion. She saw this, however, not as a bland least common denominator, but as a demanding lifetime task requiring discipline.

2. "Christendom" refers to the situation in which Christianity became the official religion of society recognized by the state. In the West, Christendom lasted from the recognition of Christianity by the emperor Constantine in the fourth century into the modern age.

3. As noted in the previous chapter, marriage patterns reflect that contrast: in traditional Colombian cities in the highlands, formal marriage in the Church is considered the norm; on the Caribbean and Pacific coasts, consensual relations are common.

4. The first written account mentioning Juan Diego dates from almost a century after the apparition. At the site of the vision, the Spaniards had destroyed a shrine to the Aztec goddess Tonantzin and built one to Mary less than a decade before the reported vision. In Extremadura, Spain, the homeland of Hernán Cortés, a dark-skinned Virgin of Guadalupe is venerated. Thus, the image may have been painted by an indigenous artist in the mid-sixteenth century, and the Juan Diego legend may be a later accretion.

5. Peter Canby (1992) offers a wonderful account of a several-day festival in Chenalhó in Chiapas in chapter 5 of *Heart of the Sky*.

6. A similar division between popular and official Catholicism existed in European Christendom, and in fact it was one of the major targets of the Reformation. Luther and the reformers attacked the practice of venerating the relics of saints and the very idea of praying to intercessors rather than to God himself. Counter-Reformation Catholicism defended such practices but sought to purify itself of distortions and excesses. Without pressure from Protestantism, Latin American Catholicism continued to be divided into popular and elite forms until the twentieth century.

7. Penny Lernoux (1982) gives many instances and conveys well the climate of the period.

8. The occasion was a talk given to priests in Chimbote, Peru; text is reproduced in Hennelly (1990); the ideas are more fully developed in Gutiérrez (1973).

9. At that moment, Óscar Romero had just been made archbishop. The killing of his friend Grande propelled his own radicalization. These events are portrayed in the film *Romero* (1989).

10. See chapter 12.

11. An exception was Chile during the Popular Unity government (1971–1973), where Christians for Socialism organized a continent-wide meeting in 1972.

12. When Cardinal Jorge Bergoglio was elected pope in 2013, the conduct of the Argentine Church resurfaced. During the "dirty war," Bergoglio was the national superior of the Jesuits. The consensus was that he was not complicit in the crimes, and intervened behind the scenes on behalf of some people arrested, but like other Church leaders, he did not challenge the dictatorship publicly. His recognition of his own shortcomings shaped his later outlook and behavior.

13. In the 1990s, the Guatemalan Catholic Church sponsored a large grassroots effort to have people come forward to testify on the slaughter of the previous decades, carried out largely by official Guatemalan forces. The multivolume report was released publicly in April 1998 at a ceremony presided over by Bishop Juan Gerardi. Two days later, he was bludgeoned to death as he was pulling into his garage, by assassins linked to retired Guatemalan military officers.

14. By comparison, all US presidents present themselves as churchgoing Christians. Indeed, virtually no members of the US Senate or House are publicly agnostic; only 1 percent list themselves as unaffiliated (as opposed to 16 percent of the general public).

15. Gang members may be victims of injustice and indeed violence, but they are also typically perpetrators of violence. Hence for many church groups, both Catholic and Protestant, the only stance is avoidance.

16. In his research in Greater Rio in the late 1980s comparing an evangelical church and a progressive Catholic parish, John Burdick found something similar among youth, when the problem was not yet gang violence: evangelical youth found it a relief to be freed from the competitiveness of normal youth behavior, particularly regarding clothes, spending money, and sexual braggadocio (Burdick 1993, chapter 5).

17. Many Guatemalans also have great devotion to San Judas Tadeo.

18. Previous such continent-wide CELAM conferences have occurred in Rio de Janeiro (1955), Medellín (1968), Puebla (1979), and Santo Domingo (1992).

19. Aparecida document (CELAM 2007, 147, 548, 397).

CHAPTER 10

1. Historians' views are generally shaped by the time in which they are writing and the types of history being written. Since the 1960s, historians of Latin America often told a story of the aspirations of people thwarted by elites and foreign forces, notably the United States, drawing on dependency theory as developed by Latin American social scientists. Today, historians are aware that older paradigms no longer work, but no new "master narrative" of Latin American history has yet gained broad acceptance.

2. Hypotheses about contacts between the Americas and Oceania or Africa by sea have been made for decades but have not been proven. Genetic analysis could offer evidence.

3. The other four arose in present-day Iraq, Egypt, India, and China. "Civilization" refers to the complexity of societal organization; it does not imply any division of peoples into superior and inferior.

4. Jared Diamond (1997) discusses the consequences of the differences between Eurasia and the Americas when they re-encountered one another at the time of the conquest.

5. The names given here are those conventionally used. Researchers have only their archaeological remains, not their language, and hence cannot know what they called themselves. That is true even of the Aztecs, who are more properly called Mexicas. The term "Inca" refers to the rulers, but it has been applied to the civilization itself.

6. The "ball game" played in Mesoamerican societies until the conquest entailed two teams on a field with sloping masonry walls; it has been compared to soccer, volleyball, and racquetball and had some ritual dimensions.

7. Recent archaeological work has revealed that the city of Teotihuacán ruled over a vast empire, extending to and perhaps into the Maya area. Although archaeologists have assumed that it would

have been ruled by powerful kings, they have been puzzled by not finding elaborate tombs. An alternate theory is that the city was ruled collectively by elites from other areas (Oaxaca, Gulf of Mexico) each of which occupied a quadrant of the city, and had its own symbol (feathered serpent, jaguar). Vance (2014) summarizes archaeological work and hypotheses about Teotihuacán.

8. Archaeologists are also studying the Beni region in northern Bolivia, where evidence indicates that it was once densely populated by peoples who built canals, causeways, and elevated settlements in a savanna subject to regular flooding; see Erickson (2008).

9. Estimates vary from as high as one hundred million to as low as ten million, all dependent on relatively scant archaeological evidence, the accounts of the first European arrivals, and assumptions about how to construe the evidence.

10. For a map of the languages spoken in South America, see http://titus.uni-frankfurt.de /didact/karten/amer/samerim.htm.

11. Frances Karttunen (1997) provides an enlightening examination of Marina (her baptismal name): how she was viewed by fellow Nahuatl speakers and by Spanish colonists, as well as how her image changed from independence to the present, when through sexist and racist lenses she is dismissed as a traitor. Karttunen helps us see her as she was: a talented, intelligent young woman of noble ancestry who pragmatically made the best of her situation and was loyal after making her choices. I am grateful to Ann Farnsworth-Alvear for alerting me to the Karttunen essay.

12. The plagues that periodically swept across Eurasia had endowed the survivors with resistances absent in the indigenous population of the Americas, who had been out of contact with Eurasia for millennia, as developed masterfully by Jared Diamond (1997).

13. In Latin American countries today, the municipality is a fundamental unit of local government. The *alcalde*, or mayor, and municipal council govern not only the town seat but the surrounding countryside extending to the boundaries of neighboring municipalities. Colombia and Panama still designate subdistricts using the colonial term *corregimiento*.

14. The prize-winning film *The Mission* (1986) tells the story of the dismantling of the "reductions," with some cinematic license.

15. This term was coined by the geographer Alfred Crosby.

CHAPTER 11

1. President Álvaro Uribe of Colombia (2002–2010) was given to demonstrating his prowess on horseback.

2. Pedro II was an honored guest at the 1876 Centennial Exposition in Philadelphia, where he examined new developments in science and industry. There he met Alexander Graham Bell, learned of the telephone, and became the first person to invest in the Bell Telephone Company.

3. The American short-story writer O. Henry coined the phrase "banana republic," which he portrayed in *Cabbages and Kings* (1904), based on his experience working in Honduras in the early 1900s.

4. In Brazil, Santos-Dumont is considered the "father" of heavier-than-air aviation. Most historians credit the Wright brothers, but it should be kept in mind that early aviation was the result of large numbers of inventors building upon one another's innovations and technological developments such as the internal combustion engine. For the life of Santos-Dumont, see Hoffman (2003).

5. Roosevelt later boasted, "I took Panama."

6. The "Halls of Montezuma" in the US Marine Corps hymn is a reference to the storming of Chapultepec Castle in Mexico City (1847).

7. In 1966, a Chilean intellectual recited this poem to me from memory as we walked along a seawall in Panama City. He had recently been in the Dominican Republic as an observer of elections, held under the guns of the US Marines, who had invaded that country the previous year under the pretext of restoring order.

8. The figure is from Thomas Anderson's careful study (1971), but the figure of thirty thousand people killed is commonly cited.

9. In response to his murder, riots broke out in Bogotá, with looting, fires, and an estimated three thousand people killed. The murder of Gaitán detonated ten years of violence, primarily in the countryside (called simply La Violencia in Colombia), that left an estimated 200,000 dead. A young Cuban named Fidel Castro was in Bogotá for a youth conference and was scheduled to meet with Gaitán later on the day he was assassinated. That experience contributed to his radicalization.

10. Similar figures include Víctor Raúl Haya de la Torre (Peru), José María Velasco Ibarra (Ecuador), and Arnulfo Arias (Panama), each of whom loomed large in his country's politics for decades in the mid-twentieth century.

11. Discussed further in chapter 15.

12. Panama abolished its armed forces in the wake of the US invasion to topple the regime of Gen. Manuel Noriega in December 1989.

13. The government offered to pay the fruit company for the land, using the values it had declared for tax purposes.

14. The coup came the year after the CIA-engineered coup in Iran, likewise against a democratically elected president, which reinstalled the Shah Reza Pahlavi, whose despotic regime was eventually overthrown by the revolution of 1979. Both events cast a long shadow over their countries and regions for the next several decades. The early stance of the Cuban Revolution toward the United States was influenced by what Ernesto ("Che") Guevara had witnessed as a visitor and sympathizer with the Arbenz government.

CHAPTER 12

1. As Jane Jacobs (1961) was pointing out at the same period, great cities thrive on mixes of residential neighborhoods and local businesses.

2. The United Nations distinguished "centrally planned" from "market" economies. Latin Americans insisted that they did not view Soviet socialism as their model, and indeed there was much discussion of what "socialism" meant or what true socialism would look like.

3. Almost from the outset, the narrative of the course of the revolution has taken one of two forms: 1. Castro and the revolutionaries took more radicalized steps in response to events that occurred, particularly the hostility of the US government, counterrevolutionary movements on the island, and the mass exodus of previous elites; or 2. They always intended to set up a communist dictatorship but hid their intentions until they had consolidated power.

4. During the Cold War, Cuba was an active member of the Non-Aligned Movement (NAM), begun by Yugoslavia and India in 1961, which included dozens of nations and about half of the world population.

5. Indeed, Christian Democratic president Eduardo Frei (1964–1970) had claimed to be leading a "Revolution in Liberty" in Chile, implicitly criticizing Cuba and its supporters, and claiming that his party could bring improved conditions without sacrificing freedom.

6. That Allende had committed suicide was the conclusion of the autopsy performed. Many did not believe in the word of the military government and assumed he had been murdered. However, Allende's family accepted the autopsy result from the beginning.

7. The personal accounts of victims of the Pinochet regime in Chile in Politzer (1989) give an idea of the psychological effects of these regimes.

8. For an overview of these struggles, with the accent on Nicaragua and El Salvador and US domestic policies, see LeoGrande (1998).

9. Reagan said that Managua was closer to Harlingen, Texas, than Harlingen was to Washington.

10. See further discussion in chapter 15.

11. The Argentine military were chagrined to find President Reagan supporting the British. They had assumed that the United States would sympathize with their cause in return for the assistance they had supplied to the Nicaraguan *contras* in Central America at the behest of the US government and the Pentagon.

12. Latin American countries were part of a worldwide "third wave" of democracy (Huntington 1991), starting with Portugal in 1974 and including countries in Asia, Africa, and Eastern Europe.

13. The plebiscite campaign is portrayed in the Oscar-nominated 2012 Chilean film *No*, directed by Pablo Larraín and starring Gael García Bernal as an advertising executive who agrees to aid the campaign in marketing.

14. The church leaders were Paulo Evaristo Cardinal Arns of São Paulo, Presbyterian pastor Jaime Wright, and the World Council of Churches. One account is in Weschler (1990).

15. As noted in chapter 9, Bishop Juan Gerardi of Guatemala was bludgeoned to death by army-connected assassins in his garage in 1998, two days after the commission that he had chaired issued its human rights report on the decades of the war, *Guatemala: Nunca más*.

16. Definitions of "civil society" vary somewhat, but the term can be said to refer to organized activity that is neither of the market nor the state, like the nonprofit sector in the United States but also like grassroots community organizations. The movements that led to the downfall of communism in Eastern Europe were said to show an emergence of "civil society."

17. US funding, particularly from the US government, was regarded with suspicion.

18. An account by Forrest Colburn about a woman in El Salvador offers a window into the process. In the 1970s and 1980s, Deysi was a member of a guerrilla organization, primarily involved in noncombat activities. In the 1990s, after the end of the war, she was working with women and started an NGO that was working on over a dozen broad issues, some economic and some matters such as combating incest. The staff worked with individual women and women's groups (Colburn 2002, 89–98).

19. Latin American economic history offers some perspective for understanding the present. As we have noted, from approximately 1870 to 1930 Latin American countries had an outward-oriented economic strategy: export commodities and import manufactured goods. They then shifted to an inward-oriented strategy, import-substitution industrialization, aimed at developing the internal market and utilizing tariffs and other barriers to protect their products. Even by the 1960s that model was showing its limitations, and a shift was almost inevitable. Indeed, it seems that Williamson's original "Washington Consensus" document was a summary of policy prescriptions already agreed upon by Latin American technocrats.

20. These trade agreements are discussed in chapter 17.

21. Books on Latin America were still bearing titles like *Falling Behind* (Fukuyama 2007) and *Left Behind* (Edwards 2010). Indeed, books on Latin America since the 1960s, including survey histories, have tended to be explanations of the failure of the region to achieve development. Those from a leftist perspective were sympathetic to revolution until around 1990; after that they critiqued "neoliberalism" and took heart in the 2000s with the advent of left-leaning governments.

CHAPTER 13

1. EMBRAPA has also developed a type of hog lower in fat and cholesterol, which could earn higher export prices, and has been working on wheat adapted to the tropics.

2. It should be noted, however, that the banana plantations, largely on the Atlantic coast, are an area in which the large companies have been able to prevail over workers' demands for better conditions, such as protection against pesticides. Repression against labor is not as violent as in Colombia or Guatemala; it has tended to take the form of imposing a model of labor union that promotes "harmony" with the company and thus stifles militancy.

3. Contraband is also central to the economy of Paraguay. Its tobacco industry is largely devoted to the manufacture of cigarettes with dozens of brands that evade taxes. Contraband in goods flourishes in the Tri-Border Area where Paraguay, Brazil, and Argentina meet.

4. Remittances are also significant in Ecuador: two million of the country's fourteen million citizens live outside the country, predominantly in Spain, and send back money to family members. The same is true of Bolivians, many of whom work in Argentina.

5. The figure for the United States was $50,700; Norway, Singapore, and Hong Kong were even

higher. "Purchasing Power Parity" seeks to measure goods and services that can be purchased in the country, not the value of the currency when traded internationally.

6. The Panamanian currency has always been the dollar (although it is called the balboa).

7. Doctrinaire US conservatives who advocate smaller government seem unaware that Latin American countries are far closer to their nirvana. For example, tax collection revenues in Guatemala are only 11 percent of GDP versus 25–40 percent in advanced countries.

8. By 2012, there were signs that the real rates of inflation in Venezuela and Argentina were considerably higher than official government figures.

9. Not all economists agree with their conclusion, and the matter continues to be debated.

10. In chapter 5, we noted that many Latin American governments are opening up areas for exploration and development of minerals, natural gas, and petroleum (and disregarding the impact on poor farmers and indigenous people).

11. One illustration is Italy, where the prosperity of the north (as compared to the south) is built on a tradition of small family businesses.

12. This section is drawn largely from Pagés (2010).

13. It might be noted that by productivity the authors mean "total factor productivity," that is, the combination of labor, capital, and human capital. The consequence is that they are not saying that the larger firm will be more productive because investment and technology per worker are greater, but rather that even holding all factors (including technology) constant, a larger company will be more productive because it can organize those factors more effectively.

14. Increased formalization and higher productivity could thus lead to higher unemployment—unless the formal economy is creating jobs.

15. This section draws on Dreher and Herzfeld (2005) and also on Mauro (1998).

16. See the biography of Hirschman by Jeremy Adelman (2013) and a collection of essays by Hirschman (2013).

17. Such considerations would matter if the investment has to do with the domestic market or depends on the quality of available labor and management talent. It would matter less if it were a mining concession in an authoritarian regime.

18. Winner of the Nobel Prize in Economic Sciences in 1993.

CHAPTER 14

1. The US founders intended to establish a "republic" (nonmonarchical government) not a "democracy." The root idea of "democracy" comes from the Greek (*demos* = "people" and *kratos* = "power"), but in antiquity it had the pejorative connotation of mob rule. It was only under President Andrew Jackson that the property requirement was dropped and the vote was extended to all white men.

2. Panamanians and Colombians speak of *la rosca* (literally a round form of bread) for the inner circle. Mexicans and others speak of needing *palanca* (lit. "lever"), or "pull" to get things done.

3. Torrijos was similar to the Venezuelan Hugo Chávez: both were children of rural schoolteachers, had careers in the military, looked different from traditional elites, and could speak to ordinary people in their own language. Panama is about one-tenth the size of Venezuela, but its "oil" is the canal and international trade.

4. The community group grew out of my work in the barrio of Chorrillo. With the approval of the government and a loan from the Inter-American Development Bank, the housing project of Nuevo Chorrillo was built in the late 1970s.

5. Even if the decision had been made in advance on its merits and the jump into the river was calculated theater, the net effect was to reinforce Torrijos's populist image.

6. A low-level and perhaps unconscious form of clientelism takes place when families choose godparents for their children from among wealthy or powerful people rather than from their own family or friends. Baptism sets up a relationship of *compadrazgo* (a sort of fictive kinship) between the parents and godparents, who become "patrons," a resource to be drawn on in case of need.

7. In Guatemala in the 1970s, I had difficulty understanding how the right-wing Movimiento de Liberación Nacional (MLN; National Liberation Movement) party, which had grown out of the 1954 coup and had sponsored death squads since the 1960s, could win many votes, especially among the poor. Then one day I heard political leaders in a rural town talk about how they planned to win back the local mayor's position, and I realized that the MLN's history and ideology meant little to them: it was a vehicle by which to gain some power locally and then dispense favors, especially through employment.

8. As an example of the problems of clientelism, initially the Bolsa Familia (family allowance) program in Brazil was being managed through local political figures, who had the funds distributed to their supporters rather than to those most in need. In response, the Lula government set up a means test, and then bypassed traditional politicians by providing recipients with a card whereby they could withdraw their payments directly from ATMs.

9. The formal names of two of the countries are "The Federative Republic of Brazil" and "The United Mexican States."

10. In the decades before the 1973 coup, the Christian Democratic Party played the role of a center between the right-wing Nationalist and left-wing Socialist parties.

11. The PRI is identified not so much by an ideological position as by its many decades of holding a political quasi-monopoly and its ability to wield power.

12. That description of proportional representations is broadly true of Latin American political party systems, although the details may vary from one country to another. Such a system is arguably more democratic than a winner-take-all system. In the United States, for example, a Democrat in a heavily Republican state would never feel that his or her vote counted for congress or the presidency. In a proportional-representation system, if voters in a district or state lined up 40 percent Democratic and 60 percent Republican, the representation in Washington would be similar.

13. Outsiders might find it hard to understand how anyone could vote for Pérez Molina, who had commanded troops during the dirty wars of the 1980s when civilians were slaughtered wholesale. Twenty-five or thirty years later, however, his campaign photos showed him looking avuncular and his major promise was to deal harshly with crime, which was perhaps the greatest concern of citizens. In 2015 Pérez Molina resigned the presidency because of corruption charges against him and his associates and pressure from street demonstrations.

14. This finding confirms my own experience. While living in Panama, Ecuador, and Guatemala in the 1960s and 1970s, I paid no attention to what transpired in legislatures, because it seemed to me that the real power lay with the president, the army, and business groups, such as the Guatemalan CACIF (Comité de Asociaciones Agrícolas, Comerciales, Industriales y Financieras—Coordinating Committee of Agricultural, Commercial, Industrial and Financial Associations), an umbrella business organization of chambers of agroexporters, industrialists, and business owners.

15. Activists used the English word "lobby(ing)" or the neologism "*cabildeo*," from "*cabildo*," the word for local councils of notables formed in the later colonial period.

16. The exceptions are Argentina—36 percent, Brazil—29 percent, and Venezuela—19 percent (data from 1997).

17. US labor unions resisted free trade agreements and tried to insist on a condition that minimum labor rights be part of such agreements. A notable case was Colombia, where hundreds of union members have been murdered with impunity.

18. The process was so unusual that the Brazilians used the English term "impeachment," since there was no obvious Portuguese expression for it.

19. One of the beneficiaries has been Colombia, where Venezuelan experts have played a critical role in developing new petroleum deposits.

20. See Jon Lee Anderson (2013) for descriptions of crime and poverty in Caracas, where the Chávez government seemed absent or irrelevant.

21. The rate of taxation of economic activity in Mexico is low (around 11% of GDP); oil revenues are crucial to government spending.

22. That situation is changing in Brazil, where tens of millions of middle-class households are now filing income-tax returns.

23. Although the US civil service system was created in 1883, it did not become fully effective until a half century later.

CHAPTER 15

1. Portrayed effectively in the Venezuelan film *Secuestro Express* (2005).

2. In 2005, the US Department of Justice estimated that the United States had 30,000 gangs, with 800,000 members in 2,500 communities (especially in Los Angeles, New York City, and northern Virginia; Mateo 2011, 93).

3. One experimenter was Sigmund Freud, who used himself as his subject.

4. The film *Maria Full of Grace* (2004) presents a gripping picture of the trade from Colombia to US streets.

5. Drug organizations are not "cartels" in the proper sense of the term, which is small, closed groups of businesses that collude to keep prices high, but the term has become conventional and so is used here.

6. The Colombian drug war must be set within the larger story of political violence in Colombia. Even in the 1960s, the Colombian army, with US advice, encouraged the formation of paramilitary groups to combat leftist guerrillas. In the 1980s, landholders formed a paramilitary group in response to left-wing kidnappings for ransom. Such groups then spread throughout the country, generally with the tolerance or support of elements in the army. Thus, for decades, Colombia has had various "armed actors": the military, police, left-wing guerrillas, and right-wing paramilitaries, all with ties to armed drug traffickers. Left-wing guerrillas have claimed to protect small farmers and have "taxed" large landowners and companies. Right-wing paramilitaries have been responsible for 80 percent or more of the political violence, most often against peasants, union organizers, and others, and they are primarily responsible for the estimated four million Colombians displaced since 1985.

7. It is commonly said that they got their idea from left-wing guerrillas with whom they were imprisoned.

8. An estimated one hundred community leaders were killed between 1992 and 2001, and another one hundred were forced out of their communities. The effect of drug trafficking on the favelas is portrayed in the highly praised film *City of God* (2002) and the less well known *City of Men*, which appeared as a television series and then a feature film (2007). For an oral history of a "drug dealer's woman" in Rio, see Gay (2005).

9. See Latin American Commission on Drugs and Democracy (2009) for a statement by literary figures and former presidents urging a paradigm shift on combating drugs.

10. In the US media, the summit itself was overshadowed by the scandal of US Secret Service agents having hired prostitutes in the city of Cartagena prior to the meeting.

11. For the 2011 report, information was gathered on thirteen different indicators of corruption, and by assigning numerical values to these indicators, each country could be assigned a value from 1 to 10. Of 183 countries on the list, the highest scoring was New Zealand (9.5) and the lowest, Somalia (1.0), tied with North Korea for last place.

12. It is perhaps significant that there is no Spanish or Portuguese word that easily translates the English word "accountability"; a common version is *rendición de cuentas*, literally, "rendering of accounts."

13. In travels in Brazil, Mexico, Cuba, Peru, Chile, Argentina, Colombia, Ecuador, and Bolivia, and throughout Central America in the past dozen years, only once have I been the victim of a crime (when my backpack was cleverly stolen in a Managua bus station).

14. For example, policies of mass incarceration of Central American youth gang members, often with no evidence of a crime, have actually transformed them into behaving more like members of criminal organizations.

15. In 2005, a chance event led to the discovery of National Police archives in Guatemala tracing back to the nineteenth century, totaling an estimated 75 million pages. A team of investigators set out to give priority to checking and scanning documents from the 1975–1985 period for evidence of police involvement in repressive actions, especially in Guatemala City.

16. Years ago, Jaime Wright, a Protestant church leader who had fought for human rights during the Brazilian dictatorship, told me with pain in his voice that he and Cardinal Arns of São Paulo were vilified for advocating for prisoners' rights after the 1992 uprising at Carandiru Penitentiary in which 111 were killed, most by prison guards. They thought their work was in logical continuity with what they had done earlier for victims of the military regime, but their critics, including many who had applauded their earlier human rights work, accused them of coddling criminals.

CHAPTER 16

1. Certainly not the United States, as evidenced by health-care costs far higher than those in other developed countries yet with inferior results.

2. In 1969, I was in a village in northeastern Brazil where parasitical worms had been found in all 250 children.

3. Medical researchers regard longevity as a proxy indicator for the overall health of a population.

4. Relative positions in the rankings are not too significant, since many countries cluster around 77–78 years. Note that in 2010, the United States at 78.2 years was behind twenty-eight other countries, mainly European but including Jordan. Although the ranking by itself might be used as evidence of a relative US decline, the figures might be read as evidence of worldwide success.

5. The life expectancy of 113th-ranking Iran (69.8) is the same as that of the United States in 1968.

6. Early chapters covered home cures and popular beliefs, and others went on to explain how to examine a sick person; the right and wrong use of modern medicines, including antibiotics; how to measure and give injections; first aid; nutrition; diseases that need special attention; problems of skin, eyes, teeth, urinary system, and genitals; information for midwives; family planning; diseases of children and of older people; and finally the items in the standard medicine kit.

7. For the current English version, see Werner, Thuman, and Maxwell 2013.

8. In 2004, there were three thousand health promoters in El Salvador, and a study showed that a majority of rural people were familiar with the program and had had dealings with the promoters.

9. These figures are expressed in PPP (purchasing power parity) dollars, that is, the figures are based on what can be bought inside the country in question, eliminating distortions from exchange rates.

10. Reasons for this include inefficiencies in the mix of delivery systems (insurance companies; for-profit and not-for-profit hospitals and clinics; federal, state, and local governments; physicians in private practice), the relatively high cost of medications, insurance costs driven by litigation, and costly catastrophic and end-of-life interventions.

11. WHO criteria: life expectancy (50%), responsiveness (25%), and fair financial cost (25%). Bloomberg criteria: life expectancy (60%), relative per capita cost (30%), absolute per capita cost (10%).

12. "Brazil's AIDS Programme: A Conflict of Goals," *The Economist* 2007a.

13. On a world scale, the number of overweight people is 1.4 billion, as opposed to 870 million suffering hunger.

14. Despite his meager formal schooling, Lula is not "uneducated"; by the time he became president, he had spent twenty years in the company of Brazilian intellectuals, social scientists, and politicians, sometimes in three-day seminars focused on major issues facing the country.

15. Freire frequently invoked philosophers, particularly those in the phenomenology tradition. His approach may be regarded as that of a humanistic philosopher who regarded everything said

about "man" in the Western philosophical tradition from Plato to the existentialists as applicable to poor peasants.

16. *Deschooling Society* (1970), Ivan Illich's critique of the modern school, helped spur a generation of critics to question existing education models in Europe and North America. Illich's Center for Inter-Cultural Communication in Cuernavaca, Mexico, provided a forum for Freire during the early years of his exile and published some of his early writings. Illich was partly driven by what he observed in Mexico, an unquestioning acceptance of rich-world assumptions about development and institutions like schools.

17. The United States' ranking was: mathematics, 31; sciences, 23; reading, 17.

18. Until that moment, her political power seemed to be second only to the president's.

19. Kenny (2014) reports that poor parents in Asia and Africa are opting to use their scarce incomes on private schools.

20. It may be noted that US higher education expanded similarly starting with veterans returning from World War II (the GI Bill) and lasting several decades thereafter. The evidence can be seen on campuses by noting the construction dates and architectural styles of the various buildings.

21. A ranking published by Quacquarelli Symonds, one of three such international rankings of universities.

22. These rankings are heavily based on the citations of works by professors, and on the judgment of academics at other institutions. MIT and Harvard are numbers 1 and 2 and almost all the top 20 are from the US and the UK. Such rankings, it should be pointed out, may be useful if they help institutions identify problematic areas and may help students choose where to study. They can become counterproductive if institutions become obsessed about their "brand."

23. Universidad Centro Americana José Simeón Cañas (José Simeón Cañas Central American University), often referred to as the UCA.

24. An early example was a book-length study of the 1972 election, in which the official party prevailed through electoral fraud. Others were several studies of land reform in the mid-1970s. In the midst of the civil war of the 1980s, the UCA served as a venue for public forums to discuss how to end hostilities. The monthly review *Estudios Centroamericanos* has provided a forum for serious studies and critiques of national issues.

CHAPTER 17

1. ALBA is a play on ALCA (Área de Libre Comercio de América), the Spanish acronym for the FTAA. *Alba* also means "dawn."

2. One reason for this is US farm subsidies, which reduce the risks of crop failure and price fluctuations, thus lowering overall production cost.

3. The "China Price" assumes an absence of tariffs or other protections.

4. Brazilian manufacturers have charged China with "dumping" bikes (selling unfairly at below the normal price) and have sought higher tariff protection.

5. This section draws on Stolte (2012).

6. It is also seeking political support for becoming a permanent member of the UN Security Council, a long-standing objective of the nation.

7. Similarly, Japanese and European governments cite the noneconomic value of retaining the tradition of family farming as a reason for protecting their domestic farmers.

8. Analysts contrasted the alliance to MERCOSUR. The alliance is based on concrete steps and is market friendly; MERCOSUR is protectionist vis-à-vis nonmember countries and seems to be driven as much by politics as economics.

9. *Los gauchos judíos* (*The Jewish Gauchos*; 1920), by Alberto Gerchunoff, which presents stories of Jewish immigrant farmers from Russia and Eastern Europe, is considered a classic in Argentine literature and in Jewish literature in Spanish.

10. In the words of the *corrido* sung by Los Tigres del Norte: "We didn't cross the border; the border crossed us."

11. In 2012, a *New York Times* report portrayed a Mexico that was actually attracting immigrants from Korea, Europe, and even the United States, particularly entrepreneurs who were drawn by investment opportunities (Cave 2013).

12. The merits and demerits of the terms "Hispanic" and "Latino" have been debated for decades. Neither term is satisfactory, especially when treated as a "racial" classification.

13. His previous book *Clash of Civilizations* had helped foster an "us-vs.-them" animus against Islam as a whole, as opposed to a discriminating approach to combating clandestine stateless terrorist organizations.

14. Brazilians and Brazilian Americans in the United States (who are not "Hispanic" but possibly "Latino") are estimated to be several hundred thousand.

15. The main characters in Héctor Tobar's novel *The Barbarian Nurseries* are Scott Torres, a software entrepreneur, and his wife, Maureen, who live in a gated Orange County community whose streets have faux Spanish names, and their live-in domestic, Araceli Ramírez. The main action ensues when both spouses leave the house after a fight and Araceli takes two of their children on an odyssey across Southern California searching for their Mexican grandfather. Their encounters along the way culminate in Huntington Park, now heavily Latino, and expose a Los Angeles invisible even to many Southern California residents. Tobar himself was born in Los Angeles to Guatemalan parents in 1963; he is fully American but Latino, as are the characters he portrays. His Southern California is a kaleidoscope of many shiny pieces, but it is an American kaleidoscope.

16. In mid-1990, a public relations officer at the Southern Command (then still in the Panama Canal Zone), showed me a slide show that contrasted the Pentagon's old mission to its new one: "Old Enemy: Communism," "New Enemy: Drug trafficking."

17. That has been disconcerting for academics specializing in Latin America, whose work had seemed policy-relevant for a half century. For decades they had opposed CIA meddling, Pentagon training of Latin American militaries, and US support for dictatorships and repressive regimes, and had argued on behalf of a more enlightened policy, including ending the blockade against Cuba. Academics took part in local solidarity groups and opposed Latin America policy, during both Democratic and Republican administrations.

18. It should be noted that Zelaya had lost the support of congress, including his own party, and at least some Hondurans argued that the removal was constitutional.

References

Adelman, Jeremy. 2013. *Worldly Philosopher: The Odyssey of Albert O. Hirschman.* Princeton, NJ: Princeton University Press.

Adese, Carlos. 2006. "Tuning In: Lower-Income Consumers Are Fueling Business in Latin America, Which Is Good News for Advertisers." *Latin Trade* (October).

Albó, Xavier. 2011. "El Alto in Flux." *ReVista, the Harvard Review of Latin America* 11, no. 1 (Fall): 18–20.

Althaus, Dudley. 2013. "Mexico Takes Title of 'Most Obese' from America." *Global Post,* July 8.

Alvarez, Sonia E., Evelina Dagnino, and Arturo Escobar, eds. 1998. *Cultures of Politics, Politics of Cultures: Re-Visioning Latin American Social Movements.* Boulder: Westview Press.

Americas Quarterly: Education. 2010. Vol. 4, no. 4 (Fall).

Americas Quarterly: Health Care. 2010. Vol. 4, no. 3 (Summer).

Americas Quarterly: Latin America's Real Middle Class: What They Believe, What They Purchase, What They Want. 2012. Vol. 6, no. 4 (Fall).

Americas Quarterly: Natural Resource Extraction in Latin America. 2013. Vol. 7, no. 1 (Winter).

Americas Quarterly: Our Cities, Our Future. 2014. Vol. 8, no. 1 (Winter).

Amnesty International. 2010. "Amnesty International Joins the Campaign to Decriminalize Abortion in Latin America and the Caribbean." Public statement, September 28.

Anderson, Jon Lee. 2013. "Letter from Caracas." *New Yorker,* January 28.

Anderson, Thomas P. 1971. *Matanza: El Salvador's Communist Revolt of 1932.* Lincoln: University of Nebraska Press.

Andrews, George Reid. 2004. *Afro-Latin America, 1800–2000.* Oxford: Oxford University Press.

Araujo, Kathya, and Mercedes Prieto, eds. 2008. *Estudios sobre sexualidades en América Latina.* Quito: FLACSO, Sede Ecuador.

Armenta, Amira, Pien Metaal, and Martin Jelsma. 2012. "A Breakthrough in the Making? Shifts in the Latin American Drug Policy Debate." Transnational Institute, Series on Legislative Reform of Drug Policies No. 21, June.

Armstrong, Karen. 2010. *Twelve Steps to a Compassionate Life.* New York: Knopf.

Arnson, Cynthia J., ed. 2012. *In the Wake of War: Democratization and Internal Armed Conflict in Latin America.* Stanford: Stanford University Press.

———. 2013. "Setting Priorities for U.S. Policy in Latin America." Wilson Center policy brief, January.

Arnson, Cynthia, Marcelo Bergman, and Tasha Fairfield, eds. 2012. "Taxation and Equality in Latin America." Woodrow Wilson Center Update on the Americas. http://www.wilsoncenter.org/sites/default/files/Taxation_0.pdf.

Astill, James. 2011. "Seeing the Wood: A Special Report on Forests." *The Economist*, September 25.

Aziakou, Gerard. 2012. "Brazil Bids to Become World's Third IT Market by 2022." AFP, August 28.

Barber, Benjamin. 2013. *If Mayors Ruled the World: Dysfunctional Nations, Rising Cities*. New Haven: Yale University Press.

Barnes, Taylor. 2012. "Franchising Boom in Latin America and the Challenge of Adapting to Local Tastes." *Latin Trade* (March/April): 44–49.

Barnitz, Jacqueline. 2011. *Twentieth-Century Art of Latin America*. Austin: University of Texas Press.

Bateman, Joseph, and Viviane Brochardt, with contributions from Silvio Porto. 2013. "Brazil's Lessons in Rural Development: Family Agriculture, Access to Water, and Civic Engagement." WOLA (Washington Office on Latin America), February.

Bauer, Arnold J. 2001. *Goods, Power, History: Latin America's Material Culture*. Cambridge: Cambridge University Press.

Bebbington, Anthony. 2013. "Crossing Boundaries." *Americas Quarterly: Natural Resource Extraction in Latin America*. Vol. 7, No. 1 (Winter).

Beltrán, Adriana, and Laurie Freeman. 2007. "Hidden in Plain Sight: Violence Against Women in Mexico and Guatemala." WOLA (Washington Office on Latin America), March.

Berdegué, Julio A., and Ricardo Fuentealba. 2011. "Latin America: The State of Smallholders in Agriculture." Conference on New Directions for Smallholder Agriculture, January 24–25, Rome, IFAD (International Fund for Agricultural Development) HQ. http://www.ifad.org/events /agriculture/doc/papers/berdegue.pdf.

Berry, Albert. 2002. "The Role of the Small and Medium Enterprise Sector in Latin America and Similar Developing Economies." *Seton Hall Journal of Diplomacy and International Relations* 3 (Winter/Spring): 104.

Berryman, Phillip. 1994. *Stubborn Hope: Religion, Politics, and Revolution in Central America*. Maryknoll, NY: Orbis Books.

———. 1995. "Is Latin America Turning Pluralist? Recent Writings on Religion." *Latin American Research Review* 30, no. 3: 107–122.

———. 1996. *Religion in the Megacity: Catholic and Protestant Portraits from Latin America*. Maryknoll, NY: Orbis Books.

Bethell, Leslie, ed. 1989. *Latin America: Economy and Society, 1870–1930*. Cambridge: Cambridge University Press.

Biles, James J. 2008. "Wal-Mart and the 'Supermarket Revolution' in Mexico." *Geographische Rundschau International Edition* 4, no. 2: 44–49.

———. 2009. "Informal Work in Latin America: Competing Perspectives and Recent Debates." *Geography Compass* 3, no. 1: 214–236. DOI: 10.1111/j.1749-8198.2008.00188x.

Birdsall, Nancy. 2012. "A Note on the Middle Class in Latin America." Working Paper 303. Washington, DC: Center for Global Development, August.

Birdsall, Nancy, Nora Lustig, and Christian J. Meyer. 2013. "The Strugglers: The New Poor in Latin America?" Working Paper 337. Washington, DC: Center for Global Development, August.

Birdsall, Nancy, Nora Lustig, and Darryl McLeod. 2011. "Declining Inequality in Latin America: Some Economics, Some Politics." Working Paper 251. Washington, DC: Center for Global Development, May.

Black, Jan Knippers, ed. 2011. *Latin America: Its Problems and Its Promise: A Multidisciplinary Introduction*. 5th ed. Boulder, CO: Westview Press.

Bloomberg. 2014. "Most Efficient Health Care 2014: Countries." http://www.bloomberg.com /visual-data/best-and-worst/most-efficient-health-care-2014-countries, accessed May 4, 2015.

Boggs, Clay, and Geoff Thale. 2013. "Government Investment in Family Agriculture: New Opportunities in Mexico and Central America." WOLA (Washington Office on Latin America), May.

Brainard, Lael, and Leonardo Martinez-Diaz, eds. 2009. *Brazil as an Economic Superpower? Understanding Brazil's Changing Role in the Global Economy*. Washington, DC: Brookings Institution.

Brands, Hal. 2010. *Latin America's Cold War*. Cambridge, MA: Harvard University Press.

Bratton, William J., and William Andrews. 2010. "Eight Steps to Reduce Crime." *Americas Quarterly: Transnational Crime and Security* (Spring).

Brenneman, Robert. 2015. "Violence, Religion, and Institutional Legitimacy in Northern Central America." In Wilde, *Religious Responses*.

Brown, Anna, and Eileen Patten. 2014a. "Portrait of the Foreign-Born Population in the United States, 2012." April 29. http://www.pewhispanic.org/2014/04/29/statistical-portrait-of-the -foreign-born-population-in-the-united-states-2012/.

———. 2014b. "Statistical Portrait of Hispanics in the United States." April 29. http://www .pewhispanic.org/2014/04/29/statistical-portrait-of-hispanics-in-the-united-states-2012/.

Bruneau, Thomas, Lucía Dammert, and Elizabeth Skinner, eds. 2011. *Maras: Gang Violence and Security in Central America*. Austin: University of Texas Press.

Bulmer-Thomas, Victor. 1994. *The Economic History of Latin America since Independence*. Cambridge: Cambridge University Press.

Burdick, John. 1993. *Looking for God in Brazil: The Progressive Catholic Church in Urban Brazil's Religious Arena*. Berkeley: University of California Press.

Burkholder, Mark A., and Lyman L. Johnson. 1993. *Colonial Latin America*. 3rd ed. Oxford: Oxford University Press.

Burns, E. Bradford. 1994. *Latin America: A Concise Interpretive History*. 6th ed. Englewood Cliffs, NJ: Prentice Hall.

Butler, Rhett A. 2009. "Activists Target Brazil's Largest Driver of Deforestation: Cattle Ranching." Interview with Roberto Smeraldi, September 8. http://news.mongabay.com/2009/0908 -smeraldi.html.

Buvinic, Mayra, and Vivian Roza. 2004. "Women, Politics and Democratic Prospects in Latin America." Washington, DC: Inter-American Development Bank, Sustainable Development Department Technical Papers series; WID-108.

Byerlee, Derek, Alain de Janvry, and Elisabeth Sadoulet. 2009. "Agriculture for Development: Toward a New Paradigm." *Annual Review of Resource Economics* 1, no. 1: 15–35. http://are.berkeley .edu/~esadoulet/papers/Annual_Review_of_ResEcon7.pdf.

Cadena, Andres, et al. 2011. *Building Globally Competitive Cities: The Key to Latin American Growth*. McKinsey Global Institute, August. http://www.mckinsey.com/insights/urbanization /building_competitive_cities_key_to_latin_american_growth.

Camus, Manuela. 2011. "Primero de Julio: Urban Experiences of Class Decline and Violence." In O'Neill and Thomas, *Securing the City*, 49–66.

Canby, Peter. 1992. *Heart of the Sky: Travel among the Maya*. New York: HarperCollins.

———. 1999. "The Truth About Rigoberta Menchú." *The New York Review of Books*, April 8. http:// www.nybooks.com/articles/archives/1999/apr/08/the-truth-about-rigoberta-menchu/.

Capizzani, Mario, Felipe Javier Ramírez Huerta, and Paulo Rocha e Oliveira. 2012a. "Consumer Credit in Latin America: Trends and Opportunities in Credit and Store Cards." IESE Business School, University of Navarra, Occasional Paper OP-200, April. http://www.iese.edu/research /pdfs/OP-0200-E.pdf.

———. 2012b. "Retail in Latin America: Trends, Challenges and Opportunities." IESE Business School, University of Navarra, Study 170, April. http://www.iese.edu/research/pdfs /ESTUDIO-170-E.pdf.

Capp, Joe, Heinz-Peter Elstrodt, and William Bebb Jones Jr. 2005. "Reining in Brazil's Informal Economy." *McKinsey Quarterly*, January. http://www.swisscam.com.br/files_news/McKinsey _Brazil_Informal_Economy_RIB.pdf.

Carmack, Robert M., Janine L. Gasco, and Gary H. Gossen. 2007. *The Legacy of Mesoamerica: History and Culture of a Native American Civilization*. 2nd ed. Upper Saddle River, NJ: Pearson Prentice Hall.

Carranza, Elías. 2009. "Penal Reform and Prison Overcrowding in Latin America and the Caribbean. What to Do, What Not to Do. The Good Examples of Costa Rica and the Dominican

Republic." Presentation at workshop on penal reform and prison overcrowding at 18th Session of the United Nations Commission on Crime Prevention and Criminal Justice, Vienna International Centre, April 15. Translated from Spanish by Orlando García Valverde. http://www.unafei.or.jp/english/pdf/Congress_2010/14Elias_Carranza.pdf.

Carrión M., Fernando. 2010. *Ciudad, memoria y proyecto*. Quito: Olacchi.

Carrión M., Fernando, Jenny Pontón C., and Blanca Armijos V. 2009. *120 estrategias y 36 experiencias de seguridad ciudadana*. Quito: FLACSO.

Casanova, Lourdes, and Anne Dumas. 2010. "Corporate Social Responsibility and Latin American Multinationals: Is Poverty a Business Issue?" *Universia Business Review* 25: 132–145.

Casanova, Lourdes, and Matthew Fraser. 2009. *From Multilatinas to Global Latinas: The New Latin American Multinationals. Compilation Case Studies*. Washington, DC: Inter-American Development Bank.

Casas-Zamora, Kevin. 2010. "Dirty Money: How to Break the Link between Organized Crime and Politics." *Americas Quarterly: Trafficking and Transnational Crime* 3, no. 2 (Spring). http://www.americasquarterly.org/casas-zamora.

———. 2011. "The Travails of Development and Democratic Governance in Central America." Foreign Policy at Brookings. Policy Paper Number 28, June. http://www.brookings.edu/~/media/research/files/papers/2011/6/central-america-casaszamora/06_central_america_casaszamora.pdf.

———. 2012. "Venezuela's Crime Debacle: A Cautionary Tale." Brookings Institution Opinion, February 3. http://www.brookings.edu/research/opinions/2012/02/03-venezuela-casaszamora.

Castañeda, Jorge G. 1993. *Utopia Unarmed: The Latin American Left After the Cold War*. New York: Alfred A. Knopf.

———. 2011. *Mañana Forever?: Mexico and the Mexicans*. New York: Vintage.

Castañeda, Jorge G., and Marco A. Morales. 2008. *Leftovers: Tales of the Latin American Left*. New York: Routledge.

Castelli, Irene. 2012. "'Beggars Sitting on a Sack of Gold?' Ecuadoreans Protest Mining." *Christian Science Monitor*, March 22. http://www.csmonitor.com/World/Americas/2012/0322/Beggars-sitting-on-a-sack-of-gold-Ecuadoreans-protest-mining.

Castro Martín, Teresa. 2010. "Cohabitación y fecundidad no matrimonial en América Latina: Una perspectiva comparada." Seminario Internacional Nupcialidad y Familia en América Latina, Barcelona, October 7–9. http://www.ced.uab.es/worldfam/teresa_castro.pdf.

Castro Martín, Teresa, Clara Cortina, Teresa Martín García, and Ignacio Pardo. 2010. "La fecundidad no matrimonial en América Latina: Indicadores y análisis comparativos a partir de datos censales." Paper presented at the 9th Jornadas de Investigación de la Facultad de Ciencias Sociales, UdelaR, Montevideo, September 13–15. http://www.fcs.edu.uy/archivos/Mesa_46_Castro%20Mart%C3%ADn%20et%20al.pdf.

Cave, Damien. 2012a. "Lush Walls Rise to Fight a Blanket of Pollution." *New York Times*, April 9.

———. 2012b. "Migrants' New Paths Reshaping Latin America." *New York Times*, January 5.

———. 2013. "For Migrants, New Land of Opportunity Is Mexico." *New York Times*, September 21.

CELAM (Latin American Episcopal Conference). 2007. "The Aparecida Document." Aparecida, Brazil. http://www.celam.org/aparecida/Ingles.pdf.

Charles, Dan. 2008. "The Supermarket Revolution Moves into Honduras." NPR Report, August 5. http://www.npr.org/templates/story/story.php?storyId=93050486.

Chasteen, John Charles. 2007. *Born in Blood and Fire: A Concise History of Latin America*. 2nd ed. New York: W. W. Norton.

Chestnut, R. Andrew. 2003. *Competitive Spirits: Latin America's New Religious Economy*. New York: Oxford University Press.

Children's Defense Fund. 2012. "Portrait of Inequality 2012: Hispanic Children in America." November. http://www.childrensdefense.org/library/data/a-portrait-of-inequality-2012.pdf.

Chomsky, Aviva, Barry Carr, and Pamela Maria Smorkaloff, eds. 2006. *The Cuba Reader: History, Culture, Politics*. Durham: Duke University Press.

Clawson, David L. 2006. *Latin America and the Caribbean: Lands and Peoples*. 4th ed. Oxford: Oxford University Press.

Cleary, Edward L. 1997. *The Struggle for Human Rights in Latin America*. Westport, CT: Praeger.

———. 2007. *Mobilizing for Human Rights in Latin America*. Bloomfield, CT: Kumarian Press.

Cleary, Edward L., and Timothy J. Steigenga, eds. 2004. *Resurgent Voices in Latin America: Indigenous Peoples, Political Mobilization, and Religious Change*. New Brunswick, NJ: Rutgers University Press.

Colburn, Forrest D. 1994. *The Vogue of Revolution in Poor Countries*. Princeton, NJ: Princeton University Press.

———. 2002. *Latin America at the End of Politics*. Princeton, NJ: Princeton University Press.

———. 2006. "Defending the Market in Latin America: Appreciating Costa Rica's Success." *Journal of Business Research* 59: 349–355.

Collinson, Helen, ed. 1996. *Green Guerrillas: Environmental Conflicts and Initiatives in Latin America and the Caribbean. A Reader*. London: Latin America Bureau.

Comisión Ecuménica de Derechos Humanos. 2006. *Poblaciones afectadas por industrias extractivas en Ecuador: La defensa de sus derechos*. Quito: Comisión Ecuménica de Derechos Humanos.

Conroy, Michael E. 2007. *Branded! How the 'Certification Revolution' Is Transforming Global Corporations*. Gabriola Island, British Columbia, Canada: New Society Publishers.

Constable, Pamela, and Arturo Valenzuela. 1991. *A Nation of Enemies: Chile under Pinochet*. New York: W. W. Norton.

Contreras, Joseph. 2009. *In the Shadow of the Giant: The Americanization of Modern Mexico*. New Brunswick, NJ: Rutgers University Press.

Corchado, Alfredo. 2013. *Midnight in Mexico: A Reporter's Journey through a Country's Descent into Darkness*. New York: Penguin Books.

Corrales, Javier. 2009. "Gays in Latin America: Is the Closet Half Empty?" *Foreign Policy*, February 18.

D'Andrea, Guillermo, E. Alejandro Stengel, and Anne Goebel-Krstelj. 2004. "6 Truths about Emerging-Market Consumers." *Strategy+Business* 34 (Spring). http://www.strategy-business.com/article/04106?pg=all.

Davis, Mike. 2006. *Planet of Slums*. New York: Verso.

Dawson, Alexander. 2011. *Latin America since Independence: A History with Primary Sources*. New York: Routledge.

DeHart, Monica C. 2010. *Ethnic Entrepreneurs: Identity and Development Politics in Latin America*. Stanford: Stanford University Press.

De la Dehasa, Rafael. 2010. *Queering the Public Sphere in Mexico and Brazil: Sexual Rights Movements in Emerging Democracies*. Durham: Duke University Press.

De la Torre, Carlos, and Cynthia J. Arnson, eds. 2013. *Latin American Populism in the Twenty-First Century*. Washington DC: Woodrow Wilson Center Press.

Del Sarto, Ana, Alicia Ríos, and Abril Trigo, eds. 2004. *The Latin American Cultural Studies Reader*. Durham: Duke University Press.

DeShazo, Peter, and Juan Enrique Vargas. 2006. *Judicial Reform in Latin America: An Assessment*. Policy Papers on the Americas Vol. XVII, Study 2. Washington, DC: Center for Strategic and International Studies, September.

de Soto, Hernando. 1989. *The Other Path: The Invisible Revolution in the Third World*. New York: Harper and Row.

Devlin, Robert, and Ricardo Ffrench-Davis. 1995. "The Great Latin America Debt Crisis: A Decade of Asymmetric Adjustment." *Revista de Economia Política* 15, no. 3 (July–September): 117–142.

DeVos, Susan. 2000. "Nuptiality in Latin America: The View of a Sociologist and Family Demographer." CDE Working Paper No. 98–21. Madison, WI: Center for Demography and Ecology.

Diamond, Jared. 1997. *Guns, Germs, and Steel: The Fates of Human Societies*. New York: W. W. Norton.

Díaz-Briquets, Sergio, and Jorge Pérez-López. 2010. "Cuba: Corruption at a Crossroads." In Morris and Blake, *Corruption and Politics*, 113–136.

Dimitri, Carolyn, Anne Effland, and Neilson Conklin. 2005. "The 20th Century Transformation of U.S. Agriculture and Farm Policy." U.S. Department of Agriculture, Economic Research Service, Economic Information Bulletin No. 3, Electronic Report, June. http://www.ers.usda.gov/media/259572/eib3_1_.pdf.

Dolan, Kerry A. 2011. "Arcos Dorados IPO Creates First McDonald's Billionaire." *Forbes*, April 28. http://www.forbes.com/sites/kerryadolan/2011/04/28/arcos-dorados-ipo-creates-first-mcdonalds-billionaire/.

Dreher, Alex, and Thomas Herzfeld. 2005. "The Economic Costs of Corruption: A Survey and New Evidence." June. http://128.118.178.162/eps/pe/papers/0506/0506001.pdf.

Dudley, Steven. 2013. "The El Salvador Gang Truce and the Church: What Was the Role of the Catholic Church?" Washington, DC: Center for Latin American and Latino Studies, American University; and InSight Crime. CLALS White Paper Series No. 1, May 5.

Duncan, Emma. 2013. "All creatures great and small." Special Report: Biodiversity. *The Economist*, September 14.

Durand, Francisco. 2007. *El Perú fracturado: Formalidad, informalidad y economía delictiva*. Lima: Fondo Editorial del Congreso del Perú.

Durand, Jorge. 2009. "Processes of Migration in Latin America and the Caribbean (1950–2008)." United Nations Development Programme. Human Development Reports Research Paper 2009/24, July.

Dussel Peters, Enrique. 2007. "What Does China's Integration to the World Market Mean for Latin America? The Mexican Experience." Paper presented at LASA Congress, Montreal, September 5–8.

Eakin, Marshall C. 2007. *The History of Latin America: Collision of Cultures*. New York: Palgrave Macmillan.

Ebrard, Marcelo. 2014. "Cleaning Up 'Makesicko' City." *Americas Quarterly: Our Cities, Our Future* 8, no. 1 (Winter): 66–72.

Eckstein, Susan Eva, ed. 1989. *Power and Popular Protest: Latin American Social Movements*. Berkeley: University of California Press.

Eckstein, Susan Eva, and Timothy P. Wickham-Crowley, eds. 2003. *What Justice? Whose Justice? Fighting for Fairness in Latin America*. Berkeley: University of California Press.

ECLAC (Economic Commission for Latin America and the Caribbean). 2013. *Social Panorama of Latin America 2012*. New York: United Nations.

The Economist Intelligence Unit. 2008. "Latin America's Small and Medium-sized Enterprises: The Human Capital Challenge." July. http://graphics.eiu.com/PDF/SAP.LatinAm.Human.pdf.

———. 2010. *Latin American Green City Index: Assessing the Environmental Performance of Latin America's Major Cities*. Munich, Germany: Siemens AG. http://www.siemens.com/entry/cc/features/greencityindex_international/all/en/pdf/report_latam_en.pdf.

———. 2011. "Latin America Business: Heading for the mall." March 16. http://apportal.ey1.dedicated.nines.nl/wp-content/uploads/2011/04/Latin-America-business-Heading-for-the-mall.pdf.

The Economist. 1999. "Latin American Gays: Living la vida loca," December 16.

———. 2007a. "Brazil's AIDS Programme: A Conflict of Goals," May 10.

———. 2007b. "Gay Rights in Latin America: Out of the Closet," March 8.

———. 2008. "Brazil: Half the Nation, a Hundred Million Citizens Strong," September 11.

———. 2010. "Brazilian Agriculture: The Miracle of the Cerrado," August 26.

———. 2011. "Regional Integration in Latin America: The Pacific Players Go to Market," April 7.

———. 2012a. "Prisons in Latin America: A Journey into Hell," September 22.

———. 2012b. "Señores, Start Your Engines," November 24.

———. 2013a. "Latin American Geoeconomics: A Continental Divide," May 18.

———. 2013b. "Obesity in Latin America: Battle of the Bulge," July 27.

ECosociAL (Encuesta de Cohesión Social en América Latina). 2007. "Nueva Agenda de Cohesión Social para América Latina." September. http://www.cieplan.org/media/publicaciones /archivos/22/Conferencia_de_Prensa_ECosociAL.pdf.

Edlin, Mari. 2009. "Chile's Healthcare Offers Public and Private Plans: Chronic Care Has Guarantees." *Managed Healthcare Executive*, December 1.

Edwards, Sebastian. 2010. *Left Behind: Latin America and the False Promise of Populism*. Chicago: University of Chicago Press.

Eidt, Jack. 2010. "Destructive Progress: Brazil-Peru Transoceanic Highway." *WilderUtopia*, November 3. http://www.wilderutopia.com/international/destructive-progress-brazil-peru -transoceanic-highway-by-jack-eidt/.

Elkin, Judith Laikin. 1914. *The Jews of Latin America*. 3rd ed. Boulder, CO: Lynne Rienner.

Ellacuría, Ignacio. 1991. "Is a Different Kind of University Possible?" In John J. Hasset and Hugh Lacey, eds., *Towards a Society That Serves Its People: The Intellectual Contribution of El Salvador's Murdered Jesuits*, 177–207. Washington, DC: Georgetown University Press.

Erickson, Clark L. 2008. "Amazonia: The Historical Ecology of a Domesticated Ecology." In Helaine Silverman and William H. Isbell, eds., *The Handbook of South American Archaeology*, 157–182. New York: Springer. http://www.sas.upenn.edu/anthropology/system/files /EricksonAmazonia2008b.pdf.

Estevadeordal, Antoni, and Theodore Kahn. 2012. *Pathways to China: The Story of Latin American Firms in the Chinese Market*. Washington, DC: Inter-American Development Bank.

FAO (Food and Agriculture Organization of the United Nations). 2011. *Panorama de la seguridad alimentaria y nutricional en América Latina y el Caribe 2011*. FAO. http://www.fao.org/docrep/014 /am865s/am865s00.pdf.

Fatheuer, Thomas. 2011. *Buen Vivir: A Brief Introduction to Latin America's New Concepts for the Good Life and the Rights of Nature*. Series on Ecology. Berlin: Heinrich Böll Foundation.

Felbab-Brown, Vanda. 2011. "Bringing the State to the Slum: Confronting Organized Crime and Urban Violence in Latin America." Brookings Institution Research Paper, December 5. http:// www.brookings.edu/research/papers/2011/12/05-latin-america-slums-felbabbrown.

Fernandes, Rubem César. 1998. "Urban Violence and Civic Action: The Experience of Viva Rio." http://tinyurl.com/ppvo3bn.

Fernández, Francisco de Asís, ed. 1986. *Poesía política nicaragüense*. Managua: Ministerio de Cultura.

Fernández-Armesto, Felipe. 2003. *The Americas: A Hemispheric History*. New York: Modern Library.

Ferreira, Francisco H. G., Julian Messina, Jamele Rigolini, Luis-Felipe López-Calva, Maria Ana Lugo, and Renos Vakis. 2012. *Economic Mobility and the Rise of the Latin American Middle Class*. Washington, DC: World Bank.

FIDH (International Federation for Human Rights). 2012. "Colombia: The War Is Measured in Litres of Blood. False Positives, Crimes against Humanity: Those most Responsible Enjoy Impunity." Paris: FIDH. https://www.fidh.org/IMG/pdf/rapp_colombie__juin_2012_anglais_def.pdf.

Figueiredo, Angela. 2010. "Out of Place: The Experience of the Black Middle Class." In Reiter and Mitchell, *Brazil's New Racial Politics*, 51–63.

Fisher, Jo. 1993. *Out of the Shadows: Women, Resistance and Politics in South America*. London: Latin American Bureau.

Franco, Rolando, Martín Hopenhayn, and Arturo León. 2011. "The Growing and Changing Middle Class in Latin America: An Update." *Cepal Review* 103 (April): 7–25.

Franko, Patrice. 2007. *The Puzzle of Latin American Economic Development*. 3rd ed. Lanham, MD: Rowman and Littlefield.

Frank-Vitale, Amelia. 2015. "*Fui migrante y me hospedaste*": The Catholic Church's Response to Violence against Central American Migrants in Mexico." In Wilde, ed., *Religious Responses to Violence*.

Fraser, Barbara. 2012. "Melting in the Andes: Goodbye Glaciers." *Nature* 491, no. 7423 (November): 180–182.

Freire, Paulo. 1970. *Pedagogy of the Oppressed*. New York: Continuum.

———. 1973. *Education for Critical Consciousness*. New York: Continuum.

Frenk, Julio, Octavio Gómez-Dantés, and Felicia Marie Knaul. 2009. "The Democratization of Health in Mexico: Financial Innovations for Universal Coverage." *Bulletin of the World Health Organization* 87: 542–548.

Friedman-Rudovsky, Jean. 2007. "Abortion Under Siege in Latin America." *Time*, August 9.

———. 2012. "The Bully from Brazil." *Foreign Policy*, July 20.

Fuentes Vásquez, Lya Yaneth. 2002. *El origen de una política: Mujeres jefas de hogar en Colombia, 1990–1998*. Bogotá: Universidad Nacional de Colombia.

Fukuyama, Francis, ed. 2007. *Falling Behind: Explaining the Development Gap Between Latin America and the United States*. New York: Oxford University Press.

Galeano, Eduardo. 1973. *Open Veins of Latin America: Five Centuries of the Pillage of a Continent*. New York: Monthly Review Press.

———. 1985. *Genesis*. Vol. 1 of *Memory of Fire* trilogy. Translated by Cedric Belfrage. New York: Pantheon.

———. 1987. *Faces and Masks*. Vol. 2 of *Memory of Fire* trilogy. Translated by Cedric Belfrage. New York: Pantheon.

———. 1988. *Century of the Wind*. Vol. 3 of *Memory of Fire* trilogy. Translated by Cedric Belfrage. New York: Pantheon.

Gallagher, Kevin P. 2012. "Capitalizing on the China Cycle: Time Is Running Out for Latin America." Inter-American Dialogue Economics Brief, December 7. http://www.thedialogue.org/page.cfm ?pageID=32&pubID=3174

Gallagher, Kevin P., and Roberto Porzecanski. 2010. *The Dragon in the Room: China and the Future of Latin American Industrialization*. Stanford: Stanford University Press.

Gallup, John Luke, Alejandro Gaviria, and Eduardo Lora, eds. 2003. *Is Geography Destiny? Lessons from Latin America*. Stanford: Stanford University Press and the World Bank.

Gallup, John Luke, and Jeffrey D. Sachs. 2000. "Agriculture, Climate, and Technology: Why Are the Tropics Falling Behind?" *American Journal of Agricultural Economics* 82, no. 3 (August): 731–737.

García-Valdivieso, Gonzalo. 2006. *Arco iris en el tiempo: Salgamos del clóset*. Bogotá: Icono.

Garzón, Juan Carlos. 2008. *Mafia and Company: The Criminal Networks in Mexico, Brazil, and Colombia*. Washington, DC: Woodrow Wilson International Center for Scholars.

Gates, Henry Louis, Jr. 2011. *Black in Latin America*. New York: New York University Press.

Gay, Robert. 2005. *Lucia: Testimonies of a Brazilian Drug Dealer's Woman*. Philadelphia: Temple University Press.

Gerchunoff, Alberto. 2003. *Los gauchos judíos*. Buenos Aires: Arenal.

Giedion, Ursula, and Manuela Villar Uribe. 2009. "Colombia's Universal Health Insurance System." *Health Affairs* 28, no. 3 (May/June): 853–863.

Gilbert, Alan. 1994. *The Latin American City*. London: Latin America Bureau.

Global Footprint Network. 2013. "Footprint for Nations." http://www.footprintnetwork.org/en /index.php/GFN/page/footprint_for_nations/ (accessed October 3).

Goetzal, Ted G. 2011. *Brazil's Lula: The Most Popular Politician on Earth*. Boca Raton, FL: Brown Walker Press.

Goldman, Francisco. 2007. *The Art of Political Murder: Who Killed the Bishop?* New York: Grove Press.

Grandin, Greg, Deborah T. Levenson, and Elizabeth Oglesby, eds. 2011. *The Guatemala Reader: History, Culture, Politics*. Durham: Duke University Press.

Green, Duncan, with Sue Branford. 2013. *Faces of Latin America*. 4th ed. New York: Monthly Review Press. Originally published 1991.

Greenpeace International. 2009. "Slaughtering the Amazon." June. http://www.greenpeace.org /international/en/publications/reports/slaughtering-the-amazon/.

Grindle, Merilee S. 2010. "Constructing, Deconstructing, and Reconstructing Career Civil Service Systems in Latin America." Harvard Kennedy School. Faculty Research Working Paper Series RWP10–025, June.

Guedes, Patricia Mota, and Nilson Vieira Oliveira. 2006. "The Democratization of Consumption: Life and Its Aspirations on the Outskirts of Greater São Paulo." Braudel Papers, No. 38. São Paulo: Fernand Braudel Institute of World Economics. http://pt.braudel.org.br/publicacoes /braudel-papers/downloads/ingles/bp39_en.pdf.

Guillermoprieto, Alma. 1994. *The Heart That Bleeds: Latin America Now*. New York: Alfred A. Knopf.

———. 2001. *Looking for History*. New York: Vintage.

———. 2010a. "Mexican Saints." *National Geographic*, May (follow-up in May 2013).

———. 2010b. "The Murderers of Mexico." *The New York Review of Books*, October 28.

———. 2010c. "Poverty of Opportunity: Crime's Breeding Ground." *Americas Quarterly: Trafficking and Transnational Crime* 4, no. 2 (Spring): 50–55.

———. 2012. "Drugs: The Rebellion in Cartagena." *The New York Review of Books*, June 7.

Gutiérrez, Gustavo. 1973. *A Theology of Liberation: History, Politics, and Salvation*. Translated by Caridad inda and John Eagleson. Maryknoll, NY: Orbis Books. Originally published as *Teología de la liberación*. Lima: CEP, 1971.

———. 1993. *Las Casas: In Search of the Poor of Jesus Christ*. Translated by Robert R. Barr. Maryknoll, NY: Orbis Books.

Guttmacher Institute. 2012. "Facts on Abortion in Latin America and the Caribbean." New York and Washington, DC: In Brief. http://www.guttmacher.org/pubs/IB_AWW-Latin-America.pdf.

Gwynne, Robert N., and Cristobal Kay, eds. 1999. *Latin America Transformed: Globalization and Modernity*. London: Arnold.

Haar, Jerry, and John Price, eds. 2008. *Can Latin America Compete? Confronting the Challenges of Globalization*. New York: Palgrave Macmillan.

Haber, Stephen, Herbert S. Klein, Noel Maurer, and Kevin J. Middlebrook. 2008. *Mexico since 1980*. Cambridge: Cambridge University Press.

Hagedorn, John M. 2008. "Making Sense of Central American Maras." *Air & Space Power Journal* 20, no. 2 (June): 42–48.

Hagopian, Frances, ed. 2009a. *Religious Pluralism, Democracy, and the Catholic Church in Latin America*. Notre Dame, IN: University of Notre Dame Press.

———. 2009b. "Social Justice, Moral Values, or Institutional Interests?: Church Responses to the Democratic Challenge in Latin America." In Hagopian, *Religious Pluralism*, 257–331.

Haight, Colleen. 2011. "The Problem with Fair Trade Coffee." *Stanford Social Innovation Review* (Summer). http://www.ssireview.org/articles/entry/the_problem_with_fair_trade_coffee.

Hakim, Peter, and Kimberly Covington. 2012. "What Is US Drug Policy?" Inter-American Dialogue Working Paper, July 16. http://www.thedialogue.org/uploads/Drug_Policy/IAD _USDrugPolicyPaper_web.pdf.

Hale, Lindsay. 2009. "Umbanda." In Lee M. Penyak and Walter J. Petry, eds., *Religion and Society in Latin America: Interpretive Essays from Conquest to Present*, 225–242. Maryknoll, NY: Orbis Books.

Hall-Jones, Peter. 2007. "Unionism and Economic Performance." New Unionism News Wire. http://www.newunionism.net/library/member%20contributions/news/Unionism%20and%20 Economic%20Performance.htm.

Halperin Donghi, Tulio. 1993. *The Contemporary History of Latin America*. Durham: Duke University Press.

Hammergren, Linn. 2008. "Twenty-Five Years of Latin American Judicial Reforms: Achievements, Disappointments, and Emerging Issues." *The Whitehead Journal of Diplomacy and International Relations* (Winter/Spring): 89–104.

Hart, Hillary. 2008. "Nelsa Curbelo, Former Nun and Schoolteacher, Takes on Ecuador's Toughest Criminals." Originally in *Ode Magazine*, reprinted in *Huffington Post*, July 2. http://www .huffingtonpost.com/2008/06/24/nelsa-curbelo-former-nun_n_108869.html.

Hecht, Susanna B., and Charles C. Mann. 2008. "How Brazil Outfarmed the American Farmer." *Fortune*, January 19.

Heckenberger, Michael J. 2009. "Lost Cities of the Amazon." *Scientific American* 301 (October): 64–71.

Hellinger, Daniel C. 2011. *Comparative Politics of Latin America: Democracy at Last?* New York: Routledge.

Helwege, Ann. 2011. "Latin America 2060: Securing Economic Development for the Longer-Range Future." In *Latin America 2060: Consolidation or Crisis?*, 9–20. Boston University, Pardee Center Task Force Report, September.

Helwege, Ann, and Melissa B. L. Birch. 2007. "Declining Poverty in Latin America? A Critical Analysis of New Estimates by International Institutions." Global Development and Environment Institute Working Paper No. 07–02. Medford, MA: Global Development and Environment Institute, September.

Hennelly, Alfred T. 1990. *Liberation Theology: A Documentary History*. Maryknoll, NY: Orbis Books.

Herring, Hubert. 1972. *A History of Latin America: From the Beginnings to the Present*. New York: Alfred A. Knopf.

Hillman, Richard S., and Thomas J. D'Agostino, eds. 2011. *Understanding Contemporary Latin America*. 4th ed. Boulder, CO: Lynne Rienner.

Hirschman, Albert O. 2013. *The Essential Hirschman*. Edited by Jeremy Adelman. Princeton, NJ: Princeton University Press.

Hoffman, Paul. 2003. *Wings of Madness: Alberto Santos-Dumont and the Invention of Flight*. New York: Hyperion.

Holden, Robert H., and Rina Villars. 2013. *Contemporary Latin America: 1970 to the Present*. West Sussex, UK: Wiley-Blackwell.

Hongxian, Huang. 2012. "In Ecuador, Home Truths for China." Chinadialogue, August 6. http://www.chinadialogue.net/article/show/single/en/4966-In-Ecuador-home-truths-for-China.

Hornbeck, J. F. 2011. "U.S.-Latin America Trade: Recent Trends and Policy Issues." CRS Report for Congress. Congressional Research Service, February 8. http://fas.org/sgp/crs/row/98-840.pdf.

Htun, Mala. 2009. "Life, Liberty, and Family Values: Church and State in the Struggle over Latin America's Social Agenda." In Hagopian, *Religious Pluralism*, 257–364.

Huntington, Samuel P. 1991. *The Third Wave: Democratization in the Late 20th Century*. Norman: University of Oklahoma Press.

———. 2004. *Who Are We? The Challenges to America's National Identity: The Clash of Civilizations and the Remaking of World Order*. New York: Simon and Schuster.

Husain, Saima. 2006. "The Whole Is Greater Than the Sum of the Parts: Citizen-Police Cooperation in the Implementation of Community-Orientated Policing in Brazil." Paper presented at the meeting of the Latin American Studies Association, San Juan, Puerto Rico, March 15–18.

Hyland, Steven. 2011. "The Shifting Terrain of Latin American Drug Trafficking." *Origins* 4, no. 12 (September).

Illich, Ivan. 1971. *Deschooling Society*. New York: Harper and Row.

Inter-American Development Bank. 2010. "Stagnant productivity causing poor growth in Latin America and the Caribbean." http://www.iadb.org/en/news/news-releases/2010-03-20/stagnant-productivity-causing-poor-growth-in-latin-america-and-the-caribbean-bid,6696.html.

Inter-American Dialogue. 2012. "Remaking the Relationship: The United States and Latin America." Inter-American Dialogue Policy Report, April 11. http://www.thedialogue.org/PublicationFiles/IAD2012PolicyReportFINAL.pdf.

Israel, Franz. 2013. "2013 Digital Trends in Latin America." Digital Media Bloggers, June 29. http://digitalmediabloggers.com/es/2013-digital-trends-in-latin-america.

Jackson, Norma Lozano, and Peter Jackson, translators. 2007. "Law 70 of Colombia (1993): In Recognition of the Right of Black Colombians to Collectively Own and Occupy Their Ancestral

Lands." April. http://www.benedict.edu/exec_admin/intnl_programs/other_files/bc-intnl
_programs-law_70_of_colombia-english.pdf.

Jacobs, Jane. 1961. *The Death and Life of Great American Cities*. New York: Random House.

Jaff, Hanna. 2010. "The Right to Health in Mexico: Seguro Popular." World Poverty and Human
Rights Online, March 27. http://archive.today/Q4gHc.

Jaquette, Jane S., ed. 2009. *Feminist Agendas and Democracy in Latin America*. Durham: Duke
University Press.

Johnson, Andrew. 2015. "The Politics of Presence: Evangelical Ministry in Brazilian Prisons."
In Wilde, *Religious Responses*.

Joyce, Helen. 2013. "Grounded." Special Report: Brazil. *The Economist*, September 26.

Karttunen, Frances. 1997. "Rethinking Malinche." In Susan Schroeder, Stephanie Wood, Robert Stephen Haskett, eds., *Indian Women of Early Mexico*, 291–312. Norman: University of
Oklahoma Press.

Keefe, Patrick Radden. 2012a. "Cocaine Incorporated." *New York Times Magazine*, June 15.

———. 2012b. "Reversal of Fortune." *The New Yorker*, January 9.

———. 2014. "The Hunt for El Chapo." *The New Yorker*, May 5.

Keen, Benjamin. 1986. *Latin American Civilization: History and Society, 1492 to the Present*. 4th ed.
Boulder, CO: Westview Press.

Kenny, Charles. 2014. "Learning Curve: Why More and More Parents in Poor Countries Are Paying
to Send Their Kids to Private School." *Foreign Policy*, March 12, 30–31.

Kimerling, Judith. 1993. *Crudo amazónico*. Quito: Abya Yala.

———. 2013. "Oil, Contact, and Conservation in the Amazon: Indigenous Huaorani, Chevron,
and Yasuni." *Colorado Journal of International Environmental Law and Policy* 24, no. 1: 43–115.

Kimmelman, Michael. 2012. "A City Rises, along with Its Hopes." *New York Times*, May 18.

King, John, ed. 2004. *The Cambridge Companion to Modern Latin American Culture*. Cambridge:
Cambridge University Press.

Klaiber, Jeffrey, S.J. 1998. *The Church, Dictatorships, and Democracy in Latin America*. Maryknoll, NY:
Orbis Books.

Klein, Herbert S., and Ben Vinson III. 2007. *African Slavery in Latin America and the Caribbean*. 2nd
ed. Oxford: Oxford University Press.

Kopenawa, Davi. 2013. *The Falling Sky: Words of a Yanomami Shaman*. Cambridge, MA: Belknap/
Harvard University Press.

Krauze, Enrique. 1997. *Mexico: Biography of Power—A History of Modern Mexico, 1810–1996*.
Translated by Hank Heifetz. New York: HarperCollins.

———. 2012. "Mexico at War." Translated from the Spanish by Hank Heifetz. *New York Review of
Books*, September 27.

Larraín, Soledad. 1999. "Curbing Domestic Violence: Two Decades of Action." In Andrew R. Morrison and María Loreto Biehl, eds., *Too Close to Home: Domestic Violence in the Americas*, 105–130.
Washington, DC: Inter-American Development Bank.

Latin American Commission on Drugs and Democracy. 2009. "Drugs and Democracy: Toward a
Paradigm Shift." http://www.ungassondrugs.org/images/stories/towards.pdf.

Latinamerica Press. 2005. *The Impact of Mining on Latin America*. Special Number. Lima:
Comunicaciones Aliadas. http://www.lapress.org/informes.asp?inf=2.

"Latin 500." 2010. *Latin Trade* (July–August): 22–56.

Le Breton, Binka. 2008. *The Greatest Gift: The Courageous Life and Martyrdom of Sister Dorothy Stang*.
New York: Doubleday.

Lehmann, David. 2000. "Female-Headed Households in Latin America and the Caribbean:
Problems of Analysis and Conceptualization." In François Couzet and Denis Rolland, eds., *Pour
l'histoire du Brésil: Hommage à Katia de Queiros Mattoso*, Paris: L'Harmattan. http://tinyurl.com
/b7b5eet.

LeoGrande, William M. 1998. *Our Own Backyard: The United States in Central America, 1977–1992.* Chapel Hill: University of North Carolina Press.

Lernoux, Penny. 1982. *Cry of the People: The Struggle for Human Rights in Latin America.* New York: Penguin.

Levenson, Deborah T. 2011. "Living Guatemala City, 1930s–2000s." In O'Neill and Thomas, *Securing the City*, 25–48.

Levine, Daniel H. 2012. *Politics, Religion and Society in Latin America.* Boulder, CO: Lynne Rienner.

Levine, Daniel H., and José E. Molina, eds. 2011. *The Quality of Democracy in Latin America.* Boulder, CO: Lynne Rienner.

Levine, Robert M., and John J. Crocitti, eds. 1999. *The Brazil Reader: History, Culture, Politics.* Durham: Duke University Press.

Lida, David. 2008. *First Stop in the New World: Mexico City, the Capital of the 21st Century.* New York: Penguin.

López, Julie. 2010. "Guatemala's Crossroads: Democratization of Violence and Second Chances." Woodrow Wilson International Center for Scholars. Working Paper Series on Organized Crime in Central America, December.

Lopez, Mark Hugo, and Ana Gonzalez-Barrera. 2013. "What Is the Future of Spanish in the United States?" Pew Research Center, September 5.

Lora, Eduardo, ed. 2006. *The State of State Reform in Latin America.* Washington, DC: Inter-American Development Bank.

Loyka, Mark. 2011. "Inequality and Poverty in Latin America: Can the Decline Continue?" COHA (Council on Hemispheric Affairs), July 21.

Mainwaring, Scott, and Timothy R. Scully, eds. 2010. *Democratic Governance in Latin America.* Stanford: Stanford University Press.

Maldonado, Rene, and Maria Luisa Hayem. 2013. "Remittances to Latin America and the Caribbean in 2012: Differing Behavior across Subregions." Washington, DC: Multilateral Investment Fund, Inter-American Development Bank. http://idbdocs.iadb.org/wsdocs/getDocument.aspx?DOCNUM=37735715.

Mann, Charles. 2005. *1491: New Revelations of the Americas Before Columbus.* New York: Knopf.

———. 2011. *1493: Uncovering the New World Columbus Created.* New York: Knopf.

Marowits, Ross. 2013. "Dorel to Assemble Bikes after Buying Brazil's Largest Bicycle Maker." *The Canadian Press*, August 22.

Marti Puig, Salvador. 2010. "The Emergence of Indigenous Movements in Latin America and Their Impact on the Latin American Political Scene: Interpretive Tools at the Local and Global Levels." *Latin American Perspectives* 37, no. 6 (November): 74–92.

Martin, Cheryl E., and Mark Wasserman. 2005. *Latin America and Its People.* One-volume ed. New York: Pearson.

Massey, Douglas S., and María Aysa-Lastra. 2011. "Social Capital and International Migration from Latin America." *International Journal of Population Research* 2011. Article ID 834145.

Mateo, Joanna. 2011. "Street Gangs of Honduras." In Bruneau, Dammert, and Skinner, *Maras*, 87–104.

Mauro, Paolo. 1998. "Corruption: Causes, Consequences, and Agenda for Further Research." *Finance & Development* 35 (March): 11–14. http://www.imf.org/external/pubs/ft/fandd/1998/03/pdf/mauro.pdf.

Maxfield, Sylvia. 2005. "Women on the Verge: Corporate Power in Latin America." Report of the Women's Leadership Conference of the Americas. Inter-American Dialogue and Simmons College, April. http://thedialogue.org/PublicationFiles/Women%20on%20the%20Verge.pdf.

Maxfield, Sylvia, María Consuelo Cárdenas, and Lidia Heller. 2008. *Mujeres y vida corporativa en Latinoamérica: Retos y dilemas.* Bogotá: Universidad de los Andes.

McCann, Bryan. 2008. *The Throes of Democracy: Brazil since 1989.* London: Zed Books.

McGuirk, Justin. 2014. *Radical Cities: Across Latin America in Search of a New Architecture*. London: Verso.

Menchú, Rigoberta. 1984. Edited by Elisabeth Burgos-Debray; translated by Ann Wright. *I, Rigoberta Menchú: An Indian Woman in Guatemala*. New York: Verso.

Menjívar, Cecilia. 2011. *Enduring Violence: Ladina Women's Lives in Guatemala*. Berkeley: University of California Press.

Mertens, Richard. 2008. "Can't See the Forest for the Trees." *University of Chicago Magazine* (September–October). http://magazine.uchicago.edu/0810/features/the_forest.shtml.

Miniwatts Marketing Group. 2014. "Internet World Stats. Internet Users in the Americas by Geographic Region – June 2014." http://www.internetworldstats.com/stats2.htm.

Mollmann, Marianne. 2012. "Fatal Consequences: Women, Abortion, and Power in Latin America." International Planned Parenthood Federation, March 13. https://www.ippfwhr.org/en/blog/fatal-consequences-women-abortion-and-power-in-latin-america.

Moreira Alves, Maria Helena, and Philip Evanson. 2011. *Living in the Crossfire: Favela Residents, Drug Dealers, and Police Violence in Rio de Janeiro*. Philadelphia: Temple University Press.

Morris, Stephen D. 2010. "Mexico: Corruption and Change." In Morris and Blake, eds. *Corruption and Politics*, 137–164.

Morris, Stephen D., and Charles H. Blake, eds. 2010. *Corruption and Politics in Latin America: National and Regional Dynamics*. Boulder, CO: Lynne Rienner.

Morrison, Tony, and John Forrest. 2012. "The InterOceanic Highway: The Missing Link in the Exploitation of Amazonia?" Presentation to the Anglo-Peruvian Society in London, November. Available at *Andean Air Mail & Peruvian Times*, March 23, 2013. http://www.peruviantimes.com/23/the-interoceanic-highway-the-missing-link-in-the-exploitation-of-amazonia/18555/.

Moser, Caroline O. N. 1993. "Adjustment from Below: Low-income Women, Time and the Triple Role in Guayaquil, Ecuador." In Radcliffe and Westwood, *'Viva,'* 173–196.

———. 2009. *Ordinary Families, Extraordinary Lives: Assets and Poverty Reduction in Guayaquil, 1978–2004*. Washington, DC: Brookings Institution Press.

Moser, Caroline O. N., and Cathy McIlwaine. 2006. "Latin American Urban Violence as a Development Concern: Towards a Framework for Violence Reduction." *World Development* 34, no. 1: 89–112.

Moya, Jose C., ed. 2010. *The Oxford Handbook of Latin American History*. Oxford: Oxford University Press.

Msangi, Siwa, and Mark W. Rosegrant. 2011. "Feeding the Future's Changing Diets: Implications for Agriculture Markets, Nutrition, and Policy." 2020 Conference Paper 3. 2020 Conference: Leveraging Agriculture for Improving Nutrition and Health, February 10–12, New Delhi, India.

Munck, Ronaldo. 2003. *Contemporary Latin America*. New York: Palgrave Macmillan.

Mundy, Liza. 2012. *The Richer Sex: How the New Majority of Female Breadwinners Is Transforming Sex, Love, and Family*. New York: Simon and Schuster.

North, Douglass C. 1992. "The New Institutional Economics and Development." Paper presented at the American Economic Association meetings, January. http://www.deu.edu.tr/userweb/sedef.akgungor/Current%20topics%20in%20Turkish%20Economy/north.pdf.

Nouzeilles, Gabriela, and Graciela Montaldo, eds. 2002. *The Argentina Reader: History, Culture, Politics*. Durham: Duke University Press.

O'Connor, Anne-Marie. 2010. "Mexico City Drastically Reduced Air Pollutants since 1990s." *Washington Post*, April 1.

O'Conor, Tania. 2013. "Chinese Investment in Brazil: An Overview of Shifting Trends." Inter-American Dialogue, September 9.

O'Neill, Kevin Lewis, and Kedron Thomas, eds. 2011. *Securing the City: Neoliberalism, Space, and Insecurity in Postwar Guatemala*. Durham: Duke University Press.

Oppenheimer, Andrés. 2007. *Saving the Americas: The Dangerous Decline of Latin America and What the U.S. Must Do*. Mexico City: Random House Mondadori.

———. 2010. *Basta de historias! La obsesión latinoamericana con el pasado y las doce claves del futuro*. New York: Vintage Especial.

Orozco, Manuel. 2012. "Future Trends in Remittances to Latin America and the Caribbean." Washington, DC: Inter-American Dialogue Remittances and Development Program Report, May.

Pagés, Carmen, ed. 2010. *The Age of Productivity: Transforming Economies from the Bottom Up*. New York: Inter-American Development Bank/Palgrave-MacMillan.

Paim, Jairnilson, Claudia Travassos, Celia Almeida, Ligia Bahia, and James Macinko. 2011. "The Brazilian Health System: History, Advances, and Challenges." *The Lancet* 377, no. 9779 (May): 1778–1797.

Parker, Cristián. 2009. "Education and Increasing Religious Pluralism in Latin America: The Case of Chile." In Hagopian, *Religious Pluralism*, 131–181.

Patroni, Viviana, and Manuel Poitras. 2002. "Labor in Neoliberal Latin America: An Introduction." *LABOUR, Capital and Society* 35, no. 2 (November): 207–220.

Paus, Eva. 2011. "Latin America's Middle Income Trap." *Americas Quarterly: Free Trade and Market Access* 5, no. 1 (Winter): 70–76. http://www.americasquarterly.org/node/2142.

Peñalosa, Enrique. 2003. "La ciudad y la igualdad." *El Malpensante* 45 (March 16–April 30). http://elmalpensante.com/articulo/1804/la_ciudad_y_la_igualdad.

Penyak, Lee M., and Walter J. Petry, eds. 2009. *Religion and Society in Latin America: Interpretative Essays from Conquest to Present*. Maryknoll, NY: Orbis Books.

Pérez-Stable, Marifeli. 1999. *The Cuban Revolution: Origins, Course, and Legacy*. New York: Oxford University Press.

Perlman, Janice. 1976. *The Myth of Marginality: Urban Poverty and Politics in Rio de Janeiro*. Berkeley: University of California Press.

———. 2010. *Favela: Four Decades of Living on the Edge in Rio de Janeiro*. New York: Oxford University Press.

Perry, Guillermo E., William F. Maloney, Omar S. Arias, Pablo Fajnzylber, Andrew D. Mason, and Jaime Saavedra-Chanduvi. 2007. *Informality: Exit and Exclusion*. Washington, DC: World Bank. For a summary of key points, see "Overview: Informality: Exit and Exclusion," 1–20. http://siteresources.worldbank.org/INTLAC/Resources/CH0.pdf.

Peterson, Anna L., and Manuel A. Vásquez. 2008. *Latin American Religions: Histories and Documents in Context*. New York: New York University Press.

Pew Research Center. 2013a. "Diverse Origins: The Nation's 14 Largest Hispanic-Origin Groups." Pew Research Center, June 19. http://www.pewhispanic.org/files/2013/06/summary_report _final.pdf.

———. 2013b. "Second-Generation Americans: A Portrait of the Adult Children of Immigrants." Pew Research Center, February 7. http://www.pewsocialtrends.org/2013/02/07/second -generation-americans/.

Piñera, Sebastián. 2010. "We, the Bicentennials." *The World in 2011*, special issue of *The Economist*, November 22.

Piovesan, Flávia. 2009. "Violence against Women in Brazil." In Jaquette, *Feminist Agendas*, 113–128.

Politzer, Patricia. 1989. *Fear in Chile: Lives under Pinochet*. New York: Pantheon.

Power, Thomas M. 2009. "Metals Mining and Sustainable Development in Central America: An Assessment of Benefits and Costs." Boston: Oxfam America. http://www.oxfamamerica.org /static/media/files/metals-mining-and-sustainable-development-in-central-america.pdf.

Prahalad, C. K., and Stuart L. Hart. 2002. "The Fortune at the Bottom of the Pyramid." *Strategy + Business*. First Quarter, no. 26. http://www.strategy-business.com/article/11518?pg=0.

Preston, Julia, and Samuel Dillon. 2004. *Opening Mexico: The Making of a Democracy*. New York: Farrar, Strauss and Giroux.

Prevost, Gary, and Harry Vanden. 2010. *Latin America: An Introduction*. New York: Oxford University Press.

Price, John. 2011. "Globalization Is Here to Stay: Why Latin America Must Accept Its Globalized

Destiny and Ready Itself to Compete." Center for Hemispheric Policy, University of Miami, October 19. http://americasmi.com/archivos/pdf/Price-GlobalizationTFPaper.pdf.

Puryear, Jeffrey, and Mariellen Malloy Jewers. 2009. "How Poor and Unequal Is Latin America and the Caribbean?" Policy Brief No. 1. Washington, DC: Inter-American Dialogue, November. http://www.thedialogue.org/PublicationFiles/Social%20Policy%20Brief%20No%201%20-%20 Poverty%20and%20Inequality%20in%20LAC.pdf.

Rabinovitch, Jonas, and Josef Leitman. 1996. "Urban Planning in Curitiba." *Scientific American*, March.

Radcliffe, Sarah A., and Sallie Westwood, eds. 1993. *'Viva': Women and Popular Protest in Latin America*. London and New York: Routledge.

Ramírez, Sergio. 1999. *Adiós muchachos: Una memoria de la revolución sandinista*. Mexico City: Aguilar.

Ravelo Blancas, Patricia, Sergio Sánchez Díaz, and Javier Melgoza Valdivia. 2012. "Femicidio y violencias urbanas en la Frontera Norte: Ciudad Juárez/El Paso." Paper presented at LASA Congress, San Francisco, CA.

Reardon, Thomas, and Julio A. Berdegué. 2002. "The Rapid Rise of Supermarkets in Latin America: Challenges and Opportunities for Development." *Development Policy Review* 20 (4): 371–388.

Reardon, Thomas, and Ashok Gulati. 2008. "The Supermarket Revolution in Developing Countries: Policies for 'Competitiveness with Inclusiveness.'" IFPRI Policy Brief 2, June. http://www.ifpri .org/sites/default/files/publications/bp002.pdf.

Rebolledo González, Loreto. 2008. "Del padre ausente al padre próximo: Emergencias de nuevas formas de paternidad en el Chile actual." In Araujo and Prieto, *Estudios sobre sexualidades*, 123–140.

Reid, Michael. 2007. *Forgotten Continent: The Battle for Latin America's Soul*. New Haven: Yale University Press.

———. 2010. "Nobody's Backyard: The Rise of Latin America." Special Report: Latin America. *The Economist*, September 9.

———. 2014. *Brazil: The Troubled Rise of a Global Power*. New Haven: Yale University Press.

Reider, Susan. 2010. "Challenging the Standard Narrative: Myth-making and Accountability in Ecuadorian Environmental and Indigenous Politics." Hershey, PA: Terra Group. http://terra -group.net/pdfs/ChallengingTheStandardNarrative.pdf.

Reiter, Bernd, and Gladys L. Mitchell. 2010. *Brazil's New Racial Politics*. Boulder, CO: Lynne Rienner.

ReVista: Harvard Review of Latin America. 2003. *Cityscapes: Latin America and Beyond* (Winter). http://revista.drclas.harvard.edu/book/cityscapes-latin-america-and-beyond-winter-2003.

———. 2007. *Brazil: The Search for Equity* (Spring). http://revista.drclas.harvard.edu/book /brazil-search-equity-spring-2007.

———. 2008. *Venezuela: The Chávez Effect* (Fall). http://revista.drclas.harvard.edu/book /venezuela-ch%C3%A1vez-effect.

———. 2011. *Bolivia: Revolutions and Beyond* (Fall). http://revista.drclas.harvard.edu/book /bolivia-fall-2011.

———. 2012a. *Universities* (Fall). http://revista.drclas.harvard.edu/book/universities-fall-2012.

———. 2012b. *Organized Crime: Beyond Drug Trafficking* (Winter). http://revista.drclas.harvard.edu /book/organized-crime-beyond-drug-trafficking-winter-2012.

———. 2013a. *Memory: In Search of History and Democracy* (Fall). http://revista.drclas.harvard.edu /book/memory-fall-2013.

———. 2013b. *Water* 12, no. 2 (Winter). http://revista.drclas.harvard.edu/book/water-winter-2013.

———. 2014. *Mining* 13, no. 2 (Winter). http://revista.drclas.harvard.edu/book/mining-winter-2014.

Rice, Paul. 2011. "Fair Trade: A Model for Sustainable Development." *Stanford Social Innovation Review*, June 23.

Rivera Andueza, Raúl. 2011. *Nuestra Hora: Los latinoamericanos en el siglo XXI*. Santiago: Prentice-Hall.

Robles, Fernando, Nila M. Wiese, and Gladys Torres-Baumgarten. 2014. *Business in Emerging Latin America*. New York and London: Routledge.

Rodrik, Dani. 2007. *One Economics, Many Recipes: Globalization, Institutions, and Economic Growth*. Princeton, NJ: Princeton University Press.

Rohter, Larry. 2012. *Brazil on the Rise: The Story of a Country Transformed*. New York: Palgrave-Macmillan.

Romero, Simon. 2010. "Venezuela, More Deadly Than Iraq, Wonders Why." *New York Times*, August 22.

Romig, Shane. 2012. "Latin America Gears Up as Bike Hub." *Wall Street Journal*, August 9.

Rosenberg, Tina. 2007. "The Perils of Petrocracy." *New York Times Magazine*, November 4.

Ross, Jen. 2004. "Illegal Abortions Rampant in Latin America." *WeNews*, November 28.

Sachs, Jeffrey D., and Andrew M. Warner. 1995. "Natural Resource Abundance and Economic Growth." NBER Working Paper 5398, National Bureau of Economic Research, December. http://www.nber.org/papers/w5398.

Salamon, Lester M. 2010. *Rethinking Corporate Social Engagement: Lessons from Latin America*. Sterling, VA: Kumarian Press.

Santiso, Javier. 2006. *Latin America's Political Economy of the Possible: Beyond Good Revolutionaries and Free-Marketeers*. Cambridge, MA: MIT Press.

———. 2013. *The Decade of the Multilatinas*. Cambridge: Cambridge University Press.

Scartascini, Carlos, Ernesto Stein, and Mariano Tommasi, eds. 2010. *How Democracy Works: Politics, Institutions, Actors, and Arenas in Latin American Policymaking*. Washington, DC, and Cambridge, MA: Inter-American Development Bank.

Schemo, Diana Jean. 1999. "The Last Tribal Battle." *New York Times Magazine*, October 31.

Schneider, Friedrich, Andreas Buehn, and Claudio E. Montenegro. 2010. "Shadow Economies All Over the World: New Estimates for 162 Countries from 1999 to 2007 (Revised Version)." Policy Research Working Paper 5356. The World Bank Development Research Group, Poverty and Inequality Research Team and Europe and Central Asia Region, Human Development Economics Unit, July. https://openknowledge.worldbank.org/bitstream/handle/10986/3928/WPS5356.pdf?sequence=1.

Schwartz, Hugh. 2004. *Urban Renewal, Municipal Revitalization: The Case of Curitiba, Brazil*. Alexandria, VA: Hugh Schwartz.

Schwerin, Karl M. 2011. "The Indian Populations of Latin America." In Black, ed., *Latin America: Its Problems and Its Promise*, 39–55.

Scott, John F. 1999. *Latin American Art: Ancient to Modern*. Gainesville: University Press of Florida.

Seelke, Clare Ribando. 2008. "Afro-Latinos in Latin America and Considerations for U.S. Policy." CRS (Congressional Research Service) Report for Congress, updated November 21. https://www.fas.org/sgp/crs/row/RL32713.pdf.

———. 2012. "Trafficking in Persons in Latin America and the Caribbean." CRS (Congressional Research Service) Report for Congress, January 23. https://www.fas.org/sgp/crs/row/RL33200.pdf.

Sherman, Scott. 2012. "The Brawl over Fair Trade Coffee." *The Nation*, September 10.

Sirkin, Harold L. 2010. "Enter the 'Multilatinas.'" *Bloomberg Businessweek*, December 28.

Skidmore, Thomas E., and Peter H. Smith. 1992. *Modern Latin America*. 3rd ed. New York: Oxford University Press.

Snodgrass Godoy, Angelina. 2013. *Of Medicines and Markets: Intellectual Property and Human Rights in the Free Trade Era*. Stanford: Stanford University Press.

Soubbotina, Tatyana P. 2004. *Beyond Economic Growth: An Introduction to Sustainable Development*. Washington, DC: World Bank Publications.

Sreeharsha, Vinod. 2013. "The World's Top 10 Most Innovative Companies in South America." *Fast Company*, February 11. http://www.fastcompany.com/most-innovative-companies/2013/industry/south-america.

Steigenga, Timothy J., and Edward L. Cleary, eds. 2007. *Conversion of a Continent: Contemporary Religious Change in Latin America*. New Brunswick, NJ: Rutgers University Press.

Stein, Ernesto, ed. 2006. *The Politics of Policies: Economic and Social Progress in Latin America. 2006 Report*. Washington, DC, and Cambridge, MA: Inter-American Development Bank and David Rockefeller Center for Latin American Studies.

Stoll, David. 1990. *Is Latin America Turning Protestant? The Politics of Evangelical Growth*. Berkeley: University of California Press.

———. 1999. *Rigoberta Menchú and the Story of All Poor Guatemalans*. Boulder, CO: Westview Press.

———. 2010. "From Wage Migration to Debt Migration? Easy Credit, Failure in El Norte, and Foreclosure in a Bubble Economy of the Western Guatemalan Highlands." *Latin American Perspectives* 37, no. 1 (January): 123–142.

Stolte, Christina. 2012. "Brazil in Africa: Just Another BRICS Country Seeking Resources?" Chatham House Briefing Paper, November 1, 2012. London: Chatham House, The Royal Institute of International Affairs. http://www.chathamhouse.org/publications/papers/view/186957#.

Suarez, Ray. 2013. *Latino Americans: The 500-Year Legacy That Shaped a Nation*. New York: Penguin.

Suska, Marta-Laura. 2012. "Military Police as a Generator of Trust? The Pacification Police Unit in Violence-ridden Favelas of Rio de Janeiro." Paper presented at LASA Congress, San Francisco, May. http://www.academia.edu/9199641/Military_Police_as_a_generator_of_trust_The_Pacification_Police_Unit_in_violence-ridden_favelas_of_Rio_de_Janeiro.

Symmes, Patrick. 2002. "Blood Wood." *Outside*, October 1. http://www.outsideonline.com/outdoor-adventure/Blood-Wood.html.

Taylor, Matthew M. 2010. "Brazil: Corruption as Harmless *Jeitinho* or Threat to Democracy?" In Morris and Blake, *Corruption and Politics*, 89–112.

Taylor, Paul, Mark Hugo Lopez, Jessica Martinez, and Gabriel Velasco. 2012. "When Labels Don't Fit: Hispanics and Their Views of Identity." Washington, DC: Pew Research Center, Hispanic Trends Project, April 4. http://www.pewhispanic.org/2012/04/04/when-labels-dont-fit-hispanics-and-their-views-of-identity/.

Tegel, Simeon. 2012. "Ecuador's Green President Pushes Massive Chinese Mine." *GlobalPost*, March 30. http://www.globalpost.com/dispatch/news/regions/americas/120329/ecuador-indigenous-protest-chinese-mirador-copper-mine.

Telles, Edward E. 2004. "Rethinking Brazilian Race Relations." In *Race in Another America: The Significance of Skin Color in Brazil*. Princeton, NJ: Princeton University Press.

Terborgh, John. 2012. "Out of Contact." *The New York Review of Books*, April 5.

Terrazas, Aaron. 2010. "Salvadoran Immigrants in the United States." *Migration Information Source*, January 5. http://www.migrationpolicy.org/article/salvadoran-immigrants-united-states.

Thorp, Rosemary. 1998. *Progress, Poverty and Exclusion: An Economic History of Latin America in the 20th Century*. New York and Baltimore: Inter-American Development Bank and the Johns Hopkins University Press.

Thorp, Rosemary, José Carlos Orihuela, and Maritza Paredes. 2013. "Avoiding the Resource Curse." *Americas Quarterly: Natural Resource Extraction in Latin America* 7, no. 1 (Winter): 52–59.

Tiano, Susan. 2011. "Women, Work, and Politics." In Hillman and D'Agostino, eds., *Understanding Contemporary Latin America*, 285–384.

Tobar, Héctor. 2011. *The Barbarian Nurseries: A Novel*. New York: Farrar, Straus and Giroux.

Tokman, Victor E. 2010. "Domestic Workers in Latin America: Statistics for New Policies." WIEGO Working Paper (Statistics) No. 17, June. http://wiego.org/sites/wiego.org/files/publications/files/Tokman_WIEGO_WP17.pdf.

Torche, Florencia, and Luis Felipe López-Calva. 2011. "Middle Classes, Education and Mobility." *Americas Quarterly* 5, no. 1 (Winter): 39–43.

Torres, Fernando, Nila M. Wiese, and Gladys Torres-Baumgarten. 2015. *Business in Emerging Latin America*. New York: Routledge.

Traba, Marta. 1994. *Art of Latin America: 1900–1980*. Washington, DC: Inter-American Development Bank.

Transparency International. 2014. *Corruption Perceptions Index*. http://www.transparency.org/cpi2014/results/.

UNCTAD (United Nations Trade and Development Organization). 1960 and 2010. "Life Expectancy at Birth—Demographic indicators—UNCTAD Handbook of Statistics—Country Comparison." http://www.nationsencyclopedia.com/WorldStats/UNCTAD-indicators-life-expectancy-birth.html.

United Nations. 2013. "Latin America and the Caribbean Make Progress on Child Health and Gender Equality." Press release, June 23.

United Nations Development Programme. 2013. *Human Development Report 2013: The Rise of the South—Human Development in a Diverse World*. New York: United Nations Development Programme. http://www.unodc.org/documents/gsh/pdfs/2014_GLOBAL_HOMICIDE_BOOK_web.pdf.

———. 2014. *Human Development Report 2014: Sustaining Human Progress: Reducing Vulnerabilities and Building Resilience*. New York: United Nations Development Programme. http://hdr.undp.org/en/content/human-development-report-2014.

United Nations Office on Drugs and Crime. 2014. *Global Study on Homicide 2013: Trends, Context, Data*. New York: UNODC.

Uribe Díaz, Patricia Isabel. 2007. "Familias monoparentales con jefatura femenina, una de las expresiones de las familias contemporáneas." *Revista Tendencia y Retos* 12 (October): 81–90.

Urquieta C., Patricia, ed. 2011. *Ciudades en transformación: Disputas por el espacio, apropiación de la ciudad y prácticas de ciudadanía*. La Paz: CIDES-UMSA.

Valenzuela, J. Samuel, Timothy R. Scully, and Nicolás Somma. 2009. "Social and Political Effects of Religiosity and Religious Identities in Latin America." Kellogg Working Paper No. 362, December.

Vance, Erik. 2014. "Gods of Blood and Stone." *Scientific American* 311, no. 1 (June): 48–55.

Vanden, Harry E., and Gary Prevost. 2009. *The Politics of Latin America: The Power Game*. 3rd ed. New York: Oxford University Press.

Vargas Llosa, Álvaro. 2005. *Liberty for Latin America: How to Undo Five Hundred Years of State Oppression*. New York: The Independent Institute.

Vaughn, Adam. 2009. "Carbon Emissions per Person, by Country." *The Guardian*, Datablog, September 2. http://www.theguardian.com/environment/datablog/2009/sep/02/carbon-emissions-per-person-capita.

Viana, Virgilio M. 2010. *Sustainable Development in Practice: Lessons Learned from Amazonas*. London: International Institute for Environment and Development.

Vidal Luna, Francisco, and Herbert S. Klein. 2006. *Brazil Since 1980*. Cambridge: Cambridge University Press.

Villarreal, M. Angeles. 2010. "NAFTA and the Mexican Economy." CRS Report for Congress. Congressional Research Service, June 3.

Von Wobeser, Gisela, ed. 2010. *Historia de México*. Mexico City: Academia Mexicana de la Historia, Fondo de Cultura Económica, and Secretaría de Educación.

Wainwright, Tom. 2012. "Going Up in the World." Special Report: Mexico. *The Economist*, November 24.

Walker, Harry. 2012. *Under a Watchful Eye: Self, Power, and Intimacy in Amazonia*. Berkeley: University of California Press.

Walker, Ignacio. 2013. *Democracy in Latin America: Between Hope and Despair*. Translated by Krystin Krause, Holy Bird, and Scott Mainwaring. Notre Dame, IN: University of Notre Dame.

Wallace, Scott. 2007. "Last of the Amazon." *National Geographic*, January.

Weatherford, Jack. 1988. *Indian Givers: How the Indians of the Americas Transformed the World*. New York: Fawcett Columbine.

Weitzman, Hal. 2013. "Resource Nationalism: Beyond Ideology." *Americas Quarterly: Natural Resource Extraction in Latin America* 7, no. 1 (Winter): 120–124.

Werner, David, Carol Thuman, and Jane Maxwell. 2013. *Where There Is No Doctor: A Village Health Care Handbook.* Berkeley, CA: Hesperian Foundation. Originally published in Spanish as *Donde no hay doctor* in 1973.

Weschler, Lawrence. 1990. *A Miracle, A Universe: Settling Accounts with Torturers.* Chicago: University of Chicago Press.

WHO (World Health Organization). 2010. http://en.wikipedia.org/wiki/List_of_countries_by_total_health_expenditure_%28PPP%29_per_capita.

Wilde, Alexander, ed. 2015. *Religious Responses to Violence: Human Rights in Latin America Past and Present.* Notre Dame, IN: University of Notre Dame Press.

Winn, Peter. 2006. *Americas: The Changing Face of Latin America and the Caribbean.* 3rd ed. Berkeley: University of California Press. Originally published 1992.

Wise, Carol. 2012. "China's Free Trade Agreements in South America." Economics Brief. Inter-American Dialogue, November.

WOLA (Washington Office on Latin America). 2011. "Tackling Urban Violence in Latin America: Reversing Exclusion through Smart Policing and Social Investment." June 13. http://www.wola.org/publications/tackling_urban_violence_in_latin_america_reversing_exclusion_through_smart_policing_and.

Wolf, Sonja. 2011. "Street Gangs of El Salvador." In Bruneau, Dammert, and Skinner, *Maras*, 43–69.

Wolseth, Jon. 2011. *Jesus and the Gang: Youth Violence and Christianity in Urban Honduras.* Tucson: University of Arizona Press.

World Bank. 2008. *World Development Report 2008: Agriculture for Development.* Washington, DC: World Bank.

———. 2014. "Proportion of Seats Held by Women in National Parliaments (%)." http://data.worldbank.org/indicator/SG.GEN.PARL.ZS.

———. 2015. "GDP per Capita (Current US$)." http://data.worldbank.org/indicator/NY.GDP.PCAP.CD.

World Bank Group. 2015. "Economy Rankings." Ease of Doing Business Rankings. http://www.doingbusiness.org/rankings.

World Bank—LAC. 2011. "Crime and Violence in Central America: A Development Challenge." Washington, DC: World Bank. http://siteresources.worldbank.org/INTLAC/Resources/FINAL_VOLUME_I_ENGLISH_CrimeAndViolence.pdf.

World Commission on Environment and Development. 1987. *Our Common Future.* Oxford: Oxford University Press.

Young, Clifford. 2007. "The Mugging of Latin America." *Americas Quarterly: Coping with (In)Security* 1, no. 2 (Fall).

Youngers, Coletta A. 2013. "The Drug Policy Reform Agenda in the Americas." London: International Drug Policy Consortium, May.

Zepeda, Eduardo, Timothy A. Wise, and Kevin P. Gallagher. 2009. "Rethinking Trade Policy for Development: Lessons from Mexico under NAFTA." Washington, DC: Carnegie Endowment for International Peace, December.

Zirin, Dave. 2014. *Brazil's Dance with the Devil: The World Cup, the Olympics, and the Fight for Democracy.* Chicago: Haymarket Books.

Index

bus rapid transit (BRT), 32, 82, 319

cable cars, 35, 270
caboclos, 144
Cabral, Pedro Álvares, 161, 167
CACIF (Coordinating Committee of Agricultural, Commercial, Industrial and Financial Associations), 332
cacique, 160
Cádiz, 167
Calderon, Felipe, 95, 258, 269, 270
Cali, 30, 64, 65, 82, 255
Cali cartel, 256, 270
California, 12, 165, 305, 308
callampas, 23
Calles, Plutarco Elías, 181
Canada, 14, 29, 61, 88, 207, 217, 233, 295–296, 303, 304, 314
Canal Zone, Panama, 178, 198, 217, 232, 336
Canby, Peter, 326
Cancún, 296
Candelária, 29
Candomblé, 144
Canelones (Uruguay), 128
capitalism, 51
capoeira, 110
Caracas, 12, 21, 30, 32, 220, 332
Caral, 155
Carambiru Penitentiary, 334
carbon emissions, 70, 73, 83
Cardenal, Ernesto, 7, 141
Cárdenas, Lázaro, 181, 186
Cardoso, Fernando Henrique, 42, 147, 208
Caribbean, 14, 39,118, 160, 162, 181, 255, 257, 259, 270
Carneiro, Mario, 58
Carrefour, 36, 73
Carrera, Rafael, 173
Carrión, Francisco, 32, 322
Cartagena, 333
cartels, 257, 259
Carter, Jimmy, 198
Casa de las Américas, 195
Casa do Pão de Queijo, 58
Castaneda, Jorge, 85
Castillo Armas, Carlos, 188
Castro Martin, Teresa, 119
Castro, Fidel, 191, 192, 193, 241, 263, 306, 315, 329
Castro, Raúl, 315
Catatombo River, 68

Catholic Church, 6, 100, 108, 122, 131, 134–142, 150–151, 165–167, 173, 326
Catholic University of Chile, 292
católico a mi manera (Catholic in my own way), 146
cattle, 38, 73
caudillos, 171, 173, 174, 197
CELAC (Community of Latin American and Caribbean States), 313–314
CELAM (Latin American Bishops Council), 150, 326
cell phones, 247
CEMEX, 60
census (racial classification), 113,
Central America, 12, 14, 49, 63, 68, 74, 118, 141, 142, 149, 304, 306, 316; crime and corruption, 252, 259, 270; history, 170, 173, 180, 199–201; politics and governance, 215, 229, 238, 240, 24
cerrado, 14, 44–45, 214
Cerrejón, 79
Chagas disease, 13
Chapultepec Castle, 328
Charismatic Renewal, Catholic, 143–144
Chávez, Carlos, 182
Chavez, Cesar, 135, 311
Chávez, Hugo, 220, 239, 241–243, 272, 313, 321, 331
Chavín de Huáutar, 156
Chevron, 105, 325
Chiapas, 108
Chicago boys, 213
Chile, 1, 7, 8, 12, 17, 23, 32, 37, 42, 54, 60, 63, 64, 79, 82, 86, 88, 95, 140, 141, 279, 284, 290, 293, 299, 313, 324; crime and justice system, 252, 262, 263, 264, 271–272, 273; economy and trade, 212, 213–214, 215, 216, 217, 220, 223, 225, 226, 227, 229, 230, 303, 304; gender, 117, 119, 122, 123, 126, 127, 128, 130, 131; history, 154, 158, 167, 174, 176, 177, 180; politics and governance, 232, 233, 234, 236, 237, 238, 240, 242, 245, 246, 249; recent history, 196, 198, 203
Chilean miracle, 213
Chimbote, 326
"China price," 300, 335
China, 2, 3, 14, 45, 57, 77, 83, 206, 208, 212, 214, 215, 221, 295, 299–303, 317, 319
Chorrillo (Panama City), 331
Christian base communities, 140, 148
Christian Congregation, 142